Practical Python Data Wrangling and Data Quality

Susan E. McGregor

Beijing · Boston · Farnham · Sebastopol · Tokyo

Practical Python Data Wrangling and Data Quality

by Susan E. McGregor

Published by O'Reilly Media, Inc., 1005 Gravenstein Highway North, Sebastopol, CA 95472.

O'Reilly books may be purchased for educational, business, or sales promotional use. Online editions are also available for most titles (*http://oreilly.com*). For more information, contact our corporate/institutional sales department: 800-998-9938 or *corporate@oreilly.com*.

Acquisitions Editor: Jessica Haberman	**Indexer:** nSight, Inc.
Development Editor: Jeff Bleiel	**Interior Designer:** David Futato
Production Editor: Daniel Elfanbaum	**Cover Designer:** Jose Marzan Jr.
Copyeditor: Sonia Saruba	**Illustrator:** Kate Dullea
Proofreader: Piper Editorial Consulting, LLC	

December 2021:   First Edition

Revision History for the First Edition

2021-12-02:   First Release

See *http://oreilly.com/catalog/errata.csp?isbn=9781492091509* for release details.

978-1-492-09150-9

[LSI]

Table of Contents

Preface

Welcome! If you've picked up this book, you're likely one of the many millions of people intrigued by the processes and possibilities surrounding "data"—that incredible, elusive new "currency" that's transforming the way we live, work, and even connect with one another. Most of us, for example, are vaguely aware of the fact that data—collected by our electronic devices and other activities—is being used to shape what advertisements we see, what media is recommended to us, and which search results populate first when we look for something online. What many people may not appreciate is that the tools and skills for accessing, transforming, and generating insight from data are readily available to them. This book aims to help those people— you, if you like—do just that.

Data is not something that is only available or useful to big companies or governmental number crunchers. Being able to access, understand, and gather insight from data is a valuable skill whether you're a data scientist or a day care worker. The tools needed to use data effectively are more accessible than ever before. Not only can you do significant data work using only free software and programming languages, you don't even need an expensive computer. All of the exercises in this book, for example, were designed and run on a Chromebook that cost less than $500. You can even just use free online platforms through the internet connection at your local library.

The goal of this book is to provide the guidance and confidence that data novices need to begin exploring the world of data—first by accessing it, then evaluating its quality. With those foundations in place, we'll move on to some of the basic methods of analyzing and presenting data to generate meaningful insight. While these latter sections will be far from comprehensive (both data analysis and visualization are robust fields unto themselves), they will give you the core skills needed to generate accurate, informative analyses and visualizations using your newly cleaned and acquired data.

Who Should Read This Book?

This book is intended for true beginners; all you need are a basic understanding of how to use computers (e.g., how to download a file, open a program, copy and paste, etc.), an open mind, and a willingness to experiment. I especially encourage you to take a chance on this book if you are someone who feels intimidated by data or programming, if you're "bad at math," or imagine that working with data or learning to program is too hard for you. I have spent nearly a decade teaching hundreds of people who didn't think of themselves as "technical" the exact skills contained in this book, and I have never once had a student who was genuinely unable to get through this material. In my experience, the most challenging part of programming and working with data is not the difficulty of the material but the quality of the instruction.[1] I am grateful both to the many students over the years whose questions have helped me immeasurably in finding ways to convey this material better, and for the opportunity to share what I learned from them with so many others through this book. While a book cannot truly replace the kind of support provided by a human teacher, I hope it will at least give the tools you need to master the basics—and perhaps the inspiration to take those skills to the next level.

Folks who have some experience with data wrangling but have reached the limits of spreadsheet tools or want to expand the range of data formats they can easily access and manipulate will also find this book useful, as will those with frontend programming skills (in JavaScript or PHP, for example) who are looking for a way to get started with Python.

> ## Where Would You like to Go?
>
> In the preface to media theorist Douglas Rushkoff's book *Program or Be Programmed* (OR Books), he compares the act of programming to that of driving a car. Unless you learn to program, Rushkoff writes, you are a perpetual passenger in the digital world, one who "is getting driven from place to place. Only the car has no windows and if the driver tells you there is only one supermarket in the county, you have to believe him."
>
> "You can relegate your programming to others," Rushkoff continues, "but then you have to trust them that their programs are really doing what you're asking, and in a way that is in your best interests." More and more these days, the latter assertion is being thrown into question (*https://www.theguardian.com/technology/2021/sep/14/facebook-aware-instagram-harmful-effect-teenage-girls-leak-reveals*).
>
> Over the years, I've asked several hundred students if they believe anyone can learn to drive, and the answer has always been yes. At the same time, I have met few people,

---

1 For a *long* time, installing the tools was also a huge obstacle. Now all you need is an internet connection!

apart from myself, who truly believe that *anyone* can program. Yet driving a motor vehicle is, in reality, vastly more complex than programming a computer. Why, then, do so many of us imagine that programming will be "too hard" for us?

For me, this is where the real strength of Rushkoff's analogy shows, because his "windowless car" doesn't just hide the outside world from the passenger—it also hides the "driver" from passersby. It's easy to believe that anyone can drive a car because we actually *see* all kinds of people driving cars, every day.

When it comes to programming, though, we rarely get to see who is "behind the wheel," which means our ideas about who *can* and *should* program are largely defined by media that portray programmers as typically white and overwhelmingly male (*https://www.npr.org/sections/money/2014/10/21/357629765/when-women-stopped-coding*). As a result, those characteristics have come to dominate who *does* program—but there's no reason why it should. Because if you can drive a car—or even punctuate a sentence—I promise you can program a computer, too.

Who Shouldn't Read This Book?

As noted previously, this book is intended for beginners. So while you may find some sections useful if you are new to data analysis or visualization, this volume is not designed to serve those with prior experience in Python or another data-focused programming language (like R). Fortunately, O'Reilly has many specialized volumes that deal with advanced Python topics and libraries, such as Wes McKinney's *Python for Data Analysis* (O'Reilly) or the *Python Data Science Handbook* by Jake VanderPlas (O'Reilly).

What to Expect from This Volume

The content of this book is designed to be followed in the order presented, as the concepts and exercises in each chapter build on those explored previously. Throughout, however, you will find that exercises are presented in two ways: as code "notebooks" and as "standalone" programming files. The purpose of this is twofold. First, it allows you, the reader, to use whichever approach you prefer or find more accessible; second, it provides a way to compare these two methods of interacting with data-driven Python code. In my experience, Python "notebooks" are extremely useful for getting up and running quickly but can become tedious if you develop a reliable piece of code that you wish to run repeatedly. Since the code from one format often cannot simply be copied and pasted to the other, both are provided in the accompanying GitHub repo. Data files, too, are available via Google Drive. As you follow along with the exercises, you will be able to use the format you prefer and will also have the option of seeing the differences in the code for each format firsthand.

Although Python is the primary tool used in this book, effective data wrangling and analysis are made easier through the smart use of a range of tools, from text editors (the programs in which you will actually write your code) to spreadsheet programs. Because of this, there are occasional exercises in this book that rely on other free and/or open source tools besides Python. Wherever these are introduced, I will offer some context as to why that tool has been chosen, along with sufficient instructions to complete the example task.

Conventions Used in This Book

The following typographical conventions are used in this book:

Italic
> Indicates new terms, URLs, email addresses, filenames, and file extensions.

`Monospaced`
> Used for program listings, as well as within paragraphs to refer to program elements such as variable or function names, databases, data types, environment variables, statements, and keywords.

`Monospaced bold`
> Shows commands or other text that should be typed literally by the user.

`Monospaced italic`
> Shows text that should be replaced with user-supplied values or by values determined by context.

This element signifies a tip or suggestion.

This element signifies a general note.

This element indicates a warning or caution.

Using Code Examples

Supplemental material (code examples, exercises, etc.) is available for download at *https://github.com/PracticalPythonDataWranglingAndQuality*.

If you have a technical question or a problem using the code examples, please send email to *bookquestions@oreilly.com*.

The code in this book is here to help you develop your skills. In general, if example code is offered with this book, you may use it in your programs and documentation. You do not need to contact us for permission unless you're reproducing a significant portion of the code. For example, writing a program that uses several chunks of code from this book does not require permission. Selling or distributing examples from O'Reilly books does require permission. Answering a question by citing this book and quoting example code does not require permission. Incorporating a significant amount of example code from this book into your product's documentation does require permission.

We appreciate, but generally do not require, attribution. An attribution usually includes the title, author, publisher, and ISBN. For example: "*Practical Python Data Wrangling and Data Quality* by Susan E. McGregor (O'Reilly). Copyright 2022 Susan E. McGregor, 978-1-492-09150-9."

If you feel your use of code examples falls outside fair use or the permission given above, feel free to contact us at *permissions@oreilly.com*.

O'Reilly Online Learning

 For more than 40 years, *O'Reilly Media* has provided technology and business training, knowledge, and insight to help companies succeed.

Our unique network of experts and innovators share their knowledge and expertise through books, articles, and our online learning platform. O'Reilly's online learning platform gives you on-demand access to live training courses, in-depth learning paths, interactive coding environments, and a vast collection of text and video from O'Reilly and 200+ other publishers. For more information, visit *http://oreilly.com*.

How to Contact Us

Please address comments and questions concerning this book to the publisher:

O'Reilly Media, Inc.
1005 Gravenstein Highway North
Sebastopol, CA 95472
800-998-9938 (in the United States or Canada)
707-829-0515 (international or local)
707-829-0104 (fax)

We have a web page for this book, where we list errata, examples, and any additional information. You can access this page at *https://www.oreilly.com/library/view/practical-python-data/9781492091493*.

Email *bookquestions@oreilly.com* to comment or ask technical questions about this book.

For news and information about our books and courses, visit *http://oreilly.com*.

Find us on Facebook: *http://facebook.com/oreilly*

Follow us on Twitter: *http://twitter.com/oreillymedia*

Watch us on YouTube: *http://www.youtube.com/oreillymedia*

Acknowledgments

As I mentioned previously, this book owes much to my many students over the years who were brave enough to try something new and ask sincere questions along the way. The process of writing this book (to say nothing of the text itself) was made immeasurably better by my editor, Jeff Bleiel, whose pleasantness, flexibility, and light touch tempered my excesses while making space for my personal style. I am also grateful for the thoughtful and generous comments of my reviewers: Joanna S. Kao, Anne Bonner, and Randy Au.

I would also like to thank Jess Haberman, who offered me the chance to make this material my own, as well as Jacqueline Kazil and Katharine Jarmul, who helped put me in her way. I'd also like to thank Jeannette Wing and Cliff Stein and the staff at Columbia University's Data Science Institute, whose interest in this work has already helped it generate exciting new opportunities. And of course, I want to thank my friends and relations for their interest and support, even—and especially—when they had no idea what I was talking about.

Finally, I'd want to thank my family (including the children too young to read this) for staying supportive even when the Sad SpongeBob days set in. You make the work worth doing.

# CHAPTER 1

Introduction to Data Wrangling and Data Quality

These days it seems like data is the answer to everything: we use the data in product and restaurant reviews to decide what to buy and where to eat; companies use the data about what we read, click, and watch to decide what content to produce and which advertisements to show; recruiters use data to decide which applicants get job interviews; the government uses data to decide everything from how to allocate highway funding to where your child goes to school. Data—whether it's a basic table of numbers or the foundation of an "artificial intelligence" system—permeates our lives. The pervasive impact that data has on our experiences and opportunities every day is precisely why data wrangling is—and will continue to be—an essential skill for anyone interested in understanding and influencing how data-driven systems operate. Likewise, the ability to assess—and even improve—data quality is indispensable for anyone interested in making these sometimes (deeply) flawed systems work better.

Yet because both the terms *data wrangling* and *data quality* will mean different things to different people, we'll begin this chapter with a brief overview of the three main topics addressed in this book: data wrangling, data quality, and the Python programming language. The goal of this overview is to give you a sense of my approach to these topics, partly so you can determine if this book is right for you. After that, we'll spend some time on the necessary logistics of how to access and configure the software tools and other resources you'll need to follow along with and complete the exercises in this book. Though all of the resources that this book will reference are free to use, many programming books and tutorials take for granted that readers will be coding on (often quite expensive) computers that they own. Since I *really* believe that anyone who wants to can learn to wrangle data with Python, however, I wanted to make sure that the material in this book can work for you even if you don't have access to a full-featured computer of your own. To help ensure this, all of the solutions you'll find here and in the following chapters were written and tested on a Chromebook; they can also be run using free, online-only tools using either your own device or a shared computer, for example, at school or a public library. I hope that by illustrating how accessible not just the knowledge but also the tools of data wrangling can be will encourage you to explore this exciting and empowering practice.

What Is "Data Wrangling"?

Data wrangling is the process of taking "raw" or "found" data, and transforming it into something that can be used to generate insight and meaning. Driving every substantive data wrangling effort is a *question*: something about the world you want to investigate or learn more about. Of course, if you came to this book because you're really excited about learning to program, then data wrangling can be a great way to get started, but let me urge you now not to try to skip straight to the programming without engaging the data quality processes in the chapters ahead. Because as much as data wrangling may benefit from programming skills, it is about much more than simply learning how to access and manipulate data; it's about making judgments, inferences, and selections. As this book will illustrate, most data that is readily available is not especially good *quality*, so there's no way to do data wrangling without making choices that will influence the substance of the resulting data. To attempt data wrangling without considering data quality is like trying drive a car without steering: you may get *somewhere*—and fast!—but it's probably nowhere you want to be. If you're going to spend time wrangling and analyzing data, you want to try to make sure it's at least *likely* to be worth the effort.

Just as importantly, though, there's no better way to learn a new skill than to connect it to something you genuinely *want* to get "right," because that personal interest is what will carry you through the inevitable moments of frustration. This doesn't mean that question you choose has to be something of global importance. It can be a question about your favorite video games, bands, or types of tea. It can be a question about your school, your neighborhood, or your social media life. It can be a question about economics, politics, faith, or money. It just has to be something that *you* genuinely care about.

Once you have your question in hand, you're ready to begin the data wrangling process. While the specific steps may need adjusting (or repeating) depending on your particular project, in principle data wrangling involves some or all of the following steps:

1. Locating or collecting data
2. Reviewing the data
3. "Cleaning," standardizing, transforming, and/or augmenting the data

4. Analyzing the data

5. Visualizing the data

6. Communicating the data

The time and effort required for each of these steps, of course, can vary considerably: if you're looking to speed up a data wrangling task you already do for work, you may already have a dataset in hand and know basically what it contains. Then again, if you're trying to answer a question about city spending in your community, collecting the data may be the most challenging part of your project.

Also, know that, despite my having numbered the preceding list, the data wrangling process is really more of a cycle than it is a linear set of steps. More often than not, you'll need to revisit earlier steps as you learn more about the meaning and context of the data you're working with. For example, as you analyze a large dataset, you may come across surprising patterns or values that cause you to question assumptions you may have made about it during the "review" step. This will almost always mean seeking out more information—either from the original data source or completely new ones—in order to understand what is really happening before you can move on with your analysis or visualization. Finally, while I haven't explicitly included it in the list, it would be a little more accurate to start each of the steps with *Researching and*. While the "wrangling" parts of our work will focus largely on the dataset(s) we have in front of us, the "quality" part is almost all about research and context, and both of these are integral to every stage of the data wrangling process.

If this all seems a little overwhelming right now—don't worry! The examples in this book are built around real datasets, and as you follow along with coding and quality-assessment processes, this will all begin to feel much more organic. And if you're working through your own data wrangling project and start to feel a little lost, just keep reminding yourself of the question you are trying to answer. Not only will that remind you why you're bothering to learn about all the minutiae of data formats and API access keys,[1] it will also almost always lead you intuitively to the next "step" in the wrangling process—whether that means visualizing your data or doing just a *little* more research in order to improve its context and quality.

What Is "Data Quality"?

There is plenty of data out in the world and plenty of ways to access and collect it. But all data is not created equal. Understanding data quality is an essential part of data wrangling because any data-driven insight can only be as good as the data it was built upon.[2] So if you're trying to use data to understand something meaningful about

---

1 We'll cover these in detail in Chapters 4 and 5, respectively.

the world, you have to first make sure that the data you have accurately reflects that world. As we'll see in later chapters (Chapters 3 and 6, in particular), the work of improving data quality is almost never as clear-cut as the often tidy-looking, neatly labeled rows and columns of data you'll be working with.

That's because—despite the use of terms like *machine learning* and *artificial intelligence*—the only thing that computational tools can do is follow the directions given to them, using the data provided. And even the most complex, sophisticated, and abstract data is irrevocably human in its substance, because it is the result of human decisions about what to measure and how. Moreover, even today's most advanced computer technologies make "predictions" and "decisions" via what amounts to large-scale pattern matching—patterns that exist in the particular selections of data that the *humans* "training" them provide. *Computers do not have original ideas or make creative leaps*; they are fundamentally bad at many tasks (like explaining the "gist" of an argument or the plot of a story) that humans find intuitive. On the other hand, computers excel at performing repetitive calculations, very very fast, without getting bored, tired, or distracted. In other words, while computers are a fantastic complement to human judgment and intelligence, they can only amplify them—not substitute for them.

What this means is that it is up to the humans involved in data collection, acquisition, and analysis to ensure its quality so that the outputs of our data work actually *mean* something. While we will go into significant detail around data quality in Chapter 3, I do want to introduce two distinct (though equally important) axes for evaluating data quality: (1) the integrity of the data itself, and (2) the "fit" or appropriateness of the data with respect to a particular question or problem.

Data Integrity

For our purposes, the *integrity* of a dataset is evaluated using the data values and descriptors that make it up. If our dataset includes measurements over time, for example, have they been recorded at consistent intervals or sporadically? Do the values represent direct individual readings, or are only averages available? Is there a *data dictionary* that provides details about how the data was collected, recorded, or should be interpreted—for example, by providing relevant units? In general, data that is *complete*, *atomic*, and *well-annotated*—among other things—is considered to be of higher integrity because these characteristics make it possible to do a wider range of more conclusive analyses. In most cases, however, you'll find that a given dataset is lacking on any number of data integrity dimensions, meaning that it's up to you to try to understand its limitations and improve it where you can. While this often means augmenting a given dataset by finding others that can complement, contextualize, or

---

2 In the world of computing, this is often expressed as "garbage in/garbage out."

extend it, it almost *always* means looking beyond "data" of any kind and reaching out to experts: the people who designed the data, collected it, have worked with it previously, or know a lot about the subject area your data is supposed to address.

Data "Fit"

Even a dataset that has excellent integrity, however, cannot be considered high quality unless it is *also* appropriate for your particular purpose. Let's say, for example, that you were interested in knowing which Citi Bike station has had the most bikes rented and returned in a given 24-hour period. Although the real-time Citi Bike API (*http:// gbfs.citibikenyc.com/gbfs/gbfs.json*) contains high-integrity data, it's poorly suited to answering the particular question of which Citi Bike station has seen the greatest turnover on a given date. In this case, you would be much better off trying to answer this question using the Citi Bike "trip history" data (*https://s3.amazonaws.com/trip data/index.html*).

Of course, it's rare that a data fit problem can be solved so simply; often we have to do a significant amount of integrity work before we can know with confidence that our dataset *is* actually fit for our selected question or project. There's no way to bypass this time investment, however: shortcuts when it comes to either data integrity or data fit will inevitably compromise the quality and relevance of your data wrangling work overall. In fact, many of the harms caused by today's computational systems are related to problems of data fit. For example, using data that describes one phenomenon (such as income) to try to answer questions about a potentially related —but fundamentally different—phenomenon (like educational attainment) can lead to distorted conclusions about what is happening in the world, with sometimes devastating consequences. In some instances, of course, using such proxy measures is unavoidable. An initial medical diagnosis based on a patient's observable symptoms may be required to provide emergency treatment until the results of a more definitive test are available. While such substations are sometimes acceptable at the individual level, however, the gap between any proxy measure and the real phenomenon multiplies with the scale of the data and the system it is used to power. When this happens, we end up with a massively distorted view of the very reality our data wrangling and analysis hoped to illuminate. Fortunately, there are a number of ways to protect against these types of errors, as we'll explore further in Chapter 3.

Unpacking COMPAS

One high-profile example of the harms that can be caused by using bad proxy data in a large-scale computational system was demonstrated a number of years ago by a group of journalists at ProPublica, a nonprofit investigative news organization.[3] In the series "Machine Bias" (*https://propublica.org/article/machine-bias-risk-assessments-in-criminal-sentencing*), reporters examined discrepancies in the way that an algorithmic tool called the Correctional Offender Management Profiling for Alternative Sanctions, or COMPAS, made re-offense predictions for Black and white defendants who were up for parole. In general, Black defendants with similar criminal histories to white defendants were given higher risk scores, in large part because the data used to predict—or "model"—their risk of re-offense treated arrest rates as a proxy for crime rates. But because patterns of arrest were *already* biased against Black Americans (i.e., Black people were being arrested for "crimes"—like walking to work (*https://fusion.tv/story/5568/florida-citys-stop-frisk-nabs-thousands-of-kids-finds-5-year-olds-suspicious*)—that white people were not being arrested for), the risk assessments the tool generated were biased, too.[4]

Unfortunately, similar examples of how poor data "fit" can create massive harms are not hard to come by. That's why assessing your data for both integrity *and* fit is such an essential part of the data wrangling process: if the data you use is inappropriate, your work may not be just wrong but actively harmful.

Why Python?

If you're reading this book, chances are you've already heard of the Python programming language, and you may even be pretty certain that it's the right tool for starting—or expanding—your work on data wrangling. Even if that's the case, I think it's worth briefly reviewing what makes Python especially suited to the type of data wrangling and quality work that we'll do in this book. Of course if you *haven't* heard of Python before, consider this an introduction to what makes it one of the most popular and powerful programming languages in use today.

Versatility

Perhaps one of the greatest strengths of Python as a general programming language is its versatility: it can be easily used to access APIs, scrape data from the web,

---

3 Disclosure: many ProPublica staffers, including the lead reporter on this series, are former colleagues of mine.

4 The "Machine Bias" series generated substantial debate in the academic community, where some took issue with ProPublica's definition of *bias*. Much more importantly, however, the controversy spawned an entirely new area of academic research: fairness and transparency in machine learning and intelligence.

perform statistical analyses, and generate meaningful visualizations. While many other programming languages do some of these things, few do all of them as well as Python.

Accessibility

One of Python creator Guido van Rossum's goals in designing the language was to make "code that is as understandable as plain English" (*https://en.wikipedia.org/wiki/Guido_van_Rossum#Python*). Python uses English keywords where many other scripting languages (like R and JavaScript) use punctuation. For English-language readers, then, Python may be both easier and more intuitive to learn than other scripting languages.

Readability

One of the core tenets of the Python programming language is that "readability counts" (*https://en.wikipedia.org/wiki/Zen_of_Python*). In most programming languages, the visual layout of the code is irrelevant to how it functions—as long as the "punctuation" is correct, the computer will understand it. Python, by contrast, is what's known as "whitespace dependent": without proper tab and/or space characters indenting the code, it actually won't do anything except produce a bunch of errors. While this can take some getting used to, it enforces a level of readability in Python programs that can make reading other people's code (or, more likely, your own code after a little time has passed) much less difficult. Another aspect of readability is *commenting* and otherwise documenting your work, which I'll address in more detail in "Documenting, Saving, and Versioning Your Work" on page 24.

Community

Python has a very large and active community of users, many of whom help create and maintain "libraries" of code that enormously expand what you can quickly accomplish with your own Python code. For example, Python has popular and well-developed code libraries like *NumPy* and *Pandas* that can help you clean and analyze data, as well as others like *Matplotlib* and *Seaborn* to create visualizations. There are even powerful libraries like *Scikit-Learn* and *NLTK* that can do the heavy lifting of machine learning and natural language processing. Once you have a handle on the essentials of data wrangling with Python that we'll cover in this book (in which we will use many of the libraries just mentioned), you'll probably find yourself eager to explore what's possible with many of these libraries and just a few lines of code. Fortunately, the same folks who write the code for these libraries often write blog posts, make video tutorials, and share code samples that you can use to expand your Python work.

Similarly, the size and enthusiasm of the Python community means that finding answers to both common (and even not-so-common) problems and errors that you may encounter is easy—detailed solutions are often posted online. As a result, troubleshooting Python code can be easier than for more specialized languages with a smaller community of users.

Python Alternatives

Although Python has much to recommend it, you may also be considering other tools for your data-wrangling needs. The following is a brief overview of some tools you may have heard of, along with why I chose Python for this work instead:

R

The R programming language is probably Python's nearest competitor for data work, and many teams and organizations rely on R for its combination of data wrangling, advanced statistical modeling, and visualization capabilities. At the same time, R lacks some of the accessibility and readability of Python.

SQL

Simple Query Language (SQL) is just that: a language designed to "slice and dice" database data. While SQL can be powerful and useful, it requires data to exist in a particular format to be useful and is therefore of limited use for "wrangling" data in the first place.

Scala

Although Scala is well suited for dealing with large datasets, it has a much steeper learning curve than Python, and a much smaller user community. The same is true of Julia.

Java, C/C++

While these have large user communities and are very versatile, they lack the natural language and readability bent of Python and are oriented more toward building software than doing data wrangling and analysis.

JavaScript

In a web-based environment, JavaScript is invaluable, and many popular visualization tools (e.g., D3) are built using variations of JavaScript. At the same time, JavaScript does not have the same breadth of data analysis features as Python and is generally slower.

Writing and "Running" Python

To follow along with the exercises in this book, you'll need to get familiar with the tools that will help you write and run your Python code; you'll also want a system for backing up and documenting your code so you don't lose valuable work to an errant keystroke,[5] *and* so that you can easily remind yourself what all that great code can do, even when you haven't looked at it for a while. Because there are multiple toolsets for solving these problems, I recommend that you start by reading through the following sections and then choosing the approach (or combination of approaches) that works best for your preferences and resources. At a high level, the key decisions will be whether you want to work "online only"—that is, with tools and services you access via the internet—or whether you can and want to be able to do Python work *without* an internet connection, which requires installing these tools on a device that you control.

We all write differently depending on context: you probably use a different style and structure when writing an email than when sending a text message; for a job application cover letter you may use a whole different tone entirely. I know I also use different tools to write depending on what I need to accomplish: I use online documents when I need to write and edit collaboratively with coworkers and colleagues, but I prefer to write books and essays in a super-plain text editor that lives on my device. More particular document formats, like PDFs, are typically used for contracts and other important documents that we don't want others to be able to easily change.

Just like natural human languages, Python can be written in different types of documents, each of which supports slightly different styles of writing, testing, and running your code. The primary types of Python documents are *notebooks* and *standalone files*. While either type of document can be used for data wrangling, analysis, and visualization, they have slightly different strengths and requirements. Since it takes some tweaking to convert one format to the other, I've made the exercises in this book available in both formats. I did this not only to give you the flexibility of choosing the document type that you find easiest or most useful but also so that you can compare them and see for yourself how the translation process affects the code. Here's a brief overview of these document types to help you make an initial choice:

Notebooks
> A Python *notebook* is an interactive document used to run chunks of code, using a web browser window as an interface. In this book, we'll be using a tool called "Jupyter" to create, edit, and execute our Python notebooks.[6] A key advantage of using notebooks for Python programming is that they offer a simple way to write, run, and document your Python code all in one place. You may prefer notebooks if you're looking for a more "point and click" programming experience or if working entirely online is important to you. In fact, the same Python notebooks can be used on your local device or in an online coding environment with minimal changes, meaning that this option may be right for you if you (1) don't

---

5 Remember that even a misplaced space character can cause problems in Python.

6 This same software can also be used to create notebooks in R and other scripting languages.

have access to a device where you're able to install software, or (2) you can install software but you *also* want to be able to work on your code when you don't have your machine with you.

Standalone files

A *standalone* Python file is really any plain-text file that contains Python code. You can create such standalone Python files using any basic text editor, though I strongly recommend that you use one specifically designed for working with code, like Atom (I'll walk through setting this up in "Installing Python, Jupyter Notebook, and a Code Editor" on page 14). While the software you choose for writing and editing your code is up to you, in general the only place you'll be able to *run* these standalone Python files is on a physical device (like a computer or phone) that has the Python programming language installed. You (and your computer) will be able to recognize standalone Python files by their *.py* file extension. Although they might seem more restrictive at first, standalone Python files can have some advantages. You don't need an internet connection to run standalone files, and they don't require you to upload your data to the cloud. While both of those things are also true of locally run notebooks, you *also* don't have to wait for any software to start up when running standalone files. Once you have Python installed, you can run standalone Python files instantly from the *command line* (more on this shortly)—this is especially useful if you have a Python script that you need to run on a regular basis. And while notebooks' ability to run bits of code independently of one another can make them feel a bit more approachable, the fact that standalone Python files also always run your code "from scratch" can help you avoid the errors or unpredictable results that can occur if you run bits of notebook code out of order.

Of course, you don't have to choose just one or the other; many people find that notebooks are especially useful for *exploring* or *explaining* data (thanks to their interactive and reader-friendly format), while standalone files are better suited for *accessing, transforming*, and *cleaning* data (since standalone files can more quickly and easily run the same code on different datasets, for example). Perhaps the bigger question is whether you want to work *online* or *locally*. If you don't have a device where you can install Python, you'll need to work in cloud-based notebooks; otherwise you can choose to use either (or both!) notebooks or standalone files on your device. As noted previously, notebooks that can be used either online or locally, as well as standalone Python files, are available for all the exercises in this book to give you as much flexibility as possible, and also so you can compare how the same tasks get done in each case!

Working with Python on Your Own Device

To understand and run Python code, you'll need to install it on your device. Depending on your device, there may be a downloadable installation file available, or you may need to use a text-based interface (which you'll need to use at some point if you're using Python on your device) called the *command line*. Either way, the goal is to get you up and running with at least Python 3.9.[7] Once you've got Python up and running, you can move on to installing Jupyter notebook and/or a code editor (instructions included here are for Atom (*https://atom.io*)). If you're planning to work only in the cloud, you can skip right to "Working with Python Online" on page 19 for information on how to get started.

Getting Started with the Command Line

If you plan to use Python locally on your device, you'll need to learn to use the *command line* (also sometimes referred to as the *terminal* or *command prompt*), which is a text-based way of providing instruction to your computer. While in principle you can do anything in the command line that you can do with a mouse, it's particularly efficient for installing code and software (especially the Python libraries that we'll be using throughout the book) and backing up and running code. While it may take a little getting used to, the command line is often faster and more straightforward for many programming-related tasks than using a mouse. That said, I'll provide instructions for using both the command line and your mouse where both are possible, and you should feel free to use whichever you find more convenient for a particular task.

To get started, let's open up a command line (sometimes also called the *terminal*) interface and use it to create a folder for our data wrangling work. If you're on a Chromebook, macOS, or Linux machine, search for "terminal" and select the application called Terminal; on a Windows PC, search for "powershell" and choose the program called Windows PowerShell.

 To enable Linux on your Chromebook, just go to your Chrome OS settings (click the gear icon in the Start menu, or search for "settings" in the Launcher). Toward the bottom of the lefthand menu, you'll see a small penguin icon labeled "Linux (Beta)." Click this and follow the directions to enable Linux on your machine. You may need to restart before you can continue.

---

7 The numbers here are called *version numbers*, and they increase sequentially as the Python language is changed and upgraded over time. The first number (3) indicates the "major" version, and the second number (9) indicates the "minor" version. Unlike regular decimals, it's possible for the minor version to be higher than 9, so in the future you might encounter a Python 3.12.

Once you have a terminal open, it's time to make a new folder! To help you get started, here is a quick glossary of useful command-line terms:

ls
> The "list" command shows files and folders in the current location. This is a text-based version of what you would see in a finder window.

cd *foldername*
> The "change directory" command moves you from the current location into *foldername*, as long as *foldername* is shown when you use the ls command. This is equivalent to "double-clicking" on a folder within a finder window using your mouse.

cd ../
> "Change directory" once again, but the ../ moves your current position to the containing folder or location.

cd ~/
> "Change directory," but the ~/ returns you to your "home" folder.

mkdir *foldername*
> "Make directory" with name *foldername*. This is equivalent to choosing New → Folder in the context menu with your mouse and then naming the folder once its icon appears.

 When using the command line, you never actually have to type out the full name of a file or folder; think of it more like search, and just start by typing the first few characters of the (admittedly case-sensitive) name. Once you've done that, hit the Tab key, and the name will autocomplete as much as possible.

For example, if you have two files in a folder, one called *xls_parsing.py* and one called *xlsx_parsing.py* (as you will when you're finished with Chapter 4), and you wanted to run the latter, you can type **python xl** and then hit Tab, which will cause the command line to autocomplete to **python xls**. At this point, since the two possible filenames diverge, you'll need to supply either an x or an _, after which hitting Tab one more time will complete the rest of the filename, and you're good to go!

Any time you open a new terminal window on your device, you'll be in what's known as your "home" folder. On macOS, Windows, and Linux machines, this is often the "User" folder, which is *not* the same as the "desktop" area you see when you first log in. This can be a little disorienting a first, since the files and folders you'll see when you first run `ls` in a terminal window will probably be unfamiliar. Don't worry; just point your terminal at your regular desktop by typing:

```
cd ~/Desktop
```

into the terminal and hitting Enter or Return (for efficiency's sake, I'll just refer to this as the Enter key from here on out).

On Chromebooks, Python (and the other programs we'll need) can only be run from inside the *Linux files* folder, so you can't actually navigate to the desktop and will have to open a terminal window.

Next, type the following command into your terminal window and hit Enter:

```
mkdir data_wrangling
```

Did you see the folder appear? If so, congratulations on making your first folder in the command line! If not, double-check the text at the left of the command line prompt ($ on Chromebook, % on macOS, or > on Windows). If you don't see the word `Desktop` in there, run `cd ~/Desktop` and then try again.

Don't Leave Space!

Although most operating systems will let you do it, I strongly recommend against using either spaces or any punctuation marks apart from the underscore character (_) in your folder and filenames. As you'll see firsthand in Chapter 2, both the command line and Python (along with most programming languages) rely on whitespace and punctuation as shorthand for specific functionality, which means these characters have to be "escaped"—usually by preceding them with some additional character, like a backslash (\)—if they are part of a file or folder name you want to access. In fact, you can't even *do* this from the command line; if you were to type:

```
mkdir data wrangling
```

you'd just end up with two new folders: one called *data* and another called *wrangling*. If you really wanted to force it and you used your mouse to create a folder called *data wrangling*, moreover, to access it from the command line, you'd need to type:

```
cd data\ wrangling/
```

Not impossible, of course, but more trouble than it's worth. To avoid this hassle, it's easier to just get in the habit of not using spaces or punctuation other than underscores when naming files, folders, and, soon, Python variables!

Now that you've gotten a little bit of practice with the command line, let's see how it can help when installing and testing Python on your machine.

Installing Python, Jupyter Notebook, and a Code Editor

To keep things simple, we're going to use a software *distribution manager* called Miniconda, which will automatically install both Python and Jupyter Notebook. Even if you don't plan to use notebooks for your own coding, they're popular enough that being able to view and run *other* people's notebooks is useful, and it doesn't take up that much additional space on your device. In addition to getting your Python and Jupyter Notebook tools up and running, installing Miniconda will also create a new command-line function called conda, which will give you a quick and easy way to keep both your Python and Jupyter Notebook installations up to date.[8] You can find more information about how to do these updates in Appendix A.

If you're planning to do most of your Python programming in a notebook, I also still recommend installing a code editor. Even if you never use them to write a single line of Python, code editors are indispensable for viewing, editing, and even creating your own data files more effectively and efficiently than most devices' built-in text-editing software. Most importantly, code editors do something called *syntax highlighting*, which is basically built-in grammar checking for code and data. While that may not sound like much, the reality is that it will make your coding and debugging processes *much* faster and more reliable, because you'll know (literally) where to look when there's a problem. This combination of features makes a solid code editor one of the most important tools for both Python programming *and* general data wrangling.

In this book I'll be using and referencing the Atom (*https://atom.io*) code editor, which is free, multiplatform, and open source. If you play around with the settings, you'll find many ways to customize your coding environment to suit your needs. Where I reference the color of certain characters or bits of code in this book, they reflect the default "One Dark" theme in Atom, but use whatever settings work best for you.

 You'll need a strong, stable internet connection and about 30–60 minutes to complete the following setup and installation processes. I also strongly recommend that you have your device plugged into a power source.

Chromebook

To install your suite of data wrangling tools on a Chromebook, the first thing you'll need to know is whether your version of the Chrome OS operating system is 32-bit or 64-bit.

---

8 Miniconda is a smaller version of the popular "Anaconda" software, but since the latter installs the R programming language and a number of other items we won't need, we'll use Miniconda to save space on our device.

To find this information, open up your Chrome settings (click the gear icon in the Start menu, or search "settings" in the Launcher) and then click on "About Chrome OS" at the lower left. Toward the top of the window, you'll see the version number followed by either (32-bit) or (64-bit), as shown in Figure 1-1.

Figure 1-1. Chrome OS version detail

Make a note of this information before continuing with your setup.

Installing Python and Jupyter Notebook. To get started, download the Linux installer (*https://docs.conda.io/en/latest/miniconda.html#latest-miniconda-installer-links*) that matches the bit format of your Chrome OS version. Then, open your *Downloads* folder and drag the installer file (it will end in *.sh*) into your *Linux files* folder.

Next, open up a terminal window, run the `ls` command, and make sure that you see the Miniconda *.sh* file. If you do, run the following command (remember, you can just type the beginning of the filename and then hit the Tab key, and it will autocomplete!):

```
bash _Miniconda_installation_filename_.sh
```

Follow the directions that appear in your terminal window (accept the license and the `conda init` prompt), then close and reopen your terminal window. Next, you'll need to run the following:

```
conda init
```

Then close and reopen your terminal window again so that you can install Jupyter Notebook with the following command:

```
conda install jupyter
```

Answer yes to the subsequent prompts, close your terminal one last time, and you're all set!

Installing Atom. To install Atom on your Chromebook, you'll need to download the *.deb* package from *https://atom.io* and save it in (or move it to) your *Linux files* folder.

To install the software using the terminal, open a terminal window and type:

```
sudo dpkg -i atom-amd64.deb
```

Hit Enter.[9] Once the text has finished scrolling and the *command prompt* (which ends with a $) is back, the installation is complete.

Alternatively, you can context-click on the *.deb* file in your *Linux files* folder and choose the "Install with Linux" option from the top of the context menu, then click "Install" and "OK." You should see a progress bar on the bottom right of your screen and get a notification when the installation is complete.

Whichever method you use, once the installation is finished, you should see the green Atom icon appear in your "Linux apps" bubble in the Launcher.

macOS

You have two options when installing Miniconda on macOS: you can use the terminal to install it using a *.sh* file, or you can install it by downloading and double-clicking the *.pkg* installer.

Installing Python and Jupyter Notebook. To get started, go to the Miniconda installer links page (*https://docs.conda.io/en/latest/miniconda.html#latest-miniconda-installer-links*). If you want to do your installation with the terminal, download the Python 3.9 "bash" file that ends in *.sh*; if you prefer to use your mouse, download the *.pkg* file (you may see a notification from the operating system during the download process warning, "This type of file can harm your computer"; choose "Keep").

Whichever method you select, open your *Downloads* folder and drag the file onto your desktop.

If you want to try installing Miniconda using the terminal, start by opening a terminal window and using the cd command to point it to your desktop:

```
cd ~/Desktop
```

Next, run the **ls** command, and make sure that you see the Miniconda *.sh* file in the resulting list. If you do, run the following command (remember, you can just type the beginning of the filename and then hit the Tab key, and it will autocomplete!):

```
bash _Miniconda_installation_filename_.sh
```

Follow the directions that appear in your terminal window:

---

9 If you have a 32-bit Chromebook, the filename might be slightly different.

- Use the space bar to move through the license agreement a full page at a time, and when you see (END), hit Return.
- Type **yes** followed by Return to accept the license agreement.
- Hit Return to confirm the installation location, and type **yes** followed by Return to accept the conda init prompt.

Finally, close your terminal window.

If you would prefer to do the installation using your mouse, just double-click the *.pkg* file and follow the installation instructions.

Now that you have Miniconda installed, you need to open a new terminal window and type:

```
conda init
```

Then hit Return. Next, close and reopen your terminal window, and use the following command (followed by Return) to install Jupyter Notebook:

```
conda install jupyter
```

Answer yes to the subsequent prompts.

Installing Atom. To install Atom on a Mac, visit *https://atom.io* and click the large yellow Download button to download the installer.

Click on the *atom-mac.zip* file in your *Downloads* folder and then drag the Atom application (which will have a green icon next to it) into your *Applications* folder (this may prompt you for your password).

Windows 10+

To install your suite of data wrangling tools on Windows 10+, the first thing you'll need to know is whether your version of the Windows 10 operating system is 32-bit or 64-bit.

To find this information, open up your Start menu, then select the gear icon to go to the Settings menu. In the resulting window, choose System → About in the lefthand menu. In the section titled "Device specifications," you'll see "System type," which will specify whether you have a 32-bit or 64-bit system. For the official instructions, see Microsoft's related FAQ (*https://support.microsoft.com/en-us/windows/32-bit-and-64-bit-windows-frequently-asked-questions-c6ca9541-8dce-4d48-0415-94a3faa2e13d*).

Make a note of this information before continuing with your setup.

Installing Python and Jupyter Notebook. To get started, go to the Miniconda installer links page (*https://docs.conda.io/en/latest/miniconda.html#latest-miniconda-installer-links*) and download the Python 3.9 installer appropriate for your system (either 32-bit or 64-bit). Once the *.exe* file has downloaded, click through the installer menus, leaving the preselected options in place (you can skip the recommended tutorials and the "Anaconda Nucleus" sign-up at the end).

Once the installation is complete, you should see two new items in your Start menu in the "Recently added" list at the top: "Anaconda Prompt (miniconda3)" and "Anaconda Powershell Prompt (miniconda3)," as shown in Figure 1-2. While both will work for our purposes, I recommend you use Powershell as your "terminal" interface throughout this book.

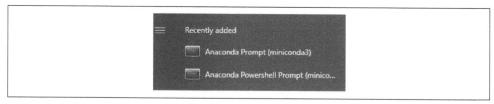

Figure 1-2. Anaconda options in the Start menu

Now that you have Miniconda installed, you need to open a new terminal (Powershell) window and type:

```
conda init
```

Then hit Return. Next, close and reopen your terminal window as instructed, and use the following command (followed by Return) to install Jupyter Notebook:

```
conda install jupyter
```

Answer yes (by typing **y** and then hitting the Enter key) to the subsequent prompts.

Installing Atom. To install Atom on a Windows 10+ machine, visit *https://atom.io* and click the large yellow "Download" button to download the installer.

Click on the *Atom-Setup-x64.exe* file,[10] and wait for the installation to finish; Atom should launch automatically. You can answer Yes to the blue pop-up that asks about registering as the default *atom://* URI handler.

---

10 The installer filename may have a different number if you are on a 32-bit system.

Testing your setup

To make sure that both Python and Jupyter Notebook are working as expected, start by opening a terminal window and pointing it to the *data_wrangling* folder you created in "Getting Started with the Command Line" on page 11, then running the following command:[11]

```
cd ~/Desktop/data_wrangling
```

Then, run:

```
python --version
```

If you see something like:

```
Python 3.9.4
```

this means that Python was installed successfully.

Next, test out Jupyter Notebook by running:

```
jupyter notebook
```

If a browser window opens[12] that looks something like the image in Figure 1-3, you're all set and ready to go!

Figure 1-3. Jupyter Notebook running in an empty folder

Working with Python Online

If you want to skip the hassle of installing Python and code editor on your machine (and you plan to only use Python when you have a strong, consistent internet connection), working with Jupyter notebooks online through Google Colab is a great option. All you'll need to get started is an unrestricted Google account (you can create a new one if you prefer—make sure you know your password!). If you have those elements in place, you're ready to get wrangling with "Hello World!" on page 20!

---

11 Unless otherwise noted, all terminal commands should be followed by hitting Enter or Return.

12 If you get a prompt asking about how you want to "open this file," I recommend selecting Google Chrome.

Hello World!

Now that you've got your data wrangling tools in place, you're ready to get started writing and running your first Python program. For this, we'll bow to programming tradition and create a simple "Hello World" program; all it's designed to do is print out the words "Hello World!" To get started, you'll need a new file where you can write and save your code.

Using Atom to Create a Standalone Python File

Atom works just like any other text-editing program; you can launch it using your mouse or even using your terminal.

To launch it with your mouse, locate the program icon on your device:

Chromebook
Inside the "Linux apps" applications bubble.

Mac
In *Applications* or in the Launchpad on Mac.

Windows
In the Start menu or via search on Windows. If Atom doesn't appear in your start menu or in search after installing it for the first time on Windows 10, you can find troubleshooting videos on YouTube (*https://youtube.com/watch? v=N4liFqsK9nM*).

Alternatively, you can open Atom from the terminal by simply running:

```
atom
```

The first time you open Atom on a Chromebook, you'll see the "Choose password for new keyring" prompt. Since we'll just be using Atom for code and data editing, you can click Cancel to close this prompt. On macOS, you'll see a warning that Atom was downloaded from the internet—you can also click past this prompt.

You should now see a screen similar to the one shown in Figure 1-4.

By default, when Atom launches, it shows one or more "Welcome" tabs; you can just close these by clicking the x close button that appears to the right of the text when you hover over it with your mouse. This will move the *untitled* file toward the center of your screen (if you like, you can also collapse the Project panel on the left by hovering over its right edge until the < appears and then clicking on that).

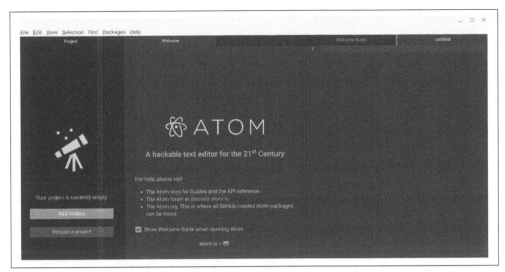

Figure 1-4. Atom welcome screen

Before we start writing any code, let's go ahead and save our file where we'll know where to find it—in our *data_wrangling* folder! In the File menu, select "Save As…" and save the file in your *data_wrangling* folder with the name *HelloWorld.py*.

When saving standalone Python files, it's essential to make sure you add the *.py* extension. While your Python code will still work properly without it, having the correct extension will let Atom do the super-useful syntax highlighting I mentioned in "Installing Python, Jupyter Notebook, and a Code Editor" on page 14. This feature will make it *much* easier to write your code correctly the first time!

Using Jupyter to Create a New Python Notebook

As you may have noticed when you tested Jupyter Notebook, in "Testing your setup" on page 19, the interface you're using is actually just a regular browser window. Believe it or not, when you run the `jupyter notebook` command, your regular computer is actually creating a tiny web server on your device![13] Once that main Jupyter window is up and running, you can use your mouse to create new Python files and run other commands right in your web browser!

To get started, open a terminal window and use the command:

```
cd ~/Desktop/data_wrangling/
```

---

13 Don't worry, it's not visible on the internet!

to move into the *data_wrangling* folder on your Desktop. Next, run:

```
jupyter notebook
```

You'll see a lot of code run past on the terminal window, and your computer should automatically open a browser window that will show you an empty directory. Under New in the upper-righthand corner, choose "Python 3" to open a new notebook. Double-click the word *Untitled* in the upper-lefthand corner next to the Jupyter logo to name your file *HelloWorld*.

 Because Jupyter Notebook is actually running a web server (yes, the same kind that runs regular websites) on your local computer, it's essential that *you leave that terminal window open and running* for as long as you are interacting with your notebooks. If you close that particular terminal window, your notebooks will "crash."

Fortunately, Jupyter notebooks autosave every two minutes, so even if something does crash, you probably won't lose much work. That being said, you may want to minimize the terminal window you use to launch Jupyter, just to avoid accidentally closing it while you're working.

Using Google Colab to Create a New Python Notebook

First, sign in to the Google account you want to use for your data wrangling work, then visit the Colab website (*https://colab.research.google.com*). You'll see something similar to the overlay shown in Figure 1-5.

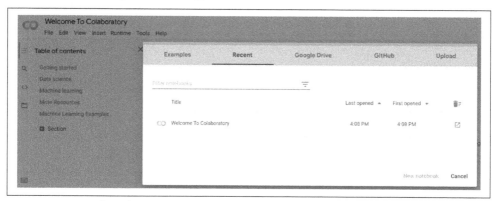

Figure 1-5. Google Colab landing page (signed in)

In the bottom-right corner, choose New notebook, then double-click at the top left to replace *Untitled0.ipynb* with *HelloWorld.ipynb*.[14]

Adding the Code

Now, we'll write our first bit of code, which is designed to print out the words "Hello World." No matter which type of Python file you're using, the code shown in Example 1-1 is the same.

Example 1-1. hello_world.py

```
# the code below should print "Hello World!"
print("Hello World!")
```

In a Standalone File

All you need to do is copy (or type) the code in Example 1-1 into your file and save it!

In a Notebook

When you create a new file, there is one empty "code cell" in it by default (in Jupyter Notebook, you'll see In [ ] to the left of it; in Google Colab, there's a little "play" button). Copy (or type) the code in Example 1-1 into that cell.

Running the Code

Now that we've added and saved our Python code in our file, we need to *run* it.

In a Standalone File

Open a terminal window and move it into your *data_wrangling* folder using:

```
cd ~/Desktop/data_wrangling
```

Run the **ls** command and make sure you see your *HelloWorld.py* file listed in response. Finally, run:

```
python HelloWorld.py
```

You should see the words Hello World! print out on their own line, before the command prompt returns (signaling that the program has finished running).

---

14 Early versions of Jupyter Notebook were known as "iPythonNotebook," which is where the *.ipynb* file extension comes from.

In a Notebook

Hit the "play" button to the left of the cell. You should see the words `Hello World!` print out beneath it.

If everything worked as expected—congratulations! You've now written your first bit of Python code!

Documenting, Saving, and Versioning Your Work

Before we really dive into Python in Chapter 2, there are a few more bits of preparation to do. I know these may seem tedious, but making sure you've laid the groundwork for properly documenting your work will save you dozens of hours of effort and frustration. What's more, carefully commenting, saving, and versioning your code is a crucial part of "bulletproofing" your data wrangling work. And while it's not exactly enticing right now, pretty soon all of these steps will be second nature (I promise!), and you'll see how much speed and efficiency it adds to your data work.

Documenting

You may have noticed that the first line you wrote in your code cell or Python file in "Hello World!" on page 20 *didn't* show up in the output; the only thing that printed was `Hello World!`. That first line in our file was a *comment*, which provides a plain-language description of what the code on the following line(s) will do. Almost all programming languages (and some data types!) provide a way to include comments, precisely because they are an excellent way to provide anyone reading your code[15] with the context and explanation necessary to understand what the specific program or section of code is doing.

Though many individual programmers tend to overlook (read: skip) the commenting process, it is probably the single most valuable programming habit you can develop. Not only will it save you—and anyone you collaborate with—an enormous amount of time and effort when you are looking through a Python program, but commenting is also *the single best way* to really internalize what you're learning about programming more generally. So even though the code samples provided with this book will already have comments, I *strongly* encourage you to rewrite them in your own words. This will help ensure that when future you returns to these files, they'll contain a clear walk-through of how you understood each particular coding challenge the first time.

The other essential documentation process for data wrangling is keeping what I call a "data diary." Like a personal diary, your data diary can be written and organized however you like; the key thing is to capture *what you are doing as you are doing*

---

15 Especially "future you"!

---

it. Whether you're clicking around the web looking for data, emailing experts, or designing a program, you need somewhere to keep track of everything, because you *will* forget.

The first entry in your "diary" for any data wrangling project should be *the question you are trying to answer*. Though it may be a challenge, try to write your question as a single sentence, and put it at the top of your data wrangling project diary. Why is it important that your question be a single sentence? Because the process of real data wrangling will inevitably lead you down enough "rabbit holes"—to answer a question about your data's origin, for example, or to solve some programming problem—that it's very easy to lose track of what you were originally trying to accomplish (and why). Once you have that question at the top of your data diary, though, you can always come back to it for a reminder.

Your data diary question will also be invaluable for helping you make decisions about how to spend your time when data wrangling. For example, your dataset may contain terms that are unfamiliar to you—should you try to track down the meaning of every single one? Yes, *if* doing so will help answer your question. If not, it may be time to move on to another task.

Of course, once you succeed in answering your question (and you will! at least in part), you'll almost certainly find you have more questions you want to answer, or that you want to answer the same question again, but a week, a month, or a year later. Having your data diary on hand as a guide will help you do it *much* faster and more easily the next time. That's not to say that it doesn't take effort: in my experience, keeping a thorough data diary makes a project take about 40% longer to complete the first time around, but it makes doing it again (with a new version of the dataset, for example) at least twice as fast. Having a data diary is also a valuable proof of work: if you're ever looking for the process by which you got your data wrangling results, your data diary will have all the information that you (or anyone else) might need.

When it comes to *how* you keep your data diary, however, it's really up to you. Some folks like to do a lot of fancy formatting; others just use a plain old text file. You may even want to use a real gosh-for-sure paper notebook! Whatever works for you is fine. While your data diary will be an invaluable reference when it comes time to communicate with others about your data (and the wrangling process), you should organize it however suits you best.

Saving

In addition to documenting your work carefully through comments and data diaries, you'll want to make sure you save it regularly. Fortunately, the "saving" process is essentially built in to our workflow: notebooks autosave regularly, and to run the code in our standalone file, we have to save our changes first. Whether you rely on keyboard shortcuts (for me, hitting Ctrl+S is something of a nervous habit) or use mouse-driven menus, you'll probably want to save your work every 10 minutes or so at least.

 If you are using standalone files, one thing to get familiar with is how your code editor indicates that a file has unsaved changes. In Atom, for example, a small colored dot appears in the document tab just to the right of the filename when there are unsaved changes to the file. If the code you're running isn't behaving as you expect, double-check that you have it saved first and then try again.

Versioning

Programming—like most writing—is an iterative process. My preferred approach has always been to write a little bit of code, test it out, and if it works, write a little more and test again. One goal of this approach is to make it easier to backtrack in case I add something that accidentally "breaks" the code.[16]

At the same time, it's not always possible to guarantee that your code will be "working" when you have to step away from it—whether because the kids just got home, the study break is over, or it's time for bed. You always want to have a "safe" copy of your code that you can come back to. This is where version control comes in.

Getting started with GitHub

Version control is basically just a system for backing up your code, both on your computer and in the cloud. In this book, we'll be using GitHub for version control; it's a hugely popular website where you can back up your code for free. Although there are many different ways to interact with GitHub, we'll use the command line because it just takes a few quick commands to get your code safely tucked away until you're ready to work on it again. To get started, you'll need to create an account on GitHub, install Git on your computer, and then connect the accounts to one another:

1. Visit the GitHub website at *https://github.com* and click "Sign Up." Enter your preferred username (you may need to try a few to find one that's available), your email address, and your chosen password (make sure to write this down or save it to your password manager—you'll need it soon!).

2. Once you've logged in, click the New button on the left. This will open the "Create a new repository" page shown in Figure 1-6.

3. Give your repository a name. This can be anything you like, but I suggest you make it something descriptive, like *data_wrangling_exercises*.

---

16 Meaning that I no longer get the output I expect, or that I get errors and no output at all!

4. Select the Private radio button, and select the checkbox next to the option that says "Add a README file."

5. Click the"Create repository" button.

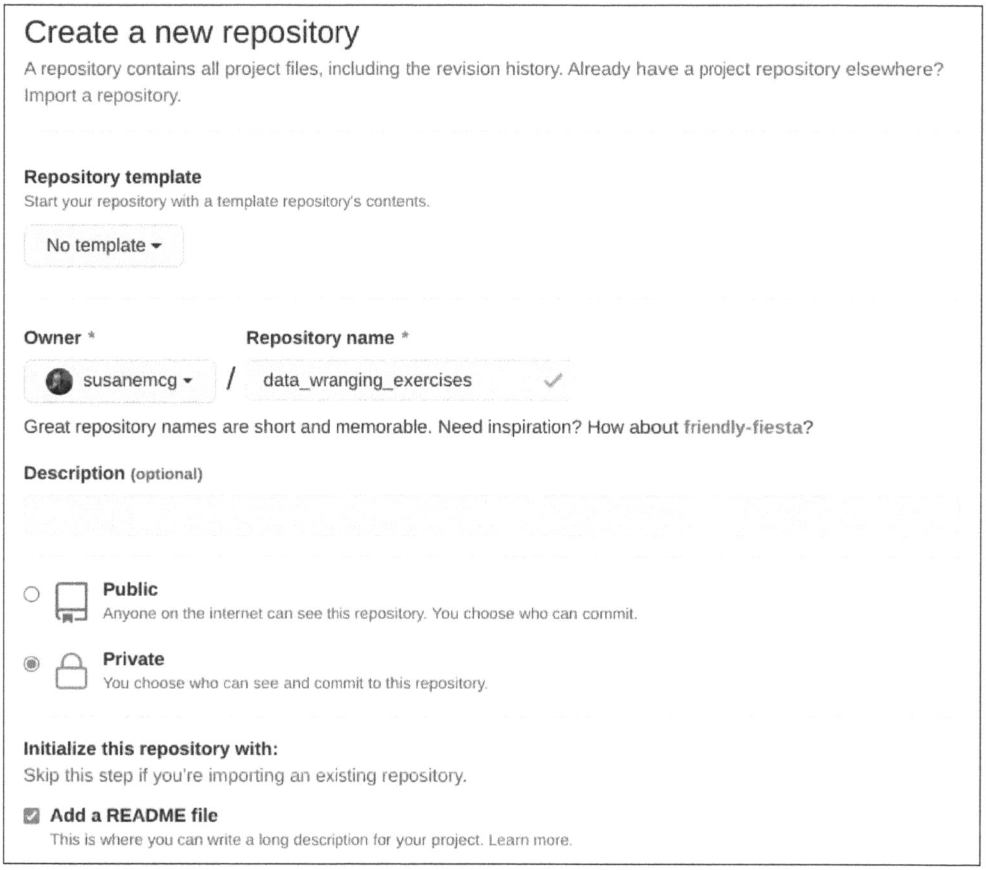

Figure 1-6. Creating a new repository (or "repo") on GitHub.com

You'll now see a page that shows *data_wrangling_exercises* in large type, with a small pencil icon just above and to the right. Click on the pencil and you'll see an editing interface where you can add text. This is your *README* file, which you can use to describe your repository. Since we'll be using this repository (or "repo" for short) to store exercises from this book, you can just add a sentence to that effect, as shown in Figure 1-7.

Scroll to the bottom of the page and you'll see your profile icon with an editable area to the right that says "Commit changes," and below that some default text that says "Update README.md." Replace that default text with a brief description of what you did; this is your "commit message." For example, I wrote: "Added description of repo contents," as shown in Figure 1-8. Then click the"Commit changes" button.

Figure 1-7. Updating the README file on GitHub

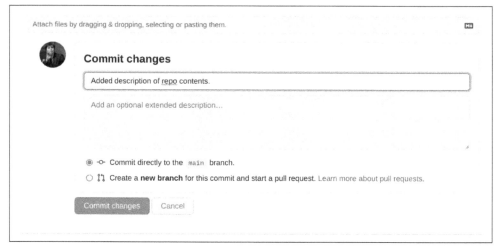

Figure 1-8. Adding a commit message to the README file changes

When the screen refreshes, you'll now see the text you added to the main file underneath the original *data_wrangling_exercises* title. Just above that, you should be able to see the text of your commit message, along with the approximate amount of time that's passed since you clicked "Commit changes." If you click on the text that says "2 commits" to the right of that, you'll see the "commit history," which will show you all the changes (so far just two) that have been made to that repo, as shown in Figure 1-9. If you want to see how a commit changed a particular file, just click on the six-character code to the right, and you'll see what's known as a *diff* (for "difference") view of the file. On the left is the file as it existed before the commit, and on the right is the version of the file in this commit.

Figure 1-9. A brief commit history for our new repo

By this point, you may be wondering how this relates to backing up code, since all we've done is click some buttons and edit some text. Now that we've got a "repo" started on GitHub, we can create a copy of it on our local machine and use the command line to make "commits" of working code and back them up to this website with just a few commands.

For backing up local files: installing and configuring Git. Like Python itself, Git is software that you install on your computer and run via the command line. Because version control is such an integral part of most coding processes, Git comes built in on macOS and Linux; instructions for Windows machines can be found on GitHub (*https://github.com/git-guides/install-git*), and for ChromeBooks, you can install Git using the Termux app (*https://techrepublic.com/article/how-to-use-github-in-chrome-os*). Once you've completed the necessary steps, open up a terminal window and type:

```
git --version
```

Followed by 'enter'. If *anything* prints, you've already got Git! You'll still, however, want to set your username and email (you can use any name and email you like) by running the following commands:

```
git config --global user.email your_email@domain.com
git config --global user.name your_username
```

Now that you have Git installed and have added your name and email of choice to your local Git account, you need to create an *authentication key* on your device so that when you back up your code, GitHub knows that it really came from you (and not just someone on the other side of the world who figured out your username and password).

To do this, you'll need to create what's known as an *SSH key*—which is a long, unique string of characters stored on your device that GitHub can use to identify it. Creating these keys with the command line is easy: just open up a terminal window and type:

```
ssh-keygen -t rsa -b 4096 -C "your_email@domain.com"
```

When you see the "Enter a file in which to save the key" prompt, just press the Enter or Return key, so it saves the default location (this will make it easier to find in a minute, when we want to add it to GitHub). When you see the following prompt:

```
Enter passphrase (empty for no passphrase):
```

definitely add a passphrase! And *don't* make it the password to your GitHub (or any other) account. However, since you'll need to supply this passphrase every time you want to back your code up to GitHub,[17] it needs to be memorable—try something like the first three words of the second verse of your favorite song or poem, for example. As long as it's at least 8–12 characters long, you're set!

Once you've reentered your passphrase for confirmation, you can copy your key to your GitHub account; this will let GitHub match the key on your account to the one on your device. To do this, start by clicking on your profile icon in the upper-righthand corner of GitHub and choosing Settings from the drop-down menu. Then, on the lefthand navigation bar, click on the "SSH and GPG Keys" option. Toward the upper right, click the "New SSH key" button, as shown in Figure 1-10.

Figure 1-10. SSH key landing page on GitHub.com

To access the SSH key you just generated, you'll need to navigate to the main user folder on your device (this is the folder that a new terminal window will open in) and set it (temporarily) to show hidden files:

---

17 Depending on your device, you can save this password to your "keychain." For more information, see the docs on GitHub (*https://docs.github.com/en/github/authenticating-to-github/connecting-to-github-with-ssh/working-with-ssh-key-passphrases*).

Chromebook

Your main user folder is just the one called *Linux files*. To show hidden files, just click the three stacked dots at the top right of any Files window and choose "Show hidden files."

macOS

Use the Command-Shift-. keyboard shortcut to show/hide hidden files.

Windows

Open File Explorer on the taskbar, then choose View → Options → "Change folder and search options." On the View tab in "Advanced settings," select "Show hidden files, folders, and drives," then click OK.

Look for the folder (it actually is a folder!) called *.ssh* and click into it, then using a basic text editor (like Atom), open the file called *id_rsa.pub*. Using your keyboard to select and then copy everything in the file, paste it into the empty text area labeled Key, as shown in Figure 1-11.

Figure 1-11. Uploading your SSH key to your GitHub.com account

Finally, give this key a name so you know what device it's associated with, and click the"Add new SSH key" button—you will probably have to reenter your main GitHub password. That's it! Now you can go back to leaving hidden files hidden and finish connecting your GitHub account to your device and/or Colab account.

I recommend using keyboard shortcuts to copy/paste your SSH key because the *exact* string of characters (including spaces) actually matters; if you use a mouse, something might get dragged around. If you paste in your key and GitHub throws an error, however, there are a couple of things to try:

- Make sure you're uploading the contents of the *.pub* file (you never really want to do anything with the other one).
- Close the file (without saving) and try again.

If you still have trouble, you can always just delete your whole .ssh folder and generate new keys—since they haven't been added to anything yet, there's no loss in just starting over!

Tying it all together. Our final step is to create a linked copy of our GitHub repo on our local computer. This is easily done via the `git clone` command:

1. Open a terminal window, and navigate to your *data_wrangling* folder.
2. On GitHub, go to *your_github_username/data_wrangling_exercises*.
3. Still on GitHub, click theCode button toward the top of the page.
4. In the "Clone with SSH" pop-up, click the small clipboard icon next to the URL, as shown in Figure 1-12.

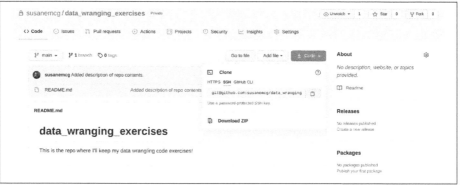

Figure 1-12. Retrieving the repo's SSH location

5. Back in your terminal window, type **git clone** and then paste the URL from your clipboard (or type it directly if needed). It will look something like:

```
git clone git@github.com:susanemcg/data_wrangling_exercises.git
```

6. You may get a prompt asking if you would like to add the destination to the list of known hosts. Type **yes** and hit Return. If prompted, provide your SSH password.

7. When you see the "done" message, type **ls**. You should now see *data_wrangling_exercises* in your *data_wrangling* folder.

8. Finally, type **cd data_wrangling_exercises** and hit Enter to move your terminal into the copied repo. Use the **ls** command to have the terminal show the *README.md* file.

Whew! That probably seems like a lot, but keep in mind that you only ever need to create an SSH key once, and you'll only have to go through the cloning process once per repo (and all the exercises in this book can be done in the same repo).

Now let's see how this all works in action by adding our Python file to our repo. In a finder window, navigate to your *data_wrangling* folder. Save and close your *HelloWorld.py* or *HelloWorld.ipynb* file, and drag it into the *data_wrangling_exercises* folder. Back in terminal, use the **ls** command to confirm that you see your Python file.

Our final step is to use the **add** command to let Git know that we want our Python file to be part of what gets backed up to GitHub. We'll then use a **commit** to save the current version, followed by the **push** command to actually upload it to GitHub.

To do this, we're going to start by running **git status** in the terminal window. This should generate a message that mentions "untracked files" and shows the name of your Python file. This is what we expected (but running **git status** is a nice way to confirm it). Now we'll do the adding, committing, and pushing process described previously. Note that the **add** commands produce output messages in the terminal:

1. In terminal, run **git add** *your_python_filename*.

2. Then run **git commit -m "Adding my Hello World Python file."** *your_python_filename*. The -m command indicates that the quoted text should be used as the commit message—the command-line equivalent of what we entered on GitHub for our *README* update a few minutes ago.

3. Finally, run **git push**.

The final command is what uploads your files to GitHub (note that this clearly will not work if you don't have an available internet connection, but you can make commits anytime you like and run the **push** command whenever you have internet again). To confirm that everything worked correctly, reload your GitHub repo page, and you'll see that your Python file and commit message have been added!

For backing up online Python files: connecting Google Colab to GitHub. If you're doing all of your data wrangling online, you can connect Google Colab directly to your GitHub account. Make sure you're logged in to your data wrangling Google account and then visit *https://colab.research.google.com/github*. In the pop-up window, it will ask you to sign in to your GitHub account, and then to "Authorize Colaboratory." Once you do so, you can select a GitHub repo from the drop-down menu on the left, and any Jupyter notebooks that are in that repo will appear below.

> The Google Colab view of your GitHub repos will *only* show you Jupyter notebooks (files that end in *.ipynb*). To see all files in a repo, you'll need to visit it on the GitHub website.

Tying it all together. If you're working on Google Colab, all you have to do to add a new file to your GitHub repo is to choose File → Save a copy in GitHub. After automatically opening and closing a few pop-ups (this is Colab logging in to your GitHub account in the background), you'll once again be able to choose the GitHub repo where you want to save your file from the drop-down menu at the top left. You can then choose to keep (or change) the notebook name and add a commit message. If you leave "Include a link to Colaboratory" checked in this window, then the file in GitHub will include a little "Open in Colab" label, which you'll be able to click to automatically open the notebook in Colab from GitHub. Any notebooks that you don't explicitly back up in GitHub this way will be in your Google Drive, inside a folder called *Colab Notebooks*. You can also find them by visiting the Colab website (*https://colab.research.google.com*) and selecting the Google Drive tab at the top.

Folders, Directories, and Repos: Oh My!

You may have noticed over the course of this chapter that there doesn't seem to be much difference between "folders," "directories," and even "repos." In fact, the first two are just different names for the same thing, while the last specifically refers to folders where at least some of the files are tracked by Git.

In other words, you can still interact with all of them, using your mouse and regular finder windows, to add, remove, and open files. The only difference is that, in the case of a repo, you'll need to use Git commands like add and rm to keep everything in order—but we'll address each of these situations as they arise in future chapters.

Conclusion

The goal of this chapter was to provide you with a general overview of what you can expect to learn in this book: what I mean by data wrangling and data quality, and why I think the Python programming language is the right tool for this work.

In addition, we covered all the setup you'll need to get started (and keep going!) with Python for data wrangling, by offering instructions for setting up your choice of programming environment: working with "standalone" Python files or Jupyter notebooks on your own device, or using Google Colab to use Jupyter notebooks online. Finally, we covered how you can use version control (no matter which setup you have) to back up, share, and document your work.

In the next chapter, we'll move far beyond our "Hello World" program as we work through the foundations of the Python programming language and even tackle our first data wrangling project: a day in the life of New York's Citi Bike system.

# CHAPTER 2

Introduction to Python

Can you read this? If so, I have good news for you: you won't have any trouble learning to program. Why? Because computer programming languages in general—and Python in particular—are much less complex than natural human languages. Programming languages are designed by humans to be read, for the most part, by computers, so they have simpler grammar and far fewer "parts of speech" than natural languages. So if you feel reasonably comfortable reading English—a language notorious for its large vocabulary and irregular spellings and pronunciation—rest assured that learning the fundamentals of Python is well within your reach.

By the end of this chapter, you'll have all the Python skills you need to begin doing basic data wrangling with the common data formats that we'll cover in Chapter 4. To get to that point, we'll start by doing some basic coding exercises that cover the following:

- Essential Python "parts of speech" and its basic grammar/syntax
- How the computer reads and interprets your Python code
- How to use code "recipes" that are built by others (and yourself!) to quickly expand what your own code can do

Throughout this chapter, you'll find code snippets that illustrate each concept, which are also collected in the accompanying Jupyter notebooks and standalone Python files on GitHub; these can be pulled into Google Colab or downloaded and run on a computer. While these files will let you see this chapter's code in action, however, I *strongly* suggest that you create a new Colab/Jupyter notebook or standalone Python file and practice writing, running, and commenting this code for yourself (for a refresher on how to do this, see "Hello World!" on page 20). While you might think this is silly, there is actually nothing more useful for building your data wrangling skills and confidence than setting up a Python file "from scratch" and then seeing code you wrote yourself make the computer do what you want—even if you are "just" retyping it from another file. Yes, you will encounter more hiccups this way, but that's sort of the point: doing good data wrangling is not really about learning to do anything "right," *it's about learning how to recover when things go wrong.* Giving yourself room to make little mistakes early on (and learning how to recognize and fix them) is how you'll truly make progress as both a data wrangler and programmer. You'll never get that experience if all you do is run already-working code.

Because these little mistakes are so important, I've included some "Fast Forward" sections in this chapter, which will offer you ways to take the code examples I've provided one step further—which often involves intentionally "breaking" the code. By the end of this chapter, you'll be ready to combine the basics we've covered into a full-fledged data wrangling program that relies on real-world data. For each example, I'll also include some explicit reminders about the kinds of things you'll want to include in your data diary, when you'll want to back up your code to GitHub, and so on so that you can begin to get really comfortable with those processes and also start to develop a feel for when you'll want to take those steps during your own data wrangling projects.

Now that you know where we're headed—let's get started!

The Programming "Parts of Speech"

Different human languages use different vocabularies and syntax structures, but there are many fundamental concepts that they typically share. For example, let's take a look at the following two sentences:

```
My name is Susan.         // English

Je m'appelle Susan.       // French
```

Both of these sentences express essentially the same thing: they state what my name is. And though each language uses different words and slightly different grammatical structures, they both include parts of speech like subjects, objects, verbs, and modifiers. They also both follow similar grammar and *syntax* rules, in that they organize words and ideas into structures like sentences, paragraphs, and so on.

Many programming languages also share key structural and organizational elements that roughly parallel those found in natural languages. To get a better idea of how this works, let's start in the same way that we might when learning a new human language: by exploring programming languages' "parts of speech."

Nouns ≈ Variables

In the English language, nouns are often described as any word that refers to a "person, place, or thing." Though this isn't a super-precise definition, it is a handy way of illustrating the different types of entities that nouns can be. In programming languages, it is *variables* that are used to hold and refer to the different data *types* that we use to write our programs. Instead of "people, places, and things," however, variables in the Python programming language can be one of five main data types:

- Number
- String
- List
- Dictionary (dict)
- Boolean

As with human languages, there is a lot of overlap in types of variables that different programming languages support: what in Python we call *lists* are known as *arrays* in JavaScript or C, for example; JavaScript *objects*, on the other hand, are officially known as *maps* (or *dictionaries*) in Python.[1]

Having read the data types list, you can probably already guess what at least some of these data types will look like. The good news is that, unlike nouns in the real world, every data type in Python can be reliably identified by its formatting and punctuation—so there's no need to worry that you'll mix up your *dicts* and your *lists*, as long as you take the time to look closely at the symbols that surround your data.

To get a sense of the unique punctuation structure of each data type, take a look at Example 2-1. In particular, make sure you open or make a copy of this code in your code editor or notebook, so you can see the *syntax highlighting* in action. Numbers should be a different color than strings, for example, and the brackets, braces, and comments (on the lines that begin with a #) should all be another color as well.

Example 2-1. parts_of_speech.py

```
# a number is just digits
25

# a string is anything surrounded by matching quotation marks
"Hello World"

# a list is surrounded by square brackets, with commas between items
```

---

1 There are also many language-specific data types (such as Python's *tuple* data type) that are not as relevant to our data wrangling efforts, so we won't address these in detail.

```
# note that in Python, the first item in a list is considered to be
# in position `0`, the next in position `1`, and so on
["this","is",1,"list"]

# a dict is a set of key:value pairs, separated by commas and surrounded
# by curly braces
{"title":"Practical Python for Data Wrangling and Data Quality",
 "format": "book",
 "author": "Susan E. McGregor"
}

# a boolean is a data type that has only two values, true and false.
True
```

Of course, this list is far from exhaustive; just as human languages support "complex nouns" (like "haircut" and "bedroom"), it is possible to build more complex data types in programming languages as well. As you'll soon see, however, there's quite a lot that we can get done even with just this handful of basic types.

In the real world we also often give names to the many unique instances of "people, places, and things" in our lives, to reference and communicate about them more easily. We do this in programming, too, and for exactly the same reason: naming our variables lets us reference and modify specific pieces of data in a way the computer can understand. To see how this works, let's try translating a simple English sentence into Python code:

```
The author is Susan E. McGregor
```

After reading this sentence, you will associate the name "Susan E. McGregor" with the label "author." If someone asks you who wrote this book, you will (hopefully) remember this and say "Susan E. McGregor." The equivalent "sentence" in Python code is shown in Example 2-2.

Example 2-2. Naming a Python variable

```
author = "Susan E. McGregor"
```

This code tells the computer to set aside a box in memory, label it author, and then put the string "Susan E. McGregor" into that box. Later on in our program, if we asked the computer about the author variable, it would tell us that it contains the string "Susan E. McGregor", as shown in Example 2-3.

Example 2-3. Printing the contents of a Python variable

```
# create a variable named author, set its contents to "Susan E. McGregor"
author = "Susan E. McGregor"
```

```
# confirm that the computer "remembers" what's in the `author` variable
print(author)
```

What's in a name?

In Example 2-3, I chose to name my variable `author`, but there is nothing magical about that choice. In principle, you can name variables almost anything you want—the only "hard-and-fast" rules are that variable names cannot:

- Begin with a digit
- Contain punctuation marks other than underscores (_)
- Be "reserved" words or "keywords" (like Number or Boolean, for example)

For example, I could just as easily have called the variable in Example 2-3 `nyc_resi dent` or even `fuzzy_pink_bunny`. What matters most is that you, as the programmer, follow the few restrictions listed previously, *and* that you use *exactly* the same variable name when trying to access its contents later (capitalization counts!). For example, create a new Python file containing the code in Example 2-4, and then run it to see what results you get.

Example 2-4. noun_examples.py

```
# create a variable named nyc_resident, set its contents to "Susan E. McGregor"
nyc_resident = "Susan E. McGregor"

# confirm that the computer "remembers" what's in the `nyc_resident` variable
print(nyc_resident)

# create a variable named fuzzyPinkBunny, set its contents to "Susan E. McGregor"
fuzzyPinkBunny = "Susan E. McGregor"

# confirm that the computer "remembers" what's in the `fuzzyPinkBunny` variable
print(fuzzyPinkBunny)

# but correct capitalization matters!
# the following line will produce an error
print(fuzzypinkbunny)
```

Best practices for naming variables

While all of the examples used in Example 2-4 are *legitimate* variable names, not all of them are especially *good* variable names. As we'll see throughout this book, writing good code—like any other kind of writing—is about more than just writing code that "works"; it's also about how useful and intelligible that code is to both computers *and* people. Because of this, I consider naming variables well an essential part of good programming. In practice, *good* variable names are:

- Descriptive
- Unique (within a given file or program)
- Readable

Because achieving the first two properties often requires using more than one word, programmers typically use one of two stylistic conventions to help ensure that their variable names also remain *readable*, both of which are shown in Example 2-4. One approach is to add underscores (_) between words (e.g., nyc_residents) or use "camel case," in which the first letter of every word (except the first) is capitalized (e.g., fuzzyPinkBunny). In general, you should use one style and stick to it, though your code will work fine (and mostly meet the readability criteria) even if you mix them together. In this book, we'll mostly use underscores, which also happen to be considered more "Pythonic."

Verbs ≈ Functions

In the English language, verbs are often described as "actions" or "states of being." We've already seen a programming language equivalent of the latter: the equals sign (=) and the print() function used in the preceding examples. In English, we use forms of the verb "to be" to describe what something *is*; in Python (and many other programming languages), the value of a variable *is* whatever appears on the righthand side of the equals sign. This is why the equals sign is also sometimes described as the *assignment operator*.

In programming, the equivalent of "action verbs" are *functions*. In Python and many other programming languages, there are *built-in functions*, which represent tasks—like printing output via the print() function—that the language "just knows" how to do. While similar, *methods* are special functions that are designed to work with a particular data type and need to be "called on" a variable of that data type in order to work. The methods available for a given data type tend to reflect common tasks you might want to perform with it. So just as most humans can walk, talk, eat, drink, and grasp objects, most programming languages have *string methods* that can do tasks like stick two strings together (known as *concatenation*), split two strings apart, and so on. But since it doesn't make sense to "split" the number 5, the Number data type *doesn't* have a split() method.

What is the difference between a built-in function and a method in practice? Not much, except for the way we include these "verbs" in our Python "sentences" or *statements*. With a built-in function, we can simply write the function name and pass along any "ingredients" it needs, by placing them between the round parentheses. For example, if you recall our Example 1-1, all we had to do was pass the string Hello World! to the print() function, like this:

```
print("Hello World!")
```

In the case of the split() method, however, *we have to attach the method to a specific string*. That string can either be a *literal* (that is, a series of characters surrounded by quotation marks), or it can be a variable whose value is a string. Try the code in Example 2-5 in a standalone file or notebook, and see what kind of output you get!

Example 2-5. method_madness.py

```
# splitting a string "literal" and then printing the result
split_world = "Hello World!".split()
print(split_world)

# assigning a string to a variable
# then printing the result of calling the `split()` method on it
world_msg = "Hello World!"
print(world_msg.split())
```

Note that if you try to run the split() method by itself or on a data type where it doesn't make sense, you'll get an error. Try each of these out in succession (or in two different cells if you're using a notebook) and see what happens:

```
# the following will produce an error because
# the `split()` method must be called on a string in order to work!
split("Hello World!")

# the following will produce an error because
# there is no `split()` method for numbers!
print(5.split())
```

Just like data types, methods and functions are recognizable thanks to their typography and punctuation. A built-in function (like print()) will turn a specific color in your code editor or notebook. In Atom's default One Dark theme, for example, variable names are light gray, operators like = are purple, and built-in functions like print() are aqua. You can also recognize functions by their associated punctuation: anywhere you see text *immediately* followed by round parentheses (e.g., print()), you are looking at a function. The same is true of methods, except that these are always preceded by an appropriate data type or variable name, and separated from it by a period (.).

In a programming language like Python, you can actually get a fair bit done with just operators, methods, and built-in functions—especially if you are mostly doing tasks like basic math. When it comes to data wrangling, however, we need a little bit more sophistication. In exactly the same way we can think about complex tasks like playing a piano or kicking a ball as "just" a careful combination of many simpler actions—like moving our fingers or feet, for example—very sophisticated programming functions can be built by thoughtfully composing relatively simple operators, methods, and built-in functions. These *user-defined functions* are where we can start to really amplify the power of our code by making what are essentially code "recipes" that can be used again and again.

For example, let's say we wanted to print out the same greeting to two different people. We could simply use the `print()` function as we have been, as shown in Example 2-6.

Example 2-6. basic_greeting.py

```
# create a variable named author
author = "Susan E. McGregor"

# create another variable named editor
editor  = "Jeff Bleiel"

# use the built-in print function to output "Hello" messages to each person
print("Hello "+author)
print("Hello "+editor)
```

There are a couple of things to notice about the code in Example 2-6. First, using the `print()` function works just fine; this code totally gets the job done. And that's great! The first time we write code for something (including a given data wrangling task), that's pretty much our main goal: get it to work correctly.

Once we've accomplished that, though, we can start to think about some simple ways to make our code "cleaner" and more useful. In the previous example, the two print statements are identical, except for the variable being used. Any time we see this type of repetition in our code, it's a clue that we may want to make our own user-defined function instead, as in Example 2-7.

Example 2-7. greet_me.py

```
# create a function that prints out a greeting
# to any name passed to the function

def greet_me(a_name):
    print("Hello "+a_name)

# create a variable named author
author = "Susan E. McGregor"

# create another variable named editor
editor  = "Jeff Bleiel"

# use my custom function, `greet_me` to output "Hello" messages to each person
greet_me(author)
greet_me(editor)
```

Pretty nifty, right? In some ways, we didn't change much at all—but there's actually quite a lot going in Example 2-7. We'll take a few moments now to highlight some of the new concepts being used here, but don't worry if it doesn't all make sense right away—we'll continue to revisit these ideas throughout the book.

The main thing we've done in Example 2-7 is write our first custom function, `greet_me()`. We did this by using a few different syntax structures and typographic indicators to let the computer know that we want it to create and remember this function for future use. Some of these conventions match what we've already seen for creating our own custom variables (for example, using the descriptive name `greet_me()`), as well as the conventions of built-in functions and methods, like following the name of our function immediately with round parentheses (`()`).

In Figure 2-1, I've diagrammed the code for our `greet_me()` function in order to highlight what's happening on each line.

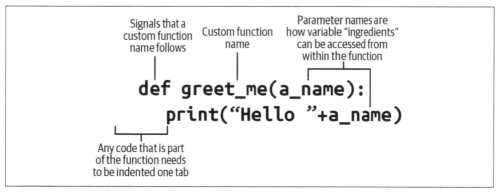

Figure 2-1. Components of a custom function

As you can see from Figure 2-1, creating a custom function means including multiple signposts to the computer:

- The `def` keyword (short for *define*) tells the computer that what comes next is a function name.
- The round parentheses immediately following the function name reinforce that this is a function and are used to enclose the function's *parameters* (if there are any).
- The colon (`:`) indicates that the indented lines of code that follow are part of the function.

- If we want to access the variable that was passed into our function as an *argument*, we use the "local" *parameter* name that appears between the round parentheses in the function definition.

- We can use any type of functions (both built-in and custom) or methods *inside* our custom function. This is key strategy for building efficient, flexible code.

When it comes to using or "calling" our function, we can simply write the name of the function (`greet_me()`), making sure that we put the same number of "ingredients" between the parentheses that appear in the function definition. Since we have defined `greet_me()` to take exactly *one* argument "ingredient" (in this case, the `a_name` parameter), we have to provide *exactly* one argument when we want to use it—otherwise, we'll get an error.

Fast Forward

We'll discuss errors a little more in-depth in "Understanding Errors" on page 55, but you should *always* feel free to play around with the code in these examples to see what happens when something goes "wrong" with your code. For the code in Example 2-7, here are a few ways to start experimenting:

- Without any parameter "ingredients," e.g., `greet_me()`

- With *too many* parameter "ingredients," e.g., `greet_me(author,editor)`

- With something that isn't a variable, e.g., `greet_me("Samantha")`

- With something that isn't a string, e.g., `greet_me(14)`

In each case, notice what happens when you try to run the code. If it produces an error message, see if you can connect the contents of that message to the changes you made. While programming error messages are not brilliantly descriptive, it's usually possible to glean at least *some* useful information from them about why the computer is complaining. We'll walk through *debugging*—the process of methodically fixing "broken" code—in detail soon, but this is a great way to get started now!

Cooking with Custom Functions

As you may have noticed, I like to think of user-defined or "custom" functions as programming "recipes." Like food recipes, they provide the computer with reusable instructions for transforming one or more raw data "ingredients" into some other useful resource. Sometimes there is only one parameter or "ingredient," as in our `greet_me()` recipe; sometimes there are many parameters of many different data types. There's no strictly "right" or "wrong" way to write a custom function—much as there's no right or wrong way to write a cooking recipe; everyone will have their own

---

style. At the same time, when it comes to strategies for deciding what should go into a given function, it can help to think about how we tend to use (or maybe even write!) recipes for cooking food.

For example, it's obviously *possible* to write a single cooking recipe called "Thanksgiving" that describes how to make an entire holiday meal from start to finish. Depending on your holiday style, it might take anywhere from 2 to 72 hours to "run," and it would be very useful once a year—and almost never otherwise. If you *did* want to make just part of that massive recipe—perhaps you want to serve your Thanksgiving mashed potatoes at New Year's—you'd first have to dig through the Thanksgiving instructions to identify and piece together *just* the ingredients and steps for making mashed potatoes. That would mean investing a lot of work before you ever even got cooking!

So while we want our custom functions to do things that are *somewhat* more complex than what the computer can do already, we generally don't want them to be truly *complicated*. Like a "Thanksgiving" recipe, making giant functions (or even programs) limits how effectively they can be reused. Creating simple, focused functions actually makes our code more useful and flexible in the long run—a process we'll explore in more detail in Chapter 8.

Libraries: Borrowing Custom Functions from Other Coders

If custom functions are programming recipes, then *libraries* are programming cookbooks: large collections of *other people's* custom functions that *we* can use to transform our raw data ingredients without having to figure out and write our own recipe "from scratch." As I mentioned in Chapter 1, the large community of coders who have written useful Python libraries is one of the reasons we're using Python in the first place—and as you'll see in "Hitting the Road with Citi Bike Data" on page 62 at the end of this chapter, using them is both useful and powerful.

Before we can really take advantage of libraries, however, we need to cover two more essential grammatical structures of Python: *loops* and *conditionals*.

Taking Control: Loops and Conditionals

As we have discussed, writing Python code is similar to writing in English in many ways. In addition to relying on some basic "parts of speech," Python code is written from left to right and read essentially from top to bottom. But the path that the computer takes through a data wrangling program is much more like a "Choose Your Own Adventure" book (*https://en.wikipedia.org/wiki/Choose_Your_Own_Adventure*) than a traditional essay or article: depending on the commands that you, as the programmer, provide, some bits of code may be skipped or repeated based on your data or other factors.

In the Loop

When we're data wrangling with Python, one of our most common goals will be to do *something* to every record in a dataset. For example, let's say we wanted to add together a list of numbers to find their sum:

```
# create a list that contains the number of pages in each chapter
# of a fictional print version of this book

page_counts = [28, 32, 44, 23, 56, 32, 12, 34, 30]
```

If you needed to total a group of numbers like this without programming, you would have several options: you could use the calculator program on a computer, a physical calculator, or even (gasp!) a pencil and paper. If you know how to use a spreadsheet program, you could enter each data item there and use a SUM() function, too. For short lists, any of these solutions would probably be fine, but they don't *scale* well: sure, adding up 10 numbers by hand (or by calculator) might not take too long, but adding up 100 numbers would. The spreadsheet solution is somewhat better in terms of time, but it still requires a number of external steps—like copying and pasting the data into a spreadsheet and more or less manually selecting which rows or columns should be summed. With a programmatic solution, we can avoid almost all of those drawbacks—and whether we need to add 10 rows or 10 million, it will take no more work on our part, and only slightly longer for the computer to actually calculate.

Because programming is still writing, of course, there are multiple ways we can express the instructions we give to the computer. One way is to have the computer look at each number in the list and keep a running total, as shown in Example 2-8.

Example 2-8. page_count_loop.py

```
# fictional list of chapter page counts
page_counts = [28, 32, 44, 23, 56, 32, 12, 34, 30]

# variable for tracking total page count; starting value is 0
total_pages = 0

# for every item in the list, perform some action
for a_number in page_counts:

    # in this case, add the number to our "total_pages" variable
    total_pages = total_pages + a_number

print(total_pages)
```

Before we look at some other ways we could tell the computer to do this task, let's break down Example 2-8. Obviously, we start with the list of numbers. Next, we create a variable to keep track of total_pages, to which we have to explicitly assign a value of 0 to start out (most calculator programs do this more or less implicitly). Finally, we begin going through our list:

```
for a_number in page_counts:
```

To me, the easiest way to understand this line of code is to say it out loud like an English sentence: "For every a_number in the list, page_counts do the following." And in fact, that's exactly what happens. For every item in the page_counts list, the computer follows the instructions in the code indented under the for...in...: statement. In this case, that means adding together the current value of total_pages and the value of a_number and storing that back in total_pages again.

In some ways, this is straightforward: we've already told the computer, very explicitly, the values of both page_counts (that's our list of numbers) and total_pages. But what about a_number? Where did that come from, and how does the computer know where to find it?

Like the print() statement or the def...function_name(): construction, the for...in...: configuration is built into the Python language, which is why we don't have to give it quite as many instructions as we usually will when coding. In this case, what we have to provide the for...in...: statement to work are two things: a list-like variable (in this case, page_counts) and a name that the computer can use to refer to the current item in the list (in this case, a_number), as shown in Figure 2-2.

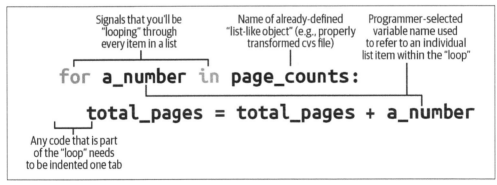

Figure 2-2. Structure of a for loop

As with all variable names, there is nothing "magic" about the variable name a_number—I thought that was a good option because it's descriptive and readable. What matters is that when I want the computer to do something with each list item, the variable name I use in my indented code has to match what I've written in that top for...in...: statement.

In programming lingo, this for...in...: construction is known as a *for loop*—and every commonly used programming language has one. The reason why it's known as a "loop" is because for every item in the list provided, the computer runs every relevant line of code—in the case of Python, every indented line below the for...in...: statement—and then moves to the next item and "loops" back to the first indented line of code again. This is a little hard to see when our "loop" only has one line of code, so let's add a few more lines to better illustrate what's going on, as shown in Example 2-9.

Example 2-9. page_count_printout.py

```python
# fictional list of chapter page counts
page_counts = [28, 32, 44, 23, 56, 32, 12, 34, 30]

# variable for tracking total page count; starting value is 0
total_pages = 0

# for every item in the list, perform some action
for a_number in page_counts:
    print("Top of loop!")
    print("The current item is:")
    print(a_number)
    total_pages = total_pages + a_number
    print("The running total is:")
    print(total_pages)
    print("Bottom of loop!")

print(total_pages)
```

By now you might be thinking, "This seems like a lot of work just to sum a list of numbers." And there is, of course, a more efficient way to complete this *specific* task: Python has a built-in sum() function that will take our list of numbers as an argument (Example 2-10).

Example 2-10. Using the sum() function

```
# fictional list of chapter page counts
page_counts = [28, 32, 44, 23, 56, 32, 12, 34, 30]

# `print()` the result of using the `sum()` function on the list ❶
print(sum(page_counts))
```

❶ Try adding this to your existing program on your own!

Even though we could have used the sum() function from the start, I took this opportunity to introduce for loops, for a couple of reasons. First, because it's a good reminder that even when it comes to simple programming tasks, there's always more than one approach. Second, because for loops are an essential part of data wrangling (and, really, all programming), for...in...: loops are one of the key tools we'll use to filter, evaluate, and reformat data.

One Condition…

The for loop gives us a straightforward way to look at every item in a dataset, but data wrangling requires making *decisions* about our data as well. Usually, that means evaluating some aspect of the data and doing one thing if the data has a certain value and otherwise something (or nothing!) else. For example, what if we wanted to know how many chapters in this book have more than 30 pages and how many have fewer than 30 pages? We'd need a way to:

1. Check whether a particular number in our page_counts list is more than 30.

2. Add 1 to an over_30 counter if it's more than 30.

3. Otherwise, add 1 to our under_30 counter.

Fortunately, Python has a built-in grammatical structure for doing exactly this kind of evaluation and decision-making: the if...else statement. Let's see how it works by modifying the for loop in Example 2-9 to also track the number of chapters that are more and less than 30 pages.

Example 2-11. page_count_conditional.py

```python
# fictional list of chapter page counts
page_counts = [28, 32, 44, 23, 56, 32, 12, 34, 30]

# create variables to keep track of:
# the total pages in the book
total_pages = 0

# the number of chapters with more than 30 pages,
under_30 = 0

# the number of chapters with fewer than 30 pages
over_30 = 0


# for every item in the page_counts list:
for a_number in page_counts:

    # add the current number of pages to our total_pages count
    total_pages = total_pages + a_number

    # check if the current number of pages is more than 30
    if a_number > 30:

        # if so, add 1 to our over_30 counter
        over_30 = over_30 + 1

    # otherwise...
    else:
        # add 1 to our under_30 counter
        under_30 = under_30 + 1


# print our various results
print(total_pages)
print("Number of chapters over 30 pages:")
print(over_30)
print("Number of chapters under 30 pages:")
print(under_30)
```

As with `for` loops, I think the easiest way to understand what's happening in an `if...else` conditional is to say it out loud as a sentence (and, just as importantly, write that sentence in the comments of your code): "if the current number of pages is more than 30, add one to the `over_30` counter. Otherwise (`else`), add one to the `under_30` counter."

While hopefully this makes some sense intuitively, I want to slow down again and go through what's happening in a bit more detail, since `if...else` statements are another programming structure that we'll come back to over and over.

First, let's look at the indenting structure of the preceding example: everything that's part of the `for` loop is indented one tab from the left margin; that's how the computer knows that code is "inside" that loop. Similarly, the code that belongs to each part of the `if...else` statement is indented one tab *more*. In Python, this process of progressive indentation is actually *required* for the code to work properly—if the indenting isn't correct, Python will complain.[2] This mechanism is often referred to as *nesting*. A more visual way to think about what's happening is shown in Figure 2-3.

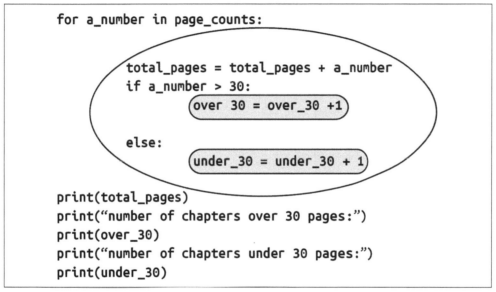

Figure 2-3. Code "nesting"

There are a number of implications of nesting that we'll address later in this book, but the main takeaway for now is that in order to make a line of code "belong" to a function, loop, or conditional, *it must be indented one tab to the right of the structure you want it to be part of.* To see this in action, let's bring together everything we've done up to this point to create a Python program that uses a loop, a conditional, and a custom-defined function, as shown in Example 2-12.

---

2 In many other programming languages, curly braces are used to indicate which pieces of code belong inside a loop or a conditional statement. As we mentioned in "Readability" on page 7, however, Python is *whitespace dependent*.

Example 2-12. page_count_custom_function.py

```python
# fictional list of chapter page counts
page_counts = [28, 32, 44, 23, 56, 32, 12, 34, 30]

# define a new `count_pages()` function that takes one ingredient/argument:
# a list of numbers
def count_pages(page_count_list):  ❶

    # create variables to keep track of:
    # the total pages in the book
    total_pages = 0

    # the number of chapters with more than 30 pages,
    under_30 = 0

    # the number of chapters with fewer than 30 pages
    over_30 = 0


    # for every item in the page_count_list:
    for a_number in page_count_list:  ❷

        # add the current number of pages to our total_pages count
        total_pages = total_pages + a_number

        # check if the current number of pages is more than 30
        if a_number > 30:

            # if so, add 1 to our over_30 counter
            over_30 = over_30 + 1

        # otherwise...
        else:
            # add 1 to our under_30 counter
            under_30 = under_30 + 1


    # print our various results
    print(total_pages)
    print("Number of chapters over 30 pages:")
    print(over_30)
    print("Number of chapters under 30 pages:")
    print(under_30)

# call/execute this "recipe", being sure to pass in our
# actual list as an argument/ingredient
count_pages(page_counts)  ❸
```

❶ We can "wrap" our existing code into a new function (here called `count_pages()`) by indenting one tab and adding the function definition line.

❷ We have to match the name of the list variable the `for` loop references to the parameter name provided between the round parentheses in the function definition in ❶.

❸ A function does not *do* anything until it is actually *called* or *executed*. At this point, we need to provide it with the specific argument/ingredient we want it to work on.

If you compare Example 2-12 to Example 2-11, you'll see that I actually just copied the code from Example 2-11 and did three things:

1. I added the function defining statement `def count_pages(page_count_list):`.
2. I indented all the existing code one additional tab so that the computer views it as "belonging" to our new `count_pages()` function. In Atom, you can do this all at once by highlighting all the lines of code you want to move and hitting the Tab key. I also updated the variable referenced at the top of the `for` loop to match the parameter name provided between the round parentheses on the `def` line of the function.
3. I made sure to "call" the function at the end, giving it the `page_counts` variable as an "ingredient" or *argument*. Notice that the `count_pages(page_counts)` statement isn't indented at all.

Hopefully, you're starting to get a little bit of a handle on how all this fits together. Before we start using these tools to do some real-world data wrangling, though, we need to spend some time talking about what happens when code goes wrong.

Understanding Errors

As we've mentioned in Chapter 1, computers are *very* good at doing repetitive tasks quickly (and usually accurately). This lets us write programs that *scale* well: the same code that can sum or sort a list that's 10 items long (like our `page_counts` example) can also be used pretty effectively on a list that's 10,000 items long.

At the same time, however, computers are truly, importantly, and irretrievably stupid. Computers can't really infer or innovate—they can only choose paths through their code based on the instructions and data that humans provide to them. As a result, there are many ways in which writing code is like giving instructions to a toddler: you have to be extremely literal and very explicit, and if something unexpected happens, you should expect a tantrum.[3]

For example, when humans encounter a spelling or grammatical error in a written sentence, we often don't even notice it: based on the context of the surrounding sentence or paragraph, much of the time we'll infer the appropriate meaning without even really trying. In fact, even if almost *all* of the letters in *all* of the words in a sentence are rearranged, we can uusally siltl raed it wihtuot too mcuh erfoft.[4] Computers, by contrast, will just complain loudly and stop reading altogether if your code has even a comma out of place.

Because of this, errors in programming aren't just inevitable, they're *expected*. No matter how much you program, any chunk of code you write that's longer than a few lines will have errors in it of one kind or another. Rather than worrying about how to *avoid* errors, it is much more useful to learn how to *interpret* and *correct* errors. Throughout this book, I will at times intentionally generate errors (or encourage you to do so, as in "Fast Forward" on page 46 and "Fast Forward" on page 50) so that you can get familiar with them and begin to develop your own process for working through them. As a starting point, we'll discuss the three main *types* of errors that occur in programming: syntax errors, runtime errors, and logic errors.

Syntax Snafus

Grammatical or *syntax* errors in programming may simultaneously be the simplest and most frustrating type of error you'll encounter—in part because they happen very frequently and because the computer complains loudly about them. The example I gave earlier about a comma being out of place is an example of a syntax error: in one way or another, your code has violated the grammatical rules of the programming language.

The reason I describe these errors as "simple" is that they almost always are. In my experience, most syntax errors—and, by extension, programming errors—are basically typos: a comma or quotation mark gets forgotten, or a line of code gets indented too much or not enough. Unfortunately, many newer programmers I've worked with seem to find these errors especially frustrating precisely because they are simple—and because they feel silly for making them.

In truth, experienced programmers experience syntax errors all the time. If you're just starting out, the main thing you can learn from syntax errors is how *not* to let them derail you. In fact, one of the reasons why I've included the preceding "Fast Forward"

---

3 Unlike computers, of course, toddlers are capable of genuine originality and learning.

4 For more, see Scott Rosenberg's Wordyard blog post about the topic (*http://wordyard.com/2003/09/15/if-u-cn-rd-ths-msg-u-r-jst-lke-vryne-lse*).

sections on how to "break" your code intentionally is to help illustrate how easily errors can happen—and be fixed. In some ways one of the greatest skills you'll learn when programming is how to be wrong a *lot* and not let it discourage you.

Get Your Game On

One thing that can help make programming errors less frustrating—especially early on—is to approach the process sort of like a video game: beating a difficult level often means attempting it (at least) dozens of times. Sometimes you'll have to retry because an enemy (or problem) is truly difficult, but sometimes you just make a mistake and fall down a hole (or forget a comma). In both cases, the key thing is to try again—up to a point. While you certainly don't want to give up on a programming task as soon as you get an error, you can definitely burn out in a programming session the same way you might when you're trying to beat a hard level on a game. When that happens, try to take a break for at least 20 or 30 minutes before trying again. Over time, you'll start to develop a sense for when you need a break—another programming skill that will be invaluable in the long run.

If you run a piece of code that has a syntax error, you'll know because the last line of the (usually multiline) error message will say SyntaxError. But more useful than this when actually *fixing* the error will be the part of the error message that tells you *which file* the error is in and *which line* the error is on. Over time, just going to that line of code and looking for problems (typically missing punctuation: commas, brackets, colons, and quotation marks) will be enough for you to spot what's wrong. While the error message will also include the (presumably) offending line of code with a caret (^) below the spot where Python believes the missing character might belong, this isn't foolproof. For instance, Example 2-13 shows a Python dict that is missing a comma on one line.

Example 2-13. Introducing an error

```
1 # although the actual error is on line 4 (missing comma)
2 # the error message points to line 5
3 book = {"title":"Practical Python for Data Wrangling and Data Quality",
4  "format": "book"
5  "author": "Susan E. McGregor"
6 }
```

And here is the error output:

```
    File "ObjectError.py", line 5
      "author": "Susan E. McGregor"
              ^
    SyntaxError: invalid syntax
```

As you can see, even though the code in Example 2-13 is missing a comma after the value `"book"` on line 4, the computer reports the error as being on line 5 (because that's the point at which the computer has realized there is a problem). In general, though, you can usually find a syntax error on the line (or the line before) wherever the computer has reported it.

Runtime Runaround

A *runtime* error in programming is used to describe any type of problem that crops up in the process of "running" or *executing* your code. Like syntax errors, a large portion of runtime errors are *also* essentially typos, such as incorrectly copied variable names. For example, anytime you see an error that includes the phrase `some_variable is not defined`, you've almost certainly got mismatched variable names somewhere in your code (remember: capitalization counts!). Since reading the entire "traceback" error can get a little convoluted (they tend to reference the inner workings of the Python programming language more than I, personally, find strictly useful), I recommend copying the variable name directly from the error and then doing a case-*insensitive* search for it in your code (this is the default behavior in Atom). This approach will highlight similar (but not *quite* identical) spellings of a variable name, speeding up your search for the mismatch.

For example, in Example 2-14 the parameter name provided in the function definition for `greet_me(a_name)` doesn't *precisely* match what's used within the body of the function definition on the next line.

Example 2-14. Slightly mismatched variable names will generate runtime errors

```
# create a function that prints out a greeting to any name passed to the function

def greet_me(a_name):
    print("Hello "+A_name)

# create a variable named author
author = "Susan E. McGregor"

# pass my `author` variable as the "ingredient" to the `greet_me` function
greet_me(author)
```

Because the parameter name that appears inside the round parentheses of the function definition always takes precedence, running the code in Example 2-14 generates the following error:

```
    File "greet_me_parameter_mismatch.py", line 10, in <module>
      greet_me(author)
    File "greet_me_parameter_mismatch.py", line 4, in greet_me
      print("Hello "+A_name)
  NameError: global name 'A_name' is not defined
```

Note that, as usual, the last few lines of the error message are giving us the most help-ful information. The last line lets us know that we're trying to use the variable name A_name without having defined it first, and the line above contains the actual code where it appears. With these two pieces of information (plus our search strategy), it probably won't take too long before we see where we went wrong.

Another very common type of runtime error occurs when you try to do something with a particular data type that it wasn't designed for. In the "Fast Forward" on page 46, you may have tried running the code greet_me(14). In this case, the last line of the error output will include the word TypeError, which means that some part of our code received a different data type than it was expecting. In that example, the problem is that the function expects a string (which can be "added" or *concatenated* to another string using the + sign), but we provided it with a number, in this case, 14.

The challenge with fixing this kind of error is that identifying exactly where the problem lies can be a bit tricky, because it involves a mismatch between where a variable's value was *assigned* and where that variable (and therefore its value) was actually *used*. Especially as your programs grow more sophisticated, these two processes may be nowhere near each other in your code. Looking at the error output from Example 2-14, for example, you can see that it reports two locations. The first is a line where the variable was passed into the function, and so where the available value was *assigned*:

```
File "greet_me_parameter_mismatch.py", line 10, in <module>
```

The second is the line where the value passed to it was *used*:

```
File "greet_me_parameter_mismatch.py", line 4, in greet_me
```

As I have mentioned already, starting your debugging work with where a problematic variable or value was *used* and then working backward through your code to see where the value was assigned is helpful; just know that the line of code where the value was assigned may or may *not* actually appear in the error output. This is part of what makes these kinds of runtime errors more difficult to track down than your average syntax error.

The fact that runtime errors are some of the harder ones to diagnose is a key reason why I recommend both saving and testing your code frequently. The source of a new runtime error is much easier to identify if you've only written a few new lines of code since you last tested it, because the problem *must* be in that little bit of new code. With this sort of write, run, repeat approach, you'll have much less ground to cover when it comes to looking for the source of any new errors, and you'll probably be able to fix them relatively quickly.

Except…

One of the realities of data wrangling is that our code will often come up against inappropriate or unpredictable input, because the data we're working with may have missing or invalid values. For example, a column of otherwise numerical values may have some that are empty. As we'll see in Chapter 6 in particular, those empty values won't automatically be converted to a number like zero.[5] This means that those empty values may generate errors if your code is only written to handle numerical values.

In Python, this kind of unfortunate-but-foreseeable error is known as an *exception*, because it happens when your program encounters an "exceptional" or unexpected situation—like an inappropriate data type. While especially common in data wrangling work, it is possible to write our programs to "handle" exceptions—that is, to tell our code to do something *other* than throw an error and stop running.

While handling exceptions can be useful, we won't be spending a lot of time on it in this book. The reason is that our goal here is not simply to create programs that can *work* on a given set of data but to ensure the *quality* of that data as well. As a result, most of the time we'll actually *want* to know when and where our data is not what we expect, rather than writing our code to just roll past those problems without stopping. So it usually makes more sense for us to deal with runtime errors as they arise, rather than trying to plan for (and handle) all possible errors in advance.[6]

Of course, it *is* possible to write Python exceptions that can help us meaningfully assess data quality; it's just that in most cases we won't need to do this directly because the Python libraries we'll use (again, especially in Chapter 6) do much of this work for us. We'll also minimize the likelihood of needing exceptions by taking an incremental approach to writing our data wrangling code: we'll start by designing and testing our code on a subset of our target dataset, and then we'll run the program on the entire dataset (or versions of the entire dataset) to see how it performs. This will help us balance speed and scale by allowing us to quickly assess the quality of a given dataset while still creating code that can handle the entire dataset if things work out.

Logic Loss

By far the trickiest type of programming problem is the *logic* error, which is broadly used to describe what happens when your program *works*, just *not how you intended*. These errors are especially insidious because—from the computer's perspective—everything is fine: your code is not trying to do anything it finds confusing or "wrong." But computers are stupid, remember, so they will happily let your program

---

5 This is actually a good thing, as we'll see in Chapter 3.

6 For information on code coverage best practices, see "Code Coverage Best Practices" on the Google Testing Blog (*https://testing.googleblog.com/2020/08/code-coverage-best-practices.html*).

do things that produce meaningless, nonsensical, or even misleading results. In precisely the same way that one can do correct math on bad data (as we'll discuss in Chapter 3), it's very possible to write functioning code that does something inappropriate or incorrect. In fact, we already have!

If you look back at Example 2-12, you'll notice that there's actually a slight disconnect between what our comments *say* we wanted to accomplish and what our code actually *does*. The output of that example looks like this:

```
291
Number of chapters over 30 pages:
5
Number of chapters under 30 pages:
4
```

But our data looks like this:

```
page_counts = [28, 32, 44, 23, 56, 32, 12, 34, 30]
```

See the problem? While it's true that we have 5 chapters whose page count is more than 30, we actually have only 3 chapters whose page count is *under* 30—there's one chapter with exactly 30 pages.

Right now, this may not seem like a particularly significant error—after all, how important is it if one 30-page chapter gets lumped in with chapters that are fewer than 30 pages? But imagine that instead of counting chapter pages, this code was being used to determine voting eligibility? If that code was counting only people who were "over 18," hundreds of thousands of people would be disenfranchised.

Fixing this error is not difficult or complicated in terms of the code we need to adjust. All we have to do is change this:

```
# check if the current number of pages is more than 30
if a_number > 30:
```

To this:

```
# check if the current number of pages is greater than or equal to 30
if a_number >= 30:
```

The challenge this type of error presents is that it relies entirely on our diligence as programmers to make sure that as we *design* our programs, we don't overlook some possible data value or discrepancy that can result in incorrect measurements or results. Because the computer cannot warn us about logic errors, the only reliable way to avoid them is to plan our programs carefully in the first place, and to carefully "sanity check" the results. In "Hitting the Road with Citi Bike Data" on page 62, we'll see what this process looks like when we write a program to deal with a real-world dataset.

Phew! Now that we've covered all the fundamentals of Python programming (really!), we're ready to move on from our "toy" examples using data that is (sort of) about this book. To get our feet wet with a data wrangling task using a real dataset, we'll turn to information from the New York City bike-sharing system, Citi Bike.

Hitting the Road with Citi Bike Data

Every month, millions of people use bike-sharing systems to navigate cities and towns around the world. New York City's Citi Bike program launched in 2013 with 6,000 bikes, and in 2020, the system saw its 100 millionth ride (*https://citibike nyc.com/about*).

Citi Bike provides freely accessible data about its system operations that is both real-time and historical. To see what it takes to do data wrangling with a real-world dataset, we're going to use Citi Bike data to answer a simple question: how many rides each day are taken by different types of Citi Bike riders?

We need our Python skills to answer this question because Citi Bike riders take hundreds of thousands of rides per day—meaning that just one day of this data has too many rows for either Microsoft Excel or Google Sheets to handle. But even on a Chromebook, Python will have no problem working with this amount of data.

To think about how to approach this, let's revisit the steps of data wrangling outlined in "What Is "Data Wrangling"?" on page 2:

1. Locating or collecting data
2. Assessing the data's quality
3. "Cleaning," standardizing, and/or transforming the data
4. Analyzing the data
5. Visualizing the data
6. Communicating the data

For this exercise, we're going to focus on steps 1–4, though as you'll see, I've done some preparation that will cut down on how long we spend with certain steps. For example, I've already located the Citi Bike system data (*https://citibike nyc.com/system-data*) and downloaded the September 2020 trip history data (*https:// s3.amazonaws.com/tripdata/index.html*), confirmed that the only values that appear in the User Type column are Customer and Subscriber, and cut down the whole September dataset to *just* the rides that began on September 1, 2020. While we'll delve into how to do all of these processes in subsequent chapters, for now I want to focus on how to apply the lessons from this chapter to data that we didn't make up for ourselves.[7]

Starting with Pseudocode

One of the best ways to get started with a data wrangling project of any size is to plan out your approach in advance and include that program outline in you Python file through a process known as *pseudocoding*. Pseudocoding basically means writing, in regular English (though you could certainly pseudocode in another natural language if you prefer!), what your program will do, step by step. In addition to giving you space to think through what your program needs to accomplish without worrying about how to code it, pseudocoding will give you a valuable reference for what to

---

[7] All of the code for this exercise can be found in the *hitting_the_road_with_citibike.py* and *hitting_the_road_with_citibike.ipynb* files. However, I strongly encourage you to create new files of your own and enter the provided code yourself.

work on next when you need to take a break from your project and come back to it later. Although you'll no doubt meet many professional programmers who *don't* do this part of the process regularly, I can guarantee that it will help you finish your wrangling projects more quickly—and that it's the kind of habit that is welcome in any professional programming or data science setting.

I prefer to put my program outline and pseudocode right at the top of my Python file, in a large block of comments. To start out, I'm going to do three things:

1. State my question.
2. Describe how I will "answer" my question.
3. Outline in plain language the steps my program will take.

This means that the first thing I'm going to do is write a *lot* of comments in my file, as you can see in Example 2-15.

Example 2-15. hitting_the_road_with_citibike.py

```
# question: How many Citi Bike rides each day are taken by
# "subscribers" versus "customers"?

# answer: Choose a single day of rides to examine.
# the dataset used for this exercise was generated from the original
# Citi Bike system data found here: https://s3.amazonaws.com/tripdata/index.html
# filename: 202009-citibike-tripdata.csv.zip

# program Outline:
# 1. read in the data file: 202009CitibikeTripdataExample.csv
# 2. create variables to count: subscribers, customers, and other
# 3. for each row in the file:
#        a. If the "User Type" is "Subscriber," add 1 to "subscriber_count"
#        b. If the "User Type" is "Customer," add 1 to "customer_count"
#        c. Otherwise, add 1 to the "other" variable
# 4. print out my results
```

Now that the program outline is all squared away, it's time to get started with the first part of our program: reading in our data.

Anytime you start a new file like this, remember that even if it's saved inside a local Git repo folder, you'll need to run `git add` to have Git back up any changes you make (you can't `commit` a file until you `add` it, remember). These steps are outlined in "Don't Forget Git!" on page 62, in case you'd like a refresher. While how often you `commit` is up to you, for this exercise I recommend that you `commit` your code (with a descriptive commit message, of course!) after each code block in this section. As you get more comfortable with the coding and Git `commit` process, of course, you'll find a frequency and rhythm for backing up your code that works best for you.

Loading different data formats, as we'll see in-depth in Chapter 4, can actually be one of the trickier aspects of data wrangling. Fortunately, there are many Python libraries available to help, and we're going to make use of one right now! I mentioned libraries briefly in "Libraries: Borrowing Custom Functions from Other Coders" on page 47; they are essentially cookbooks of code. For this project, we're going to use the code "recipes" from the *csv* library, which is mostly designed to deal with—you guessed it!—.*csv* files. The file extension .*csv* stands for *comma-separated value*, and if you haven't seen it before, don't worry. We'll go into (significant) detail about file types in Chapter 4. Right now, having the *csv* library on hand means that we don't actually *need* to know too much about this file type in order to work with it, because the library's code recipes are going to do a lot of the work for us!

If you're following along in your own file, you'll want to add the code in Example 2-16 to the program outline.

Example 2-16. hitting_the_road_with_citibike.py (continued)

```
# import the `csv` library ❶
import csv

# open the `202009CitibikeTripdataExample.csv` file in read ("r") mode
# this file should be in the same folder as our Python script or notebook
source_file = open("202009CitibikeTripdataExample.csv","r") ❷

# pass our `source_file` as an ingredient to the `csv` library's
# DictReader "recipe".
# store the result in a variable called `citibike_reader`
citibike_reader = csv.DictReader(source_file)

# the DictReader method has added some useful information to our data,
# like a `fieldnames` property that lets us access all the values
# in the first or "header" row
print(citibike_reader.fieldnames) ❸
```

❶ The *csv* library includes a range of handy code recipes for dealing with our data files.

❷ open() is a built-in function that takes a file name and a "mode" as parameters. In this example, the target file (*202009CitibikeTripdataExample.csv*) should be in the same folder as our Python script or notebook. Values for the "mode" can be "r" for "read" or "w" for "write."

❸ By printing out the citibike_reader.fieldnames values, we can see that the exact label for the "User Type" column is usertype.

At this point, we could actually run this script, and we should see output that looks something like this:

```
['tripduration', 'starttime', 'stoptime', 'start station id', 'start station
  name', 'start station latitude', 'start station longitude', 'end station id',
  'end station name', 'end station latitude', 'end station longitude', 'bikeid',
  'usertype', 'birth year', 'gender']
```

We've also now succeeded in completing the first step of our outline: we've read in our data. But we've also used the *csv* library to transform that data and even generate some *metadata* about it. Importantly, we now know that the *precise* name of the column containing our "User Type" information is actually usertype. This will help us when it comes time to write our if...else statements. To confirm that things are working as you expect, be sure to save and run your code. If it works as expected (that is, it prints out a list of column headers), now is a good time to do a git commit cycle:

```
git status
git commit -m "Commit message here" filename_with_extension
git push
```

Remember that if you are working on Google Colab, you can commit your code directly to GitHub by choosing File → "Save a copy in GitHub" and entering your commit message in the overlay window that appears.

Now that we've completed step one successfully, let's go on to step two, as shown in Example 2-17.[8]

Example 2-17. hitting_the_road_with_citibike.py (continued again)

```
# create a variable to hold the count of each type of Citi Bike user
# assign or "initialize" each with a value of zero (0)
subscriber_count = 0
```

---

[8] Once again—and from here on out—add this code to your file below the last line of the previous block.

```
customer_count = 0
other_user_count = 0
```

Pretty simple, right? On to step three! Since we need to check each row of data in the file, we'll need to write a for...in loop, which will need to have an if...else inside of it to test for specific values in the usertype column. To help keep track of what each line of code is doing, I'm going to write a *lot* of comments explaining the code in English, as shown in Example 2-18.

Example 2-18. hitting_the_road_with_citibike.py (still rolling)

```
# step 3: loop through every row of our data
for a_row in citibike_reader: ❶

    # step 3a: if the value in the `usertype` column
    # of the current row is "Subscriber"
    if a_row["usertype"] == "Subscriber": ❷

        # add 1 to `subscriber_count`
        subscriber_count = subscriber_count +1

    # step 3b: otherwise (else), if the value in the `usertype` column
    # of the current row is "Customer"
    elif a_row["usertype"] == "Customer": ❸

        # add 1 to `subscriber_count`
        customer_count = customer_count + 1

    # step 3c: the `usertype` value is _neither_ "Subscriber" nor "Customer",
    # so we'll add 1 to our catch-all `other_user_count` variable
    else: ❹
        other_user_count = other_user_count + 1
```

❶ We want to make sure our for loop is working with the data that's already been transformed by our DictReader recipe, so we want to make sure we're referencing our citibike_reader variable here.

❷ In order for my if statements to be "inside" my loop, they have to be indented one more tab to the right.

❸ Because we need to use "else" here—but also need another "if" statement—we're using the compound keyword elif, which is short for "else if."

❹ This final else will "catch" any rows of data where the value of usertype was not one of the values we checked for explicitly (in this case, "Subscriber" or "Customer"). This serves as a (very) basic data quality check: if this data column contains any unexpected values, other_user_count will be greater than zero (0), and we need to look at our original data more closely.

OK, there is a *lot* going on in Example 2-18—or at least it looks like there is! Really, all we did was check whether the value in each row's usertype column was "Subscriber" or "Customer" and added one to (or *incremented*) the corresponding count variable if it was. If the usertype value was *neither* of those, we added one to the other_user_count variable.

While it may seem strange that we've added so many more lines of comments than code, this is actually pretty normal—even good! After all, while the computer never "forgets" how to read Python code, *you* will *absolutely* forget what this code is doing and why if you don't explain it in the comments. And that's not a bad thing! After all, memorizing all of your code would make programming pretty inefficient. By writing detailed comments, you ensure that you can easily understand your code in the future, without having to do the work of translating Python to English all over again!

Before we move on, make sure to run your code. Since "no news is good news" for our most common types of errors, if you don't get any errors, go ahead and do a git commit cycle. Otherwise, now is a good time to pause and troubleshoot any issues you've encountered. Once those are resolved, you'll see there's only one very simple step left: printing! Let's just go the most straightforward route and use built-in print statements, as shown in Example 2-19.

Example 2-19. hitting_the_road_with_citibike.py (we've arrived!)

```
# step 4: print out our results, being sure to include "labels" in the process:
print("Number of subscribers:") ❶
print(subscriber_count)
print("Number of customers:")
print(customer_count)
print("Number of 'other' users:")
print(other_user_count)
```

❶ Note that these print() statements are left justified, because we only want to print values once the for loop has finished going through the entire dataset.

When you've added the code in Example 2-19 to your file, save and run it. Your output should look something like this:

```
['tripduration', 'starttime', 'stoptime', 'start station id', 'start station
 name', 'start station latitude', 'start station longitude', 'end station id',
 'end station name', 'end station latitude', 'end station longitude', 'bikeid',
 'usertype', 'birth year', 'gender']
Number of subscribers:
58961
```

```
Number of customers:
17713
Number of 'other' users:
0
```

If that's what you see—congratulations! You've successfully written your first real-world data wrangling program. Make sure to do a `git commit` cycle to back up your great work!

Seeking Scale

In writing this script, we've accomplished a number of things:

1. We've successfully and precisely counted the number of "Subscribers" and "Customers" who used Citi Bikes on a single day in September 2020.

2. We've confirmed that there are no other values in the `usertype` column (because the value in our `other_user_count` variable was 0).

If you've done data wrangling before using spreadsheet or database programs, for example, but this was your first time working in Python, chances are this process took longer than your previous method, all things considered. But as I've mentioned a few times already, a key advantage that coding offers over many other methods is the ability to *scale* almost seamlessly. That scale works in two ways. First, it does the same work on a larger dataset almost as fast as a smaller one. For example, on my Chromebook, the *hitting_the_road_with_citibike.py* script completes in about half a second. If I run the same script on the data from *the entire month of September*, it takes about 12 seconds. Most software programs that could even handle the entire month's data would probably need that long just to *open* the file, much less do any work to it. So, using Python helps us scale because we can handle larger datasets much more quickly and effectively. You can test this out for yourself by changing the line:

```
source_file = open("202009CitibikeTripdataExample.csv","r")
```

to:

```
source_file = open("202009-citibike-tripdata.csv","r")
```

If you're working in a standalone Python file, you can even measure how long it takes to run your script on the new file by adding the `time` keyword before your `python` command:

```
time python _your_filename_.py
```

This illustrates the second type of scale we achieve with Python, which has to do with the *marginal effort* required to have the computer do the same task on a different dataset (with the same structure) once we have written our program, and this is where Python (and programming in general) really shines. In order to run my script on data from the whole month of September 2020, *all I had to do was load a different data file.* By changing the target filename that I opened with my `source_file =` statement, I was able to process *all* of the September data instead of just the data from one day. In other words, the additional (or "marginal") effort to process hundreds of thousands of additional rows of data was exactly as long as it took me to copy and paste the filename. Building on that example, I could process an entire year of data in a few minutes (or less, as we'll see in Chapter 8). That is something that is nearly impossible to achieve with any noncoding data wrangling method.

The complete script we've built in this section is an example of how, even using just the basic structures we've covered in this chapter, you can do some really useful and efficient data wrangling with Python. Though there are many new data formats and challenges to explore in the remaining chapters, I hope this has given you a sense of how much you can achieve with even these "basic" Python tools and just a little effort and attention to detail. Imagine what else you can accomplish if you keep going!

Conclusion

Believe it or not, in this chapter we've covered *all* the essential Python tools you'll need to do data wrangling—as well as almost any other kind of Python programming! To recap what we've covered, we learned about:

Data types
> These are the "nouns" of programming: numbers, strings, lists, dicts, and Booleans.

Functions
> These are the "verbs" of programming: operators, built-in functions, and user-defined functions.

Using `for...in...` *loops*
> These let us run a particular chunk of code on every item in a list.

Using `if...else` *conditionals*
> These let us to make "decisions" about what code should be run, based (usually) on the attributes of our data.

Errors
> We explored the different types of errors that we're likely to encounter when programming and how to best address and prevent them.

We also practiced combining and composing these concepts to create a basic program to work with some sample data from the New York Citi Bike system. While we'll expand on this example and explore others in future chapters, our next task is to understand more about how to evaluate data itself as part of our data wrangling work.

# CHAPTER 3

Understanding Data Quality

Data is everywhere. It's automatically generated by our mobile devices, our shopping activities, and our physical movements. It's captured by our electric meters, public transportation systems, and communications infrastructure. And it's used to estimate our health outcomes, our earning potential, and our credit worthiness.[1] Economists have even declared that data is the "new oil,"[2] given its potential to transform so many aspects of human life.

While data may be plentiful, however, the truth is that *good* data is scarce. The claim of "the data revolution" is that, with enough data, we can better understand the present and improve—or even predict—the future. For any of that to even be possible, however, the data underlying those insights has to be high quality. Without good-quality data, all of our efforts to wrangle, analyze, visualize, and communicate it will, at best, leave us with no more insight about the world than when we started. While that would be an unfortunate waste of effort, the consequences of failing to recognize that we have poor-quality data is even worse, because it can lead us to develop a seemingly rational but dangerously distorted view of reality. What's more, because data-driven systems are used to make decisions at scale, the harms caused by even a small amount of bad data can be significant. Sure, data about hundreds or even thousands of people may be used to "train" a machine learning model. But if that data is not representative of the population to which the model will be applied, the repercussions of that system can affect hundreds or thousands of times the number of people in the original dataset. Because the stakes are so high, ensuring data quality

---

1 For example, see "The Secret Bias Hidden in Mortgage-Approval Algorithms" (*https://themarkup.org/denied/ 2021/08/25/the-secret-bias-hidden-in-mortgage-approval-algorithms*) by Emmanuel Martinez and Lauren Kirschner (*The Markup*) .

2 "The World's Most Valuable Resource Is No Longer Oil, but Data," in *The Economist* (*https://econo mist.com/leaders/2017/05/06/the-worlds-most-valuable-resource-is-no-longer-oil-but-data*).

is an essential part of data wrangling. But what does it mean for data to be "high quality"? My view is that data is high quality only if it is both *fit* for purpose and has high internal *integrity*.

What does each of those terms actually mean? That is exactly what we'll explore, in depth, in this chapter. We'll begin by discussing the concept of data *fit*, which relates to the appropriateness of data for use in a particular context, or to answer a particular question. We'll then break down the many aspects of data *integrity*: the characteristics of a dataset that influence both its fitness for purpose and the types of analyses we can responsibly use it for. Finally, we'll discuss some tools and strategies for finding and working with data that can help you maximize its overall quality, lending confidence and credibility to the work that you produce with it.

In case you start to find any of this tedious, let me repeat my exhortations from "What Is "Data Wrangling"?" on page 2: trying to "skip over" the work of assessing data quality can only undermine your data wrangling efforts. At best, you'll go to share your work and encounter questions about your process that you don't have answers for. At worst, you'll end up promoting "insights" that are both wrong and do active harm. Along the way, you'll *also* be cheating yourself out of good technical skills, because solving data quality problems is where you'll expand your programming knowledge the most. If you truly want to be good at the work of data wrangling, assessing data quality *has* to be part of your practice.

Don't Forget to Document

While thoroughly commenting your code is a sound time investment if you want to improve your coding skills *and* get more value out of that code in the future, with enough time and effort it's almost always possible to retranslate computer code later on if you need to.

The same is *not* true for your work on data quality: the documentation in your data diary is actually irreplaceable. The conclusion that you reach about a dataset being representative or valid will, in most cases, be informed by everything from your own reading and research to conversations with experts to additional datasets you've located. But without good documentation of who said what or how you came across the information, any attempt to repeat or confirm your previous work will almost certainly fail.

Why? Because information sources—especially on the internet[3]—move, change, and disappear. Even in the course of just a few months, many of the links I originally included in this book moved or stopped working. The expert you spoke to six months

---

[3] For example, see "Raiders of the Lost Web" by Adrienne LaFrance in *The Atlantic* (*https://theatlantic.com/technology/archive/2015/10/raiders-of-the-lost-web/409210*).

ago may no longer be available, or the search you conducted may return different results. While the way you approach it is up to you, I cannot state emphatically enough how important it is to document your data wrangling work, especially as it pertains to data quality (which is pretty much all of it). Without a detailed description of your process, you may find you're on uncertain footing when it's time to share the results of your work—forcing you to start from the beginning all over again.

Assessing Data Fit

Perhaps one of the most common misconceptions about data wrangling is that it is a predominantly *quantitative* process, that is, that data wrangling is mostly about working with numbers, formulas, and code. In fact, irrespective of the type of data you're dealing with—it could be anything from temperature readings to social media posts—the core work of data wrangling involves making judgment calls: from whether your data accurately represents the phenomenon you're investigating, to what to do about missing data points and whether you have enough data to generate any real insight at all. That first concept—the extent to which a given dataset accurately represents the phenomenon you're investigating—is broadly what I mean by its *fit*, and assessing your dataset's *fit*ness for purpose is much more about applying informed judgment than it is about applying mathematical formulas. The reason for this is quite simple: the world is a messy place, and what may seem like even the simplest data about it is always filtered through some kind of human lens. Take something as straightforward as measuring the temperature in your workspace over the course of a week. In theory, all you need to do is get a thermometer, put it in the space, and note down the reading every day. Done, right?

Or are you? Let's start with your equipment. Did you use a digital thermometer or a mercury thermometer? Where in the space did you place it? Is it near a door, a window, or a heating or cooling source? Did you take the reading at the same time every day? Is the thermometer ever in direct sunlight? What is the typical humidity level?

You may think I'm introducing a contrived level of complexity here, but if you've ever lived in a shared space (like an apartment building), you've probably been through the experience of *feeling* like it's much warmer or colder than what some thermometer said. Likewise, if you've ever looked after a child who's ill, you're likely all too familiar with the different body temperature readings that you'll get with different types of thermometers—or even with the same one, just minutes apart.

In other words, there are a huge number of factors contributing to that two- or three-digit temperature you record—and the number itself doesn't provide information about any of them. That's why when you begin the process of trying to answer a question with data, it's not enough to know just what is in the dataset; you need to know about the processes and mechanisms used to *collect* it. Then, given everything you know about how the data was gathered, you need to determine if it can really be used to answer your specific question in a meaningful way.

Of course, this problem is neither new nor unique; it's the same challenge that all scientific fields face in their efforts to discover new information about the world. Cancer research could hardly advance if every single researcher had to conduct every single study themselves; without the ability to build on the work of others, scientific and technological progress would grind to a halt (if not go off the rails entirely). Because of this, over time the scientific community has developed three key metrics for determining the appropriateness or fit of a dataset for answering a given question: *validity*, *reliability*, and *representativeness*.

Validity

At its most basic, *validity* describes the extent to which something measures what it is supposed to. In our room temperature example, this would mean ensuring that the type of thermometer you've chosen will actually measure the air temperature rather than something else. For example, while traditional liquid-in-glass thermometers will probably capture air temperature well, infrared thermometers will tend to capture the temperature of whatever surface they're pointed at. So even with something as seemingly basic as room temperature, you need to understand the tools and methods used to collect your data readings in order to ensure their *validity* with respect to your question.

Unsurprisingly, things only get more involved when we're not collecting data about common physical phenomena. *Construct validity* describes the extent to which your data measurements effectively capture the (usually abstract) *construct*, or idea, you're trying to understand. For example, let's say you want to know which are the "best" schools in your area. What data can help you answer that question? First we have to recognize that the term *best* is imprecise. Best in what way? Are you interested in which school has the highest graduation rate? Standardized test scores? School-assigned grades? Teacher evaluations? Student satisfaction? Extracurricular participation?

In order to use data to begin to answer this question, you first need to articulate two things. First, "best" *for whom*? Are you trying to answer this question for your own child? A friend's? Having answered that, you'll be better able to complete the second task, which is *operationalizing* your specific idea of "best." If your friend's child loves sports, for example, extracurricular activities might be more important than academics.

In data analysis, this process of selecting measures is known as *operationalizing a construct*, and it inevitably requires choosing among—and balancing—proxies for the idea or concept you are trying to understand. These proxies—like graduation rates, test scores, extracurricular activities, and so on—are things *about which you can collect data* that you are choosing to use to represent an abstract concept ("best" school) *that cannot be measured directly*. Good-quality data, to say the least, must have good *construct validity* with respect to your question, otherwise your data wrangling results will be meaningless.

How? And for Whom?

Once you begin thinking about the *construct validity* of your own data wrangling questions, you'll likely find yourself much more curious about it anywhere you encounter data being used to make decisions or "predictions" about the world. More than likely, you'll find many situations where imprecise claims (like "best") are being made, with little or no explanation being offered about *how* the concept of "best" was defined. Similarly, the designers of data-driven systems may initially answer the question of "for whom?" with an enthusiastic "for everyone!" The real answer lies in their choice of proxies, which they may well have selected heuristically based only on their own tastes or preferences. In those instances, the *real* answer to the question "for whom?" is "for people like me."

Of course, sometimes you may be told that there's simply no way to know how "best" is being defined, because the system being used to make the decisions or predictions is a so-called "black box"—which is how unsupervised machine learning systems are often described. As I mentioned in "What Is "Data Quality"?" on page 3, however, this is somewhat misleading. Though it's true that we can't currently say with confidence precisely how such a machine learning system has weighted or prioritized certain things when making predictions, we *do* know that it will *always* replicate and amplify the patterns that exist within the data on which it was "trained." In those instances, then, it's the composition of the training data that will tell you both "how?" and "for whom?"—if the people who made the system are confident enough to share it.

The other type of validity that is important for data fit is *content validity*. This type of validity has to do with how complete your data is for a given proxy measurement. In the "best" school example, let's say you have determined that grades are relevant for determining what school is best, but you only have grades for history and physical education courses available. Though for many people grade data might, in principle, have *construct validity* for identifying the best school, having grade data for only two types of courses wouldn't be sufficient to satisfy the requirement for *content validity*— and for high-quality data, you need to have *both*.

Reliability

Within a dataset, the *reliability* of a given measure describes its *accuracy* and *stability*. Together, these help us assess whether the same measure taken twice in the same circumstances will give us the same—or at least very similar—results. To revisit our temperature example: taking a child's temperature with an oral thermometer is not likely to be very *reliable*, because the process requires that the child keep their mouth closed for a relatively long time (which, in my experience, they're not great at). By contrast, taking a child's temperature under their arm might be more reliable— because you can hug them to keep the thermometer in place—but it may not provide as *accurate* a reading of the child's true internal body temperature as some other methods. This is why most medical advice lists different temperature thresholds for a fever in children, depending on which method you use to take their temperature.

With abstract concepts and real-world data, determining the reliability of a data measure is especially tricky, because it is never really possible to collect the data more than once—whether because the cost is prohibitive, the circumstances can't be replicated, or both. In those cases, we typically estimate reliability by comparing one similar group to another, using either previously or newly collected data. So even though a dramatic fluctuation in a school's standardized test scores from one year to the next indicates that those scores may not be a *reliable* measure of school quality, this inconsistency itself is only part of the story. After all, those test scores *might* reflect the quality of teaching, but they might also reflect a change in the test being administered, how it was scored, or some other disruption to the learning or test-taking environment. In order to determine whether the standardized test data is *reliable* enough to be part of your "best" school assessment, you would need to look at comparison data from other years or other schools, in addition to learning more about the broader circumstances that may have led to the fluctuation. In the end, you may conclude that *most* of the test score information is reliable enough to be included but that a few particular data points should be removed, or you may conclude that the data is too unreliable to be part of a high-quality data process.

Representativeness

The key value proposition for data-driven systems is that they allow us to generate insights—or even predictions—about people and phenomena that are too massive or too complex for humans to reason about effectively. By wrangling and analyzing data, the logic goes, we can make decisions faster and more fairly. Given the powerful computational tools that even individuals—to say nothing of companies—have access to these days, there's no doubt that data-driven systems can generate "decisions" more quickly than humans can. Whether those insights are an accurate portrait of a particular population or situation, however, depends directly on the *representativeness* of the data being used.

Whether a dataset is sufficiently representative depends on a few things, the most significant of which goes back to the "for whom?" question we discussed in "Validity" on page 74. If you're trying to design a new course schedule for a specific grade school, you may be able to collect data about its entire population. If all the other criteria for data fitness have been met, then you already know that your data is representative, because you have collected data directly from or about the entire population to which it will apply.

But what if you're trying to complete the same task for an entire city's worth of schools? It's deeply unlikely that you'll succeed in collecting data about every single student in every single school, which means that you'll be relying on input from only a subset of the students when you try to design the new schedule.

Anytime you're working with a subset or *sample* in this way, it's crucial to make sure that it is *representative* of the broader population to which you plan to apply your findings. While proper sampling methodology is beyond the scope of this book,[4] the basic idea is that in order for your insights to accurately generalize to a particular community of people, the data sample you use must proportionally reflect that community's makeup. That means that you need to invest the time and resources to understand a number of things about that community *as a whole* before you can even know if your sample is representative.

At this point you may be thinking: wait, if we could already get information about the whole population, we wouldn't need a sample in the first place! And that's true—sort of. In many cases, it's possible to get *some* information about an entire community—just not precisely the information we need. In our school-scheduling scenario, for example, we would ideally get information about how—and how long—students travel to and from school each day, as well as some sense of their caretakers' schedules. But the information we might *have* about the entire school population

---

4 For a highly readable overview, see "Statistics Without Tears" by Amitav Banerjee and Suprakash Chaudhury (*https://ncbi.nlm.nih.gov/pmc/articles/PMC3105563*).

(if we are working cooperatively with the school system) will probably include only things like home address, school address, and perhaps the type of transportation support (*https://schools.nyc.gov/school-life/transportation/bus-eligibility*). Using this information, likely in conjunction with some additional administrative information, we could begin to create estimates for the proportion of certain types of student commuters that exist in the *entire* population, and then seek to replicate those proportions in selecting a *representative sample* from our survey results. Only at that point would we be ready to move on to the next step of the data wrangling process.

As you can see, ensuring representativeness demands that we carefully consider which characteristics of a population are relevant to our data wrangling question *and* that we seek out enough additional information to ensure that our dataset proportionally represents those characteristics. Perhaps unsurprisingly, this is the data fitness test that many data-driven goods and services fail on, again and again. While companies and researchers may tout the *quantity* of data they use to develop in their systems, the reality is that most datasets that are readily available to companies and researchers tend to *not* be representative of, say, the US or global population. For example, data about search engine trends, social media activity, public transit usage, or smartphone ownership, for example, are all extremely *unlikely* to be representative of the broader population, since they are inevitably influenced by things like internet access and income level. This means that communities are *over*represented in these datasets while others are (sometimes severely) *under*represented. The result is systems that don't *generalize*—like facial recognition systems that cannot "see" Black faces (*http://proceedings.mlr.press/v81/buolamwini18a/buolamwini18a.pdf*).

If you are faced with nonrepresentative data, what do you do? At the very least, you will need to revise (and clearly communicate) your "for whom?" assessment to reflect whatever population it *does* represent; this is the only community for whom your data wrangling insights will be valid. Also keep in mind that representativeness can only ensure that the outcome of your data wrangling efforts accurately reflects reality; it is not a value judgment on whether that reality should be *perpetuated*. If the outcome of your data wrangling effort will be used to make changes to a system or organization, the end of your data wrangling process is really just the starting point for thinking about what should be done with your insights, especially with respect to complex issues like fairness (*https://youtube.com/watch?v=jIXIuYdnyyk*).

This is true even if you have data about an entire population. For example, if you want to know which organizations have received a certain type of grant, then the "population" or community you're interested in is just those grant recipients. At the same time, checking your data for representativeness against the population at large still has value: if one or more communities are over- or underrepresented in your population of grant recipients, it may hint at hidden factors influencing who receives that money.

Assessing Data Integrity

Data *fit* is essentially about whether you have the right data for answering your data wrangling question. Data *integrity*, on the other hand, is largely about whether the data you have can support the analyses you'll need to perform in order to answer that question. As you'll see throughout this section, there are a *lot* of different aspects of the data to consider when performing an integrity assessment. But does a given dataset need to have *all* of them in order to be high integrity, and therefore high quality? Not necessarily. While some are essential, the importance of others depends on your specific question and the methods you'll need to answer it. And with rare exceptions, many are characteristics of the data that you will enhance and develop as part of your data wrangling process.

In other words, while ensuring data *fit* is nonoptional, the types and degree of *integrity* that your particular data wrangling project requires will vary. Of course, the more of these requirements your data meets, the more useful it will be—both to you and others.

In general, a high-integrity dataset will, to one degree or another, be:[5]

Necessary, but not sufficient
- Of known provenance
- Well-annotated

Important
- Timely
- Complete
- High volume
- Multivariate
- Atomic

Achievable
- Consistent
- Clear
- Dimensionally structured

As I have already mentioned, however, not all of these data integrity characteristics are equally important. Some of them are nonnegotiable, while others are almost always the *result* of certain steps in the data wrangling process, not precursors to it. And while the goal is for your data to have as many of these characteristics as possible before you begin your analysis, there is always a balance to be struck between more fully elaborating your data and completing your work in time for your insights to be useful.

In this sense, assessing data integrity can be a useful way to prioritize your data wrangling efforts. For example, if a dataset is missing either of the "necessary, but not sufficient" characteristics, you may as well move on from it entirely. If it's missing one or two of the characteristics in "Important" on page 82, it may still be possible to salvage the data you're working with by combining it with others or limiting the scope of your analyses—and claims. Meanwhile, developing the characteristics in "Achievable" on page 85 is often the *goal* of your data wrangling process's "cleaning"

---

5 This list is adapted from Stephen Few's excellent book *Now You See It: Simple Visualization Techniques for Quantitative Analysis* (Analytics Press), with adjustments based on my own data wrangling experience.

step, rather than something you can expect most real-world data to have when you first encounter it.

In the end, the degree to which your dataset embodies many of the characteristics that follow will depend on the time you have to invest in your data wrangling project, but without a good solid majority of them, your insights will be limited. As will be illustrated (in detail!) in Chapter 6, this variability is precisely why data wrangling and data quality are so thoroughly intertwined.

Necessary, but Not Sufficient

Most of the time, the data we're wrangling was compiled by someone else—or a whole collection of people and processes that we don't have direct access to. At the same time, we need to be able to stand behind both our data wrangling process and any insights we derive from it. This means that there are a couple of data characteristics that are really *essential* to a successful data wrangling process.

Of known provenance

As discussed in "What Is "Data Quality"?" on page 3, data is the output of human decisions about what to measure and how. This means that using a dataset collected by others requires putting a significant amount of trust in them, especially because independently verifying *every single data point* is rarely possible; if it were, you would probably just collect your own data instead. This is why knowing the *provenance* of a dataset is so important: if you don't know who compiled the data, the methods that they used, and/or the purpose for which they collected it, you will have a very hard time judging whether it is *fit* for your data wrangling purpose, or how to correctly interpret it.

Of course, this doesn't mean you need to know the birthdays and favorite colors of everyone who helped build a given dataset. But you *should* try to find out enough about their professional backgrounds, motivations for collecting the data (is it legally mandated, for example?), and the methods they employed so that you have some sense of which measures you'll want to corroborate versus those that might be okay to take at face value. Ideally, both information about the data authors and sufficient documentation about these processes will be readily enough available that you can answer all of these questions about the data's *provenance* fairly quickly. If they prove hard to locate, however, you may wish to move on; since you need this information to assess data *fit*, your time may be better spent looking for a different dataset or even collecting the data yourself.

Well-annotated

A well-annotated dataset has enough surrounding information, or *metadata*, to make interpretation possible. This will include everything from high-level explanations of the data collection methodology to the "data dictionaries" that describe each data measure right down to its units. While this may seem straightforward, there are not always well-accepted standards for how such annotation information should be provided: sometimes it appears directly in data files or data entries themselves, and sometimes the information might be contained in separate files or documents in a location totally separate from where you retrieved the data.

However they are structured or provided, robust data annotation documents are an essential component of high-integrity data because without them, it's impossible to apply any analyses or draw any inferences from it. For example, imagine trying to interpret a budget without knowing if the figures provided refer to dollars, thousands of dollars, or millions of dollars—it's clearly impossible. Or for a very American expression of the importance of annotation documents like data dictionaries, know that they sometimes require a lawsuit (*https://trac.syr.edu/foia/ice/20210805*) to get.

USDA Data Sleuthing

The USDA's Agricultural Marketing Service provides daily reports (*https://www.ams.usda.gov/market-news/custom-reports*) about the food moving through 16 terminal markets around the world. Each day, USDA experts walk through the markets, noting the size, price, condition, origin, and other aspects of the goods for sale, such as apples. While the data has many high-integrity features—it is clean, richly segmented, and high volume—the meaning of some of the data values is unclear. What do "FINEAPPEAR" and "FRAPPEAR" mean? Fortunately, knowing that this data is compiled by the USDA about the terminal markets makes answering that question much simpler. Halfway down the page of web search results for "USDA Terminal Market" is a link for a Los Angeles terminal market report (*https://www.ams.usda.gov/mnreports/hc_fv020.txt*) that includes a phone number. One quick phone call, and the mystery is solved!

Important

While it's hard to get *anywhere* with data wrangling unless you have sufficient provenance and metadata information about a dataset, you're still not going to get very far unless you have enough data, from the right time period(s), and at the right level of detail. That said, the following data characteristics are ones that we may often assess—and sometimes improve—with our own data wrangling work. So while it will certainly be easier to work with datasets that have these characteristics already, even those that fall short on a few of these may still be worth exploring.

Timely

How up to date is the data that you're using? Unless you're studying a historical period, ensuring that your data is recent enough to meaningfully describe the *current* state of the world is important—though how old is "too old" will depend on both the phenomenon you're exploring and the frequency with which data about it is collected and released.

For example, if you're interested in neighborhood demographics but your most recent data is several years old, there's a strong likelihood that things may have changed considerably since. For unemployment data, data older than a month will no longer be timely, while for stock market data, it takes just a few seconds for information to be considered too old to inform trades. Unless it's about a field you're already familiar with, assessing whether your data is timely will likely require some research with experts as well as the data publisher.

Complete

Does the dataset contain all of the data values it should? In the USDA apple data in "USDA Data Sleuthing" on page 82, for example, only a few of the rows contain appearance descriptions, while most are left blank. Can we still generate useful data insights when parts of the data are so incomplete? Addressing this question means first answering two others. First, *why* is the data missing? Second, do you *need* that data measure in order to perform a specific analysis needed for your data wrangling process?

For example, your data may be incomplete because individual values are missing, or because the data has been reported irregularly—perhaps there is a half-year gap in data that is usually recorded every month. The dataset may also have been truncated, which is a common problem when large datasets are opened in a spreadsheet program. Whatever the reason, discovering *why* some part of the data is missing is essential in order to know how to proceed. In "USDA Data Sleuthing" on page 82, we could potentially ignore the "appearance" category if our primary interest is in the way that different varietals of apples are priced, or we could contact the terminal market again to clarify if blank values in the appearance column actually correspond to some default value that they don't bother to indicate explicitly. Even truncated data may not be a problem if what we have available covers a sufficient time period for our purposes, but it is still useful to learn the true number of records and date range of the data for context. And while there are statistical tricks that can sometimes make gaps in data collection less problematic, learning that the recording gap is due to some disruptive event may change the type of analysis you do, or even the question you're pursuing altogether.

In other words, while having *complete* data is always preferable, once you know *why* that data is missing, you may be able to proceed with your data wrangling process, regardless. But you should always find out—and be sure to document what you learn!

High volume

How many data points are "enough"? At minimum, a dataset will need to have sufficient records to support the type of analysis needed to answer your particular question. If what you need is a *count*—for example, the number of 311 calls that involved noise complaints in a particular year—then having "enough" data means having records of *all* of the 311 calls for that particular year.

If your question is about general or generalizable patterns or trends, however, what counts as "enough" is a little less clear. For example, if you wanted to determine which Citi Bike station is the "busiest," how long a time period should you consider? A week? A month? A year? Should only weekdays be considered, or all days? The correct answer will partly depend on more thoroughly specifying your question. Are you interested in the experiences of commuters or visitors? Are you trying to generate insights to drive transit planning, retail placement, or service quality? Also, are you *really* interested in what station is "busiest," or is it really more about a particular rate of turnover? As is so often the case, the correct answer is largely about specifying the question correctly—and that requires being, in most cases, *very* specific.

One of the trickiest parts of assessing data "completeness," however, is that accounting for factors that may influence the trend or pattern you're investigating is difficult without knowing the subject area pretty well already. For example, while we might easily expect that Citi Bike usage might vary across seasons, what about a reduction in public transit service? An increase in fares? These changes *might* have implications for our analysis, but how can we know that when we're still starting out?

The answer—as it is so often—is (human) experts. Maybe fare increases temporarily increase bike share ridership, but only for a few months. Maybe bicycle commuters are prepared for bad weather and stick with their patterns even when it's snowing. With infinite time and infinite data, we might be able to answer these questions for ourselves; talking to *humans* is just so much faster and so much more informative. And believe it or not, there is an expert in almost everything. For example, a quick search on Google Scholar for "seasonal ridership bike sharing" returns everything from blog posts to peer-reviewed research on the topic.

What does this mean for data completeness? Existing research or—even better—a real-time conversation with a subject matter expert (see "Subject Matter Experts" on page 376 for more on this) will help you decide which factors you're going to include in your analysis, and as a result, how much data you need for your chosen analysis in order for it to be complete.

Multivariate

Wrangling real-world data inevitably means encountering real-world complexity, where a huge range of factors may influence the phenomenon we're trying to investigate. Our "busiest" Citi Bike station is one example: beyond seasonality and transit service, the surrounding terrain (*https://www.sciencedirect.com/science/article/abs/pii/S136192091731057X*) or the density of stations could play a role. If our Citi Bike data contained only information about how many trips started and ended at a particular station, then it would be very difficult to create an analysis that could say more than "this station had the most bikes removed and returned" in a given time period.

When data is multivariate, though, it means that it has multiple *attributes* or *features* associated with each record. For the historical Citi Bike data (*https://citibikenyc.com/system-data*), for example, we know we have all of the following, thanks to our little bit of wrangling in "Hitting the Road with Citi Bike Data" on page 62:

```
['tripduration', 'starttime', 'stoptime', 'start station id', 'start station
 name', 'start station latitude', 'start station longitude', 'end station id',
 'end station name', 'end station latitude', 'end station longitude', 'bikeid',
 'usertype', 'birth year', 'gender']
```

That's 15 different features about each recorded ride, any number of which might be able to leverage toward a more meaningful or nuanced way to understand which Citi Bike station is the "busiest."

Atomic

Atomic data is highly granular; it is both measured precisely and not aggregated into summary statistics or measures. In general, summary measures like rates and averages aren't great candidates for further analysis, because so much of the underlying data's detail has already been lost. For example, the *arithmetic average* or *mean* of both of the following sets of numbers is 30: 20, 25, 30, 45 and 15, 20, 40, 45. While summary statistics are often helpful when making comparisons across different datasets, they offer too little insight into the data's underlying structure to support further analysis.

Achievable

No matter how a dataset appears at first, the reality is that truly clean, well-organized, and error-free data is a near impossibility—in part just because, as time goes by, some things (like dollar values) simply *become* inconsistent. As a result, there are data quality characteristics that, as data wranglers, we should just always expect we'll need to review and improve. Fortunately, this is where the flexibility and reusability of Python really shines—meaning these tasks will get easier and faster over time as we build up our programming skills.

Consistent

High-integrity data needs to be consistent in a number of different ways. Often the most obvious type of consistency in a dataset has to do with the frequency of data that has been collected over time. Are the time intervals between individual records *consistent*? Are there gaps? Irregular intervals between data records are important to investigate (if not resolve) in part because they can be a first indicator of disruptions or disparities within the data collection process itself. Another source of pervasively *in*consistent data tends to turn up anytime a data field has text involved: fields that contain names or descriptors will almost inevitably contain multiple spellings of what is supposed to be the same term. Even fields that might seem straightforward to standardize may contain varying degrees of detail. For example, a "zip code" field might contain both five-digit zip code entries and more precise "Zip+4" values.

Other types of consistency may be less obvious but no less important. Units of measure, for example, need to be consistent across the dataset. While this might seem obvious, it's actually easier than you might first imagine for this *not* to be the case. Let's say you're looking at the cost of an apple over a period of a decade. Sure, your data may record all of the prices in dollars, but inflation will be constantly changing what a dollar is *worth*. And while most of us are aware that Celsius and Fahrenheit "degrees" are of different sizes, it doesn't stop there: an imperial pint is about 568 ml, whereas an American pint is about 473 ml. In fact, even accounts of Napoleon Bonaparte's famously short stature is likely the result of an inconsistency (*https://bri tannica.com/story/was-napoleon-short*) between the size of the 19th-century French inch (about 2.71cm) and today's version (about 2.54 cm).

The solution to such inconsistencies is to *normalize* your data before doing any comparisons or analyses. In most cases, this is a matter of simple arithmetic: you simply have to choose which interpretation of the unit to which you will convert all others (another important moment for documentation!). This is true even of currency, which analysts often begin by converting to "real" (read: inflation-controlled) dollars, using some chosen year as a benchmark. For example, if we wanted to compare the real dollar value of the US federal minimum wage in 2009 (when it was last increased) to 2021, we could use an inflation calculator like the one maintained by the Bureau of Labor Statistics (BLS) (*https://bls.gov/data/inflation_calculator.htm*) to see that the real dollar value of $7.25 per hour in 2009 is equivalent to only $5.72 per hour in 2021.

Clear

Like our Python code, our data and its labels will ideally be easy to read and interpret. Realistically, field (and even dataset) descriptors can sometimes be little more than cryptic codes that require constant cross-referencing with a data dictionary or other resources. This is part of why this type of data integrity is almost always the *product of* rather than the *precursor to* some degree of data wrangling.

For example, is there some logic to the fact that the table code for the US Census Bureau's American Community Survey Demographic and Housing Estimates is DP05? Perhaps. But it's hardly obvious to an occasional user of Census data, any more than the column label DP05_0001E is likely to be.[6] While a download of this Census table does include multiple files that can help you piece together the meaning of the filenames and column headers, developing a clear, high-integrity dataset may well require a fair amount of relabeling, reformatting, and reindexing—especially where government-produced data is involved. As always, however, documenting your information sources and renaming processes as you go is crucial.

Dimensionally structured

Dimensionally structured data contains fields that have been grouped into or additionally labeled with useful categories, such as geographic region, year, or language. Such features often provide quick entry points for both data augmentation (which we'll address in "Data Augmentation" on page 89) and data analysis, because they reduce the correlation and aggregation effort we have to do ourselves. These features can also serve as an indicator of what the data creator thought was important to record.

For example, the dimensions of our Citi Bike data include whether a bike was checked out to the account of a "Subscriber" or a "Customer," as well as the account holder's birth year and gender—suggesting that the data's designers believed these

---

6 It indicates the total population estimate, by the way.

features might yield useful insights about Citi Bike trips and usage. As we'll see in Chapter 7, however, they did *not* choose to include any sort of "weekday/holiday" indicator—meaning that is a *dimension* of the data we'll have to derive ourselves if we need it.

Data Decoding

Although easily readable filenames and column headers are useful, coded data descriptors aren't necessarily all bad. As we'll explore later on, building robust, high-quality datasets sometimes requires combining two or more data sources. In these instances, the use of standardized—if occasionally cryptic—codes can be useful. For example, the New York State Department of Education website (*https://data.nysed.gov*) provides individual school profiles, along with multiple identifiers for each one. While these ID numbers aren't very informative in and of themselves, plugging one into a search engine can help turn up other documents and datasets, making it easier to collate multiple data sources with high confidence.

Improving Data Quality

As previously noted, many aspects of data quality are the product of a data wrangling process—whether that involves reconciling and normalizing units, clarifying the meaning of obscure data labels, or seeking out background information about the representativeness of your dataset. Part of what this illustrates is that, in the real world, ensuring data *quality* is at least partly the result of multiple, iterative data wrangling processes. While the terms for these phases of the data wrangling process vary, I usually describe them as data *cleaning* and data *augmentation*.

Data Cleaning

In reality, data "cleaning" is not so much its own step in the data wrangling process as it is a constant activity that accompanies every *other* step, both because most data is *not* clean when we encounter it and because *how* a dataset (or part of it) needs to be "cleaned" is often revealed progressively as we work. At a high level, clean data might be summarized as being free from errors or typos—such as mismatched units, multiple spellings of the same word or term, and fields that are not well separated—and missing or impossible values. While many of these are at least somewhat straightforward to recognize (though not always to correct), deeper data problems may still persist. Measurement changes, calculation errors, and other oversights—especially in system-generated data—often don't reveal themselves until some level of analysis has been done and the data has been "reality-checked" with folks who have significant expertise and/or firsthand experience with the subject.

The iterative nature of data cleaning is an example of why data wrangling is a cycle rather than a linear series of steps: as your work reveals more about the data and your understanding of its relationship to the world deepens, you may find that you need to revisit earlier work that you've done and repeat or adjust certain aspects of the data. Of course, this is just another reason why documenting your data wrangling work is so crucial: you can use your documentation to quickly identify where and how you made any changes or updates, and to reconcile them with what you now know. Without robust documentation to guide you, you may quickly find yourself needing to start from scratch.

Data Augmentation

Augmenting a dataset is the process of expanding or elaborating it, usually by connecting it with other datasets—this is really the nature of "big data" in the 21st century.[7] By using features shared among datasets, it's possible to bring together data from multiple sources in order to get a more complete portrait of what is happening in the world by filling in gaps, providing corroborating measures, or adding contextual data that helps us better assess data fit. In our "best" school example, this might mean using school codes to bring together the several types of data collected by different entities, such as the state-level standardized test scores and local building information mentioned in "Data Decoding" on page 88. Through a combination of effective research and data wrangling, data augmentation can help us build data quality and answer questions far too nuanced to address through any single dataset.

Like data cleaning, opportunities for data augmentation may arise at almost any point in the data wrangling process. At the same time, each new dataset we introduce will spawn a data wrangling process of its own. This means that *unlike* data cleaning, data augmentation has no definitive "end state"—there will *always* be another dataset we can add. This is yet another reason why specifically and succinctly stating our data wrangling question up front is so essential to the process: without a clearly articulated statement about what you're trying to investigate, it's all too easy to run out of time or other resources for your data wrangling effort. The good news is that if you've been keeping up your data diary, you'll never lose track of a promising dataset for use in a future project.

---

7 See danah boyd and Kate Crawford's "Critical Questions for Big Data" (*https://tandfonline.com/doi/full/ 10.1080/1369118X.2012.678878*) for a discussion on big data.

Conclusion

Since our hands-on work with actual data has been limited up to this point, many of the concepts discussed in this chapter may seem a little bit abstract right now. Don't worry! Things are about to get *very* hands on. In the coming chapters, we'll start wrangling data that comes in various formats and from different sources, offering an inside look at how various characteristics of data quality play into the decisions we make as we access, evaluate, clean, analyze, and present our data. And you can be confident that by the end of this volume, you'll be able to create meaningful, accurate, and compelling data analyses and visualizations to share your insights with the world!

In the next chapter, we'll start this process by working through how to wrangle data from a wide variety of formats into a structure that will let us do the cleaning, augmentation, and analyses we need. Let's dive in!

# CHAPTER 4

Working with File-Based and Feed-Based Data in Python

In Chapter 3, we focused on the many characteristics that contribute to data quality—from the completeness, consistency, and clarity of data *integrity* to the reliability, validity, and representativeness of data *fit*. We discussed the need to both "clean" and standardize data, as well as the need to augment it by combining it with other datasets. But how do we actually accomplish these things in practice?

Obviously, it's impossible to begin assessing the *quality* of a dataset without first reviewing its contents—but this is sometimes easier said than done. For decades, data wrangling was a highly specialized pursuit, leading companies and organizations to create a whole range of distinct (and sometimes proprietary) digital data formats designed to meet their particular needs. Often, these formats came with their own file extensions—some of which you may have seen: *xls*, *csv*, *dbf*, and *spss* are all file formats typically associated with "data" files.[1] While their specific structures and details vary, all of these formats are what I would describe as *file-based*—that is, they contain (more or less) historical data in static files that can be downloaded from a database, emailed by a colleague, or accessed via file-sharing sites. Most significantly, a file-based dataset will, for the most part, contain the same information whether you open it today or a week, a month, or a year from now.

Today, these file-based formats stand in contrast to the data formats and interfaces that have emerged alongside real-time web services over the past 20 years. Web-based data today is available for everything from news to weather monitoring to social media sites, and these feed-style data sources have their own unique formats and

---

[1] Contrast these with some others you might know, like *mp4* or *png*, which are usually associated with music and images, respectively.

structures. Extensions like *xml*, *json*, and *rss* indicate this type of real-time data, which often needs to be accessed via specialized application programming interfaces, or APIs. Unlike file-based formats, accessing the same web-based data location or "endpoint" via an API will always show you the most *recent* data available—and that data may change in days, hours, or even seconds.

These aren't perfect distinctions, of course. There are many organizations (especially government departments) that provide file-based data for download—but then over-write those files with new ones that have the same name whenever the source data is updated. At the same time, feed-style data formats *can* be downloaded and saved for future reference—but their source location online will not generally provide access to older versions. Despite these sometimes unconventional uses for each class of data format, however, in most cases you can use the high-level differences between file-based and feed-based data formats to help you choose the most appropriate sources for a given data wrangling project.

How do you know if you want file-based or feed-based data? In many cases, you won't have a choice. Social media companies, for example, provide ready access to their data feeds through their APIs but don't generally provide retrospective data. Other types of data—especially data that is itself synthesized from other sources or heavily reviewed before release—are much more likely to be made available in file-based formats. If you *do* have a choice between file-based and feed-based formats, then which you choose will really depend on the nature of your data wrangling question: if it hinges on having the most *recent* data available, then a feed-style format will probably be preferable. But if you're concerned about *trends*, file-based data, which is more likely to contain information collected over time, will probably be your best bet. That said, even when both formats are available, there's no guarantee they contain the same fields, which once again might make your decision for you.

One Data Source, Two Ways

We've actually already worked with a data source that is available in both a file-based and a feed-based format: our Citi Bike data from Chapter 2. In "Hitting the Road with Citi Bike Data" on page 62, we used a subset of the file-based data to examine how many "Subscriber" versus "Customer" rides were taken by Citi Bike riders on September 1, 2020. For data wrangling questions about trends in ridership and station activity, these retrospective files are invaluable.

At the same time, if we wanted information about how many bikes were available at a particular Citi Bike station *right now*, that file-based data just can't help us. But we *can* access this information using Citi Bike's real-time *json* feed (*https://gbfs.cit ibikenyc.com/gbfs/en/station_status.json*). The wall of text you'll see when you open

---

that link in most web browsers isn't especially user-friendly,[2] but it *does* contain information that the file-based data doesn't—like a count of currently available bikes and parking spots, as well as how many bikes there are not usable, etc. In order to determine the physical location of a particular `station_id`, however, you'd need to *augment* this data with information from either a different Citi Bike data feed or with the file-based data we've already used.

In other words, there are plenty of data sources where it makes sense to have both file-based and feed-based data formats—which is better for you will really depend (as always!) on your particular data wrangling question.

Over the course of this chapter, we'll work through hands-on examples of wrangling data from several of the most common file-based and feed-based data formats, with the goal of making them easier to review, clean, augment, and analyze. We'll also take a look at some of the tougher-to-wrangle data formats that you might need to work with strictly out of necessity. Throughout these processes, we'll rely heavily on the excellent variety of libraries that the Python community has developed for these purposes, including specialty libraries and programs for processing everything from spreadsheets to images. By the time we finish, you'll have the skills and sample scripts you need to tackle a huge variety of data wrangling projects, paving the way forward for your next data wrangling project!

Structured Versus Unstructured Data

Before we dive into writing code and wrangling data, I want to briefly discuss one other key attribute of data sources that can impact the direction (and speed) of your data wrangling projects—working with *structured* versus *unstructured* data.

The goal of most data wrangling projects is to generate insight and, often, to use data to make better decisions. But decisions are time sensitive, so our work with data also requires balancing trade-offs: instead of waiting for the "perfect" dataset, we may combine two or three not-so-perfect ones in order to build a valid approximation of the phenomenon we're investigating, or we may look for datasets that share common identifiers (for example, zip codes), even if that means we need to later derive the particular dimensional structure (like neighborhood) that truly interests us. As long as we can gain these efficiencies without sacrificing too much in terms of data quality, improving the timeliness of our data work can also increase its impact.

One of the simplest ways to make our data wrangling more efficient is to seek out data formats that are easy for Python and other computational tools to access and understand. Although advances in computer vision, natural language processing, and

---

2 Though you'll know how to wrangle it shortly!

machine learning have made it easier for computers to analyze data regardless of its underlying structure or format, the fact is that *structured, machine-readable* data remains—unsurprisingly, perhaps—the most straightforward type of data to work with. In truth, while anything from interviews to images to the text of books can be used as a data source, when many of us think of "data," we often think of structured, numerical data more than anything else.

What Do We Mean by "Machine-Readable"?

Believe it or not, the United States actually has a legal definition of "machine-readable" data, thanks to the Foundations for Evidence-Based Policymaking Act (*https://govinfo.gov/content/pkg/PLAW-115publ435/html/PLAW-115publ435.htm*), which went into effect in early 2019. According to the law, machine-readable data is:

> data in a format that can be easily processed by a computer without human intervention while ensuring no semantic meaning is lost.

Helpful, right? While it may seem a bit formal now, as you continue to work with data (especially if you are requesting it from government agencies), you'll begin to appreciate why this definition is important. Particularly when it comes to dealing with "unstructured" data (like text documents), for example, there is a big difference between data that was generated by a word-processing program and data that was scanned in from a piece of paper. While both are "machine-readable" in the sense that you can view them on a computer, good luck trying to access the underlying text from the scanned document programmatically![3] Since there will be times that the folks providing your data might be a little reluctant to do so, a clear (legal!) definition of what "machine-readable" means is actually very valuable.

Structured data is any type of data that has been organized and classified in some way, into some version of records and fields. In file-based formats, these are usually rows and columns; in feed-based formats they are often (essentially) lists of objects or *dicti*onaries.

Unstructured data, by contrast, may consist of a mash-up of different data types, combining text, numbers, and even photographs or illustrations. The contents of a magazine or a novel, or the waveforms of a song, for example, would typically be considered unstructured data.

If right now you're thinking, "Hang on, novels have structure! What about chapters?" then congratulations: you're already thinking like a data wrangler. We can create data about almost anything by collecting information about the world and applying

---

3 Actually, you won't need that much luck—we'll look at how to do this in "Wrangling PDFs with Python" on page 135.

structure to it.[4] And in truth, this is how *all* data is created: the datasets that we access via files and feeds are all the product of someone's decisions about how to collect and organize information. In other words, there is always more than one way to organize information, but the structure chosen influences how it can be analyzed. This is why it's a *little* ridiculous to suggest that data can somehow be "objective"; after all, it's the product of (inherently subjective) human choices.

For example, try conducting this mini-experiment: think about how you organize some collection of yours (it could be a collection of music, books, games, or varieties of tea—you name it). Now ask a friend how they organize their own collection of that item. Do you do it the same way? Which is "better"? Now ask someone else, and maybe even a third person. While you may find similarities among the systems that you and your friends use for organizing your music collections, for example, I would be very surprised if you find that any two of you do it precisely the same way. In fact, you'll probably find that everyone does it a little bit differently but *also* feels passionately that their way is "best." And it is! For *them*.

If this is reminding you of our discussion in "How? And for Whom?" on page 75, that's no coincidence, because the result of your data wrangling question and efforts will eventually be—you guessed it!—another dataset, which will reflect *your* interests and priorities. It, too, will be structured and organized, which makes working with it in certain ways easier than others. But the takeaway here is not that any given way is right or wrong, just that every choice involves trade-offs. Identifying and acknowledging those trade-offs is a key part of using data honestly and responsibly.

So a key trade-off when using *structured* data is that it requires depending on someone else's judgments and priorities in organizing the underlying information. Obviously, this can be a good—or even great!—thing if that data has been structured according to an open, transparent process that involves well-qualified experts. Thoughtfully applied data structures like this can give us early insight into a subject we may otherwise know little to nothing about. On the other hand, there is also the possibility that we will inherit someone else's biased or poorly designed choices.

Unstructured data, of course, gives us complete freedom to organize information into data structures that suit our needs best. Unsurprisingly, this requires *us* to take responsibility for engaging a robust data quality process, which may be both complex and time-consuming.

How do we know if a particular dataset is structured or unstructured up front? In this case, file extensions can definitely help us out. Feed-based data formats always

---

4 In computer science, the terms *data* and *information* are applied in exactly the opposite way: *data* is the raw facts collected about the world, and *information* is the meaningful end product of organizing and structuring it. In recent years, however, as talk about "big data" has dominated many fields, the interpretation I use here has become more common, so I'll stick with it throughout this book for clarity.

have at least *some* structure to them, even if they contain chunks of "free text," like social media posts. So if you see the file extensions *.json*, *.xml*, *.rss*, or *.atom*, the data has at least some type of record-and-field structure, as we'll explore in "Feed-Based Data—Web-Driven Live Updates" on page 118. File-based data that ends in *.csv*, *.tsv*, *.txt*, *.xls(x)*, or *.ods* tends to follow a table-type, rows-and-columns structure, as we'll see in the next section. Truly unstructured data, meanwhile, is most likely to come to us as *.doc(x)* or *.pdf*.

Smart Searching for Specific Data Types

Since search engines are the first place most of us turn when we're looking for information, wouldn't it be great to be able to use the power of search engines to more efficiently find the data sources (and formats) we need?

While using keywords, sentences, or phrases is a typical way to begin an online search, tweaking those habits just a little can make all the difference when it comes to turning up useful data formats. By mixing in one or more *search operators*, you can tell your search engine to return results from only specific websites or domain types (like *.gov*), or even results with specific file extensions. For example:

Search terms or keywords `filetype: .csv`
> You can replace `.csv` with any file extension you like, including `.tsv`, `.txt`, `.pdf`, or even `.jpg`, `.mp3`, etc. This will return files with the specified extension that also match your search terms or keywords.

Search terms or keywords `site: oreilly.com`
> This search will return only results matching your search terms or keywords from within the site *oreilly.com*. This is particularly handy if you are looking for data created or published by a particular organization. Note that you can also use this to search within an entire *top-level domain* like *.gov* or *.co.uk*.

Search terms or keywords `inurl: https`
> A handy way to locate only secure websites.

Search terms or keywords `- other search terms or keywords`
> While this won't help you find specific files, using the hyphen (`-`) can be a great way to focus your search for information when you specifically want to exclude results that would be commonly associated with your main search term. To see this in action, compare the results of the search `steve jobs` with `steve jobs -apple` on your favorite search engine.

Of course, a search engine is just one way to find data; for more ideas about locating the data you need, check out Appendix C.

Now that we've got a good handle on the different types of data sources that we're likely to encounter—and even some sense of how to locate them—let's get wrangling!

Working with Structured Data

Since the early days of digital computing, the *table* has been one of the most common ways to structure data. Even today, many of the most common and easy-to-wrangle data formats are little more than tables or collections of tables. In fact, we already worked with one very common table-type data format in Chapter 2: the *.csv* or comma-separated value format.

File-Based, Table-Type Data—Take It to Delimit

In general, all of the table-type data formats you'll typically encounter are examples of what are known as *delimited* files: each data record is on its own line or row, and the boundaries between fields or columns of data values are indicated—or *delimited*—by a specific text character. Often, an indication of *which* text character is being used as the *delimiter* in a file is incorporated into the dataset's file extension. For example, the *.csv* file extension stands for *comma-separated value*, because these files use a comma character (,) as a delimiter; the *.tsv* file extension stands for *tab-separated value*, because the data columns are separated by a tab. A list of file extensions commonly associated with delimited data follows:

.csv

> Comma-separated value files are among the most common form of table-type structured data files you'll encounter. Almost any software system that handles tabular data (such as government or corporate data systems, spreadsheet programs, and even specialized commercial data programs) can output data as a *.csv*, and, as we saw in Chapter 2, there are handy libraries for easily working with this data type in Python.

.tsv

> Tab-separated value files have been around for a long time, but the descriptive *.tsv* extension has only become common relatively recently. While data providers don't often explain why they choose one delimiter over another, tab-delimited files may be more common for datasets whose values need to include commas, such as postal addresses.

.txt

> Structured data files with this extension are often *.tsv* files in disguise; older data systems often labeled tab-separated data with the *.txt* extension. As you'll see in the worked examples that follow, it's a good idea to open and review *any* data file you want to wrangle with a basic text program (or a code editor like Atom)

before you write any code, since looking at the contents of the file is the only surefire way to know what delimiters you're working with.

.xls(x)
This is the file extension of spreadsheets produced with Microsoft Excel. Because these files can contain multiple "sheets" in addition to formulas, formatting, and other features that simple delimited files cannot replicate, they need more memory to store the same amount of data. They also have other limitations (like only being able to handle a certain number of rows) that can have implications for your dataset's integrity.

.ods
Open-document spreadsheet files are the default extension for spreadsheets produced by a number of open source software suites like LibreOffice (*https://libreoffice.org*) and OpenOffice (*https://openoffice.org/download/index.html*) and have limitations and features similar to those of *.xls(x)* files.

Before we dive into how to work with each of these file types in Python, it's worth spending just a little time thinking about when we might *want* to work with table-type data and where to find it when we do.

When to work with table-type data

Most of the time, we don't get much of a choice about the format of our source data. In fact, much of the reason we need to do data wrangling in the first place is because the data we have doesn't quite meet our needs. That said, it's still valuable to know what data format you would *prefer* to be able to work with so that you can use that to inform your initial search for data.

In "Structured Versus Unstructured Data" on page 93, we talked about the benefits and limitations of structured data, and we now know that table-type data is one of the oldest and most common forms of machine-readable data. This history means, in part, that over the years many forms of source data have been crammed into tables, even though they may *not* necessarily be well suited to table-like representations. Still, this format can be especially useful for answering questions about trends and patterns over time. In our Citi Bike exercise from Chapter 2, for example, we examined how many "Customers" versus "Subscribers" had taken Citi Bike rides over the course of a single month. If we wanted to, we could perform the same calculation for *every* available month of Citi Bike rides in order to understand any patterns in this ratio over time.

Of course, table-type data is generally not a great format for real-time data, or data where not every observation contains the same possible values. These kinds of data are often better suited to the feed-based data formats that we discuss in "Feed-Based Data—Web-Driven Live Updates" on page 118.

Where to find table-type data

Since the vast majority of machine-readable data is still in table-type data formats, it is among the easiest data formats to locate. Spreadsheets are common in every discipline, and a large number of government and commercial information systems rely on software that organizes data in this way. Almost any time you request data from an expert or organization, a table-type format is what you are likely to get. This is also true of almost every open-data portal and data-sharing site you'll find online. As we covered in "Smart Searching for Specific Data Types" on page 96, you can even find table-type data (and other specific file formats) via search engines, if you know how to look.

Wrangling Table-Type Data with Python

To help illustrate how simple it is to work with table-type data in Python, we'll walk through examples of how to read in data from all of the file types mentioned in this section—plus a few others, just for good measure. While in later chapters we'll look at how to do more with cleaning, transformation, and data quality assessments, our focus for the time being will simply be on accessing the data within each type of data file and interacting with it using Python.

Reading data from CSVs

In case you didn't follow along in Chapter 2, here's a refresher on how to read data from a *.csv* file, using a sample from the Citi Bike dataset (Example 4-1). As always, I've included a description of what the program is doing—as well as links to any source files—in the comments at the top of my script. Since we've worked with this data format before, for now we'll just worry about printing out the first few rows of data to see what they look like.

Example 4-1. csv_parsing.py

```
# a simple example of reading data from a .csv file with Python
# using the "csv" library.
# the source data was sampled from the Citi Bike system data:
# https://drive.google.com/file/d/17b461NhSjf_akFWvjgNXQfqgh9iFxCu_/
# which can be found here:
# https://s3.amazonaws.com/tripdata/index.html

# import the `csv` library ❶
import csv

# open the `202009CitibikeTripdataExample.csv` file in read ("r") mode
# this file should be in the same folder as our Python script or notebook
source_file = open("202009CitibikeTripdataExample.csv","r") ❷

# pass our `source_file` as an ingredient to the `csv` library's
```

```
# DictReader "recipe".
# store the result in a variable called `citibike_reader`
citibike_reader = csv.DictReader(source_file)

# the DictReader method has added some useful information to our data,
# like a `fieldnames` property that lets us access all the values
# in the first or "header" row
print(citibike_reader.fieldnames) ❸

# let's just print out the first 5 rows
for i in range(0,5):  ❹
    print (next(citibike_reader))
```

❶ This is our workhorse library when it comes to dealing with table-type data.

❷ open() is a built-in function that takes a filename and a "mode" as parameters. In this example, the target file (202009CitibikeTripdataExample.csv) should be in the same folder as our Python script or notebook. Values for the "mode" can be r for "read" or w for "write."

❸ By printing out the citibike_reader.fieldnames values, we can see that the exact label for the "User Type" column is usertype.

❹ The range() function gives us a way to execute some piece of code a specific number of times, starting with the value of the first argument and ending just *before* the value of the second argument. For example, the code indented below this line will be executed five times, going through the i values of 0, 1, 2, 3, and 4. For more on the range() function, see "Adding Iterators: The range Function" on page 101.

The output from running this should look something like:

```
['tripduration', 'starttime', 'StartDate', 'stoptime', 'start station id',
'start station name', 'start station latitude', 'start station longitude', 'end
station id', 'end station name', 'end station latitude', 'end station
longitude', 'bikeid', 'usertype', 'birth year', 'gender']
{'tripduration': '4225', 'starttime': '2020-09-01 00:00:01.0430', 'StartDate':
'2020-09-01', 'stoptime': '2020-09-01 01:10:26.6350', 'start station id':
'3508', 'start station name': 'St Nicholas Ave & Manhattan Ave', 'start station
latitude': '40.809725', 'start station longitude': '-73.953149', 'end station
id': '116', 'end station name': 'W 17 St & 8 Ave', 'end station latitude': '40.
74177603', 'end station longitude': '-74.00149746', 'bikeid': '44317',
'usertype': 'Customer', 'birth year': '1979', 'gender': '1'}
 ...
{'tripduration': '1193', 'starttime': '2020-09-01 00:00:12.2020', 'StartDate':
'2020-09-01', 'stoptime': '2020-09-01 00:20:05.5470', 'start station id':
'3081', 'start station name': 'Graham Ave & Grand St', 'start station
latitude': '40.711863', 'start station longitude': '-73.944024', 'end station
id': '3048', 'end station name': 'Putnam Ave & Nostrand Ave', 'end station
```

latitude': '40.68402', 'end station longitude': '-73.94977', 'bikeid': '26396',
'usertype': 'Customer', 'birth year': '1969', 'gender': '0'}

Adding Iterators: The range Function

Unlike many other programming languages, Python's for loop is designed to run through *all* values in a list or a dataset by default. While this can be handy for processing entire datasets quickly, it's not so helpful when we just want to quickly review a handful of rows.

This is where a special type of variable called an *iterator* comes in. Like any variable, you can name an iterator anything you like, though i (for *iterator!*) is traditional. As you can see from the preceding example, one place where Python *iterators* typically appear is within the range function (*https://docs.python.org/3/tutorial/control flow.html#the-range-function*)—another example of a *control flow* function that, like for loops and if statements, has special, built-in properties.

For example, the range function includes an *iterator* variable that lets us write a slightly different kind of for loop—one that goes through a certain number of rows, rather than all of them. So rather than taking the form of:

```
for item in complete_list_of_items:
```

it lets us write a for loop that starts at a particular point in our list and continues for a certain number of items:

```
for item_position in range (starting_position, >number_of_places_to_move):
```

In Example 4-1, we chose to print the first several rows of the file:

```
for i in range(0,5):
    print (next(citibike_reader))
```

One thing to note is that when the range iterates over the values specified in the parentheses, it *includes* the first number but *excludes* the second one. This means that in order to print five rows of data, we need to provide an initial value of 0, because lists in Python are what's known as *zero-indexed*—they start "counting" positions at 0 rather than 1.

Reading data from TSV and TXT files

Despite its name, the Python *csv* library is basically a one-stop shop for wrangling table-type data in Python, thanks to the DictReader function's delimiter option. Unless you tell it differently, DictReader assumes that the comma character (,) is the separator it should look for. Overriding that assumption is easy, however: you can simply specify a different character when you call the function. In Example 4-2, we specify the tab character (\t), but we could easily substitute any delimiter we prefer (or that appears in a particular source file).

Example 4-2. tsv_parsing.py

```python
# a simple example of reading data from a .tsv file with Python, using
# the `csv` library. The source data was downloaded as a .tsv file
# from Jed Shugerman's Google Sheet on prosecutor politicians: ❶
# https://docs.google.com/spreadsheets/d/1E6Z-jZWbrKmit_4lG36oyQ658Ta6Mh25HCOBaz7YVrA

# import the `csv` library
import csv

# open the `ShugermanProsecutorPoliticians-SupremeCourtJustices.tsv` file
# in read ("r") mode.
# this file should be in the same folder as our Python script or notebook
tsv_source_file = open("ShugermanProsecutorPoliticians-SupremeCourtJustices.tsv","r")

# pass our `tsv_source_file` as an ingredient to the csv library's
# DictReader "recipe."
# store the result in a variable called `politicians_reader`
politicians_reader = csv.DictReader(tsv_source_file, delimiter='\t')

# the DictReader method has added some useful information to our data,
# like a `fieldnames` property that lets us access all the values
# in the first or "header" row
print(politicians_reader.fieldnames)

# we'll use the `next()` function to print just the first row of data
print (next(politicians_reader))
```

❶ This dataset was listed in Jeremy Singer-Vine's (@jsvine) "Data Is Plural" newsletter (*https://data-is-plural.com*).

This should result in output that looks something like:

```
['', 'Justice', 'Term Start/End', 'Party', 'State', 'Pres Appt', 'Other Offices
Held', 'Relevant Prosecutorial Background']
{'': '40', 'Justice': 'William Strong', 'Term Start/End': '1870-1880', 'Party':
'D/R', 'State': 'PA', 'Pres Appt': 'Grant', 'Other Offices Held': 'US House,
Supr Court of PA, elect comm for elec of 1876', 'Relevant Prosecutorial
Background': 'lawyer'}
```

What's in a File Extension?

While having computers take care of certain things for us "automagically" can often be convenient, one thing that learning to wrangle data and program in Python will hopefully make clear is that we have much more influence over how our computers behave than it might first appear.

A perfect example of this is file extensions. Throughout the course of this chapter, I've highlighted how file extensions can give us clues about the format of a dataset and even help us search for them more efficiently. Of course, computers *also* use file

---

extensions to make inferences about the contents of a particular file, typically relying on them to select the appropriate program for opening it. This is why if you've ever *changed* a file extension—whether intentionally or by accident—you've probably seen a warning message to the effect of "Are you sure you want to change this? The file might not work properly if you do." While no doubt well-intentioned, those types of warning messages make it seem like you can actually break or corrupt your files by accidentally changing the file extension.

In fact, nothing could be further from the truth. Changing the extension of a file (for example, from *.tsv* to *.txt* or vice versa) does absolutely *nothing* to change its contents. All it does is change what your computer assumes should be done with it.

Fortunately, Python tools like the ones we're using don't make those sorts of assumptions. When we're working with table-type data, as long as the delimiter we specify matches what's actually used in the file, the extension on the data file doesn't matter either way. In fact, the *.txt* file we'll use in Example 4-3 was created simply by saving a copy of the *.tsv* file from Example 4-2 and changing the extension!

Though the *.tsv* file extension has become relatively common nowadays, many files generated by older databases that are *actually* tab-separated may reach you with a *.txt* file extension. Fortunately, as described in the preceding sidebar, this changes nothing about how we handle the file as long as we specify the correct delimiter—as you can see in Example 4-3.

Example 4-3. txt_parsing.py

```
# a simple example of reading data from a .tsv file with Python, using
# the `csv` library. The source data was downloaded as a .tsv file
# from Jed Shugerman's Google Sheet on prosecutor politicians:
# https://docs.google.com/spreadsheets/d/1E6Z-jZWbrKmit_4lG36oyQ658Ta6Mh25HCOBaz7YVrA
# the original .tsv file was renamed with a file extension of .txt

# import the `csv` library
import csv

# open the `ShugermanProsecutorPoliticians-SupremeCourtJustices.txt` file
# in read ("r") mode.
# this file should be in the same folder as our Python script or notebook
txt_source_file = open("ShugermanProsecutorPoliticians-SupremeCourtJustices.txt","r")

# pass our txt_source_file as an ingredient to the csv library's DictReader
# "recipe" and store the result in a variable called `politicians_reader`
# add the "delimiter" parameter and specify the tab character, "\t"
politicians_reader = csv.DictReader(txt_source_file, delimiter='\t') ❶

# the DictReader function has added useful information to our data,
# like a label that shows us all the values in the first or "header" row
print(politicians_reader.fieldnames)
```

```
# we'll use the `next()` function to print just the first row of data
print (next(politicians_reader))
```

❶ As discussed in "Don't Leave Space!" on page 13, whitespace characters have to be *escaped* when we're using them in code. Here, we're using the escaped character for a `tab`, which is `\t`. Another common whitespace character code is `\n` for `newline` (or `\r` for `return`, depending on your device).

If everything has gone well, the output from this script should look exactly the same as that from Example 4-2.

One question you may be asking yourself at this point is "How do I know what delimiter my file has?" While there are programmatic ways to help detect this, the simple answer is: Look! Anytime you begin working with (or thinking about working with) a new dataset, start by opening it up in the most basic text program your device has to offer (any code editor will also be a reliable choice). Especially if the file is large, using the simplest program possible will let your device devote maximum memory and processing power to actually reading the data—reducing the likelihood that the program will hang or your device will crash (closing other programs and excess browser tabs will help, too)!

Though I'll talk about some ways to inspect small parts of *really* large files later on in the book, now is the time to start practicing the skills that are essential to assessing data quality—all of which require reviewing your data and making judgments about it. So while there *are* ways to "automate away" tasks like identifying the correct delimiter for your data, eyeballing it in a text editor will often be not just faster and more intuitive, but it will help you get more familiar with other important aspects of the data at the same time.

It's All Just Text

One reason why opening *.csv*, *.tsv*, and many other data formats in a text editor is so helpful is that *most* of the data formats we will (or want to) deal with are, at the most basic level, just text. In exactly the same way that written English is organized into sentences and paragraphs through the (somewhat) standardized use of periods, spaces, capital letters, and newlines, what distinguishes one data format from another at a practical level is also just the punctuation used to organize it. As we've seen, basic table-type data is separated into fields or columns through the use of *delimiters*, and into records or rows by using newlines. Feed-type data, which we'll look at in the next section, is a bit more flexible (and involved) but ultimately follows relatively simple punctuation and structure rules of its own.

Of course, there are plenty of nontext data formats out there, which are usually the output of specialized, *proprietary* programs that are designed to make data wrangling

---

(and analysis and visualization) possible *without* writing much, if any, code. While these programs can make very specific data tasks faster or more approachable, the trade-off is that they are often expensive, challenging to learn, and sometimes inflexible. As we'll see in "XLSX, ODS, and All the Rest" on page 107 and beyond, getting data *out* of these proprietary formats can also be difficult, unreliable, or even impossible. So while Python can still help us wrangle some of the most common proprietary data formats, in some cases using alternate software (or enlisting someone else's help) is our best option.

Real-World Data Wrangling: Understanding Unemployment

The underlying dataset that we'll use to explore some of our trickier table-type data formats is unemployment data about the United States. Why? In one way or another, unemployment affects most of us, and in recent decades the US has experienced some particularly high unemployment rates. Unemployment numbers for the US are released monthly by the Bureau of Labor Statistics (BLS), and while they are often reported by general-interest news sources, they are usually treated as a sort of abstract indicator of how "the economy" is doing. What the numbers really represent is rarely discussed in-depth.

When I first joined the *Wall Street Journal* in 2007, building an interactive dashboard for exploring monthly economic indicator data—including unemployment—was my first major project. One of the more interesting things I learned in the process is that there isn't "an" unemployment rate calculated each month, there are *several* (six, to be exact). The one that usually gets reported by news sources is the so-called "U3" unemployment rate, which the BLS describes as:

> Total unemployed, as a percent of the civilian labor force (official unemployment rate).

On its surface, this seems like a straightforward definition of unemployment: of all the people who reasonably *could* be working, what percentage are not?

Yet the real story is a bit more complex. What does it mean to be "employed" or be counted as part of the "labor force"? A look at different unemployment numbers makes more clear what the "U3" number does *not* take into account. The "U6" unemployment rate is defined as:

> Total unemployed, plus all persons marginally attached to the labor force, plus total employed part time for economic reasons, as a percent of the civilian labor force plus all persons marginally attached to the labor force.

When we read the accompanying note, this longer definition starts to take shape:[5]

> NOTE: Persons marginally attached to the labor force are those who currently are neither working nor looking for work but indicate that they want and are available for a job and have looked for work sometime in the past 12 months. Discouraged workers, a subset of the marginally attached, have given a job-market related reason for not currently looking for work. Persons employed part time for economic reasons are those who want and are available for full-time work but have had to settle for a part-time schedule. Updated population controls are introduced annually with the release of January data.

In other words, if you *want* a job (and have looked for one in the past year) but haven't looked for one very recently—or if you have a part-time job but *want* a full-time job—then you don't officially count as "unemployed" in the U3 definition. This means that the economic reality of Americans working multiple jobs (who are more likely to be women and have more children)[6], and potentially of "gig" workers (recently estimated as up to 30% of the American workforce)[7], are not necessarily reflected in the U3 number. Unsurprisingly, the U6 rate is typically several percentage points higher each month than the U3 rate.

To see how these rates compare over time, we can download them from the website of the St. Louis Federal Reserve, which provides thousands of economic datasets for download in a range of formats, including table-type *.xls(x)* files and, as we'll see later in Example 4-12, feed-type formats as well.

You can download the data for these exercises from the Federal Reserve Economic Database (FRED) website (*https://fred.stlouisfed.org/series/U6RATE*). It shows the current U6 unemployment rate since the measure was first created in the early 1990s.

To add the U3 rate to this graph, at the top right choose Edit graph → ADD LINE. In the search field, type **UNRATE** and then select "Unemployment Rate" when it populates below the search bar. Finally, click Add series. Close this side window using the X at the top right, and then select Download, being sure to select the first option, Excel.[8] This will be an *.xls* file, which we'll handle last because although still widely available, this is a relatively outdated file format (it was replaced by *.xlsx* as the default format for Microsoft Excel spreadsheets in 2007).

---

5 From the US Bureau of Labor Statistics (*https://bls.gov/news.release/empsit.t15.htm*).

6 "Multiple Jobholders" by Stéphane Auray, David L. Fuller, and Guillaume Vandenbroucke, posted December 21, 2018, *https://research.stlouisfed.org/publications/economic-synopses/2018/12/21/multiple-jobholders*.

7 See "New Recommendations on Improving Data on Contingent and Alternative Work Arrangements," *https://blogs.bls.gov/blog/tag/contingent-workers*; "The Value of Flexible Work: Evidence from Uber Drivers" by M. Keith Chen et al., *Nber Working Paper Series* No. 23296, *https://nber.org/system/files/working_papers/w23296/w23296.pdf*.

8 You can also find instructions for this on the FRED website (*https://fredhelp.stlouisfed.org/fred/graphs/customize-a-fred-graph/data-transformation-add-series-to-existing-line*).

To get the additional file formats we need, just open the file you downloaded with a spreadsheet program like Google Sheets and choose "Save As," then select *.xlsx*, then repeat the process choosing *.ods*. You should now have the following three files, all containing the same information: *fredgraph.xlsx*, *fredgraph.ods*, and *fredgraph.xls*.[9]

 If you opened the original *fredgraph.xls* file, you probably noticed that it contains more than just the unemployment data; it also contains some header information about where the data came from and the definitions of U3 and U6 unemployment, for example. While doing *analysis* on the unemployment rates these files contain would require separating this metadata from the table-type data further down, remember that our goal for the moment is simply to convert all of our various files to a *.csv* format. We'll tackle the data cleaning process that would involve removing this metadata in Chapter 7.

XLSX, ODS, and All the Rest

For the most part, it's preferable to avoid processing data saved as *.xlsx*, *.ods*, and most other nontext table-type data formats directly, if possible. If you're just at the stage of exploring datasets, I suggest you review these files simply by opening them with your preferred spreadsheet program and saving them as a *.csv* or *.tsv* file format before accessing them in Python. Not only will this make them easier to work with, it will give you a chance to actually look at the contents of your data file and get a sense of what it contains.

Resaving and reviewing *.xls(x)* and similar data formats as a *.csv* or equivalent text-based file format will both reduce the file size *and* give you a better sense of what the "real" data looks like. Because of the formatting options in spreadsheet programs, sometimes what you see onscreen is substantially different from the raw values that are stored in the actual file. For example, values that appear as percentages in a spreadsheet program (e.g., 10%) might actually be decimals (.1). This can lead to problems if you try to base aspects of your Python processing or analysis on what you saw in the spreadsheet as opposed to a text-based data format like *.csv*.

Still, there will definitely be situations where you need to access *.xls(x)* and similar file types with Python directly.[10] For example, if there's an *.xls* dataset you need to wrangle on a regular basis (say, every month), resaving the file manually each time would become unnecessarily time-consuming.

---

9 You can also download copies of these files directly from my Google Drive (*https://drive.google.com/drive/u/0/folders/1cU5Tdg_fvrCcwvAAyhMOhpbEcI2fF7sb*).

10 As of this writing, LibreOffice can handle the same number of rows as Microsoft Excel (2^{20}), but far fewer columns. While Google Sheets can handle *more* columns than Excel, it can only handle about 40,000 rows.

Fortunately, that active Python community we talked about in "Community" on page 7 has created libraries that can handle an impressive range of data formats with ease. To get a thorough feel for how these libraries work with more complex source data (and data formats), the following code examples read in the specified file format and then create a *new .csv* file that contains the same data.

To make use of these libraries, however, you'll first need to install them on your device by running the following commands one by one in a terminal window:[11]

```
pip install openpyxl
pip install pyexcel-ods
pip install xlrd==2.0.1
```

In the following code examples, we'll be using the *openpyxl* library to access (or *parse*) *.xlsx* files, the *pyexcel-ods* library for dealing with *.ods* files, and the *xlrd* library for reading from *.xls* files (for more on finding and selecting Python libraries, see "Where to Look for Libraries" on page 366).

To better illustrate the idiosyncrasies of these different file formats, we're going to do something similar to what we did in Example 4-3: we'll take sample data that is being provided as an *.xls* file and create *.xlsx* and *.ods* files containing *the exact same data* by resaving that source file in the other formats using a spreadsheet program. Along the way, I think you'll start to get a sense of how these nontext formats make the process of data wrangling more (and, I would argue, unnecessarily) complicated.

We'll start by working through an *.xlsx* file in \ref (Example 4-4), using a version of the unemployment data downloaded from FRED. This example illustrates one of the first major differences between dealing with text-based table-type data files and nontext formats: because the nontext formats support multiple "sheets," we needed to include a for loop at the top of our script, *within* which we put the code for creating our individual output files (one for each sheet).

Example 4-4. xlsx_parsing.py

```
# an example of reading data from an .xlsx file with Python, using the "openpyxl"
# library. First, you'll need to pip install the openpyxl library:
# https://pypi.org/project/openpyxl/
# the source data can be composed and downloaded from:
# https://fred.stlouisfed.org/series/U6RATE

# specify the "chapter" you want to import from the "openpyxl" library
# in this case, "load_workbook"
from openpyxl import load_workbook

# import the `csv` library, to create our output file
```

---

11 As of this writing, all of these libraries are already available and ready to use in Google Colab.

```
import csv

# pass our filename as an ingredient to the `openpyxl` library's
# `load_workbook()` "recipe"
# store the result in a variable called `source_workbook`
source_workbook = load_workbook(filename = 'fredgraph.xlsx')

# an .xlsx workbook can have multiple sheets
# print their names here for reference
print(source_workbook.sheetnames) ❶

# loop through the worksheets in `source_workbook`
for sheet_num, sheet_name in enumerate(source_workbook.sheetnames): ❷

    # create a variable that points to the current worksheet by
    # passing the current value of `sheet_name` to `source_workbook`
    current_sheet = source_workbook[sheet_name]

    # print `sheet_name`, just to see what it is
    print(sheet_name)

    # create an output file called "xlsx_"+sheet_name
    output_file = open("xlsx_"+sheet_name+".csv","w") ❸

    # use this csv library's "writer" recipe to easily write rows of data
    # to `output_file`, instead of reading data *from* it
    output_writer = csv.writer(output_file)

    # loop through every row in our sheet
    for row in current_sheet.iter_rows(): ❹

        # we'll create an empty list where we'll put the actual
        # values of the cells in each row
        row_cells = [] ❺

        # for every cell (or column) in each row....
        for cell in row:

            # let's print what's in here, just to see how the code sees it
            print(cell, cell.value)

            # add the values to the end of our list with the `append()` method
            row_cells.append(cell.value)

        # write our newly (re)constructed data row to the output file
        output_writer.writerow(row_cells) ❻

    # officially close the `.csv` file we just wrote all that data to
    output_file.close()
```

❶ Like the *csv* library's `DictReader()` function, openpyxl's `load_workbook()` function adds properties to our source data, in this case, one that shows us the names of all the data sheets in our workbook.

❷ Even though our example workbook only includes one worksheet, we might have more in the future. We'll use the `enumerate()` function so we can access both an iterator *and* the sheet name. This will help us create one *.csv* file per worksheet.

❸ Each sheet in our `source_workbook` will need its own, uniquely named output *.csv* file. To generate these, we'll "open" a new file with the name `"xlsx_"+sheet_name+".csv"` and make it *writable* by passing `w` as the "mode" argument (up until now, we've used the `r` mode to *read* data from *.csvs*).

❹ The function `iter_rows()` is specific to the *openpyxl* library. Here, it converts the rows of `source_workbook` into a list that can be *iterated*, or looped, over.

❺ The *openpyxl* library treats each data cell as a Python `tuple` data type (*https://docs.python.org/3/library/stdtypes.html#tuple*). If we try to just print the rows of `current_sheet` directly, we'll get sort of unhelpful cell locations, rather than the data values they contain. To address this, we'll make *another* loop inside this one to go through every cell in every row one at a time and add the actual data values to `row_cells`.

❻ Notice that this code is left-aligned with the `for cell in row` code in the example. This means that it is *outside* that loop and so will only be run *after* all the cells in a given row have been appended to our list.

This script also begins to demonstrate the way that, just as two chefs may have different ways of preparing the same dish, library creators may make different choices about how to (re)structure each source file type—with corresponding implications for our code. The creators of the *openpyxl* library, for example, chose to store each data cell's location label (e.g., A6) and the value it contains in a Python `tuple`. That design decision is why we need a second `for` loop to go through each row of data—because we actually have to access the data cell by cell in order to build the Python list that will become a single row in our output *.csv* file. Likewise, if you use a spreadsheet program to open the *xlsx_FRED Graph.csv* created by the script in Example 4-4, you'll see that the original *.xls* file shows the values in the `observation_date` column in a YYYY-MM-DD format, but our output file shows those values in a YYYY-MM-DD HH:MM:SS format. This is because the creator(s) of *openpyxl* decided that it would automatically convert any "date-like" data strings into the Python `datetime` datatype. Obviously, none of these choices are right or wrong; we simply need to account for them in writing our code so that we don't distort or misinterpret the source data.

Now that we've wrangled the *.xlsx* version of our data file, let's see what happens when we parse it as an *.ods*, as shown in Example 4-5.

Example 4-5. ods_parsing.py

```python
# an example of reading data from an .ods file with Python, using the
# "pyexcel_ods" library. First, you'll need to pip install the library:
# https://pypi.org/project/pyexcel-ods/

# specify the "chapter" of the "pyexcel_ods" library you want to import,
# in this case, `get_data`
from pyexcel_ods import get_data

# import the `csv` library, to create our output file
import csv

# pass our filename as an ingredient to the `pyexcel_ods` library's
# `get_data()` "recipe"
# store the result in a variable called `source_workbook`
source_workbook = get_data("fredgraph.ods")

# an `.ods` workbook can have multiple sheets
for sheet_name, sheet_data in source_workbook.items():    ❶

    # print `sheet_name`, just to see what it is
    print(sheet_name)

    # create "ods_"+sheet_name+".csv" as an output file for the current sheet
    output_file = open("ods_"+sheet_name+".csv","w")

    # use this csv library's "writer" recipe to easily write rows of data
    # to `output_file`, instead of reading data *from* it
    output_writer = csv.writer(output_file)

    # now, we need to loop through every row in our sheet
    for row in sheet_data:    ❷

        # use the `writerow` recipe to write each `row`
        # directly to our output file
        output_writer.writerow(row)    ❸

    # officially close the `.csv` file we just wrote all that data to
    output_file.close()
```

❶ The *pyexcel_ods* library converts our source data into Python's `OrderedDict` data type. The associated `items()` method then lets us access each sheet's name and data as a key/value pair that we can loop through. In this case, `sheet_name` is the "key" and the entire worksheet's data is the "value."

❷ Here, `sheet_data` is already a list, so we can just loop through that list with a basic `for` loop.

❸ This library converts each row in a worksheet to a list, which is why we can pass these directly to the `writerow()` method.

In the case of the *pyexcel_ods* library, the contents of our output *.csv* file *much* more closely resembles what we see visually when we open the original *fredgraph.xls* via a spreadsheet program like Google Sheets—the `observation_date` field, for example, is in a simple YYYY-MM-DD format. Moreover, the library creator(s) decided to treat the values in each row as a list, allowing us to write each record directly to our output file without creating any additional loops or lists.

Finally, let's see what happens when we use the *xlrd* library to parse the original *.xls* file directly in Example 4-6.

Example 4-6. xls_parsing.py

```
# a simple example of reading data from a .xls file with Python
# using the "xrld" library. First, pip install the xlrd library:
# https://pypi.org/project/xlrd/2.0.1/

# import the "xlrd" library
import xlrd

# import the `csv` library, to create our output file
import csv

# pass our filename as an ingredient to the `xlrd` library's
# `open_workbook()` "recipe"
# store the result in a variable called `source_workbook`
source_workbook = xlrd.open_workbook("fredgraph.xls") ❶

# an `.xls` workbook can have multiple sheets
for sheet_name in source_workbook.sheet_names():

    # create a variable that points to the current worksheet by
    # passing the current value of `sheet_name` to the `sheet_by_name` recipe
    current_sheet = source_workbook.sheet_by_name(sheet_name)

    # print `sheet_name`, just to see what it is
    print(sheet_name)
```

```
# create "xls_"+sheet_name+".csv" as an output file for the current sheet
output_file = open("xls_"+sheet_name+".csv","w")

# use the `csv` library's "writer" recipe to easily write rows of data
# to `output_file`, instead of reading data *from* it
output_writer = csv.writer(output_file)

# now, we need to loop through every row in our sheet
for row_num, row in enumerate(current_sheet.get_rows()):  ❷

    # each row is already a list, but we need to use the `row_value()`
    # method to access them
    # then we can use the `writerow` recipe to write them
    # directly to our output file
    output_writer.writerow(current_sheet.row_values(row_num))  ❸

# officially close the `.csv` file we just wrote all that data to
output_file.close()
```

❶ Notice that this structure is similar to the one we use when working with the *csv* library.

❷ The function **get_rows()** is specific to the *xlrd* library; it converts the rows of our current worksheet into a list that can be looped over.[12]

❸ There will be some funkiness within the "dates" written to our output file.[13] We'll look at how to fix up the dates in "Decrypting Excel Dates" on page 239.

One thing we'll see in this output file is some *serious* weirdness in the values recorded in the observation_date field, reflecting the fact that, as the *xlrd* library's creators put it:[14]

> Dates in Excel spreadsheets: In reality, there are no such things. What you have are floating point numbers and pious hope.

As a result, getting a useful, human-readable date out of an *.xls* file requires some significant cleanup, which we'll address in "Decrypting Excel Dates" on page 239.

As these exercises have hopefully demonstrated, with some clever libraries and a few tweaks to our basic code configuration, it's possible to wrangle data from a wide range of table-type data formats with Python quickly and easily. At the same time, I hope

---

12 For more about **get_rows()**, see the *xlrd* documentation (*https://xlrd.readthedocs.io/en/latest/api.html#xlrd-sheet*).

13 See the *xlrd* documentation (*https://xlrd.readthedocs.io/en/latest/dates.html*) for more on this issue.

14 From Stephen John Machin and Chris Withers, "Dates in Excel Spreadsheets" (*https://xlrd.readthedocs.io/en/latest/dates.html*).

that these examples have also illustrated why working with text-based and/or open source formats is almost always preferable,[15] because they often require less "cleaning" and transformation to get them into a clear, usable state.

Finally, Fixed-Width

Though I didn't mention it at the top of this section, one of the very oldest versions of table-type data is what's known as "fixed-width." As the name implies, each data column in a fixed-width table contains a specific, predefined number of characters—and *always* that number of characters. This means that the meaningful data in fixed-width files are often padded with extra characters, such as spaces or zeroes.

Though very uncommon in contemporary data systems, you are still likely to encounter fixed-width formats if you're working with government data sources whose infrastructure may be decades old.[16] For example, the US National Oceanic and Atmospheric Administration (*https://noaa.gov/our-history*) (NOAA), whose origins date back to the early 19th century, offers a wide range of detailed, up-to-date weather information online for free through its Global Historical Climatology Network (*https://ncdc.noaa.gov/data-access/land-based-station-data/land-based-datasets/global-historical-climatology-network-ghcn*), much of which is published in a fixed-width format. For example, information about the stations' unique identifier, locations, and what network(s) they are a part of is stored in the *ghcnd-stations.txt* file (*https://www1.ncdc.noaa.gov/pub/data/ghcn/daily*). To interpret any actual weather data readings (many of which are *also* released as fixed-width files), you'll need to cross-reference the station data with the weather data.

Even more than other table-type data files, working with fixed-width data can be especially tricky if you don't have access to the metadata that describes how the file and its fields are organized. With delimited files, it's often possible to eyeball the file in a text editor and identify the delimiter used with a reasonable level of confidence. At worst, you can simply try parsing the file using different delimiters and see which yields the best results. With fixed-width files—especially large ones—if there's no data for a particular field in the sample of the data you inspect, it's easy to end up inadvertently lumping together multiple data fields.

---

15 If you open the output files from the three preceding code examples in a text editor, you'll notice that the open source *.ods* format is the simplest and cleanest.

16 As in, for example, Pennsylvania (*https://spotlightpa.org/news/2021/05/pa-unemployment-claims-overhaul-ibm-gsi-benefits-labor-industry*) or Colorado (*https://denverpost.com/2021/01/10/colorado-unemployment-benefits-new-claims-system*).

As mentioned in "File-Based, Table-Type Data—Take It to Delimit" on page 97, it's still not uncommon to come across tab-separated files that have a file extension of *.txt* —which is the same one used for fixed-width files. Since both file formats *also* rely on whitespace (spaces or tabs) to separate fields, how can you be sure which one you're working with?

This is yet another situation where opening up your data file and looking at it in a text or code editor will save you some headaches, because there are clear visual differences between these two file formats. Start by looking at the right side of the document: tab-separated files will be "ragged-right" (the data records will have different line lengths), while fixed-width files will be "justified" (all the records will end at the same point).

For example, here's how a few lines of our *.tsv* data from Example 4-2 look in Atom:

```
42      Ward Hunt         1873-1882      R      NY      Grant
43      Morrison Waite    1874-1888      R      OH      Grant
44      John Marshall Harlan   1877 1911   R      KT      Hayes
```

And here's how a few lines of the ghcnd-stations.txt file look:

```
AEM00041217  24.4330  54.6510   26.8    ABU DHABI INTL                41217
AEM00041218  24.2620  55.6090  264.9    AL AIN INTL                   41218
AF000040930  35.3170  69.0170 3366.0    NORTH-SALANG            GSN   40930
```

As you can see, not only is the fixed-width file right justified but *so are all the numbers.* This is another clue that what you're looking at is actually a fixed-width file, rather than a tab-delimited one.

Fortunately, metadata about the *ghcnd-stations.txt* file that we're using as our data source *is* included in the *readme.txt* file in the same folder on the NOAA site (*https://www1.ncdc.noaa.gov/pub/data/ghcn/daily/readme.txt*).

Looking through that *readme.txt* file, we find the heading IV. FORMAT OF "ghcnd-stations.txt", which contains the following table:

```
------------------------------
Variable   Columns   Type
------------------------------
ID           1-11    Character
LATITUDE    13-20    Real
LONGITUDE   22-30    Real
ELEVATION   32-37    Real
STATE       39-40    Character
NAME        42-71    Character
GSN FLAG    73-75    Character
```

```
HCN/CRN FLAG 77-79    Character
WMO ID       81-85    Character
-------------------------------
```

This is followed by a detailed description of what each field contains or means, including information like units. Thanks to this robust *data dictionary*, we now know not just how the *ghcnd-stations.txt* file is organized but also how to interpret the information it contains. As we'll see in Chapter 6, finding (or building) a data dictionary is an essential part of assessing or improving the quality of our data. At the moment, however, we can just focus on transforming this fixed-width file into a *.csv*, as detailed in Example 4-7.

Example 4-7. fixed_width_parsing.py

```python
# an example of reading data from a fixed-width file with Python.
# the source file for this example comes from NOAA and can be accessed here:
# https://www1.ncdc.noaa.gov/pub/data/ghcn/daily/ghcnd-stations.txt
# the metadata for the file can be found here:
# https://www1.ncdc.noaa.gov/pub/data/ghcn/daily/readme.txt

# import the `csv` library, to create our output file
import csv

filename = "ghcnd-stations"

# reading from a basic text file doesn't require any special libraries
# so we'll just open the file in read format ("r") as usual
source_file = open(filename+".txt", "r")

# the built-in "readlines()" method does just what you'd think:
# it reads in a text file and converts it to a list of lines
stations_list = source_file.readlines()

# create an output file for our transformed data
output_file = open(filename+".csv","w")

# use the `csv` library's "writer" recipe to easily write rows of data
# to `output_file`, instead of reading data *from* it
output_writer = csv.writer(output_file)

# create the header list
headers = ["ID","LATITUDE","LONGITUDE","ELEVATION","STATE","NAME","GSN_FLAG",
           "HCNCRN_FLAG","WMO_ID"] ❶

# write our headers to the output file
output_writer.writerow(headers)

# loop through each line of our file (multiple "sheets" are not possible)
for line in stations_list:
```

```
    # create an empty list, to which we'll append each set of characters that
    # makes up a given "column" of data
    new_row = []

    # ID: positions 1-11
    new_row.append(line[0:11]) ❷

    # LATITUDE: positions 13-20
    new_row.append(line[12:20])

    # LONGITUDE: positions 22-30
    new_row.append(line[21:30])

    # ELEVATION: positions 32-37
    new_row.append(line[31:37])

    # STATE: positions 39-40
    new_row.append(line[38:40])

    # NAME: positions 42-71
    new_row.append(line[41:71])

    # GSN_FLAG: positions 73-75
    new_row.append(line[72:75])

    # HCNCRN_FLAG: positions 77-79
    new_row.append(line[76:79])

    # WMO_ID: positions 81-85
    new_row.append(line[80:85])

    # now all that's left is to use the
    # `writerow` function to write new_row to our output file
    output_writer.writerow(new_row)

# officially close the `.csv` file we just wrote all that data to
output_file.close()
```

❶ Since we don't have anything *within* the file that we can draw on for column headers, we have to "hard code" them based on the information in the *readme.txt* file (*https://www1.ncdc.noaa.gov/pub/data/ghcn/daily/readme.txt*). Note that I've eliminated special characters and used underscores in place of spaces to minimize hassles when cleaning and analyzing this data later on.

❷ Python actually views lines of text as just lists of characters, so we can just tell it to give us the characters between two numbered index positions. Like the range() function, the character at the first position is included, but the second number is not. Also recall that Python starts counting lists of items at zero (often called *zero-indexing*). This means that for each entry, the first number will be one *less* than whatever the metadata says, but the righthand number will be the same.

If you run the script in Example 4-7 and open your output *.csv* file in a spreadsheet program, you'll notice that the values in some of the columns are not formatted consistently. For example, in the ELEVATION column, the numbers with decimals are left justified, but those without decimals are right justified. What's going on?

Once again, opening the file in a text editor is enlightening. Although the file we've created is *technically* comma separated, the values we put into each of our newly "delimited" columns still contain the extra spaces that existed in the original file. As a result, our new file still looks pretty "fixed-width."

In other words—just as we saw in the case of Excel "dates"—converting our file to a *.csv* does not "automagically" generate sensible data types in our output file. Determining what data type each field should have—and cleaning them up so that they behave appropriately—is part of the data cleaning process that we'll address in Chapter 7.

Feed-Based Data—Web-Driven Live Updates

The structure of table-type data formats is well suited to a world where most "data" has already been filtered, revised, and processed into a relatively well-organized collection of numbers, dates, and short strings. With the rise of the internet, however, came the need to transmit large quantities of the type of "free" text found in, for example, news stories and social media feeds. Because this type of data content typically includes characters like commas, periods, and quotation marks that affect its semantic meaning, fitting it into a traditional delimited format will be problematic at best. What's more, the horizontal bias of delimited formats (which involves lots of left-right scrolling) runs counter to the vertical-scrolling conventions of the web. Feed-based data formats have been designed to address both of these limitations.

At a high level, there are two main types of feed-based data formats: XML and JSON. Both are text-based formats that allow the data provider to define their own unique data structure, making them extremely flexible and, consequently, useful for the wide variety of content found on internet-connected websites and platforms. Whether they're located online or you save a copy locally, you'll recognize these formats, in part, by their coordinating *.xml* and *.json* file extensions:

.xml

Extensible Markup Language encompasses a broad range of file formats, including *.rss*, *.atom*, and even *.html*. As the most generic type of markup language, XML is extremely flexible and was perhaps the original data format for web-based data feeds.

.json
> JavaScript Object Notation files are somewhat more recent than XML files but serve a similar purpose. In general, JSON files are less descriptive (and therefore shorter and more concise) than XML files. This means that they can encode an almost identical amount of data as an XML file while taking up less space, which is especially important for speed on the mobile web. Equally important is the fact that JSON files are essentially large `object` data types within the JavaScript programming language—which is the language that underpins many, if not most, websites and mobile apps. This means that parsing JSON-formatted data is very easy for any site or program that uses JavaScript, especially when compared with XML. Fortunately, JavaScript `object` data types are very similar to Python `dict` data types, which also makes working with JSON in Python very straightforward.

Before we dive into how to work with each of these file types in Python, let's review when we might *want* feed-type data and where to find it when we do.

When to work with feed-type data

In a sense, feed-type data is to the 21st century what table-type data was to the 20th: the sheer volume of feed-type data generated, stored, and exchanged on the web every day is probably millions of times greater than that of all of the table-type data in the world put together—in large part because feed-type data is what powers social media sites, news apps, and everything in between.

From a data wrangling perspective, you'll generally want feed-type data when the phenomenon you're exploring is time sensitive and updated on a frequent and/or unpredictable basis. Typically, this type of data is generated in response to a human or natural process, such as (once again) posting to social media, publishing a news story, or recording an earthquake.

Both file-based, table-type data and web-based, feed-type data can contain historical information, but as we discussed at the start of this chapter, the former usually reflects the data as it stood at a fixed point in time. The latter, by contrast, is typically organized in a "reverse-chronological" (most recent first) order, with the first entry being whatever data record was most recently created at the time you accessed the data, rather than a predetermined publication date.

Where to find feed-type data

Feed-type data is found almost exclusively on the web, often at special URLs known as application programming interface (API) *endpoints*. We'll get into the details of working with APIs in Chapter 5, but for now all you need to know is that API endpoints are really just data-only web pages: you can view many of them using a regular web browser, but all you'll see is the data itself. Some API endpoints will even return different data depending on the information *you* send to them, and this is part of what makes working with feed-type data so flexible: by changing just a few words or values in your code, you can access a totally different dataset!

Finding APIs that offer feed-type data doesn't require too much in the way of special search strategies because usually the sites and services that have APIs *want* you to find them. Why? Simply put, when someone writes code that makes use of an API, it (usually) returns some benefit to the company that provides it—even if that benefit is just more public exposure. In the early days of Twitter, for example, many web developers wrote programs using the Twitter API—both making the platform more useful *and* saving the company the expense and effort of figuring out what users wanted and then building it. By making so much of their platform data available for free (at first), the API gave rise to several companies that Twitter would eventually purchase—though many more would also be put out of business when either the API or its terms of service changed.[17] This highlights one of the particular issues that can arise when working with any type of data, but especially the feed-type data made available by for-profit companies: both the data and your right to access it can change at any time, without warning. So while feed-type data sources are indeed valuable, they are also ephemeral in more ways than one.

Wrangling Feed-Type Data with Python

As with table-type data, wrangling feed-type data in Python is made possible by a combination of helpful libraries and the fact that formats like JSON already resemble existing data types in the Python programming language. Moreover, we'll see in the following sections that XML and JSON are often functionally interchangeable for our purposes (though many APIs will only offer data in one format or the other).

XML: One markup to rule them all

Markup languages are among the oldest forms of standardized document formats in computing, designed with the goal of creating text-based documents that can be easily read by both humans and machines. XML became an increasingly important part of internet infrastructure in the 1990s as the variety of devices accessing and displaying web-based information made the separation of content (e.g., text and images) from formatting (e.g., page layout) more of a necessity. Unlike an HTML document— in which content and formatting are fully commingled—an XML document says pretty much nothing about how its information should be displayed. Instead, its tags and attributes act as *metadata* about what kind of information it contains, along with the data itself.

To get a feel for what XML looks like, take a look at Example 4-8.

---

17 See Vassili van der Mersch's post, "Twitter's 10 Year Struggle with Developer Relations" from Nordic APIs (*https://nordicapis.com/twitter-10-year-struggle-with-developer-relations*).

Example 4-8. A sample XML document

```xml
<?xml version="1.0" encoding="UTF-8"?>
<mainDoc>
    <!--This is a comment-->
    <elements>
        <element1>This is some text in the document.</element1>
        <element2>This is some other data in the document.</element2>
        <element3 someAttribute="aValue" />
    </elements>
    <someElement anAttribute="anotherValue">More content</someElement>
</mainDoc>
```

There are a couple of things going here. The very first line is called the *document type* (or doc-type) declaration; it's letting us know that the rest of the document should be interpreted as XML (as opposed to any of the other web or markup languages, some of which we'll review later in this chapter).

Starting with the line:

```xml
<mainDoc>
```

we are into the substance of the document itself. Part of what makes XML so flexible is that it only contains two real grammatical structures, both of which are included in Example 4-8:

tags

Tags can be either paired (like element1, element2, someElement, or even main Doc) or self-closed (like element3). The name of a tag is always enclosed by *carets* (<>). In the case of a closing tag, the opening caret is immediately followed by a forward slash (/). A matched pair of tags, or a self-closed tag, are also described as XML *elements*.

attributes

Attributes can exist only inside of tags (like anAttribute). Attributes are a type of *key/value pair* in which the attribute name (or *key*) is immediately followed by an equals sign (=), followed by the *value* surrounded by double quotation marks ("").

An XML element is whatever is contained between an opening tag and its matching closing tag (e.g., <elements> and </elements>). As such, a given XML element may contain many tags, each of which may also contain other tags. Any tags may also have any number of attributes (including none). A self-closed tag is also considered an element.

The only other meaningful rule for structuring XML documents is that when tags appear inside other tags, *the most recently opened tag must be closed first.* In other words, while this is a legitimate XML structure:

```
<outerElement>
    <!-- Notice that that the `innerElement1` is closed
    before the `innerElement2` tag is opened -->
    <innerElement1>Some content</innerElement1>
    <innerElement2>More content</innerElement2>
</outerElement>
```

this is not:

```
<outerElement>
    <!-- NOPE! The `innerElement2` tag was opened
    before the `innerElement1` tag was closed -->
    <innerElement1>Some content<innerElement2>More content</innerElement1>
    </innerElement2>
</outerElement>
```

This principle of *last opened, first closed* is also described as *nesting*, similar to the "nested" `for...in` loops from Figure 2-3.[18] Nesting is especially important in XML documents because it governs one of the primary mechanisms that we use to read or *parse* XML (and other markup language) documents with code. In an XML document, the first element after the `doc-type` declaration is known as the *root* element. If the XML document has been formatted, the root element will always be left justified, and any element that is nested directly *within* that element will be indented one level to the right and is referred to as a *child* element. In Example 4-8, then, `<mainDoc>` would be considered the *root* element, and `<elements>` would be its child. Likewise, `<mainDoc>` is the *parent* element of `<elements>` (Example 4-9).

Example 4-9. An annotated XML document

```
<?xml version="1.0" encoding="UTF-8"?>
<mainDoc>
    <!--`mainDoc` is the *root* element, and `elements` is its *child*-->
    <elements>
        <!-- `elements` is the *parent* of `element1`, `element2`, and
        `element3`, which are *siblings* of one another -->
        <element1>This is text data in the document.</element1>
        <element2>This is some other data in the document.</element2>
        <element3 someAttribute="aValue" />
    </elements>
    <!-- `someElement` is also a *child* of `mainDoc`,
    and a *sibling* of `elements` -->
    <someElement anAttribute="anotherValue">More content</someElement>
</mainDoc>
```

---

18 Unlike Python code, XML documents do *not* have to be properly indented in order to work, though it certainly makes them more readable!

Given this trend for genealogical jargon, you might be wondering: if <elements> is the parent of <element3>, and <mainDoc> is the parent of <elements>, does that make <mainDoc> the *grandparent* of <element3>? The answer is: yes, but no. While <mainDoc> *is* the "parent" of the "parent" of <element3>, the term "grandparent" is never used in describing an XML structure—that could get complicated fast! Instead, we simply describe the relationship as exactly that: <mainDoc> is the *parent* of the *parent* of <element3>.

Fortunately, there is no such complexity associated with XML attributes: they are simply key/value pairs, and they can *only* exist within XML tags, like so:

```
<element3 someAttribute="aValue" />
```

Note that there is no space on either side of the equals sign, just as there is no space between the carets and slashes of an element tag.

Like writing in English (or in Python), the question of when to use tags versus attributes for a particular piece of information is largely a matter of preference and style. Both Examples 4-10 and 4-11, for example, contain the same information about this book, but each is structured slightly differently.

Example 4-10. Sample XML book data—more attributes

```
<aBook>
    <bookURL url="https://www.oreilly.com/library/view/practical-python-data/
    9781492091493"/>
    <bookAbstract>
    There are awesome discoveries to be made and valuable stories to be
    told in datasets--and this book will help you uncover them.
    </bookAbstract>
    <pubDate date="2022-02-01" />
</aBook>
```

Example 4-11. Sample XML book data—more elements

```
<aBook>
    <bookURL>
        https://www.oreilly.com/library/view/practical-python-data/9781492091493
    </bookURL>
    <bookAbstract>
        There are awesome discoveries to be made and valuable stories to be
        told in datasets--and this book will help you uncover them.
    </bookAbstract>
    <pubDate>2022-02-01</pubDate>
</aBook>
```

This degree of flexibility means XML is highly adaptable to a wide variety of data sources and formatting preferences. At the same time, it can easily create a situation where *every* new data source requires writing custom code. Obviously, this would be a pretty inefficient system, especially if many people and organizations were publishing pretty similar types of data.

It's not surprising, then, that there are a large number of XML *specifications* that define additional rules for formatting XML documents that are intended to hold particular types of data. I'm highlighting a few notable examples here, as these are formats you may come across in the course of your data wrangling work. Despite their various format names and file extensions, however, we can parse them all using the same method that we'll look at shortly in Example 4-12:

RSS

Really Simple Syndication is an XML specification first introduced in the late 1990s for news information. The *.atom* XML format is also widely used for these purposes.

KML

Keyhole Markup Language is an internationally accepted standard for encoding both two-dimensional and three-dimensional geographic data and is compatible with tools like Google Earth.

SVG

Scalable Vector Graphics is a commonly used format for graphics on the web, thanks to its ability to scale drawings without loss of quality. Many common graphics programs can output *.svg* files, which can then be included in web pages and other documents that will look good on a wide variety of screen sizes and devices.

EPUB

Electronic publication format (*.epub*) is the widely accepted open standard for digital book publishing.

As you can see from the preceding list, some common XML formats clearly indicate their relationship to XML; many others do not.[19]

Now that we have a high-level sense of how XML files work, let's see what it takes to parse one with Python. Although Python has some built-in tools for parsing XML, we'll be using a library called *lxml*, which is particularly good at quickly parsing large XML files (*https://nickjanetakis.com/blog/how-i-used-the-lxml-library-to-parse-xml-20x-faster-in-python#xmltodict-vs-python-s-standard-library-vs-lxml*). Even though our example files that follow are quite small, know that we could use basically the same code even if our data files got considerably larger.

---

19 Fun fact: the second *x* in the *.xlsx* format actually refers to XML!

To begin with, we'll be using an XML version of the same "U6" unemployment data that I've already downloaded from the FRED website using its API.[20] After downloading a copy of this file from Google Drive (*https://drive.google.com/file/d/ 1gPGaDTT9Nn6BtlTtVp7gQLSuocMyIaLU*), you can use the script in Example 4-12 to convert the source XML to a *.csv*. Start with the `pip install`:

```
pip install lxml
```

Example 4-12. xml_parsing.py

```
# an example of reading data from an .xml file with Python, using the "lxml"
# library.
# first, you'll need to pip install the lxml library:
# https://pypi.org/project/lxml/
# a helpful tutorial can be found here: https://lxml.de/tutorial.html
# the data used here is an instance of
# https://api.stlouisfed.org/fred/series/observations?series_id=U6RATE& \
# api_key=YOUR_API_KEY_HERE


# specify the "chapter" of the `lxml` library you want to import,
# in this case, `etree`, which stands for "ElementTree"
from lxml import etree

# import the `csv` library, to create our output file
import csv

# choose a filename
filename = "U6_FRED_data" ❶

# open our data file in read format, using "rb" as the "mode"
xml_source_file = open(filename+".xml","rb") ❷

# pass our xml_source_file as an ingredient to the `lxml` library's
# `etree.parse()` method and store the result in a variable called `xml_doc`
xml_doc = etree.parse(xml_source_file)

# start by getting the current xml document's "root" element
document_root = xml_doc.getroot() ❸

# let's print it out to see what it looks like
print(etree.tostring(document_root)) ❹

# confirm that `document_root` is a well-formed XML element
if etree.iselement(document_root):
```

---

20 Again, we'll walk through using APIs like this one step by step in Chapter 5, but using this document lets us see how different data formats influence our interactions with the data.

```
# create our output file, naming it "xml_"+filename+".csv"
output_file = open("xml_"+filename+".csv","w")

# use the `csv` library's "writer" recipe to easily write rows of data
# to `output_file`, instead of reading data *from* it
output_writer = csv.writer(output_file)

# grab the first element of our xml document (using `document_root[0]`)
# and write its attribute keys as column headers to our output file
output_writer.writerow(document_root[0].attrib.keys())  ❺

# now, we need to loop through every element in our XML file
  for child in document_root:  ❻

    # now we'll use the `.values()` method to get each element's values
    # as a list and then use that directly with the `writerow` recipe
    output_writer.writerow(child.attrib.values())

# officially close the `.csv` file we just wrote all that data to
output_file.close()
```

❶ In this instance, there's nothing within the data file (like a sheet name) that we can pull as a filename, so we'll just make our own and use it to both load our source data and label our output file.

❷ I lied! The values we've been using for the "mode" of the open() function assume we want to interpret the source file as *text*. But because the *lxml* library expects byte data rather than text, we'll use rb ("read bytes") as the "mode."

❸ There is a lot of malformed XML out there! In order to make sure that what looks like good XML actually *is*, we'll retrieve the current XML document's "root" element and make sure that it works.

❹ Because our XML is currently stored as byte data, we need to use the etree.tostring() method in order to view it as one.

❺ Thanks to the *lxml*, each XML element (or "node") in our document has a property called attrib, whose data type is a Python dictionary (dict). Using the .keys() method (*https://docs.python.org/3/library/stdtypes.html#type smapping*) returns all of our XML element's attribute keys as a list. Since all of the elements in our source file are identical, we can use the keys of the first one to create a "header" row for our output file.

❻ The *lxml* library converts XML elements to lists (*https://lxml.de/tuto rial.html#elements-are-lists*), so we can use a simple for...in loop to go through the elements in our document.

As it happens, the XML version of our unemployment data is structured very simply: it's just a list of elements, and *all* the values we want to access are stored as attributes. As a result, we were able to pull the attribute values out of each element as a list and write them directly to our *.csv* file with only one line of code.

Of course, there are many times when we'll want to pull data from more complex XML formats, especially those like RSS or Atom. To see what it takes to handle something slightly more complex, in Example 4-13 we'll parse the BBC's RSS feed of science and environment stories, which you can download a copy of from my Google Drive (*https://drive.google.com/file/d/1zOaksshLfmXxLTipoOjTTnuO6PsVQgg2*).

Example 4-13. rss_parsing.py

```python
# an example of reading data from an .xml file with Python, using the "lxml"
# library.
# first, you'll need to pip install the lxml library:
# https://pypi.org/project/lxml/
# the data used here is an instance of
# http://feeds.bbci.co.uk/news/science_and_environment/rss.xml

# specify the "chapter" of the `lxml` library you want to import,
# in this case, `etree`, which stands for "ElementTree"
from lxml import etree

# import the `csv` library, to create our output file
import csv

# choose a filename, for simplicity
filename = "BBC News - Science & Environment XML Feed"

# open our data file in read format, using "rb" as the "mode"
xml_source_file = open(filename+".xml","rb")

# pass our xml_source_file as an ingredient to the `lxml` library's
# `etree.parse()` method and store the result in a variable called `xml_doc`
xml_doc = etree.parse(xml_source_file)

# start by getting the current xml document's "root" element
document_root = xml_doc.getroot()

# if the document_root is a well-formed XML element
if etree.iselement(document_root):

    # create our output file, naming it "rss_"+filename+".csv"
    output_file = open("rss_"+filename+".csv","w")

    # use the `csv` library's "writer" recipe to easily write rows of data
    # to `output_file`, instead of reading data *from* it
    output_writer = csv.writer(output_file)
```

```python
# document_root[0] is the "channel" element
main_channel = document_root[0]

# the `find()` method returns *only* the first instance of the element name
article_example = main_channel.find('item')  ❶

# create an empty list in which to store our future column headers
tag_list = []

for child in article_example.iterdescendants():  ❷

    # add each tag to our would-be header list
    tag_list.append(child.tag)  ❸

    # if the current tag has any attributes
    if child.attrib:  ❹

        # loop through the attribute keys in the tag
        for attribute_name in child.attrib.keys():  ❺

            # append the attribute name to our `tag_list` column headers
            tag_list.append(attribute_name)

# write the contents of `tag_list` to our output file as column headers
output_writer.writerow(tag_list)  ❻

# now we want to grab *every* <item> element in our file
# so we use the `findall()` method instead of `find()`
for item in main_channel.findall('item'):

    # empty list for holding our new row's content
    new_row = []

    # now we'll use our list of tags to get the contents of each element
    for tag in tag_list:

        # if there is anything in the element with a given tag name
        if item.findtext(tag):

            # append it to our new row
            new_row.append(item.findtext(tag))

        # otherwise, make sure it's the "isPermaLink" attribute
        elif tag == "isPermaLink":

            # grab its value from the <guid> element
            # and append it to our row
            new_row.append(item.find('guid').get("isPermaLink"))

    # write the new row to our output file!
    output_writer.writerow(new_row)
```

```
# officially close the `.csv` file we just wrote all that data to
output_file.close()
```

❶ As always, we'll want to balance what we handle programmatically and what we review visually. In looking at our data, it's clear that each article's information is stored in a separate `item` element. Since copying over the individual tag and attribute names would be time-consuming and error prone, however, we'll go through *one* `item` element and make a list of all the tags (and attributes) within it, which we'll then use as the column headers for our output *.csv* file.

❷ The `iterdescendants()` method is particular to the *lxml* library. It returns *only* the *descendants* of an XML element, while the more common `iter()` method would return *both* the element itself *and* its children or "descendants." (*https:// lxml.de/api.html#iteration*)

❸ Using `child.tag` will retrieve the text of the tagname of the child element. For example, for the `<pubDate>`` element it will return `pubDate`.

❹ Only one tag in our `<item>` element has an attribute, but we still want to include it in our output.

❺ The `keys()` method will give us a list of all the keys in the list of attributes that belong to the tag. Be sure to get its name as a string (instead of a one-item list).

❻ That whole `article_example for` loop was just to build `tag_list`—but it was worth it!

As you can see from Example 4-13, with the help of the *lxml* library, parsing even slightly more complex XML in Python is still reasonably straightforward.

While XML is still a popular data format for news feeds and a handful of other file types, there are a number of features that make it less than ideal for handling the high-volume data feeds of the modern web.

First, there is the simple issue of size. While XML files can be wonderfully descriptive—reducing the need for separate data dictionaries—the fact that most elements contain both an opening tag and a corresponding closing tag (e.g., `<item>` and `</ item>`) also makes XML somewhat *verbose*: there is a lot of text in an XML document that *isn't* content. This isn't a big deal when your document has a few dozen or even a few thousand elements, but when you're trying to handle millions or billions of posts on the social web, all that redundant text can really slow things down.

Second, while XML isn't exactly *difficult* to transform into other data formats, the process also isn't exactly seamless. The *lxml* library (among others) makes parsing XML with Python pretty simple, but doing the same task with web-focused languages like JavaScript is convoluted and onerous. Given JavaScript's prevalence on the web, it's not surprising that a feed-type data format that works seamlessly with JavaScript would be developed at some point. As we'll see in the next section, many of XML's limitations as a data format are addressed by the object-like nature of the *.json* format, which is at this point the most popular format for feed-type data on the internet.

JSON: Web data, the next generation

In principle, JSON is similar to XML in that it uses nesting to cluster related pieces of information into records and fields. JSON is also fairly human readable, though the fact that it doesn't support comments means that JSON feeds may require more robust data dictionaries than XML documents.

To get started, let's take a look at the small JSON document in Example 4-14.

Example 4-14. Sample JSON document

```
{
"author": "Susan E. McGregor",
"book": {
    "bookURL": "https://www.oreilly.com/library/view/practical-python-data/
        9781492091493/",
    "bookAbstract": "There are awesome discoveries to be made and valuable
        stories to be told in datasets--and this book will help you uncover
        them.",
    "pubDate": "2022-02-01"
},
"papers": [{
    "paperURL": "https://www.usenix.org/conference/usenixsecurity15/
        technical-sessions/presentation/mcgregor",
    "paperTitle": "Investigating the computer security practices and needs
        of journalists",
    "pubDate": "2015-08-12"
},
    {
    "paperURL": "https://www.aclweb.org/anthology/W18-5104.pdf",
    "paperTitle": "Predictive embeddings for hate speech detection on
        twitter",
    "pubDate": "2018-10-31"
}
    ]
}
```

Like XML, the grammatical "rules" of JSON are quite simple: there are only three distinct data structures in JSON documents, all of which appear in Example 4-14:

Key/value pairs

Technically, everything within a JSON document is a key/value pair, with the *key* enclosed in quotes to the left of a colon (:) and the *value* being whatever appears to the right of the colon. Note that while keys must *always* be strings, *values* can be strings (as in author), objects (as in book), or lists (as in papers).

Objects

These are opened and closed using pairs of curly braces ({}). In Example 4-14, there are four objects total: the document itself (indicated by the left-justified curly braces), the book object, and the two unnamed objects in the papers list.

Lists

These are enclosed by square brackets ([]) and can only contain comma-separated objects.

While XML and JSON can be used to encode the same data, there are some notable differences in what each allows. For example, JSON files do not contain a doc-type specification, nor can they include comments. Also, while XML lists are somewhat implicit (any repeated element functions something like a list), in JSON, lists must be specified by square brackets ([]).

Finally, although JSON was designed with JavaScript in mind, you may have noticed that its structures are very similar to Python dict and list types. This is part of what makes parsing JSON very straightforward with Python as well as JavaScript (and a range of other languages).

To see just how straightforward this is, in Example 4-15 we'll parse the same data as we did in Example 4-12 but in the *.json* format also provided by the FRED API. You can download the file from this Google Drive link: *https://drive.google.com/file/d/1Mpb2f5qYgHnKcU1sTxTmhOPHfzIdeBsq/view?usp=sharing*.

Example 4-15. json_parsing.py

```
# a simple example of reading data from a .json file with Python,
# using the built-in "json" library. The data used here is an instance of
# https://api.stlouisfed.org/fred/series/observations?series_id=U6RATE& \
# file_type=json&api_key=YOUR_API_KEY_HERE

# import the `json` library, since that's our source file format
import json

# import the `csv` library, to create our output file
import csv

# choose a filename
filename = "U6_FRED_data"
```

```
# open the file in read format ("r") as usual
json_source_file = open(filename+".json","r")

# pass the `json_source_file` as an ingredient to the json library's `load()`
# method and store the result in a variable called `json_data`
json_data = json.load(json_source_file)

# create our output file, naming it "json_"+filename
output_file = open("json_"+filename+".csv","w")

# use the `csv` library's "writer" recipe to easily write rows of data
# to `output_file`, instead of reading data *from* it
output_writer = csv.writer(output_file)

# grab the first element (at position "0"), and use its keys as the column headers
output_writer.writerow(list(json_data["observations"][0].keys()))  ❶

for obj in json_data["observations"]:  ❷

    # we'll create an empty list where we'll put the actual values of each object
    obj_values = []

    # for every `key` (which will become a column), in each object
    for key, value in obj.items():  ❸

        # let's print what's in here, just to see how the code sees it
        print(key,value)

        # add the values to our list
        obj_values.append(value)

    # now we've got the whole row, write the data to our output file
    output_writer.writerow(obj_values)

# officially close the `.csv` file we just wrote all that data to
output_file.close()
```

❶ Because the *json* library interprets every object as a dictionary view object (*https://docs.python.org/3/library/stdtypes.html#dict-views*), we need to tell Python to convert it to a regular list using the list() function.

❷ In most cases, the simplest way to find the name (or "key") of the main JSON object in our document is just to look at it. Because JSON data is often rendered on a single line, however, we can get a better sense of its structure by pasting it into JSONLint (*https://jsonlint.com*). This lets us see that our target data is a list whose key is observations.

❸ Because of the way that the *json* library works, if we try to just write the rows directly, we'll get the values labeled with dict, rather than the data values themselves. So we need to make another loop that goes through every value in every `json` object one at a time and appends that value to our `obj_values` list.

Although JSON is not *quite* as human readable as XML, it has other advantages that we've touched on, like smaller file size and broader code compatibility. Likewise, while JSON is not as descriptive as XML, JSON data sources (often APIs) are usually reasonably well documented; this reduces the need to simply infer what a given key/value pair is describing. Like all work with data, however, the first step in wrangling JSON-formatted data is to understand its context as much as possible.

Wherefore Art Thou, Whitespace?

Unlike *.tsv* and *.txt* files—and the Python programming language itself—neither XML nor JSON is "whitespace dependent." As long as the carets, curly braces, and other punctuation marks are all in the right place, these data feed-type formats can have everything crushed up on a single line and still work just fine. For the sake of readability, the examples I've presented in this chapter have all been nicely formatted, but that's not how you'll usually encounter these data types, especially on the web. Though many web browsers *will* show XML in its properly indented format (for example, see *Los Angeles Times'* daily "sitemap" (*https://latimes.com/sitemap-202101.xml*)), most JSON data will be rendered as run-on lines of text (as with the Citi Bike real-time data feed (*https://feeds.citibikenyc.com/stations/stations.json*)).

Since effectively parsing either data format first requires understanding its overall structure, looking at a properly formatted version of any feed-type data file you're working with is a crucial first step. With well-structured XML, opening the file (or URL) in a web browser in usually enough.[21]

For smaller *.json* files, you can copy and paste (using keyboard shortcuts to "Select All" and "Copy" is easiest) the data straight from the source into an online formatting tool like JSONLint (*https://jsonlint.com*) or JSON formatter (*https://jsonformatter.org/json-pretty-print*). If the JSON file is especially large, or you don't have internet access, however, it's also possible to use Python in the terminal to create a new, formatted *.json* file from an unformatted source JSON file, using the following command:

```
cat ugly.json | python -mjson.tool > pretty.json
```

where `ugly.json` is your unformatted file. This will create the output file `pretty.json`, which you can then open in Atom or another text editor in order to see the structure of the document.

---

21 If a stylesheet has been applied, as in the case of the BBC feed we used in Example 4-13, you can context+click the page and select "View Source" to see the "raw" XML.

Working with Unstructured Data

As we discussed in "Structured Versus Unstructured Data" on page 93, the process of creating data depends on introducing some structure to information; otherwise we can't methodically analyze or derive meaning from it. Even though the latter often includes large segments of human-written "free" text, both table-type and feed-type data are relatively structured and, most importantly, machine readable.

When we deal with unstructured data, by contrast, our work always involves approximations: we cannot be certain that our programmatic wrangling efforts will return an accurate interpretation of the underlying information. This is because most unstructured data is a representation of content that is designed to be perceived and interpreted by humans. And, as we discussed in Chapter 2, while they can process large quantities of data much faster and with fewer errors than humans can, computers can still be tricked by unstructured data that would never fool a human, such as mistaking a slightly modified stop sign for a speed limit sign (*https://spectrum.ieee.org/cars-that-think/transportation/sensors/slight-street-sign-modifications-can-fool-machine-learning-algorithms*). Naturally, this means that when dealing with data that *isn't* machine readable, we always need to do extra proofing and verification—but Python can still help us wrangle such data into a more usable format.

Image-Based Text: Accessing Data in PDFs

The Portable Document Format (PDF) was created in the early 1990s as a mechanism for preserving the visual integrity of electronic documents—whether they were created in a text-editing program or captured from printed materials.[22] Preserving documents' visual appearance also meant that, *unlike* machine-readable formats (such as word-processing documents), it was difficult to alter or extract their contents—an important feature for creating everything from digital versions of contracts to formal letters.

In other words, wrangling the data in PDFs was, at first, somewhat difficult by design. Because accessing the data in printed documents is a shared problem, however, work in optical character recognition (OCR) actually began as early as the late *19th* century.[23] Even digital OCR tools have been widely available in software packages and online for decades, so while they are far from perfect, the data contained in this type of file is also not entirely out of reach.

---

22 See Adobe's About PDF page for more information (*https://acrobat.adobe.com/us/en/acrobat/about-adobe-pdf.html*).

23 George Nagy, "Disruptive Developments in Document Recognition," *Pattern Recognition Letters* 79 (2016): 106–112, *https://doi.org/10.1016/j.patrec.2015.11.024*. Available at *https://ecse.rpi.edu/~nagy/PDF_chrono/2016_PRL_Disruptive_asPublished.pdf*.

When to work with text in PDFs

In general, working with PDFs is a last resort (much, as we'll see in Chapter 5, as web scraping should be). In general, if you can avoid relying on PDF information, you should. As noted previously, the process of extracting information from PDFs will generally yield an *approximation* of the document's contents, so proofing for accuracy is a nonnegotiable part of any *.pdf*-based data wrangling workflow. That said, there is an enormous quantity of information that is *only* available as images or PDFs of scanned documents, and Python is an efficient way to extract a reasonably accurate first version of such document text.

Where to find PDFs

If you're confident that the data you want can only be found in PDF format, then you can (and should) use the tips in "Smart Searching for Specific Data Types" on page 96 to locate this file type using an online search. More than likely, you will request information from a person or organization, and they will provide it as PDFs, leaving you to deal with the problem of how to extract the information you need. As a result, most of the time you will not need to go looking for PDFs—more often than not they will, unfortunately, find you.

Wrangling PDFs with Python

Because PDFs can be generated both from machine-readable text (such as word-processing documents) and from scanned images, it is sometimes possible to extract the document's "live" text programmatically with relatively few errors. While it seems straightforward, however, this method can still be unreliable because *.pdf* files can be generated with a wide range of encodings that can be difficult to detect accurately. So while this *can* be a high-accuracy method of extracting text from a *.pdf*, the likelihood of it working for any *given* file is low.

Because of this, I'm going to focus here on using OCR to recognize and extract the text in *.pdf* files. This will require two steps:

1. Convert the document pages into individual images.
2. Run OCR on the page images, extract the text, and write it to individual text files.

Unsurprisingly, we'll need to install quite a few more Python libraries in order to make this all possible. First, we'll install a couple of libraries for converting our *.pdf* pages to images. The first is a general-purpose library called `poppler` that is needed to make our Python-specific library `pdf2image` work. We'll be using `pdf2image` to (you guessed it!) convert our *.pdf* file to a series of images:

```
sudo apt install poppler-utils
```

Then:

```
pip install pdf2image
```

Next, we need to install the tools for performing the OCR process. The first one is a general library called *tesseract-ocr* (*https://github.com/tesseract-ocr/tesseract*), which uses machine learning to recognize the text in images; the second is a Python library that relies on *tesseract-ocr* called *pytesseract*:

```
sudo apt-get install tesseract-ocr
```

Then:

```
pip install pytesseract
```

Finally, we need a helper library for Python that can do the computer vision needed to bridge the gap between our page images and our OCR library:

```
pip install opencv-python
```

Phew! If that seems like a lot of extra libraries, keep in mind that what we're technically using here are is *machine learning*, one of those buzzy data science technologies that drives so much of the "artificial intelligence" out there. Fortunately for us, Tesseract in particular is relatively robust and inclusive: though it was originally developed by Hewlett-Packard as a proprietary system in the early 1980s, it was open sourced in 2005 and currently supports more than 100 languages—so feel free to try the solution in Example 4-16 out on non-English text as well!

Example 4-16. pdf_parsing.py

```python
# a basic example of reading data from a .pdf file with Python,
# using `pdf2image` to convert it to images, and then using the
# openCV and `tesseract` libraries to extract the text

# the source data was downloaded from:
# https://files.stlouisfed.org/files/htdocs/publications/page1-econ/2020/12/01/ \
# unemployment-insurance-a-tried-and-true-safety-net_SE.pdf

# the built-in `operating system` or `os` Python library will let us create
# a new folder in which to store our converted images and output text
import os

# we'll import the `convert_from_path` "chapter" of the `pdf2image` library
from pdf2image import convert_from_path

# the built-in `glob`library offers a handy way to loop through all the files
# in a folder that have a certain file extension, for example
import glob

# `cv2` is the actual library name for `openCV`
import cv2
```

```python
# and of course, we need our Python library for interfacing
# with the tesseract OCR process
import pytesseract

# we'll use the pdf name to name both our generated images and text files
pdf_name = "SafetyNet"

# our source pdf is in the same folder as our Python script
pdf_source_file = pdf_name+".pdf"

# as long as a folder with the same name as the pdf does not already exist
if os.path.isdir(pdf_name) == False:

    # create a new folder with that name
    target_folder = os.mkdir(pdf_name)


# store all the pages of the PDF in a variable
pages = convert_from_path(pdf_source_file, 300)  ❶


# loop through all the converted pages, enumerating them so that the page
# number can be used to label the resulting images
for page_num, page in enumerate(pages):

    # create unique filenames for each page image, combining the
    # folder name and the page number
    filename = os.path.join(pdf_name,"p"+str(page_num)+".png")  ❷

    # save the image of the page in system
    page.save(filename, 'PNG')

# next, go through all the files in the folder that end in `.png`
for img_file in glob.glob(os.path.join(pdf_name, '*.png')):  ❸

    # replace the slash in the image's filename with a dot
    temp_name = img_file.replace("/",".")

    # pull the unique page name (e.g. `p2`) from the `temp_name`
    text_filename = temp_name.split(".")[1]  ❹

    # now! create a new, writable file, also in our target folder, that
    # has the same name as the image, but is a `.txt` file
    output_file = open(os.path.join(pdf_name,text_filename+".txt"), "w")

    # use the `cv2` library to interpret our image
    img = cv2.imread(img_file)

    # create a new variable to hold the results of using pytesseract's
    # `image_to_string()` function, which will do just that
    converted_text = pytesseract.image_to_string(img)
```

```
# write our extracted text to our output file
output_file.write(converted_text)

# close the output file
output_file.close()
```

❶ Here we pass the path to our source file (in this case, that is just the filename, because it is in the same folder as our script) and the desired dots per inch (DPI) resolution of the output images to the `convert_from_path()` function. While setting a lower DPI will be much faster, the poorer-quality images may yield significantly less accurate OCR results. 300 DPI is a standard "print" quality resolution.

❷ Here we use the *os* library's `.join` function to save the new files into our target folder. We also have to use the `str()` function to convert the page number into a string for use in the filename.

❸ Note that `*.png` can be translated to "any file ending in .png." The `glob()` function creates a list of all the filenames in the folder where our images are stored (which in this case has the value `pdf_name`).

❹ String manipulation is fiddly! To generate unique (but matching!) filenames for our OCR'd text files, we need to pull a unique page name out of `img_file` whose value starts with `SafetyNet/` and ends in `.png`. So we'll replace the forward slash with a period to get something like `SafetyNet.p1.png`, and then if we `split()` *that* on the period, we'll get a list like: `["SafetyNet", "p1", "png"]`. Finally, we can access the "page name" at position 1. We need to do all this because we can't be sure that `glob()` will, for example, pull `p1.png` from the image folder *first*, or that it will pull the images in order at all.

For the most part, running this script serves our purposes: with a few dozen lines of code, it converts a multipage PDF file first into images and then writes (most of) the contents to a series of new text files.

This all-in-one approach also has its limitations, however. Converting a PDF to images—or images to text—is the kind of task that we might need to do quite often but not always at the same time. In other words, it would probably be much more useful in the long run to have two *separate* scripts for solving this problem, and then to run them one after the other. In fact, with a little bit of tweaking, we could probably break up the preceding script in such a way that we could convert *any* PDF to images or *any* images to text without having to write *any* new code at all. Sounds pretty nifty, right?

This process of rethinking and reorganizing working code is known as *code refactoring*. In writing English, we would describe this as revising or editing, and the objective in both cases is the same: to make your work simpler, clearer, and more effective. And just like documentation, refactoring is actually another important way to scale your data wrangling work, because it makes *reusing* your code much more straightforward. We'll look at various strategies for code refactoring and script reuse in Chapter 8.

Accessing PDF Tables with Tabula

If you looked at the text files produced in the preceding section, you'll likely have noticed that there are a lot of "extras" in those files: page numbers and headers, line breaks, and other "cruft." (*https://en.wikipedia.org/wiki/Cruft*) There are also some key elements missing, like images and tables.

While our data work won't extend to analyzing images (that is a much more specialized area), it's not unusual to find tables inside PDFs that hold data we might want to work with. In fact, this problem is common enough in my home field of journalism that a group of investigative journalists designed and built a tool called Tabula (*https://tabula.technology*) specifically to deal with this problem.

Tabula isn't a Python library—it's actually a standalone piece of software. To try it out, download the installer (*https://tabula.technology/#download-install*) for your system; if you're on a Chromebook or Linux machine, you'll need to download the *.zip* file and follow the directions in *README.txt*. Whatever system you're using, you'll probably need to install the Java programming library first, which you can do by running the following command in a terminal window:

```
sudo apt install default-jre
```

Like some of the other open source tools we'll discuss in later chapters (like OpenRefine, which I used to prepare some of the sample data in Chapter 2 and cover briefly in Chapter 11), Tabula does its work behind the scenes (though some of it is visible in the terminal window), and you interact with it in a web browser. This is a way to get access to a more traditional graphical interface while still leaving most of your computer's resources free to do the heavy-duty data work.

Conclusion

Hopefully, the coding examples in this chapter have started to give you an idea of the wide variety of data wrangling problems you can solve with relatively little Python code, thanks to a combination of carefully selected libraries and those few essential Python scripting concepts that were introduced in Chapter 2.

You may also have noticed that, with the exception of our PDF text, the output of *all* the exercises in this chapter was essentially a *.csv* file. This is not by accident. Not only are *.csv* files efficient and versatile, but it turns out that to do almost any basic statistical analyses or visualizations, we need table-type data to work with. That's not to say that it isn't *possible* to analyze nontable data; that, in fact, is what much of contemporary computer science research (like machine learning) is all about. However, because those systems are often both complex and opaque, they're not really suitable for the type of data wrangling work we're focused on here. As such, we'll spend our energy on the types of analyses that can help us understand, explain, and communicate new insights about the world.

Finally, while our work in this chapter focused on file-based data and pre-saved versions of feed-based data, in Chapter 5 we'll explore how we can use Python with APIs and web scraping to wrangle data out of online systems and, where necessary, right off of web pages themselves!

Accessing Web-Based Data

The internet is an incredible source of data; it is, arguably, the reason that data has become such a dominant part of our social, economic, political, and even creative lives. In Chapter 4, we focused our data wrangling efforts on the process of accessing and reformatting file-based data that had already been saved to our devices or to the cloud. At the same time, much of it came from the internet originally—whether it was downloaded from a website, like the unemployment data, or retrieved from a URL, like the Citi Bike data. Now that we have a handle on how to use Python to parse and transform a variety of file-based data formats, however, it's time to look at what's involved in collecting those files in the first place—especially when the data they contain is of the real-time, feed-based variety. To do this, we're going to spend the bulk of this chapter learning how to get ahold of data made available through APIs— those *a*pplication *p*rogramming *i*nterfaces I mentioned early in Chapter 4. APIs are the primary (and sometimes only) way that we can access the data generated by real-time or on-demand services like social media platforms, streaming music, and search services—as well as many other private and public (e.g., government-generated) data sources.

While the many benefits of APIs (see "Why APIs?" on page 143 for a refresher) make them a popular resource for data-collecting companies to offer, there are significant costs and risks to doing so. For advertising-driven businesses like social media platforms, an outside product or project that is too comprehensive in its data collection is a profit risk. The ready availability of so much data about individuals has also significantly increased privacy risks (*https://dataprivacylab.org/projects/kanonymity/kano nymity.pdf*). As a result, accessing data via many APIs requires registering with the data collector in advance, and even completing a code-based login or *authentication* process anytime you request data. At the same time, the data accessibility that APIs offer is a powerful tool for improving the transparency of government systems[1] and accountability for private companies,[2] so the up-front work of creating an account and protecting any Python scripts you make that access API-based data is well worth the effort.

Over the course of this chapter, we'll cover how to access a range of web-based, feed-type datasets via APIs, addressing everything from basic, no-login-required resources all the way to the multistep, highly protected APIs of social media platforms like Twitter. As we'll see in "Accessing Online XML and JSON" on page 143, the simpler end of this spectrum just involves using the Python *requests* library to download a web page already formatted as JSON or XML—all we need is the URL. In "Specialized APIs: Adding Basic Authentication" on page 148, we'll move on to the process of accessing data made available through the Federal Reserve Economic Database (FRED) (*https://fred.stlouisfed.org/docs/api/fred*) API. This is the same data we looked at in Examples 4-12 and 4-15, but rather than working with example files that I've provided, you'll be programmatically downloading whatever data is most recent *whenever you run the script*.

This will require both creating a login on the FRED website as well as creating—and protecting—your own basic API "key" in order to retrieve data. Finally, in "Specialized APIs: Working With OAuth" on page 159 we'll cover the more complex API authentication process required for social media platforms like Twitter. Despite the degree of up-front work involved, learning how to programmatically interact with APIs like this has big payoffs—for the most part, you'll be able to rerun these scripts at any time to retrieve the most up-to-date data these services offer.[3] Of course, since not every data source we need offers an API, we'll wrap up the chapter with "Web Scraping: The Data Source of Last Resort" on page 173 by explaining how we can use code to *responsibly* "scrape" data from websites with the *Beautiful Soup* Python library. Though in many cases these data-access tasks *could* be accomplished with a browser and mouse, you'll quickly see how using Python helps lets us scale our data-retrieval efforts by making the process faster and more repeatable.

---

1 Like the US Treasurey, for example (*https://fiscaldata.treasury.gov/api-documentation*).

2 For two examples, see articles in *The Markup* (*https://themarkup.org/google-the-giant/2021/04/09/how-we-discovered-googles-social-justice-blocklist-for-youtube-ad-placements*) and NPR (*https://npr.org/2021/08/04/1024791053/facebook-boots-nyu-disinformation-researchers-off-its-platform-and-critics-cry-f*).

3 This is also the first step to building your own "apps"!

Why APIs?

In "Where to find feed-type data" on page 119 we touched on some of the reasons that companies and organizations provide data through APIs: when people use freely available data from a company's API to make some other product or service, they are effectively providing the company with free advertising and brand awareness. These API-based projects also act as a kind of free research and development (R&D) for the source company: apps that do well indicate a potentially profitable new business direction.

Even for government and nonprofit organizations, however, offering APIs for their data has appeal. Those organizations, too, benefit from the public exposure and unique insights that others' use of their data can provide. From a data wrangling perspective, these APIs help support transparency work, making it easier for civic technologists (volunteer or otherwise) to create more usable and accessible interfaces for public interest information. By separating the *data* from the *interface* that people use to access it, APIs provide a way to build public data tools that are also more resilient and future compatible.

Accessing Online XML and JSON

In "Wrangling Feed-Type Data with Python" on page 120, we explored the process of accessing and transforming two common forms of web-based data: XML and JSON. What we didn't address, however, was how to actually get those data files from the internet onto your computer. With the help of the versatile Python *requests* library, however, it only take a few lines of code to access and download that data without ever having to open a web browser.

For the sake of comparison, let's start by "manually" downloading two of the files we've used in previous examples: the BBC's RSS feed of articles from Example 4-13 and the Citi Bike JSON data mentioned in "One Data Source, Two Ways" on page 92.

For both of these data sources, the process is basically the same:

1. Visit the target URL; in this case, one of the following:

   - *http://feeds.bbci.co.uk/news/science_and_environment/rss.xml*
   - *https://gbfs.citibikenyc.com/gbfs/en/station_status.json*

2. Context-click (also known as "right-click" or sometime "Ctrl+click," depending on your system). From the menu that appears, simply choose "Save As" and save the file to the same folder where your Jupyter notebook or Python script is located.

That's it! Now you can run the scripts from Example 4-13 on that updated XML file or paste the Citi Bike JSON data into *https://jsonlint.com* to see what it looks like when it's properly formatted. Note that even though the BBC page looks almost like a "normal" website in your browser, true to its *.xml* file extension, it downloads as well-formatted XML.

Now that we've seen how to do this part of the process by hand, let's see what it takes to do the same thing in Python. To keep this short, the code in Example 5-1 will download and save *both* files, one after the other.

Example 5-1. data_download.py

```python
# a basic example of downloading data from the web with Python,
# using the requests library
#
# the source data we are downloading will come from the following URLs:
# http://feeds.bbci.co.uk/news/science_and_environment/rss.xml
# https://gbfs.citibikenyc.com/gbfs/en/station_status.json


# the `requests` library lets us write Python code that acts like
# a web browser
import requests

# our chosen XML filename
XMLfilename = "BBC_RSS.xml"

# open a new, writable file for our XML output
xml_output_file = open(XMLfilename,"w")

# use the requests library's "get" recipe to access the contents of our
# target URL and store it in our `xml_data` variable
xml_data=requests.get('http://feeds.bbci.co.uk/news/science_and_environment/rss.xml')

# the requests library's `get()` function puts contents of the web page
# in a property `text`
# we'll `write` that directly to our `xml_output_file`
xml_output_file.write(xml_data.text)

# close our xml_output_file
xml_output_file.close()

# our chosen JSON filename
JSONfilename = "citibikenyc_station_status.json"

# open a new, writable file for our JSON output
json_output_file = open(JSONfilename,"w")

# use the `requests` library's `get()` recipe to access the contents of our
# target URL and store it in our `json_data` variable
```

```
json_data = requests.get('https://gbfs.citibikenyc.com/gbfs/en/station_status.json')

# `get()` the contents of the web page and write its `text`
# directly to `json_output_file`
json_output_file.write(json_data.text)

# close our json_output_file
json_output_file.close()
```

Pretty simple, right? Apart from different filenames, the *.xml* and *.json* files produced by Example 5-1 are exactly the same as the ones we saved manually from the web. And once we have this script set up, of course, all we have to do to get the latest data is run it again and the new data will overwrite the earlier files.

Download by Hand, or Write a Program?

In almost every phase of our data wrangling work, there will be moments when we have to decide between doing part of a task "by hand" and writing some kind of program. In Example 4-15, for example, we didn't try to have our program "detect" too much about our JSON file structure; we simply *looked* at the data and then wrote our code to match. Now that we can *download* data using Python, we have another choice: save down the data "by hand" or do so programmatically.

For the most part, I will always recommend that you download a sample copy of your data "by hand" when you're first starting to work with it, simply because doing so is (usually) less work than writing a script to do it. Especially if your data source is XML or JSON, you'll probably have found it through a web search of some kind, so you'll already have the data open in a web browser right in front of you. At that point, you may as well just context-click and save a copy of the data to your device then and there, rather than opening up a Jupyter notebook or code editor in order to write some code. Since you'll *also* need to look through the data carefully to assess its quality, doing a first download this way almost always makes sense. Once you know it's worth looking at more closely, of course, you'll probably want to automate that download process by writing a Python script to do it.

Introducing APIs

Up until this point, most of our data wrangling work has focused on data sources whose contents are almost entirely controlled by the data provider. In fact, while the contents of spreadsheet files, and documents—and even the web pages containing XML and JSON that we accessed just now in Example 5-1—may change based on *when* we access them, we don't really have any influence on *what* data they contain.

At the same time, most of us are used to using the internet to get information that's much more tailored to our needs. Often our first step when looking for information is to enter keywords or phrases into a search engine, and we expect to receive a list of highly customized "results" based (at least in part) on our chosen combination of terms. Sure, we can't control what web pages are actually out there for our search to retrieve, but this process is so common—and so useful—for most of us that we rarely stop to think about what is happening behind the scenes.

Despite their visually oriented interfaces, search engines are actually just a special instance of APIs. They are essentially just web pages that let you *interface* with a database containing information about websites on the internet, such as their URLs, titles, text, images, videos, and more. When you enter your search terms and hit Enter or Return, the search engine *queries* its database for web content that "matches" your search in some respect and then updates the web page you're looking at to display those results in a list. Though the specialized APIs made available by social media platforms and other online services require us to authenticate *and* structure our searches in a very particular way, there are enough features shared between search engines and more specialized APIs that we can learn something useful about APIs by deconstructing a basic Google search.

Basic APIs: A Search Engine Example

Though an internet search engine is probably the most straightforward form of API around, that's not always obvious from the way we see them behave onscreen. For example, if you were to visit Google and search for "weather sebastopol," you would probably see a page that looks something like Figure 5-1.

Figure 5-1. Sample search results

While the format of the search results is probably pretty familiar, right now let's take a closer look at what's happening in the URL bar. What you see will definitely be different from the Figure 5-1 screenshot, but it should contain at least some of the same information. Specifically, look through the text that now appears in *your* URL bar to find the following:

```
q=weather+sebastopol
```

Found it? Great. Now without refreshing the page, change the text in the search box to "weather san francisco" and hit Enter. Once again look through the text in the URL to find:

```
q=weather+san+francisco
```

Finally, copy and paste the following into your URL bar and hit Enter:

```
https://www.google.com/search?q=weather+san+francisco
```

Notice anything? Hopefully, you're seeing the same (or *almost* the same) search results when you type "weather san francisco" into Google's search bar and hit Enter as when you directly visit the Google search URL with the key/value pair of `q=weather+san+francisco` appended (e.g., `https://www.google.com/search?q=weather+san+francisco`). That's because `q=weather+san+francisco` is the part of the *query string* that delivers your actual search terms to Google's database; everything else is just additional information Google tacks on for customization or tracking purposes.

While Google can (and will!) add whatever it wants to our search URL, *we* can also add other useful key/value pairs. For example, in "Smart Searching for Specific Data Types" on page 96, we looked at searching for specific file types, such as *.xml*, by adding `filetype: .xml` to our search box query; we can do the same thing directly in the URL bar by adding the corresponding key/value pair of `as_filetype=xml` to our query string:

```
https://www.google.com/search?q=weather+san+francisco&as_filetype=xml
```

Not only will this return results in the correct format, but notice that it updates the contents of the search box as well!

The behavior of the Google search engine in this situation is almost identical to what we'll see with more specialized APIs in the remainder of this chapter. Most APIs follow the general structure we're seeing in this search example, where an *endpoint* (in this case `https://www.google.com/search`) is combined with one or more *query parameters* or *key/value pairs* (such as `as_filetype=xml` or `q=weather+san+fran cisco`), which comprise the *query string* that is appended after the question mark (?). A general overview of API endpoint and query string structure is shown in Figure 5-2.

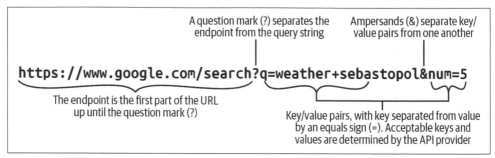

Figure 5-2. Basic query string structure

While this structure is pretty universal, here are a couple of other useful tips about query string-based APIs:

- Key/value pairs (such as `as_filetype=xml`, `num=5`, or even `q=weather+san+fran cisco`) can appear *in any order*, as long as they are added after the question mark (?) that indicates the start of the query string.

- The particular keys and values that are meaningful for a given API are determined by the API provider and can only be identified by reading the API documentation, or through experimentation (though this can present problems of its own). Anything appended to the query string that is not a recognized key or valid parameter value will probably be ignored.

While these characteristics are common to almost all APIs, the vast majority of them will not allow you to access any data at all without first identifying (or *authenticating*) yourself by creating a login and providing unique, specialized "keys" to the API along with your queries. This part of the API process is what we'll turn to next.

Specialized APIs: Adding Basic Authentication

The first step in using most APIs is creating some kind of account with the API provider. Although many APIs allow *you* to use them for free, the process of compiling, storing, searching for, and returning data to you over the internet still presents risks and costs money, so providers want to track who is using their APIs and be able to cut off your access if they want to.[4] This first part of the *authentication* process usually consists of creating an account and requesting an API "key" for yourself and/or each project, program, or "app" that you plan to have interact with the API. In a "basic" API authentication process, like the one we'll go through now, once you've

---

[4] While this is probably most likely to happen if you make too many data requests in too short a time frame, most API providers can terminate your access to their API pretty much whenever they want, and for whatever reason they want.

created your API key on the service provider's website, all you need to do to retrieve data successfully is append your key to your data request just like any other query parameter, and you're all set.

As an example, let's get set up to programmatically access the unemployment data we worked with in Example 4-15. We'll start by making an account on the FRED website and requesting an API key. Once we have that, we can just append it to our query string and start downloading data!

Getting a FRED API Key

To create an account with the Federal Reserve Economic Database (FRED), visit *https://fred.stlouisfed.org* and click on My Account in the upper-righthand corner, as shown in Figure 5-3.

Figure 5-3. FRED login link

Follow the directions in the pop-up, either creating an account with a new username and password or using your Google account to log in. Once your registration/login process is complete, clicking on the My Account link will open a drop-down menu that includes an option titled API Keys, as shown in Figure 5-4.

Figure 5-4. FRED account actions

Clicking that link will take you to a page where you can request one or more API keys using the Request API Key button. On the next page, you'll be asked to provide a brief description of the application with which the API key will be used; this can just be a sentence or two. You'll also need to read and agree to the Terms of Service by checking the provided box. Complete the process by clicking the Request API Key button.

If your request is successful (and it should be), you'll be taken to an interim page that will display the key that's been generated. If you leave that page, you can always just log in and visit *https://research.stlouisfed.org/useraccount/apikeys* to see all of your available API keys.

Using Your API key to Request Data

Now that you have an API key, let's explore how to request the data we used in Example 4-15. Start by trying to load the following URL in a browser:

```
https://api.stlouisfed.org/fred/series/observations?series_id=U6RATE&file_type=json
```

Even if you're already logged in to FRED on that browser, you'll see something like this:

```
{"error_code":400,"error_message":"Bad Request.  Variable api_key is not set.
Read https:\/\/research.stlouisfed.org\/docs\/api\/api_key.html for more
information."}
```

This is a pretty descriptive error message: it not only tells you that something went wrong, but it gives you some idea of how to fix it. Since you just created an API key, all you have to do is add it to your request as an additional parameter:

```
https://api.stlouisfed.org/fred/series/observations?series_id=U6RATE&file_type=json&
api_key=YOUR_API_KEY_HERE
```

replacing `YOUR_API_KEY_HERE` with, of course, your API key. Loading that page in a browser should return something that looks something like this:

```
{"realtime_start":"2021-02-03","realtime_end":"2021-02-03","observation_start":
"1600-01-01","observation_end":"9999-12-31","units":"lin","output_type":1,
"file_type":"json","order_by":"observation_date","sort_order":"asc","count":324,
"offset":0,"limit":100000,"observations":[{"realtime_start":"2021-02-03",
"realtime_end":"2021-02-03","date":"1994-01-01","value":"11.7"},
...
{"realtime_start":"2021-02-03","realtime_end":"2021-02-03","date":"2020-12-01",
"value":"11.7"}]}
```

Pretty nifty, right? Now that you know how to use your API key to make data requests, it's time to review how to both customize those requests *and* protect your API key when you use it in Python scripts.

Reading API Documentation

As you can see from the preceding example, once we have an API key, we can load the latest data from the FRED database whenever we want. All we need to do is construct our query string and add our API key.

But how do we know what key/value pairs the FRED API will accept and what type of information they'll return? The only really reliable way to do this is to read the API *documentation*, which should offer guidance and (hopefully) examples of how the API can be used.

Unfortunately, there's no widely adopted standard for API documentation, which means that using a new API is almost always something of a trial-and-error process, especially if the documentation quality is poor or the provided examples don't include the information you're looking for. In fact, even *finding* the documentation for a particular API isn't always straightforward, and often a web search is the simplest route.

For example, getting to the FRED API documentation from the FRED homepage (*https://fred.stlouisfed.org*) requires clicking on the Tools tab about halfway down the page, then selecting the Developer API link at the bottom right, which takes you to *https://fred.stlouisfed.org/docs/api/fred*. By contrast, a web search for "fred api documentation" will take you to the same page, shown in Figure 5-5, directly.

Figure 5-5. FRED API documentation page

Unfortunately, the list of links on this page is actually a list of *endpoints*—different base URLs that you can use to request more specific information (recall that the *endpoint* is everything before the question mark (?), which separates it from the *query string*). In the preceding example, you used the endpoint `https://api.stlouis` `fed.org/fred/series/observations` and then paired it with the key/value pairs of `series_id=U6RATE`, `file_type=json`, and, of course, your API key in order to generate a response.

Scrolling down the page in Figure 5-5 and clicking on the documentation link labeled "fred/series/observations" will take you *https://fred.stlouisfed.org/docs/api/ fred/series_observations.html*, which outlines all of the valid query keys (or *parameters*) for that particular endpoint, as well as the valid values those keys can have and some sample query URLs, as shown in Figure 5-6.

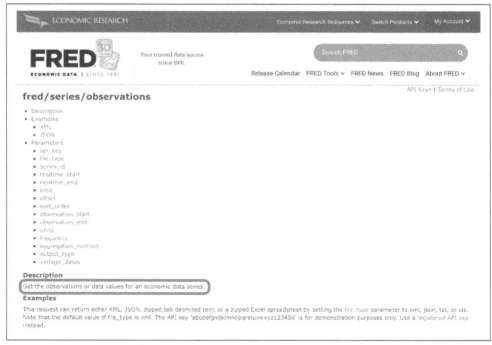

Figure 5-6. FRED API observations endpoint documentation

For example, you could limit the number of observations returned by using the `limit` parameter, or reverse the sort order of the returned results by adding `sort_order=desc`. You can also specify particular data formats (such as `file_type=xml` for XML output) or units (such as `units=pc1` to see the output as percent change from a year ago).

Protecting Your API Key When Using Python

As you may have already guessed, downloading data from FRED (or other, similar APIs) is as simple as replacing one of the URLs in Example 5-1 with your complete query, because the web page it generates is just another JSON file on the internet.

At the same time, that query contains some especially sensitive information: your API key. Remember that as far as FRED (or any other API owner) is concerned, you are responsible for any activity on their platform that uses your API key. This means that while you *always* want to be documenting, saving, and versioning your code with something like Git, you *never* want your API keys or other credentials to end up in a file that others can access.

 Properly protecting your API key takes some effort, and if you're new to working with data, Python, or APIs (or all three), you may be tempted to skip the next couple of sections and just leave your API credentials inside files that could get uploaded to the internet.[5] Don't! While right now you may be thinking, "Who's ever going to bother looking at *my* work?" or "I'm just playing around anyway— what difference does it make?" there are two things you should know.

First, as with documentation, if you don't deal with protecting your credentials correctly now, it will be *much* more difficult and time-consuming to do so later, in part because by then you'll have forgotten what exactly is involved, and in part because *it may already be too late*. Second, while few of us feel that what we're doing is "important" or visible enough that anyone *else* would bother looking at it, the reality is that bad actors don't mind who their scapegoat is—and if you make it easy, they might choose you. The fallout, moreover, might not be limited to getting you kicked off of a data platform. In 2021, the former SolarWinds CEO claimed that the massive breach of thousands of high-security systems through compromises to the company's software was made possible, in part, because of a weak password that was uploaded to a file on an intern's personal GitHub account.[6] In other words, even if you're "just practicing," you're better off practicing good security in the first place.

Protecting your API credentials is a two-part process:

1. You need to separate your API key or other sensitive information from the rest of your code. We'll do this by storing these credentials in a separate file that our main code only loads when the script is actually run.

2. You need a reliable way to ensure that as you are backing up your code using Git, for example, those credential files are *never* backed up to any online location.

---

5 For example, when you git push your code.

6 "Hackers Used SolarWinds' Dominance against It in Sprawling Spy Campaign" by Raphael Satter, Christopher Bing, and Joseph Menn, *https://reuters.com/article/global-cyber-solarwinds/hackers-at-center-of-sprawling-spy-campaign-turned-solarwinds-dominance-against-it-idUSKBN28P2N8*; "Former SolarWinds CEO Blames Intern for *solarwinds123* Password Leak" by Brian Fung and Geneva Sands, *https://www.cnn.com/2021/02/26/politics/solarwinds123-password-intern*.

We'll accomplish this by putting the word `credentials` in the name of any file that includes them and then using a `gitignore` file to make sure they don't get uploaded to GitHub.

The simplest way to achieve both of these things consistently is to define a naming convention for any file that contains API keys or other sensitive login-related information. In this case, we'll make sure that any such file has the word `credentials` somewhere in the filename. We'll then make sure to create or update a special type of Git file known as a *.gitignore*, which stores rules for telling Git which files in our repo folder should *never* be committed to our repository and/or uploaded to GitHub. By including a rule for our "credentials" file to *.gitignore*, we guarantee that no files containing sensitive login information get uploaded to GitHub by accident.

Creating Your "Credentials" File

Up until now, we've been putting all our code for a particular task—such as downloading or transforming a data file—into a single Python file or notebook. For the purposes of both security and reuse, however, when we're working with APIs, it makes much more sense to separate our functional code from our credentials. Luckily, this process is very straightforward.

First, create and save a new, empty Python file called *FRED_credentials.py*. For simplicity's sake, go ahead and put this file in the same folder where you plan to put the Python code you'll use to download data from FRED.

Then, simply create a new variable and set its value to your own API key, as shown in Example 5-2.

Example 5-2. Example FRED credentials file

```
my_api_key = "your_api_key_surrounded_by_double_quotes"
```

Now just save your file!

Using Your Credentials in a Separate Script

Now that your API key exists as a variable in another file, you can import it into any file where you want to use it, using the same method we've used previously to import libraries created by others. Example 5-3 is a sample script for downloading the U6 unemployment data from FRED using the API key stored in my *FRED_credentials.py* file.

Example 5-3. FRED_API_example.py

```python
# import the requests library
import requests

# import our API key
from FRED_credentials import my_api_key ❶

# specify the FRED endpoint we want to use
FRED_endpoint = "https://api.stlouisfed.org/fred/series/observations?"

# also specify the query parameters and their values
FRED_parameters = "series_id=U6RATE&file_type=json"

# construct the complete URL for our API request, adding our API key to the end
complete_data_URL = FRED_endpoint + FRED_parameters +"&api_key="+my_api_key

# open a new, writable file with our chosen filename
FRED_output_file = open("FRED_API_data.json","w")

# use the `requests` library's `get()` recipe to access the contents of our
# target URL and store it in our `FRED_data` variable
FRED_data = requests.get(complete_data_URL)

# `get()` the contents of the web page and write its `text`
# directly to `FRED_output_file`
FRED_output_file.write(FRED_data.text)

# close our FRED_output_file
FRED_output_file.close()
```

❶ We can make our API available to this script by using the from keyword with the name of our credentials file (notice that we *don't* include the *.py* extension here) and then telling it to import the variable that contains our API key.

What's the pycache?

When you run the script in Example 5-3, you'll probably notice that it does more than just successfully download the FRED data—it also creates a new folder called *__pycache__*, which in turn contains a single file called *FRED_credentials.cpython38.pyc* or something similar. Where did this file come from, and what is it?

When importing code from another Python file, your device first converts its contents to something called *bytecode*, which is what the device *actually* uses to run your Python script.[7] These Python bytecode files have the extension *.pyc*. Although we

---

7 That's why the program that makes Python run on your device is often called a Python *interpreter*—because it translates the code we humans write into bytecode that your device can actually understand.

haven't dealt with them directly before, there are lots of *.pyc* files already on your device associated with the libraries we have been importing—they're just stored in a tucked-away part of the computer system, so we haven't actually seen them before. In both instances, however, your system is saving resources by translating those imported files to bytecode only once and storing that translation in a *.pyc* file, rather than translating *every time* your code runs. When you import those libraries (and now, your credentials), your system relies on the pre-translated version to make the rest of your code run a little bit faster.

Fortunately, you don't have to do anything with—or about—either the *__pycache__* folder or the *.pyc* file inside it; you can even delete them if you like (though they will reappear the next time you run a Python script that imports your credentials). Since our credentials file is very small, it's not going to slow things up very much if it's regenerated each time. On the other hand, if it doesn't bother you to see it in your folder, you can just leave it alone.

Now that we've succeeded in separating our API credentials from the main part of our code, we need to make sure that our credentials file doesn't accidentally get backed up when we git commit our work and/or git push it to the internet. To do this simply and systematically, we'll make use of a special type of file known as *.gitignore*.

Getting Started with .gitignore

As the name suggests, a *.gitignore* file lets you specify certain types of files that—surprise, surprise!—you want Git to "ignore," rather than track or back up. By creating (or modifying) the pattern-matching rules in the *.gitignore* file for a repository, we can predefine which types of files our repo will track or upload. While we could *theoretically* accomplish the same thing manually—by never using git add on files we don't want to track—using a *.gitignore* file enforces this behavior[8] *and* prevents Git from "warning" us that we have untracked files every time we run git status. *Without* a *.gitignore* file, we would have to confirm which files we want to ignore every time we commit—which would quickly get tedious and easily lead to mistakes. All it would take is one hasty git add -A command to accidentally begin tracking our sensitive credentials file(s)—and getting things *out* of your Git history is much trickier than getting them in. Much better to avoid the whole problem with a little preparation.

In other words, *.gitignore* files are our friend, letting us create general rules that prevent us from accidentally tracking files we don't want to, and by making sure that Git only reports the status of files that we genuinely care about.

---

8 Even if we run, say, git add -A or git commit -a.

For the time being, we'll create a new *.gitignore* file in the same folder/repository where our *FRED_credentials.py* file is, just to get a feel for how they work.[9] To do this, we'll start by opening up a new file in Atom (or you can add a new file directly in your GitHub repo) and saving it in the same folder as your *FRED_credentials.py* with the name *.gitignore* (be sure to start the filename with a dot (.)—that's important!).

Next, add the following lines to your file:

```
# ignoring all credentials files
**credentials*
```

As in Python, comments in *.gitignore* files are started with a hash (#) symbol, so the first line of this file is just descriptive. The contents of the second line (**creden tials*) is a sort of *regular expression*—a special kind of pattern-matching system that lets us describe strings (including filenames) in the sort of generic way we might explain them to another person.[10] In this case, the expression **credentials* translates to "a file anywhere in this repository that contains the word *credentials*." By adding this line to our *.gitignore* file, we ensure that any file in this repository whose filename includes the word *credentials* will never be tracked or uploaded to GitHub.

To see your *.gitignore* in action, save the file, and then in the command line, run:

```
git status
```

While you should see the new file you created for the code in Example 5-3, you should *not* see your *FRED_credentials.py* file listed as "untracked." If you want to be really sure that the files you intend to be ignored are, in fact, being ignored, you can also run:

```
git status --ignored
```

which will show you *only* the files in your repository that are currently being ignored. Among them you'll probably also see the *__pycache__* folder, which we also don't need to back up.

Where Did My .gitignore File Go?

Once you've saved and closed your *.gitignore* file, you might be surprised to see that, well, you don't see it anymore! Whether you're looking for it in a folder on your device or via the command line, sometimes finding your *.gitignore* file can be a challenge in itself.

---

9 A repository can have different *.gitignore* files in different folders; for complete details, you can take a look at the documentation (*https://git-scm.com/docs/gitignore*).

10 We used this approach with the *glob* library in Example 4-16 and will examine it in more detail in "Regular Expressions: Supercharged String Matching" on page 229.

The reason why these files can be hard to find is that, by default, most device operating systems hide any files that begin with a dot (.). While your *.gitignore* files will always be easy to find (and edit!) on the GitHub website, if you want to change them on your device, there are a few tricks that can make finding and working with them easier.

Since your *.gitignore* file is one of the few "dot files" on your device that you'll probably ever want to see and edit, I find the easiest thing to do is look for it with the command line, by navigating to the relevant folder/repository and using the "list all" command:

```
ls -a
```

If you don't see an existing *.gitignore* file, you can, of course, create one. If it *is* there, though, how do you edit it? While you've probably been opening the Atom code editor from an icon on your device, you can actually use it to open files right from the command line by using the `atom` keyword (similar to the way we use `python`). So to open your *.gitignore* file using Atom, you can just type:

```
atom .gitignore
```

While it may take a few seconds to open (even if you have other Atom files open already), using the command line to start a program is an easy way to find and modify files—hidden or otherwise!

Specialized APIs: Working With OAuth

So far, we have everything we need to work with APIs that have what's often described as a "basic" authentication process: we create an account with the API provider and are given a key that we append to our data request, just as we did in Example 5-3.

While this process is very straightforward, it has some drawbacks. These days, APIs can do much more than just return data: they are also the way that apps post updates to a social media account or add items to your online calendar. To make that possible, they obviously need some type of access to your account—but of course you don't want to be sharing your login credentials with apps and programs willy-nilly. If you did just give apps that information, the only way to later *stop* an app from accessing your account would be to change your username and password, and then you'd have to give your updated credentials to all the apps you still *want* to use in order for them to continue working…it gets messy and complicated, fast.

The OAuth authentication workflow was designed to address these problems by providing a way to provide API access without passing around a bunch of usernames and passwords. In general, this is achieved by scripting a so-called *authorization loop*, which includes three basic steps:

1. Obtaining and encoding your API key and "secret" (each of which is just a string that you get from the API provider—just as we did with the FRED API key).

2. Sending an encoded combination of those two strings as (yet another) "key" to a special "authorization" endpoint/URL.

3. Receiving an *access token* (yet another string) from the authorization endpoint. The access token is what you actually then send along to the API's data endpoint along with your query information.

While this probably sounds convoluted, rest assured that, in practice, even this complex-sounding process is mostly about passing strings back and forth to and from certain URLs in a certain order. Yes, in the process we'll need to do some "encoding" on them, but as you may have guessed, that part will be handled for us by a handy Python library.

Despite needing to complete an authorization loop and retrieve an access token, the process of interacting with even these more specialized APIs via Python is essentially the same as what we saw in "Specialized APIs: Adding Basic Authentication" on page 148. We'll create an account, request API credentials, and then create a file that both contains those credentials and does a little bit of preparatory work to them so we can use them in our main script. Then our main script will pull in those credentials and use them to request data from our target platform and write it to an output file.

For this example, we'll be working with the Twitter API, but you'll be able to use roughly the same process for other platforms (like Facebook) that use an OAuth approach. One thing we *won't* do here is spend much time discussing how to structure specific queries, since the ins and outs of any given API could easily fill a book in and of itself! That said, once you have this authentication process down, you'll have what you need to start experimenting with a whole range of APIs and can start practicing with them in order to access the data you want. Let's get started!

Applying for a Twitter Developer Account

As it will be with (almost) every new API we want to use, our first step will be to request an API key from Twitter. Even if you already have a Twitter account, you'll need to apply for "developer access," which will take about 15 minutes (not counting the time for Twitter to review and/or approve), all told. Start by visiting the Twitter Developer API "Apply for Access" page (*https://developer.twitter.com/en/apply-for-access*), and click the "Apply for a developer account" button. Once you've logged in, you'll be prompted for more information about how you plan to use the API. For this exercise, you can select "Hobbyist" and "Exploring the API," as shown in Figure 5-7.

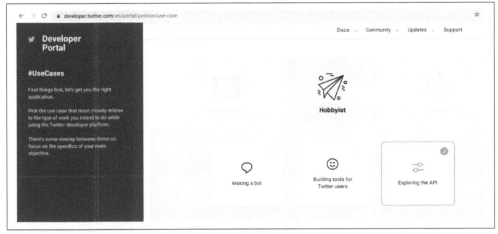

Figure 5-7. Twitter developer API use case selection

In the next step, you'll be asked to provide a 200+ character explanation of what you plan to use the API for; here you can enter something like this:

> Using the Twitter API to learn more about doing data wrangling with Python. Interested in experimenting with OAuth loops and pulling different kinds of information from public Twitter feeds and conversations.

Since our goal here is just to practice downloading data from Twitter using a Python script and an OAuth loop, you can toggle the answer to the four subsequent questions to "No," as shown in Figure 5-8, though if you begin using the API in some other way, you will need to update these answers.

Figure 5-8. Twitter developer API intended uses

On the next two screens, you'll review your previous selections and click a checkbox to acknowledge the Developer Agreement. You then click "Submit application," which will trigger a verification email. If the email doesn't arrive in your inbox within a few minutes, be sure to check your Spam and Trash. Once you locate it, click on the link in the email for your access to be confirmed!

Creating Your Twitter "App" and Credentials

Once your developer access has been approved by Twitter, you can create a new "app" by logging in to your Twitter account and visiting *https://developer.twitter.com/en/ portal/projects-and-apps*. In the center of the page, click the Create Project button.

Here you'll be taken through a mini version of the process to apply for developer access: you'll need to provide a name for your project, indicate how you intend to use the Twitter API, describe that purpose in words, and provide a name for the first app associated with that project, as shown in Figures 5-9 through 5-12.

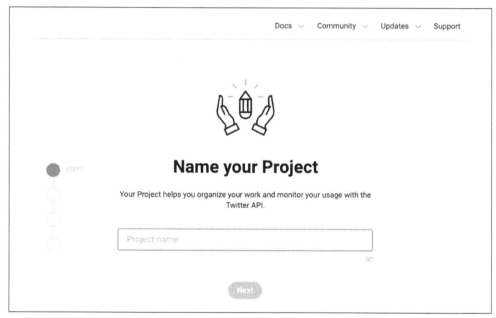

Figure 5-9. Twitter project creation: project name

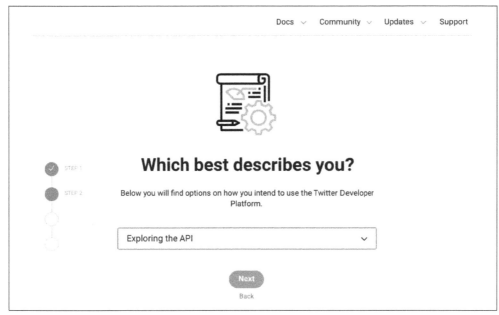

Figure 5-10. Twitter project creation: project purpose

Figure 5-11. Twitter project creation: project description

Figure 5-12. Twitter project creation: app name

Once you've added your app name, you'll see a screen that shows your API key, API secret key, and Bearer token, as shown in Figure 5-13.[11]

What's an "App" After All?

For most of us, the word *app* brings to mind phone games and services, not using Python to pull data from an API. For most API providers, however, an "app" is anything that programmatically interacts with their services—whether that's a Python script downloading tweets or a full-blown mobile app that users can install on their devices. That said, once you've got your developer account and are downloading tweets, you can honestly say that you're an "app developer." Congratulations!

---

11 These keys have since been replaced and will not work!

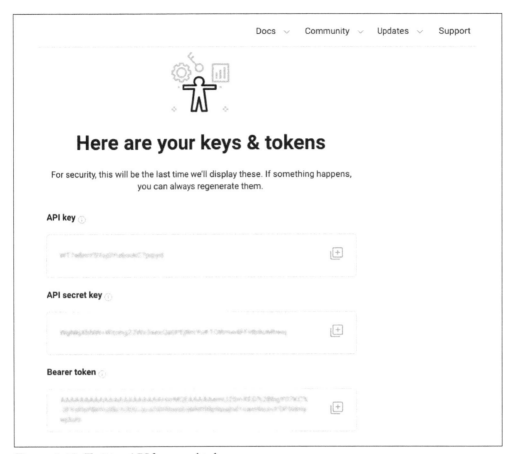

Figure 5-13. Twitter API keys and tokens screen

For security reasons, you'll only be able to view your API key and API secret key *on this screen*, so we're going to put them into a file for our Twitter credentials right away (note that in other places in the developer dashboard these are referred to as the "API Key" and "API Key Secret"—even big tech companies can have trouble with consistency!). Don't worry, though! If you accidentally click away from this screen too soon, miscopy a value, or anything else, you can always go back to your dashboard (*https://developer.twitter.com/en/portal/dashboard*) and click on the key icon next to your app, as shown in Figure 5-14.

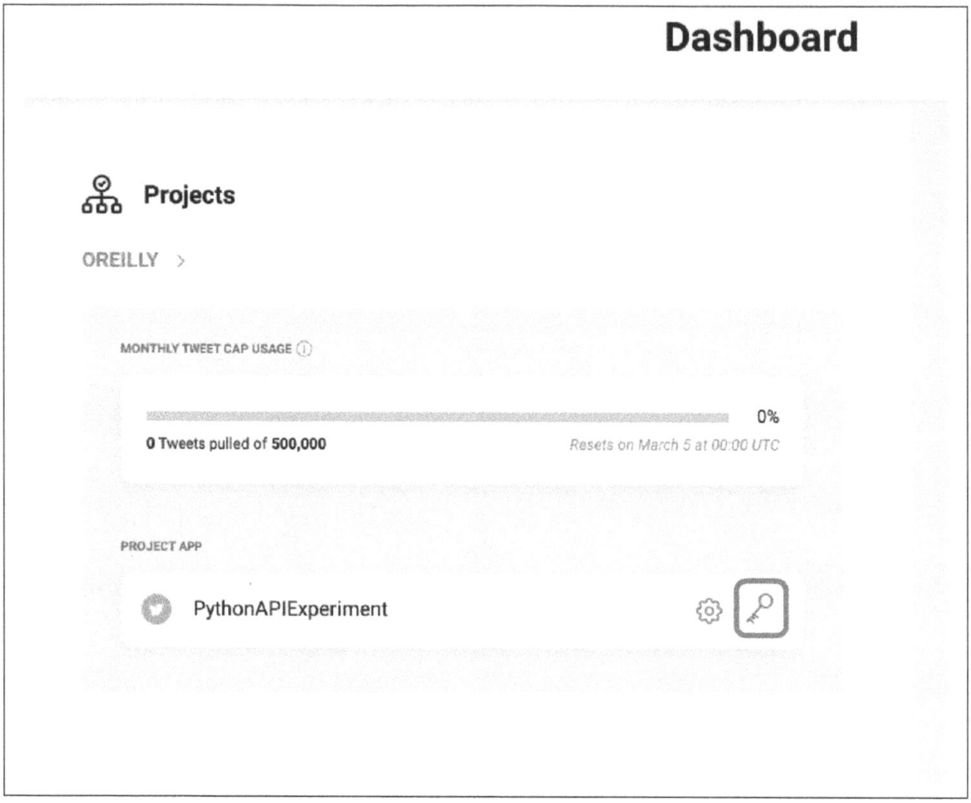

Figure 5-14. Twitter dashboard with apps

Then, just click "Regenerate" under "Consumer Keys" to get a new API Key and API Key Secret, as shown in Figure 5-15.

Now that we know how to access the API Key and API Key Secret for our app, we need to put these into a new "credentials" file, similar to the one we created for our FRED API key. To do this, create a new file called *Twitter_credentials.py* and save it in the folder where you want to put your Python script for accessing Twitter data, as shown in Example 5-4.

Example 5-4. Twitter_credentials.py

```
my_Twitter_key = "your_api_key_surrounded_by_double_quotes"
my_Twitter_secret = "your_api_key_secret_surrounded_by_double_quotes"
```

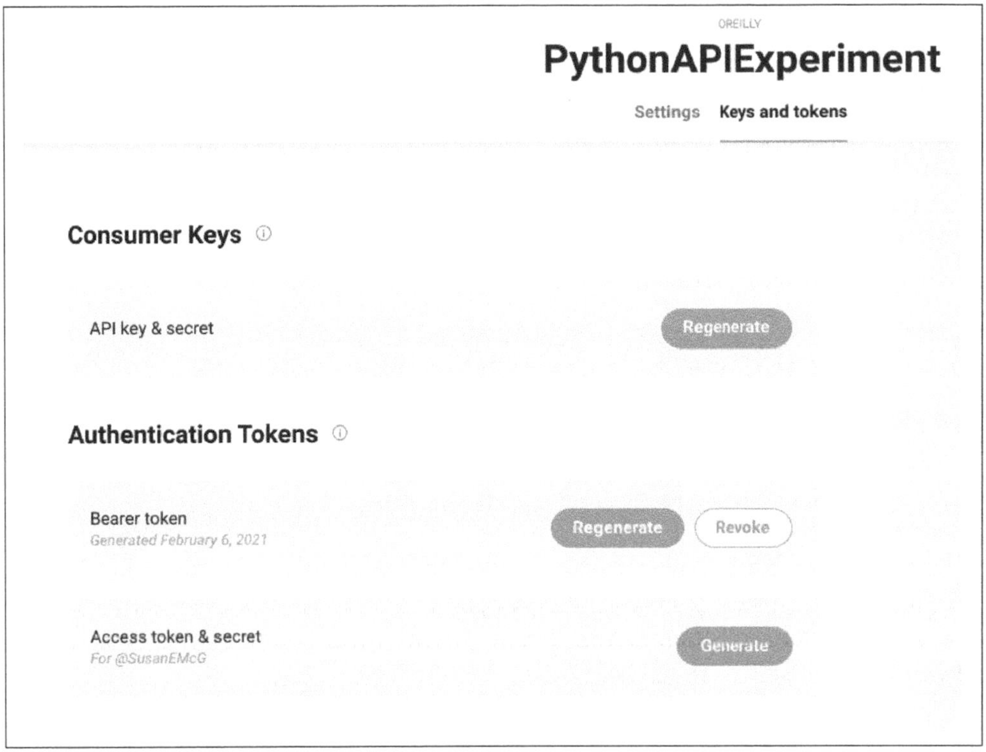

PythonAPIExperiment

Settings   **Keys and tokens**

Consumer Keys ⓘ

API key & secret   Regenerate

Authentication Tokens ⓘ

Bearer token   Regenerate   Revoke
Generated February 6, 2021

Access token & secret   Generate
For @SusanEMcG

Figure 5-15. Twitter regenerate keys

Be sure to include the word `credentials` in the name of the file where you store your Twitter API Key and API Key Secret! Recall that in "Getting Started with .gitignore" on page 157, we created a rule that ignores any file whose name includes the word `creden tials` to make sure our API keys never get uploaded to GitHub by accident. So make sure to double-check the spelling in your filename! Just to be extra sure, you can always run:

```
git status --ignored
```

in the command line to confirm that all of your credentials files are indeed being ignored.

Encoding Your API Key and Secret

So far, we haven't needed to do things *too* differently than we did for the FRED API; we've just had to create two variables in our credentials file (`my_Twitter_key` and `my_Twitter_secret`) instead of one.

Now, however, we need to do a little bit of work on these values to get them in the right format for the next step of the authentication process. While I won't go too far

---

into the details of what's happening "under the hood" in these next few steps, just know that these coding and decoding steps are necessary for protecting the raw string values of your API Key and API Key Secret so that they can be safely sent over the internet.

So, to our *Twitter_credentials.py* file we're now going to add several lines of code so that the completed file looks like Example 5-5.

Example 5-5. Twitter_credentials.py

```
my_Twitter_key = "your_api_key_surrounded_by_double_quotes"
my_Twitter_secret = "your_api_key_secret_surrounded_by_double_quotes"

# import the base64 encoding library
import base64 ❶

# first, combine the API Key and API Key Secret into a single string
# adding a colon between them
combined_key_string = my_Twitter_key+':'+my_Twitter_secret

# use the `encode()` method on that combined string,
# specifying the ASCII format (see: https://en.wikipedia.org/wiki/ASCII)
encoded_combined_key = combined_key_string.encode('ascii')

# encode the ASCII-formatted string to base64
b64_encoded_combined_key = base64.b64encode(encoded_combined_key)

# _decode_ the encoded string back to ASCII,
# so that it's ready to send over the internet
auth_ready_key = b64_encoded_combined_key.decode('ascii')
```

❶ This library will let us transform our raw API Key and API Key Secret into the correct format for sending to the Twitter authorization endpoint.

Now that we've got our API Key and API Key Secret properly encoded, we can import *just* the auth_ready_key into the script we'll use to actually specify and pull our data. After doing one request to the authorization endpoint to get our *access token*, we'll finally(!) be ready retrieve some tweets!

Requesting an Access Token and Data from the Twitter API

As we did in Example 5-3, we'll now create a Python file (or notebook) where we'll do the next two steps of our Twitter data loading process:

1. Requesting (and receiving) an access token or *bearer token* from Twitter
2. Including that bearer token in a data request to Twitter and receiving the results

Requesting an access token: get versus post

Requesting an access or bearer token from Twitter is really just a matter of sending a well-formatted request to the *authorization endpoint*, which is *https://api.twitter.com/ oauth2/token*. Instead of appending our `auth_ready_key` to the endpoint URL, however, we'll use something called a *post* request (recall that in Examples 5-1 and 5-3, the `requests` recipe we used was called `get`).

A `post` request is important here in part because it offers some additional security over `get` requests[12] but mostly because `post` requests are effectively the standard when we're asking an API to do something *beyond* simply returning data. So while in Example 5-3 the data we got back was unique to our query, the API would return that same data to *anyone* who submitted that same request. By contrast, when we use `post` to submit our `auth_ready_key`, the Twitter API will process our unique key and return a unique bearer token—so we use a `post` request.

When building our `post` request in Python, we'll need to create two `dict` objects: one that contains the request's *headers*, which will contain both our `auth_ready_key` and some other information, and another that contains the request's *data*, which in this case will specify that we're asking for credentials. Then we'll just pass these as parameters to the *requests* library's `post` recipe, rather than sticking them on the end of the URL string, as shown in Example 5-6.

Example 5-6. Twitter_data_download.py

```
# import the encoded key from our credentials file
from Twitter_credentials import auth_ready_key

# include the requests library in order to get data from the web
import requests

# specify the Twitter endpoint that we'll use to retrieve
# our access token or "bearer" token
auth_url = 'https://api.twitter.com/oauth2/token'


# add our `auth_ready_key` to a template `dict` object provided
# in the Twitter API documentation
auth_headers = {
    'Authorization': 'Basic '+auth_ready_key,
    'Content-Type': 'application/x-www-form-urlencoded;charset=UTF-8'
} ❶

# another `dict` describes what we're asking for
auth_data = {
```

---

12 For example, the contents of a post request are not saved in the browser history the way that get requests are.

```
        'grant_type': 'client_credentials'
} ❷

# make our complete request to the authorization endpoint, and store
# the results in the `auth_resp` variable
auth_resp = requests.post(auth_url, headers=auth_headers, data=auth_data)

# pull the access token out of the json-formatted data
# that the authorization endpoint sent back to us
access_token = auth_resp.json()['access_token']
```

❶ This **dict** contains the information the authorization endpoint wants in order to return an access token to us. This includes our encoded key and its data format.

❷ The format of both the **auth_headers** and the **auth_data** objects was defined by the API provider.

Actually pretty straightforward, right? If everything went well (which we'll confirm momentarily), we'll just need to add a few lines of code to this script in order to use our access token to request some actual data about what's happening on Twitter.

What About the Bearer Token in the Developer Dashboard?

When you were copying your API Key and API Key Secret out of the developer dashboard screen shown in Figure 5-13, you may have noticed that there was *also* a "Bearer Token" listed. Why aren't we just using that instead of writing code to get one?

The short answer is that while the Twitter API provides access tokens in the dashboard, many similar APIs (such as Facebook's) do not. Since the goal here is to illustrate a more general process for interacting with APIs that use OAuth, we're walking through the access/bearer token request loop so you can more easily modify and reuse this code with other APIs.

Now that we have an access token (or *bearer token*) handy, we can go ahead and make a request for some tweets. For demonstration purposes, we're going to keep our request simple: we'll do a basic search request for recent tweets that contain the word *Python*, and ask to have a maximum of four tweets returned. In Example 5-7, we're building on the script we started in Example 5-6, and we'll structure and make this request, including our newly acquired bearer token in the header. Once the response arrives, we'll write the data to a file. Since there is a *lot* in the JSON data we get back besides the text of the tweets, however, we're also going to print out *just* the text of each tweet, just to give us confidence that we got correct (if sometimes unexpected) results ;-)

Example 5-7. Twitter_data_download.py, continued

```
# now that we have an access/bearer token, we're ready to request some data!

# we'll create a new dict that includes this token
search_headers = {
    'Authorization': 'Bearer ' + access_token
}

# this is the Twitter search API endpoint for version 1.1 of the API
search_url  = 'https://api.twitter.com/1.1/search/tweets.json'

# create a new dict that includes our search query parameters
search_params = {
    'q': 'Python',
    'result_type': 'recent',
    'count': 4
} ❶

# send our data request and store the results in `search_resp`
search_resp = requests.get(search_url, headers=search_headers, params=search_params)

# parse the response into a JSON object
Twitter_data = search_resp.json()

# open an output file where we can save the results
Twitter_output_file = open("Twitter_search_results.json", "w")

# write the returned Twitter data to our output file
Twitter_output_file.write(str(Twitter_data)) ❷

# close the output file
Twitter_output_file.close()

# loop through our results and print the text of the Twitter status
for a_Tweet in Twitter_data['statuses']: ❸
    print(a_Tweet['text'] + '\n')
```

❶ In this case, our query (q) is Python, we're looking for recent results, and we want a maximum of 4 tweets back. Remember that the keys and values we can include in this object are defined by the data provider.

❷ Because the response from Twitter is a JSON object, we have to use the built-in Python str() function to convert it to a string before we can write it to our file.

❸ Because there is a *lot* of information in each result, we're going to print out the text of each tweet returned, just to get a sense of what's there. The statuses is the list of tweets in the JSON object, and the actual text of the tweets can be accessed with the key text.

Depending on how actively Twitter users have been posting about Python recently, you may see different results even if you run this script again in only a few minutes.[13] Of course you can change this search to contain any query term you want; just modify the value of the search_params variable as you like. To see all the possible parameters and their valid values, you can look through the API documentation for this particular Twitter API endpoint (*https://developer.twitter.com/en/docs/twitter-api/v1/tweets/search/api-reference/get-search-tweets*).

And that's it! While there are a number of different APIs that Twitter makes available (others allow you to actually post to your own timeline or even someone else's), for the purposes of accessing and wrangling data, what we've covered here should be enough to get you started with this and other similar APIs.

API Ethics

Now that you know how to make API requests from services like Twitter (and others that use an OAuth process), you may be imagining all the cool things you can do with the data you can collect. Before you start writing dozens of scripts to track the conversations happening around your favorite topics online, however, it's time to do both some practical and ethical reflection.

First, know that almost every API uses *rate-limiting* to restrict how many data requests you can make within a given time interval. On the particular API endpoint we used in Example 5-7, for example, you can make a maximum of 450 requests in a 15-minute time period, and each request can return a maximum of 100 tweets. If you exceed this, your data requests will probably fail to return data until Twitter determines that the next 15-minute window has begun.

Second, while you probably didn't read the Developer Agreement in detail (don't worry, you're not alone;[14] you can always find a reference copy online (*https://developer.twitter.com/en/developer-terms/agreement-and-policy*)), it includes provisions that have important practical and ethical implications. For example, Twitter's Developer Agreement *specifically* prohibits the practice of "Off-Twitter matching"—that is, combining Twitter data with other information about a user, unless that user has provided you the information directly or expressly provided their consent. It also

---

13 Remember that each time you run the script, you will also overwrite your output file, so it will only ever contain the most recent results.

14 Aleecia M. McDonald and Lorrie Faith Cranor, "The Cost of Reading Privacy Policies," *I/S: A Journal of Law and Policy for the Information Society* 4 (2008): 543, *https://kb.osu.edu/bitstream/handle/1811/72839/ISJLP_V4N3_543.pdf*, and Jonathan A. Obar and Anne Oeldorf-Hirsch, "The Biggest Lie on the Internet: Ignoring the Privacy Policies and Terms of Service Policies of Social Networking Services," *Information, Communication & Society* 23 no. 1 (2020): 128–147, *https://papers.ssrn.com/sol3/papers.cfm?abstract_id=2757465*.

---

contains rules about how you can store and display Twitter content that you may get from the API, and a whole host of other rules and restrictions.

Whether or not those terms of service are legally binding,[15] or truly ethical in and of themselves, remember that it is ultimately *your* responsibility to make sure that you are gathering, analyzing, storing, and sharing *any* data you use in an ethical way. That means taking into account the privacy and security of the people you may be using data about, as well as thinking about the implications of aggregating and sharing it.

Of course, if ethical issues were easy to identify and agree upon, we would live in a very different world. Because they aren't, many organizations have well-defined review processes and oversight committees designed to help explore and (if possible) resolve ethical issues before, for example, research and data collection impacting humans ever begins. For my own part, I still find that a good place to start when trying to think through ethical issues is the "Society of Professional Journalists' Code of Ethics" (*https://spj.org/ethicscode.asp*). While that document doesn't cover every possible ethics situation in detail, it articulates some core principles that I think all data users would do well to consider when they are collecting, analyzing, and sharing information.

In the end, however, the most important thing is that *whatever* choices you make, you're ready to stand behind them. One of the great possibilities of data access and wrangling is the ability to uncover new information and generate new insights. Just as the skills for doing that are now entirely in your control, so is the responsibility for how you use them.

Web Scraping: The Data Source of Last Resort

While APIs are designed by companies and organizations with the specific intent of providing access to often rich, diverse datasets via the internet, there is still a whole lot of information online that only exists on form-based or highly formatted web pages as opposed to an API or even as a CSV or PDF. For situations like these, the only real solution is *web scraping*, which is the process of using code to programmatically retrieve the contents of a web page and systematically extract some amount of (usually) structured data from it.

The reason why I refer to web scraping as "the data source of last resort" is that it's both a technically and ethically complex process. Creating web scraping Python scripts almost always requires manually wading through a jumble of HTML code to locate the data you're looking for, typically followed by a significant amount of trial and error to successfully separate the information you want from everything you

---

15 Victoria D. Baranetsky, "Data Journalism and the Law," *Tow Center for Digital Journalism* (2018) *https://doi.org/10.7916/d8-15sw-fy51*.

don't. It's time-consuming, fiddly, and often frustrating. And if the web page changes even a little, you may have to start from scratch in order to make your script work with the updated page.

Web scraping is also ethically complicated because, for a variety of reasons, many website owners don't *want* you to scrape their pages. Poorly coded scraping programs can overwhelm the website, making it inaccessible to other users. Making lots of scripted data requests in quick succession can also drive up the website owner's costs, because they have to pay their own service provider to return all that data in a brief period. As a result, many websites explicitly prohibit web scraping in their Terms of Service.

At the same time, if important information—especially about powerful organizations or government agencies—is *only* available via a web page, then scraping may be your *only* option even if it goes against the Terms of Service. While it is *far* beyond the scope of this book to provide even pseudolegal advice on the subject, keep in mind that even if your scripts are written responsibly and there is a good, public-interest reason for your scraping activity, you may face sanction from the website owner (such as a "cease and desist" letter) or even legal action.

Because of this, I strongly recommend that before you start down the road of writing *any* web scraping script you work through the excellent decision tree by Sophie Chou shown in Figure 5-16.[16]

---

16 The accompanying blog post is also excellent: *https://storybench.org/to-scrape-or-not-to-scrape-the-technical-and-ethical-challenges-of-collecting-data-off-the-web*.

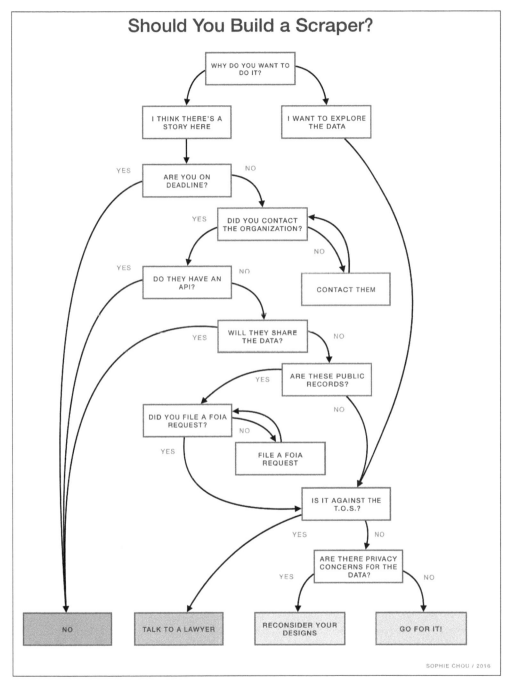

Figure 5-16. Web scraping decision tree (Sophie Chou for Storybench.org, 2016)

Once you've determined that scraping is your only/best option, it's time to get to work.

Carefully Scraping the MTA

For this example, we're going to use web scraping to download and extract data from a web page provided by New York City's Metropolitan Transit Authority (MTA), which provides links to all of the turnstile data for the city's subway stations, going back to 2010. To ensure that we're doing this as responsibly as possible, we're going to make sure that *any* Python script we write:

1. Identifies who we are and how to get in touch with us (in the example, we'll include an email address).

2. Pauses between web page requests to make sure that we don't overwhelm the server.

In addition, we'll structure and separate the parts of our script to make sure that we never download a particular web page more than absolutely necessary. To accomplish this, we'll start by downloading and saving a copy of the web page that contains the links to the individual turnstile data files. Then we'll write a separate script that goes through the *saved* version of the initial page and extracts the data we need. That way, any trial and error we go through in extracting data from the web page happens on our saved version, meaning it adds no additional load to the MTA's server. Finally, we'll write a third script that parses our file of extracted links and downloads the last four weeks of data.

Before we begin writing any code, let's take a look at the page we're planning to scrape (*http://web.mta.info/developers/turnstile.html*). As you can see, the page is little more than a header and a long list of links, each of which will take you to a comma-separated *.txt* file. To load the last several weeks of these data files, our first step is to download a copy of this index-style page (Example 5-8).

Example 5-8. MTA_turnstiles_index.py

```
# include the requests library in order to get data from the web
import requests

# specify the URL of the web page we're downloading
# this one contains a linked list of all the NYC MTA turnstile data files
# going back to 2010
mta_turnstiles_index_url = "http://web.mta.info/developers/turnstile.html"

# create some header information for our web page request
headers = {
    'User-Agent': 'Mozilla/5.0 (X11; CrOS x86_64 13597.66.0) ' + \
                  'AppleWebKit/537.36 (KHTML, like Gecko) ' + \
```

```
                'Chrome/88.0.4324.109 Safari/537.36',
    'From': 'YOUR NAME HERE - youremailaddress@emailprovider.som'
} ❶

# send a `get()` request for the URL, along with our informational headers
mta_web_page = requests.get(mta_turnstiles_index_url, headers=headers)

# open up a writable local file where we can save the contents of the web page
mta_turnstiles_output_file = open("MTA_turnstiles_index.html","w")

# write the `text` web page to our output file
mta_turnstiles_output_file.write(mta_web_page.text)

# close our output file!
mta_turnstiles_output_file.close()
```

❶ Since we're *not* using an API here, we want to proactively provide the website owner with information about who we are and how to contact us. In this case, we're describing the browser it should treat our traffic as being from, along with our name and contact information. This is data that the website owner will be able to see in their server logs.

Now you'll have a file called *MTA_turnstiles_index.html* in the same folder where your Python script was located. To see what it contains, you can just double-click on it, and it should open in your default web browser. Of course, because we only downloaded the raw code on the page and none of the extra files, images, and other materials that it would normally have access to on the web, it's going to look a little wonky, probably something like what's shown in Figure 5-17.

Fortunately, that doesn't matter at all, since what we're after here is the list of links that's stored with the page's HTML. Before we worry about how to pull that data programmatically, however, we first need to find it within the page's HTML code. To do this, we're going to use our web browser's *inspection tools*.

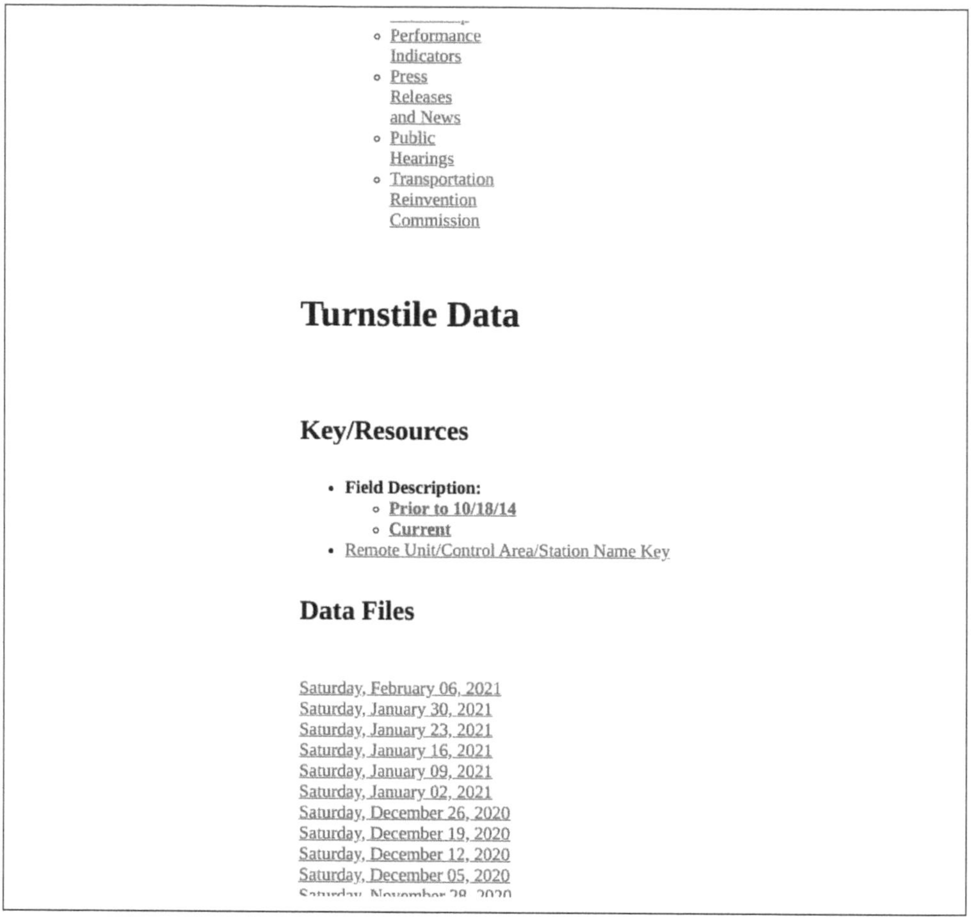

Figure 5-17. Viewing our local copy of the MTA web page in a browser

Using Browser Inspection Tools

With the local copy of the MTA turnstile data page open in a browser in front of you, scroll down until you can see the "Data Files" header, as shown in Figure 5-17. To better target *just* the information we want on this web page with our Python script, we need to try to identify something unique about HTML code that surrounds it—this will make it easier for us to have our script zero in quickly on just the content we want. The easiest way to do this is by "inspecting" the code alongside the regular browser interface.

To get started, put your mouse cursor over the "Data Files" text and context-click (also known as "right-click" or sometimes "Ctrl+click," depending on your system). At the bottom of the menu that pops up, shown in Figure 5-18, choose "Inspect."

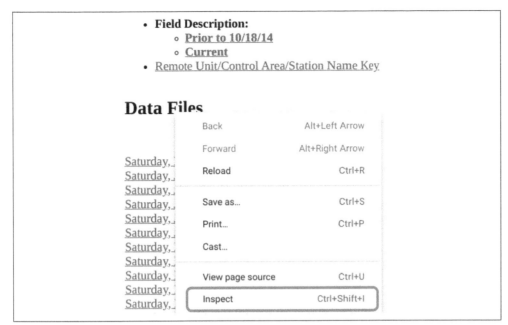

Figure 5-18. The context menu on our local copy of the MTA web page

While the precise location and shape of your particular browser's inspection tools window will vary (this screenshot is from the Chrome browser), its contents will hopefully look at least somewhat similar to the image in Figure 5-19.

Figure 5-19. Inspection tools example

Wherever your own window appears (sometimes it is anchored to the side or bottom of your browser window, and, as in Figure 5-19, there are often multiple panes of information), the main thing we want to locate in the inspection tools window are the words "Data Files." If you lost them (or never saw them in the first place!) once the window appeared, just move your mouse over those words on the web page and context-click to open the inspection tools window again.

Making the Most of Inspection Tools

Browser inspection tools can be useful in a lot of ways, but they are especially important in web scraping, when we want to find unique ways to identify specific chunks of information on a web page. Once you have them open, hovering over a piece of code will visibly highlight the part of the web page it corresponds to. By moving around the code in the inspection tools window with your mouse, you can highlight corresponding parts of the web page's visual interface, allowing you to write your script to more precisely grab the parts of the page you need.

In this case, if you use your mouse to hover over the code in the inspection tools window that says:

```
<div class="span-84 last">
```

you should see the "Data Files" section of the web page highlighted in your browser window. Based on the area highlighted, it *appears* that this bit of code includes the entire list of links we're interested in, which we can confirm by scrolling down in the inspection tools window. There we'll see that all of the data links we want (which end in *.txt*) are indeed inside this div (notice how they are indented beneath it? That's another instance of nesting at work!). Now, if we can confirm that class `span-84 last` only exists in one place on the web page, we have a good starting point for writing our Python script to extract the list of links.

The Python Web Scraping Solution: Beautiful Soup

Before we begin writing our next Python script, let's confirm that the `span-84 last` class really is unique on the page we downloaded. The simplest way to do this is to first open the page in Atom (context-click on the filename instead of double-clicking, and choose Atom from the "Open with" menu option), which will show us the page's code. Then do a regular "find" command (Ctrl+F or command+F) and search for `span-84 last`. As it turns out, even the `span-84` part only appears once in our file, so we can confine our Python script to looking for link information nested within that HTML tag.

Now we're ready to start writing the Python script that will extract the links from the web page. For this we'll install and use the *Beautiful Soup* library, which is widely used for parsing the often messy markup we find on web pages. While *Beautiful Soup* has some functionality overlap with the *lxml* library that we used in Example 4-12, the main difference between them is that *Beautiful Soup* can handle parsing even

---

less-than-perfectly-structured HTML and XML—which is what we invariably have to deal with on the web. In addition, *Beautiful Soup* lets us "grab" bits of markup by almost any feature we want—class name, tag type, or even attribute value—so it's pretty much the go-to library for pulling data out of the "soup" of markup we often find online. You can read the full documentation for the library (*https://crummy.com/ software/BeautifulSoup/bs4/doc*), but the easiest way to install it will be the same process we've used for other libraries, by using `pip` on the command line:

```
pip install beautifulsoup4
```

Now, we're ready to use Python to open the local copy of our web page and use the *Beautiful Soup* library to quickly grab all the links we need and write them to a simple *.csv* file, as shown in Example 5-9.

Example 5-9. MTA_turnstiles_parsing.py

```python
# import the Beautiful Soup recipe from the bs4 library
from bs4 import BeautifulSoup

# open the saved copy of our MTA turnstiles web page
# (original here: http://web.mta.info/developers/turnstile.html)
mta_web_page = open("MTA_turnstiles_index.html", "r")

# define the base URL for the data files
base_url = "http://web.mta.info/developers/"  ❶

# the `BeautifulSoup` recipe takes the contents of our web page and another
# "ingredient", which tells it what kind of code it is working with
# in this case, it's HTML
soup = BeautifulSoup(mta_web_page, "html.parser")

# using the "find" recipe, we can pass a tag type and class name as
# "ingredients" to zero in on the content we want.
data_files_section = soup.find("div", class_="span-84 last")  ❷

# within that div, we can now just look for all the "anchor" (`a`) tags
all_data_links = data_files_section.find_all("a")

# need to open a file to write our extracted links to
mta_data_list = open("MTA_data_index.csv","w")

# the `find_all()` recipe returns a list of everything it matches
for a_link in all_data_links:

    # combine our base URL with the contents of each "href" (link) property,
    # and store it in `complete_link`
    complete_link = base_url+a_link["href"]

    # write this completed link to our output file, manually adding a
    # newline `\n` character to the end, so each link will be on its own row
```

```
    mta_data_list.write(complete_link+"\n")

# once we've written all the links to our file, close it!
mta_data_list.close()
```

❶ If we click one of the data links on the live copy of the web page, we see that
the first part of the URL where the actual data file lives is `http://web.mta.info/developers/`, but each link only contains the latter half of the URL (in the format
`data/nyct/turnstile/turnstile_YYMMDD.txt`). So that our download script has
working links, we need to specify the "base" URL.

❷ Thanks to our work with the inspection tools, we can go straight to a `div` with
the class `span-84 last` to start looking for the links we want. Note that because
the word `class` has a special meaning in Python, Beautiful Soup appends an
underscore to the end when we're using it here (e.g., `class_`).

OK! What we should have now is a new file that contains a list of all the data links
we're interested in. Next we need to read that list in using a new script and download
the files at those URLs. However, because we want to be careful not to overload the
MTA website by downloading the files too quickly, we're going to use the built-in
Python *time* library to space out our requests by a second or two each. Also, we'll
be sure to only download the four files that we really want, rather than downloading
everything just for the sake of it. To see how this second script is organized, take a
look at Example 5-10.

Example 5-10. MTA_turnstiles_data_download.py

```
# include the requests library in order to get data from the web
import requests

# import the `os` Python library so we can create a new folder
# in which to store our downloaded data files
import os

# import the `time` library
import time ❶

# open the file where we stored our list of links
mta_data_links = open("MTA_data_index.csv","r")

# create a folder name so that we can keep the data organized
folder_name = "turnstile_data"

# add our header information
headers = {
    'User-Agent': 'Mozilla/5.0 (X11; CrOS x86_64 13597.66.0) ' + \
                  'AppleWebKit/537.36 (KHTML, like Gecko) ' + \
```

```
                    'Chrome/88.0.4324.109 Safari/537.36',
    'From': 'YOUR NAME HERE - youremailaddress@emailprovider.som'
}

# the built-in `readlines()` function converts our data file to a
# list, where each line is an item
mta_links_list = mta_data_links.readlines()

# confirm there isn't already a folder with our chosen name
if os.path.isdir(folder_name) == False:

    # create a new folder with that name
    target_folder = os.mkdir(folder_name)

# only download the precise number of files we need
for i in range(0,4):

    # use the built-in `strip()` method to remove the newline (`\n`)
    # character at the end of each row/link
    data_url = (mta_links_list[i]).strip()

    # create a unique output filename based on the url
    data_filename = data_url.split("/")[-1]  ❷

    # make our request for the data
    turnstile_data_file = requests.get(data_url, headers=headers)

    # open a new, writable file inside our target folder
    # using the appropriate filename
    local_data_file = open(os.path.join(folder_name,data_filename), "w")

    # save the contents of the downloaded file to that new file
    local_data_file.write(turnstile_data_file.text)

    # close the local file
    local_data_file.close()

    # `sleep()` for two seconds before moving on to the next item in the loop
    time.sleep(2)
```

❶ This library will let us "pause" our downloading script between data requests so that we don't overload the MTA server with too many requests in too short a time period (and possibly get in trouble).

❷ Here, we're splitting the link URL on slashes, then taking the last item from the resulting list using negative indexing (*https://w3schools.com/python/ gloss_python_string_negative_indexing.asp*), which counts backward from the end of the string. This means that the item at position -1 is the last item, which here is the *.txt* filename. This is the filename we'll use for the local copy of the data that we save.

If everything has gone well, you should now have a new folder called *turnstile_data*, with the four most recent turnstile data files saved inside it. Pretty neat, right?

Conclusion

Now that we have explored the many ways to actually *get* the data we're after and convert it into formats we can use, the next question is: what do we *do* with it all? Since the goal of all this data wrangling is to be able to answer questions and generate some insight about the world, we now need to move on from the process of *acquiring* data and start the process of assessing, improving, and analyzing it. To this end, in the next chapter we'll work through a data quality evaluation of a public dataset, with an eye toward understanding both its possibilities and limitations and how our data wrangling work can help us make the most of it.

# CHAPTER 6

Assessing Data Quality

Over the past two chapters, we've focused our efforts on identifying and accessing different formats of data in different locations—from spreadsheets to websites. But getting our hands on (potentially) interesting data is really only the beginning. The next step is conducting a thorough quality assessment to understand if what we have is useful, salvageable, or just straight up garbage.

As you may have gleaned from reading Chapter 3, crafting quality data is a complex and time-consuming business. The process is roughly equal parts research, experimentation, and dogged perseverance. Most importantly, committing to data quality means that you have to be willing to invest significant amounts of time and energy—and *still be willing to throw it all out and start over* if, despite your best efforts, the data you have just can't be brought up to par.

When it comes down to it, in fact, that last criterion is probably what makes doing really high-quality, meaningful work with data truly difficult. The technical skills, as I hope you are already discovering, take some effort to master but are still highly achievable with sufficient practice. Research skills are a bit harder to document and convey, but working through the examples in this book will help you develop many of them, especially those related to the information discovery and collation needed for assessing and improving data quality.

When it comes to reconciling yourself to the fact that, after dozens of hours of work, you may need to "give up" on a dataset because its flaws are too deep or widespread, the only advice I can offer is that you try to remember that *learning meaningful things about the world is a "long game."* That's why I always suggest that folks interested in learning about how to do data wrangling and analysis start by identifying a question about the world that is truly interesting and/or important to them. To do this work well, you have to care *more* about getting it right than about getting it "done." But it also helps if you truly value what you learn in the *process* of data wrangling—whether because you learn a new Python or data wrangling strategy or because you make contact with a new expert or discover a new information resource. In truth, the effort of doing good data work is never wasted if you really care about the topic you're exploring. It's just that it can lead you in a different direction than you expected.

Often, you will find that while a dataset cannot answer your original question, it can still shed light on some key aspect of it. Other times, you may find that there's *no* data on the subject you're exploring, and you may be able to leverage that fact to get help—discovering what data *doesn't* exist may prompt you—and others—to change focus entirely. And since there will *never* be a "perfect" dataset, there are times when you may choose to *very carefully* share data that you know has flaws, because even the partial insight it offers has important public interest benefits. What matters in every case is that you are willing to personally take responsibility for the choices you make—because no matter what the "original" data was or where it came from, the cleaned, augmented, transformed, and/or analyzed dataset is still *yours*.

If this feels a little overwhelming—well, that's not entirely an accident. We are living in a moment when it is too easy to wield powerful digital tools without considering their real-world consequences, and where the people building "advanced" technologies are writing the algorithmic rules largely in their own favor.[1] In the end, data can be a mechanism for informing *and* manipulating, for explaining *and* exploiting. Ensuring which side of those lines your work falls on is ultimately up to you.

But what does achieving data quality really mean in practice? To get a sense of this, we'll spend the remainder of this chapter evaluating real-world data in terms of the aspects of data *integrity* and data *fit* introduced in Chapter 3. The dataset we'll use for this is a single instance of loan data from the US Paycheck Protection Program (PPP), which contains information about millions of loans to small businesses during the COVID-19 pandemic. As we'll encounter firsthand throughout the remainder of this chapter, the PPP data exemplifies many of the challenges common in "found" data, whether it is compiled by government agencies or private companies: unclear terms and unexplained changes from one version of the data to the next leave room for data *fit* issues that will require additional research to address. More straightforward (though not necessarily faster to resolve) are the data *integrity* issues—like confirming whether a given bank is spelled the same way throughout the dataset or that our data file(s) contain the values and time ranges they ought to. While we will find our way through most of these challenges, in the end our insights will be high confidence, *not* incontrovertible. As with all data work, they will be the cumulative result of informed decisions, logical reasoning, and a whole *lot* of data wrangling. To get that wrangling done, the Python library we'll rely on most is *pandas*, which offers a popular and powerful set of tools for working with table-type data. Let's get started!

---

1 Even if they don't always realize it.

The Pandemic and the PPP

In the spring of 2020, the US government announced a loan program designed to help stabilize the American economy in the face of job losses related to the COVID-19 pandemic. With designated funding of nearly $1 trillion,[2] the objective of the PPP was ostensibly to help small businesses pay rent and keep paying employees despite sometimes mandatory closures and other restrictions. Although a drop in unemployment appeared to follow the first roll-out of funds, some parts of the federal government seemed determined to resist calls for transparency about where the money had gone.[3]

So did the PPP loans help save American small businesses? Now that some time has passed, one might imagine that would be a straightforward enough question to answer—but we're here to find out for ourselves. To do that we'll look at the data, of course, starting with a systematic assessment of its overall quality, in which we review our PPP loan data for each of the characteristics of data *integrity* and data *fit*, in turn. Just as importantly, we're going to *carefully document* each part of this process so that we have a record of what we did, the choices we made, and the reasoning behind them. This data diary will be a crucial resource for us in the future, especially should we need to explain or reproduce any of our work. While you can use whatever form and format you prefer, I like to keep my formatting simple and have my data diary live near my code, so I'm going to document my work in a markdown file that I can easily back up to and read on GitHub.[4] Since this file is really a running tally of everything I'm doing, I'm going to call it *ppp_process_log.md*.

Assessing Data Integrity

Should you begin your data wrangling process by assessing data integrity or data fit? Unsurprisingly: a little of both. As discussed in "What Is "Data Wrangling"?" on page 2, you should never really start a data wrangling process unless you have some sort of question you're looking to answer and some sense that a particular dataset can help you answer it—in other words, until you have some idea where your data wrangling process is going and that your data is "fit" for it. At the same time, fully assessing a dataset's fit is often difficult until its integrity has been explored. For example, if there are gaps in the data, can they be filled in somehow? Can missing metadata be located? If so, then we may be able to resolve these integrity issues and return to

---

2 See *https://en.wikipedia.org/wiki/Paycheck_Protection_Program* for details on the PPP.

3 "Who Got Half a Trillion in COVID Loans? The Trump Administration Won't Say," *https://marketplace.org/shows/make-me-smart-with-kai-and-molly/who-got-half-a-billion-in-covid-loans-the-trump-administration-wont-say.*

4 You can find a good markdown cheatsheet at *https://github.com/adam-p/markdown-here/wiki/Markdown-Here-Cheatsheet.*

the assessment of fit with more complete information. If we then find that we can improve the data's fit by augmenting it (which we'll explore in detail in Chapter 7), of course, this will initiate *another* round of data integrity assessments. And then the cycle begins again.

If you suspect that this will lead to an infinite loop of data wrangling, you're not *entirely* wrong; all good questions will generate others, so there's always more to learn. That said, the time, energy, and other resources we can dedicate to data wrangling are *not* infinite, which is why we have to make informed decisions and document them. Thoroughly assessing our data's quality will help us make those decisions well. By methodically examining your data for integrity and fit, you ensure that you not only end up with high-quality data but also that you make and document decisions that you can use to describe (and even defend, if necessary) any insights you generate. This doesn't mean that everyone will agree with your conclusions. It does, however, help ensure you can have a meaningful discussion about them—and that's what really advances knowledge.

So without further ado, let's dive into our data integrity evaluation!

Much of the data used in this chapter has since been removed from the internet and/or replaced with other files—this is not unusual. I have intentionally left the content of this chapter largely intact despite these changes, because they reflect the very real and typical challenges of trying to do data wrangling work in anything close to real time.

It also illustrates how quickly—and almost untraceably—data can evolve and change in the digital world. Something to keep in mind. In the meantime, you can find all of the datasets referenced in this chapter on this Google Drive folder (*https://drive.google.com/file/d/1EtUB0nK9aQeWWWGUOiayO9Oe-avsKvXH/view?usp=sharing*).

Is It of Known Pedigree?

At the time of this writing, the first search result for the phrase "most recent PPP loan data" is a page on the US Department of the Treasury website that links to data from August 2020.[5] The second result links to more recent data, from the Small Business Administration (SBA)—the government department charged with actually administering the funds.[6]

---

5 The original link for this content was *https://home.treasury.gov/policy-issues/cares-act/assistance-for-small-businesses/sba-paycheck-protection-program-loan-level-data*, however it is now found at *https://home.treasury.gov/policy-issues/coronavirus/assistance-for-small-businesses/paycheck-protection-program*.

6 And this second link is *https://sba.gov/funding-programs/loans/coronavirus-relief-options/paycheck-protection-program/ppp-data*.

While both of these are legitimate sites for government agencies whose work is relevant to the PPP, it makes more sense for us to work principally with data published by the SBA. Still, it was *not* the first thing I found when I first went to look for this data.

I really want to highlight this because the Treasury Department is obviously both a reasonable and reputable source for the data we were seeking, but it was still not the *best* one available. That's why it matters to evaluate not just *where* your data came from but *how* you came to find it.

Is It Timely?

If we want to use data to learn something about the state of the world as it is *now*, the first thing we need to establish is *when* our data dates from—and confirm that it's the most recent available.

If this seems like it should be straightforward, think again—many websites don't automatically date every post, so even determining when something went online is often a challenge. Alternatively, a website that *does* date its content may change it any time a change (even an insubstantial one) is made; some sites may regularly update the "published" date in an attempt to game search engine algorithms that favor more recent content.

In other words, determining what is *actually* the most recent, relevant data for your particular data wrangling problem may well require some digging. The only way to know for sure will be to try a few different search terms, click through several sets of results, and maybe reach out to an expert for advice. In the process, you'll most likely find enough references to reassure you what the most recently available data is.

Is It Complete?

So far, we know that there have been multiple data releases for the PPP. While we can be pretty confident that we've successfully located the most *recent* data, the next question is: is this *all* the data?

Since we're primarily interested in businesses that received larger loans, we only have to worry about examining one file: *public_150k_plus.csv*.[7] But how can we know if this includes all phases of the program to date, or just the loans made since the *first* data release in August 2020? Since we have access to both sets of data,[8] we have a few strategies we can use:

---

7 You can download this file at *https://drive.google.com/file/d/1EtUB0nK9aQeWWWGUOiayO9Oe-avsKvXH/ view?usp=sharing*.

8 Data for August 2020 can be found at *https://drive.google.com/file/d/11wTOapbAzcfeCQVVB- YJFIpsQVaZxJAm/view?usp=sharing*; data for February 2021 can be found at *https://drive.google.com/file/d/ 1EtUB0nK9aQeWWWGUOiayO9Oe-avsKvXH/view?usp=sharing*.

1. Find the earliest date(s) in our "recent" data file and confirm that they are *before* August 8, 2020.

2. Compare the file sizes and/or row counts of the two datasets to confirm that the more recent file is larger than the older file.

3. Compare the data they contain to confirm that all the records in the earlier file already exist in the later file.

At this point you might be thinking, "Hang on, isn't confirming the earliest date enough? Why would we do the other two? Both of those seem much more difficult." Well, sure—in *theory*, just confirming that we have data from the earlier phases should be enough. But in truth, that's a pretty cursory check. Obviously, we cannot confirm that the data the federal government has released is complete by trying to go out and collect more comprehensive data ourselves. On the other hand (and as we'll see shortly), the data collection processes of governments and large organizations (including—and perhaps especially—banks) are far from perfect.[9] Since we'll be taking ownership of this data if we use it to draw conclusions, I think it's worth being thorough.

Happily, conducting our first "completeness" check is quite simple: just by opening the data in a text editor, we can see that the first entry contains a "DateApproved" value of *05/01/2020*, suggesting that the recent dataset *does* in fact include data from the first round of PPP loans, which were disbursed in the spring of 2020, as shown in Figure 6-1.

Figure 6-1. Quick text editor view of recent PPP loan data

---

9 Following the 2008 financial crisis, for example, it became clear that many banks had not kept proper records as they repackaged and sold—or "securitized"—home mortgages, leading some courts to reject their attempts to foreclose on homeowners (*https://nytimes.com/2009/10/25/business/economy/25gret.html*).

That was easy! If we want to go a little bit further, we can always write a quick script to find the oldest and most recent LoanStatus dates in the recent data. To avoid confusion, I've renamed the more recent file *public_150k_plus_recent.csv*. Currently,[10] following the data linked from *https://home.treasury.gov/policy-issues/cares-act/assistance-for-small-businesses/sba-paycheck-protection-program-loan-level-data* leads to a *different* folder on the SBA Box account, which shows an upload date of August 14, 2020 (*https://sba.app.box.com/s/ox4mwmvli4ndbp14401xr411m8sefx3i*). We have to download the entire folder, *150k plus 0808.zip*, but we can pull out the CSV and rename it *public_150k_plus_080820.csv*.

To help us with this process, we will, as usual, be looking for a library to smooth the way—this time in the form of Pandas, a well-known Python library for manipulating table-type data. While we won't examine the *pandas* library in detail here (there is already an excellent O'Reilly book, *Python for Data Analysis*, written by the creator of Pandas, Wes McKinney!), we will definitely make use of its many helpful features in carrying out our data quality checks going forward.

To start with, we'll need to install the library by running the following from the command line:

```
pip install pandas
```

Now, let's use it to pull in the recent PPP loan data and see what the earliest and latest dates are in that file, as shown in Example 6-1.

Example 6-1. ppp_date_range.py

```
# quick script for finding the earliest and latest loan dates in the PPP loan
# data

# importing the `pandas` library
import pandas as pd ❶

# read the recent data into a pandas DataFrame using its `read_csv()` method
ppp_data = pd.read_csv('public_150k_plus_recent.csv')

# convert the values in the `DateApproved` column to *actual* dates
ppp_data['DateApproved'] = pd.to_datetime(ppp_data['DateApproved'],
                                          format='%m/%d/%Y') ❷

# print out the `min()` and `max()` values in the `DateApproved` column
print(ppp_data['DateApproved'].min())
print(ppp_data['DateApproved'].max())
```

---

10 The following links are included for posterity, as they represent the original locations from which the datasets provided with this chapter are drawn.

❶ Using the **as** keyword here lets us create a nickname for the library so that we can refer to it in fewer characters later in our code.

❷ In order to find the oldest and most recent dates, we need to first convert the (string) values in our dataset to *actual* **Date** data types. Here, we'll use the Pandas **to_datetime()** function and provide it with (1) the column we want converted (*https://pandas.pydata.org/pandas-docs/stable/reference/api/pandas.to_datetime.html*), and (2) the format of the dates (*https://docs.python.org/3/library/datetime.html#strftime-and-strptime-behavior*) as they *currently* appear in our dataset.

As we can see from the following output, the earliest loan in this dataset was made on April 3, 2020, and the most recent was made on January 31, 2021:

```
2020-04-03 00:00:00
2021-01-31 00:00:00
```

Note that while we don't *absolutely* have to pass the **format** ingredient to the Pandas **to_datetime()** function, it's always a good idea to do so; if we don't provide this information, then Pandas has to try to "guess" what date format it's looking at, which can make the actual processing take a long time. Here it only saves us about a second of processing time—but with larger datasets (or more than one), that can quickly add up!

Now let's compare the file size of the recent data with the one that was released in August 2020. Just looking at the *public_150k_plus_recent.csv* and the *public_150k_plus_080820.csv* files in a finder window, we can see that the file size of the more recent data is *much* larger than the earlier one: the August data is ~124 MB, while the recent data is several hundred megabytes. So far so good.

Drawing on the techniques we used in Example 4-7 and Example 5-10, let's write a quick script to determine how many rows of data are in each file, as shown in Example 6-2.

Example 6-2. ppp_numrows.py

```
# quick script to print out the number of rows in each of our PPP loan data files
# this is a pretty basic task, so no need to import extra libraries!

# open the August PPP data in "read" mode
august_data = open("public_150k_plus_080820.csv","r")

# use `readlines()` to convert the lines in the data file into a list
print("August file has "+str(len(august_data.readlines()))+" rows.") ❶

# ditto for the recent PPP data
recent_data = open("public_150k_plus_recent.csv","r")
```

```
# once again, print the number of lines
print("Recent file has "+str(len(recent_data.readlines()))+" rows.")
```

❶ Once the `readlines()` method has put the lines of our data file into a list, we can use the built-in `len()` method to determine how many there are. To print the result, we have to cast that number as a string with the built-in `str()` function first, or Python will yell at us.

Running this script confirms that while the file from August 2020 contains 662,516 rows, the more recent version (from February 1, 2021) contains 766,500 rows.

Finally, let's look at comparing the contents of the two files to confirm that everything in the earlier file appears in the newer file. This will undoubtedly be a multistep process, but let's start by opening up the August data file in a text editor, as shown in Figure 6-2.

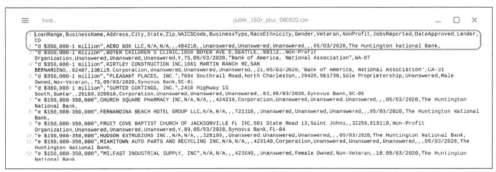

Figure 6-2. Quick text editor view of August 2020 PPP loan data

Right away it's clear there are some…differences, which will make this particular check even more complicated than we might have anticipated. First, it's clear that there are *many* more columns of data in the more recent file, which means that we'll need to devise a strategy for matching up the records from the earlier dataset to the most recent one.

First, we need to get a handle on which data columns seem to overlap between the two files. We'll do that by creating and comparing two small *sample* CSV files, each containing the first several rows of data from each dataset.

Next, we'll write a quick script that converts each of our source files into a `DataFrame` —a special Pandas data type for table-type data—and then writes the first few rows to a separate CSV, as shown in Example 6-3.

Example 6-3. ppp_data_samples.py

```
# quick script for creating new CSVs that each contain the first few rows of
# our larger data files

# importing the `pandas` library
import pandas as pd

# read the august data into a pandas DataFrame using its `read_csv()` method
august_ppp_data = pd.read_csv('public_150k_plus_080820.csv')

# the `head()` method returns the DataFrame's column headers
# along with the first 5 rows of data
august_sample = august_ppp_data.head()

# write those first few rows to a CSV called `august_sample.csv`
# using the pandas `to_csv()` method
august_sample.to_csv('august_sample.csv', index=False) ❶

# read the recent data into a pandas DataFrame using its `read_csv()` method
recent_ppp_data = pd.read_csv('public_150k_plus_recent.csv')

# the `head()` method returns the DataFrame's column headers
# along with the first 5 rows of data
recent_sample = recent_ppp_data.head()

# write those first few rows to a CSV called `recent_sample.csv`
recent_sample.to_csv('recent_sample.csv', index=False)
```

❶ The *pandas* `to_csv()` method encapsulates several steps we've previously done in plain-old Python: opening a new writable file and saving data to it. Because Pandas adds an index column (which essentially includes row numbers) to every DataFrame it creates, however, we need to include the second "ingredient" of `index=False` because we *don't* want those row numbers to appear in our output CSV.

Now that we have our two smaller file samples, let's open them up and just look through them to visually compare both the column headers and their contents. You can see screenshots of the August data in Figure 6-3, while the more recent data is shown in Figure 6-4.

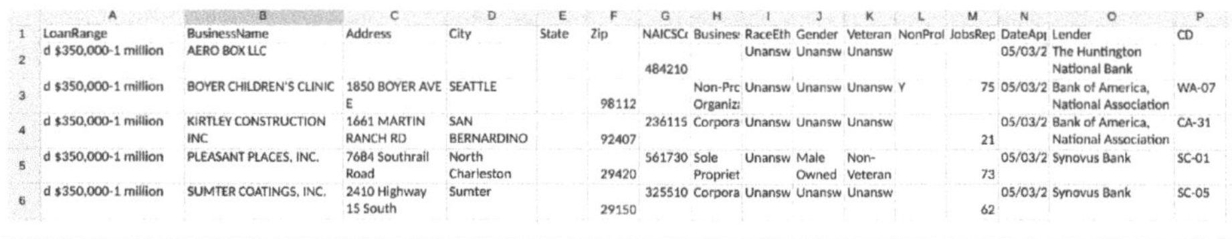

	A	B	C	D	E	F	G	H	I	J	K	L	M	N	O	P
1	LoanRange	BusinessName	Address	City	State	Zip	NAICSCo	Busines	RaceEth	Gender	Veteran	NonProf	JobsRep	DateApp	Lender	CD
2	d $350,000-1 million	AERO BOX LLC					484210		Unansw	Unansw	Unansw			05/03/2	The Huntington National Bank	
3	d $350,000-1 million	BOYER CHILDREN'S CLINIC	1850 BOYER AVE E	SEATTLE		98112		Non-Prc Organiz	Unansw	Unansw	Unansw	Y	75	05/03/2	Bank of America, National Association	WA-07
4	d $350,000-1 million	KIRTLEY CONSTRUCTION INC	1661 MARTIN RANCH RD	SAN BERNARDINO		92407	236115	Corpora	Unansw	Unansw	Unansw		21	05/03/2	Bank of America, National Association	CA-31
5	d $350,000-1 million	PLEASANT PLACES, INC.	7684 Southrail Road	North Charleston		29420	561730	Sole Propriet	Unansw	Male Owned	Non-Veteran		73	05/03/2	Synovus Bank	SC-01
6	d $350,000-1 million	SUMTER COATINGS, INC.	2410 Highway 15 South	Sumter		29150	325510	Corpora	Unansw	Unansw	Unansw		62	05/03/2	Synovus Bank	SC-05

Figure 6-3. First few lines of August PPP loan data file

	A	B	C	D	E	F	G	H	I	J	K	L	M	N	O	P	Q	R	S
1	LoanNumber	DateApproved	SBAOffic	Processi	BorrowerName	Borrow	Borrow	Borrow	Borrow	LoanSta	LoanSta	Term	SBAGua	InitialAg	Current	Undisbu	Franchis	Servicin	Servicin
2	9547507704	05/01/2020	464	PPP	SUMTER COATINGS, INC.	2410 Highway 15 Soutl	Sumter		29150-9662	12/18/2	Paid in Full	24	100	9358.78	9358.78	0			Synovus Bank
3	9777677704	05/01/2020	464	PPP	PLEASANT PLACES, INC.	7684 Southra Road	North Charlest		29420-9000		Exempti 4	24	100	6927.79	6927.79	0	19248		Synovus Bank
4	5791407702	05/01/2020	1013	PPP	BOYER CHILDREN'S CLINIC	1850 BOYER AVE E	SEATTLE		98112-2922		Exempti 4	24	100	691355	691355	0	19248		Bank of Americz Nationa Associa
5	6223567700	05/01/2020	920	PPP	KIRTLEY CONSTRUCTION INC	1661 MARTIN RANCH RD	SAN BERNAR		92407-1740		Exempti 4	24	100	499871	499871	0	9551		Bank of Americz Nationa Associa
6	9662437702	05/01/2020	101	PPP	AERO BOX LLC						Exempti 4	24	100	367437	367437	0	9551		The Hunting Nationa Bank
																	57328		

Figure 6-4. First few lines of recent PPP loan data file

Luckily, it looks like the first few rows of both files contain at least *some* of the same entries. This will make it easier for us to compare their contents and (hopefully) identify which columns we can use to match up the rows.

Let's start by choosing a single entry to work with, ideally one with as many completed fields as possible. For example, something called SUMTER COATINGS, INC. appears on line 6 of the August data sample (as labeled in the spreadsheet interface) under the column heading BusinessName. On line 2 of the recent data sample, the same value appears under the column heading BorrowerName. In the August sample file, the term Synovus Bank appears in a column called Lender, while that term appears in the recent sample file in a column called ServicingLenderName. So far so good—or is it?

Although many details between these rows seem to match across the two data files, some seemingly important ones *don't*. For example, in the August data sample, the value in the DateApproved column is 05/03/2020; in the recent data sample, it is 05/01/2020. If we look at another seemingly shared entry, we see that for the business/borrower called PLEASANT PLACES, INC. (row 5 in the August data and row 3 in the recent data), the column titled CD in both files (spreadsheet column AF in the recent file, column P in the August file) has different values, showing SC-01 in the August data and SC-06 in the recent data. What's going on?

At this point, we have to make some judgment calls about *which* column values need to match in order for us to treat a particular loan row as the same between the two. Requiring that the business name and the lender name match seems like a good starting point. Since we know that multiple rounds of loans have been made by now, we probably want to require that the values in the DateApproved column match as well (even though it seems unlikely that Synovus Bank made two loans to Sumter Coatings, Inc. two days apart). What about the mismatched congressional district? If we look at a map of South Carolina's congressional districts, it's clear that their boundaries haven't been changed since 2013,[11] though it does seem like the 1st and the 6th district share a boundary. Given that, we might conclude that the discrepancy here is just a mistake.

As you can see, we're already finding some significant data quality issues—and we've only looked at five rows of data! Since we obviously can't resolve all of these differences at once, we need to start by putting together the rows that (we hope) really match, while making sure to keep track of any that don't. To do this, we'll need to *join* or *merge* the two datasets. Because we already know there will be discrepancies, however, we need a way to keep track of those as well. In other words, we want the file created by our join process to include *every* row from *both* datasets, whether they match or not. To do this, we need what's called an *outer* join (*https://pandas.pydata.org/pandas-docs/stable/user_guide/ merging.html#brief-primer-on-merge-methods-relational-algebra*). We'll make use of this in Example 6-4.

Note that because an outer join preserves *all* data rows, it's possible that our resulting dataset could have as many rows as the individual datasets combined—in this case about *1.4 million rows*. Don't worry, though! Python can handle it. But can your device?

If you have a Macintosh or Windows machine, chances are that working with the ~500 MB of data that we need to in these examples will be no problem. If, like me, you're working on a Chromebook or something similar, now's the moment to move to the cloud.

Example 6-4. ppp_data_join.py

```
# quick script for creating new CSVs that each contain the first few rows of
# our larger data files

# importing the `pandas` library
import pandas as pd

# read the august data into a pandas DataFrame using its `read_csv()` method
august_ppp_data = pd.read_csv('public_150k_plus_080820.csv')

# read the recent data into a pandas DataFrame using its `read_csv()` method
recent_ppp_data = pd.read_csv('public_150k_plus_recent.csv')

# now that we have both files in memory, let's merge them!
merged_data = pd.merge(august_ppp_data,recent_ppp_data,how='outer',
    left_on=['BusinessName','Lender','DateApproved'],right_on=['BorrowerName',
```

---

11 For South Carolina congressional districts, see Wikipedia's page at *https://en.wikipedia.org/wiki/South_Caro lina%27s_congressional_districts#Historical_and_present_district_boundaries.*

```
    'ServicingLenderName','DateApproved'],indicator=True) ❶

# `print()` the values in the "indicator" column,
# which has a default label of `_merge`
print(merged_data.value_counts('_merge')) ❷
```

❶ We're passing the indicator=True parameter here because it will create a new column that lets us know which rows appeared in one or both files.

❷ Using indicator=True produces a column called merge, whose value for each row shows which dataset that particular row matched on. As we'll see from the output, that value will be both, left_only, or right_only.

If everything went well, you get an output like this:

```
_merge
both          595866
right_only    171334
left_only      67333
dtype: int64
```

So what does this mean? It looks like our effort to match the August data with the recent data on business name, servicing lender name, and the date of the loan successfully matched 595,866 loans. The right_only loans are the *recent* loans that weren't matched (recent_ppp_data was the second argument to our pd.merge() function, so it is considered to be in the "right"); we found 171,334 of these. This seems perfectly plausible, since we can imagine that many new loans may have been issued since August.

The troubling number here is left_only: 67,333 loans that appear in the August data that were *not* matched to any loan row contained our recent dataset. That suggests that either our recent data is incomplete or we have some serious quality issues lurking.

From our very cursory examination of the sample data earlier, we already know that the DateApproved columns may have some problems, so let's see what happens if we eliminate the need to match on date. To do this, we'll just add the snippet in Example 6-5 to Example 6-4 but without specifying that the dates need to match. Let's see what happens.

Example 6-5. ppp_data_join.py (continued)

```
# merge the data again, removing the match on `DateApproved`
merged_data_no_date = pd.merge(august_ppp_data,recent_ppp_data,how='outer',
    left_on=['BusinessName','Lender'],right_on=['BorrowerName',
    'ServicingLenderName'],indicator=True)

# `print()` the values in the "indicator" column,
```

```
# which has a default label of `_merge`
print(merged_data_no_date.value_counts('_merge'))
```

Now we get an output something like this:

```
_merge
both          671942
right_only     96656
left_only      22634
dtype: int64
```

In other words, if we only require that the business name and lender match, then we "find" another ~45,000 loans from the August data in the recent data. Of course, what we *don't* know is how many of those new "matches" are the result of data entry errors (along the lines of our 05/03/2020 versus 05/01/2020 problem) and how many of them represent multiple loans.[12] All we know is that we're down to 22,634 loans from the August data that we can't locate in the recent data.

So what if we simply check whether a given business shows up in both datasets? This seems like the most basic form of comparison: in theory, the bank or lender servicing the PPP loan could change over the course of many months, or there could be additional mismatches because of (possibly) minor data-entry differences. Remember: our goal right now is simply to evaluate how far we can trust that the *recent* data includes all of the August data.

So let's add on a final, *very* relaxed merge to see what happens. Adding the snippet in Example 6-6, we'll match *only* on business name and see what we get.

Example 6-6. ppp_data_join.py (continued)

```
# merge the data again, matching only on `BusinessName`/`BorrowerName`
merged_data_biz_only = pd.merge(august_ppp_data,recent_ppp_data,how='outer',
    left_on=['BusinessName'],right_on=['BorrowerName'],indicator=True)

# `print()` the values in the "indicator" column,
# which has a default label of `_merge`
print(merged_data_biz_only.value_counts('_merge'))
```

And now our output is the following:

```
_merge
both          706349
right_only     77064
left_only       7207
dtype: int64
```

---

12 The SBA began accepting applications for so-called "second-round" PPP loans on January 31, 2021 (*https://uschamber.com/co/run/business-financing/second-draw-ppp-loans*).

Things are looking a little bit better: out of a total of 790,620 (706,349 + 77,064 + 7,207) possible loans, we've "found" all but 7,207—a little less than 0.1%. That's *pretty good*; we might be tempted to call that quantity of missing data a "rounding error" and move on. But before we get complacent about having accounted for 99.9% of all the PPP loans, let's stop for a moment and consider what that "small" amount of missing data really represents. Even if we assume that every one of those "missing" loans was for the minimum possible amount (recall that we're only looking at loans of $150,000 or more), that still means that our recent dataset has *at least* $1,081,050,000 —over $1 billion!—in possible loans that are unaccounted for. Given how hard I work to figure (and pay) my taxes every year, I certainly hope the federal government isn't simply going to "lose" $1 billion in taxpayer money and not worry about it. But what can *we* do to account for it? This is where we get to the part of data work that can be both daunting and energizing: it's time to talk to people!

While reaching out to subject matter experts is always a great place to start your data quality investigations, in this instance we have something even better: information about the lenders and loan recipients themselves. Between the business names and locations contained in the file, we can probably track down contact information for at least a handful of our "lost" 7,207 loans from the August dataset and try to find out what happened.

Before you pick up the phone and start calling people (and yes, most of the time you should be *calling*), however, figure out what you're going to ask. While it may be tempting to imagine that something nefarious is going on (are the lenders hiding money? Are the businesses misrepresenting themselves?), there is an old (and very malleable) quote that goes something like "Never attribute to malice that which can be explained by incompetence/stupidity/neglect."[13] In other words, it's likely that these loans don't appear in the more recent data because of some data-entry error, or even because *the loans simply never came through*.

And in fact, after calling a few autobody repair and barber shops around the country, that was the story I heard most often. Multiple people I spoke with described a similar pattern: they applied for a loan, had been told it was approved, and then—the money simply never came through. While it would be impractical to try to confirm that this was the case for every single "missing" loan, hearing basically the same story from multiple businesses that are thousands of miles apart makes me *reasonably* confident that these loans don't appear in the final dataset because the money was never actually sent.[14]

---

13 Attempting to attribute axioms is always problematic, but while I prefer the phrasing of *incompetence* or *neglect*, I like the attribution of this expression as "Hanlon's Razor" found in "The Jargon File" (*https://jargon-file.org/archive/jargon-4.4.7.dos.txt*), mostly because that document explains the origin of a lot of computer/programming slang.

14 Of course, *why* it was never sent is an interesting question unto itself.

Talk to Me!

If the idea of "cold calling" an individual or business and asking for information makes you nervous, you're not alone. What helps the most is practice—but giving yourself a brief script to follow can go a long way for those first few calls. Below is a simple outline of how to approach calling a business (which mostly applies to individuals as well) to ask for information. Set your assumptions aside, and remember that you're asking busy people for their time. If you are polite and considerate, you'll get much further!

1. Identify yourself. Give your name and where you're calling from, and (briefly) what you want to speak to them about.

2. Ask if they have a moment—don't launch into the reason for your call without finding out if they're busy first.

3. If you're not sure who to ask for, ask if the owner or a manager is available. If they're not, ask when is a good time to call back.

4. Ask politely who you're speaking to, and confirm their name. Thank them for their time and hang up.

Always make sure you take notes! If/when you call back, ask for the owner/manager by name (if you have it). Mention who you spoke to the first time you called and that they mentioned this might be a good time. Offer again to call back later, or try to make an appointment if possible.

Be clear and honest about why you're getting in touch, and articulate what you'll do with the information you're asking for as you're asking for it. *Never* identify anyone in published work without clearly obtaining their permission first.

At this point, it seems fairly clear that our recent PPP loan data is, in fact, "complete" for our purposes. While this may have felt like a lot of work to test our dataset for just one of almost a dozen data integrity measures, keep in mind that in the process, we've learned valuable information that will make many of our later "tests" much faster—or even trivial—to complete. So with that, let's turn to our next criterion.

Is It Well-Annotated?

Having satisfied ourselves that our data is appropriately *timely* and *complete*, we need to turn to understanding in detail what information the data columns in our recent PPP loan data actually contain.[15] As with our completeness assessment, one place we can start is with the data itself. By looking at the column names and some of the values they contain, we can start to get a sense of what we need more information about. If the column name seems descriptive and the data values we find in that column align with our interpretation of the column name, that's a pretty good starting point.

While we have a couple of options for reviewing our column names and their corresponding values, let's go ahead and take advantage of the sample files we created earlier. Because our screen width will generally prevent us from easily printing lots of columns of data (whereas we can easily scroll down to see more rows), we're going to start by *transposing* our sample data (that is, converting the columns to row and rows to columns) to make seeing the column titles easier.[16] We're also going to apply some additional data type filtering to make it easier for us to see what data is missing. Our first pass at this can be seen in Example 6-7.

Example 6-7. ppp_columns_review.py

```
# quick script for reviewing all the column names in the PPP data
# to see what we can infer about them from the data itself

# importing the `pandas` library
import pandas as pd

# read the recent data into a pandas DataFrame using its `read_csv()` method
ppp_data_sample = pd.read_csv('recent_sample.csv')

# convert all missing data entries to '<NA>' using the `convertdtypes()` method
converted_data_sample = ppp_data_sample.convert_dtypes() ❶

# transpose the whole sample
transposed_ppp_data_sample = converted_data_sample.transpose()

# print out the results!
print(transposed_ppp_data_sample)
```

---

15 You may have noticed that in this chapter, I haven't addressed our data integrity criteria in precisely the order I listed them in Chapter 3. Because the PPP was modeled on the existing 7(a) loan program (*https://journalo faccountancy.com/news/2020/apr/paycheck-protection-program-ppp-loans-sba-details-coronavirus.html*), I made the (questionable) assumption that this data would be well-annotated. Of course, these were also the *only* datasets available about the PPP, so my options were limited (as they so often are when working with real-world data).

16 I sometimes find it easier to think of transposing data as "turning it on its side."

❶ For the sake of speed, the Pandas `read_csv()` method converts all missing entries to `NaN` (Not a Number), as described at *https://pandas.pydata.org/pandas-docs/ stable/user_guide/missing_data.html*. To get these values converted to the more general (and intuitive) *<NA>* label, we apply the `convertdtypes()` method to the entire DataFrame, as described at *https://pandas.pydata.org/pandas-docs/sta ble/user_guide/missing_data.html#missing-data-na-conversion*.

As you can see in Figure 6-5, this lets us see all of the original column names as rows, along with a couple of the original rows as columns of data. By looking through these, we can start to get a sense of what we know—and what we don't.

Thanks to their relatively descriptive names, we can start to guess at what we are likely to find in many of these columns. For example, columns like `DateApproved`, `ProcessingMethod`, `BorrowerName`, `BorrowerAddress`, `BorrowerCity`, `BorrowerCity`, `BorrowerState`, and `BorrowerZip` are fairly straightforward. In some cases, the name is descriptive but doesn't give us all the information we need. For example, while `SBAGuarantyPercentage` gives us information about both the column's content and its units (presumably the amount of the loan guaranteed by the SBA, as a percent-age), the `Term` column doesn't tell us if the value should be interpreted as 24 days, weeks, months, or years. Likewise, while the values in `BusinessAgeDescription` are themselves descriptive (e.g., `Existing or more than 2 years old`), a `LoanStatus` value of `Exemption 4` doesn't really help us understand what happened to the loan. Finally, there are column names like `LMIIndicator` that might be easy for an expert to interpret but difficult for those of us not well-versed in loan jargon to identify.

What we really need at this point is a "data dictionary"—the term sometimes used to refer to the document that describes the contents of (especially) table-type data. Data dictionaries are important because while table-type data is very handy for conducting analyses, it doesn't inherently offer a way to include the type of *metadata*—that is, data *about* the data—that we need to answer questions like "What units should be used?" or "What do coded categories mean?" which are exactly the kinds of questions that come up frequently with complex datasets.

The most likely place to find a data dictionary should be the same location where we originally obtained the data (remember that in Chapter 4, we found the description of the *ghcnd-stations.txt* file linked from the *readme.txt* file in the same folder where the data was located). In this instance, that means going back to the SBA website (*https://sba.gov/funding-programs/loans/coronavirus-relief-options/ paycheck-protection-program/ppp-data*) and seeing what we can find.

```
LoanNumber                      9547507704 ...                    9662437702
DateApproved                    05/01/2020 ...                    05/01/2020
SBAOfficeCode                          464 ...                           101
ProcessingMethod                       PPP ...                           PPP
BorrowerName          SUMTER COATINGS, INC. ...                  AERO BOX LLC
BorrowerAddress      2410 Highway 15 South ...                          <NA>
BorrowerCity                        Sumter ...                          <NA>
BorrowerState                         <NA> ...                          <NA>
BorrowerZip                     29150-9662 ...                          <NA>
LoanStatusDate                  12/18/2020 ...                          <NA>
LoanStatus                    Paid in Full ...                   Exemption 4
Term                                    24 ...                            24
SBAGuarantyPercentage                  100 ...                           100
InitialApprovalAmount            769358.78 ...                      367437.0
CurrentApprovalAmount            769358.78 ...                      367437.0
UndisbursedAmount                        0 ...                             0
FranchiseName                         <NA> ...                          <NA>
ServicingLenderLocationID            19248 ...                         57328
ServicingLenderName          Synovus Bank ...  The Huntington National Bank
ServicingLenderAddress        1148 Broadway ...                  17 S High St
ServicingLenderCity               COLUMBUS ...                      COLUMBUS
ServicingLenderState                    GA ...                            OH
ServicingLenderZip              31901-2429 ...                    43215-3413
RuralUrbanIndicator                      U ...                             U
HubzoneIndicator                         N ...                             N
LMIIndicator                          <NA> ...                          <NA>
BusinessAgeDescription Existing or more than 2 years old ...     Unanswered
ProjectCity                         Sumter ...                          <NA>
ProjectCountyName                   SUMTER ...                          <NA>
ProjectState                            SC ...                          <NA>
ProjectZip                      29150-9662 ...                          <NA>
CD                                   SC-05 ...                          <NA>
JobsReported                            62 ...                            25
NAICSCode                           325510 ...                        484210
RaceEthnicity                   Unanswered ...                    Unanswered
UTILITIES_PROCEED                     <NA> ...                          <NA>
PAYROLL_PROCEED                  769358.78 ...                      367437.0
MORTGAGE_INTEREST_PROCEED             <NA> ...                          <NA>
RENT_PROCEED                          <NA> ...                          <NA>
REFINANCE_EIDL_PROCEED                <NA> ...                          <NA>
HEALTH_CARE_PROCEED                   <NA> ...                          <NA>
DEBT_INTEREST_PROCEED                 <NA> ...                          <NA>
BusinessType                   Corporation ...                          <NA>
OriginatingLenderLocationID          19248 ...                         57328
OriginatingLender            Synovus Bank ...  The Huntington National Bank
OriginatingLenderCity             COLUMBUS ...                      COLUMBUS
OriginatingLenderState                  GA ...                            OH
Gender                          Unanswered ...                    Unanswered
Veteran                         Unanswered ...                    Unanswered
NonProfit                             <NA> ...                          <NA>
```

Figure 6-5. Recent sample data transposed

At first, things look fairly promising. Under the "All Data" section on that page, we see a link promising a summary of "key data aspects," as shown in Figure 6-6.[17]

Figure 6-6. Landing page for PPP loan data on the SBA's website

Following the link (*https://sba.gov/document/report-paycheck-protection-program-ppp-loan-data-key-aspects*) brings us to a page that (as of this writing) lists two PDF documents from the summer of 2020. Unfortunately, neither of them seems to contain what we need—they are mostly filled with disclaimer-type text about how PPP loans are processed, though they do confirm our discovery that "canceled" loans will not appear in the database, as shown in Figure 6-7.

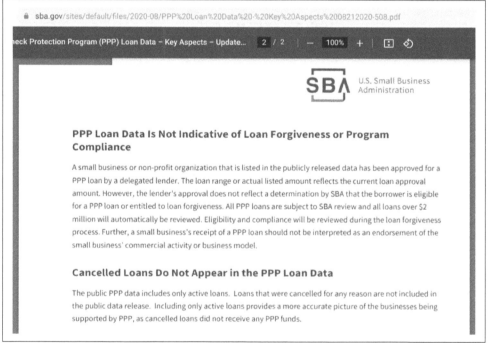

Figure 6-7. Excerpt of information to keep in mind when reviewing PPP data

---

17 This page has changed considerably since this chapter was originally written. Notably, the main data location now includes a "data dictionary"—but this was released only several months after the data was first posted.

Now what? We have a few options. We can turn to a more general research strategy in order to learn more about the PPP and hopefully fill in some of the blanks for ourselves. For example, reading enough articles on websites targeting potential PPP applicants will make clear that the appropriate units for the `Term` column is almost certainly weeks. Likewise, if we do enough web searches for the term `LMIIndicator`, `LMI Indicator`, and `LMI Indicator loans`, we'll eventually come across a Wikipedia page that suggests this term *may* be shorthand for "Loan Mortgage Insurance Indicator"—but we hardly know for sure.

In other words, it's once again time to look for some human help. But who can we reach out to? Scholars who have looked at the PPP data already are one place to start, but they might be hard to find if the data release is relatively recent. So, just as we did when trying to confirm what happened to all those missing loans from the August dataset, we're going to go straight to the source: the SBA. And fortunately, if we go back to the site where we downloaded our actual data files, as shown in Figure 6-8, it turns out there is a name attached to those uploads: Stephen Morris.[18]

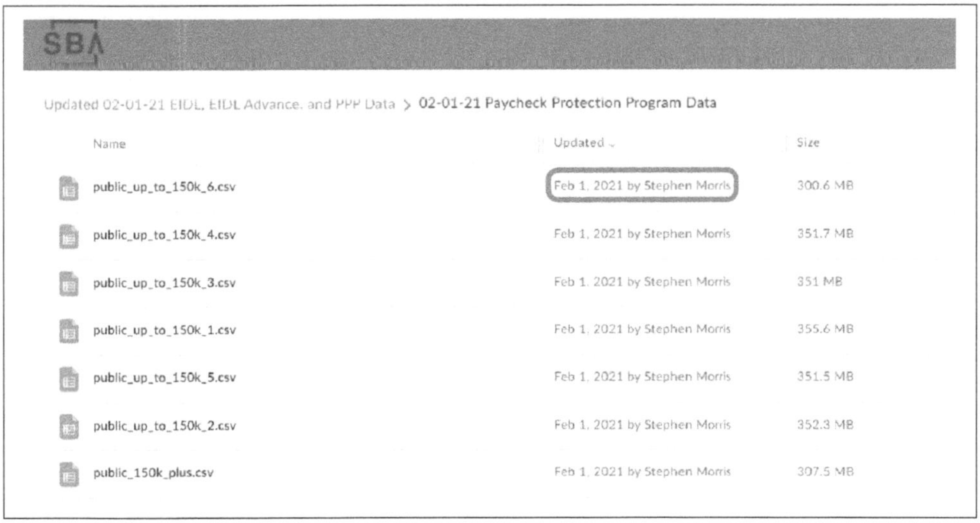

Figure 6-8. PPP data download portal

After placing a call and sending an email, I learned that, at the time of my inquiry, the SBA hadn't yet created a data dictionary for the PPP loan data, though Morris did refer me to both the original PDF and a data dictionary for the SBA's 7a loan program, on which the PPP loan structure was based. While the latter file (located at *https://data.sba.gov/dataset/7-a-504-foia*) still differed significantly from the PPP loan data columns, it did provide insight into some key elements. For example, that

---

18 It seems slightly noteworthy that this attribution was changed to SM shortly after I reached out to him.

file included a description of a column also called LoanStatus, whose possible values seem to parallel at least some of what we've found in the PPP loan data so far:

```
LoanStatus            Current status of loan:
                      • NOT FUNDED = Undisbursed
                      • PIF = Paid In Full
                      • CHGOFF = Charged Off
                      • CANCLD = Canceled
                      • EXEMPT = The status of loans that have been disbursed but
                          have not been canceled, paid in full, or charged off are
                          exempt from disclosure under FOIA Exemption 4
```

So is this data "well-annotated"? Somewhat. It's not as well annotated as, say, the NOAA data we worked with in "Finally, Fixed-Width" on page 114, but with some effort we'll probably be able to build up our own data dictionary for the PPP loan data that we can be pretty confident in.

Is It High Volume?

Since we have already finished our "completeness" review, we have largely already answered the question of whether the data we're using is *generally* high volume. There are few instances in which having more than 750,000 rows of data won't be sufficient for conducting at least *some* useful form of analysis.

At the same time, we also can't say yet exactly what types of analyses we'll be able to conduct, because the number of data rows we have doesn't matter if most of them are empty. So how can we check this? For columns where we only expect to find a few possible values, like LoanStatus, we can use the Pandas value_counts() method to summarize the contents. For columns that have very diverse values (such as BorrowerName or BorrowerAddress), we'll need to instead check specifically for *missing* values and then compare that to the total row count to get a sense of how much data might be missing. To start off with, we'll summarize the columns we expect will only contain a handful of distinct values, as shown in Example 6-8. We'll also count the NA entries in a more varied column—in this case, BorrowerAddress.

Example 6-8. ppp_columns_summary.py

```python
# quick script for reviewing all the column names in the PPP data
# to see what we can infer about them from the data itself

# importing the `pandas` library
import pandas as pd

# read the recent data sample into a pandas DataFrame
ppp_data = pd.read_csv('public_150k_plus_recent.csv')

# print the summary of values that appear in the `LoanStatus` column
print(ppp_data.value_counts('LoanStatus'))
```

```
# print the total number of entries in the `LoanStatus` column
print(sum(ppp_data.value_counts('LoanStatus')))

# print the summary of values that appear in the `Gender` column
print(ppp_data.value_counts('Gender'))

# print the total number of entries in the `Gender` column
print(sum(ppp_data.value_counts('Gender')))

# print how many rows do not list a value for `BorrowerAddress`
print(ppp_data['BorrowerAddress'].isna().sum())
```

The output from Example 6-8, shown in Example 6-9, starts to paint a picture of what kind of data is actually contained in our dataset's ~750,000 rows. For example, the status of most loans is "Exemption 4," which we know from our annotation investigation means it is "exempt from disclosure under FOIA Exemption 4."[19] Similarly, we can see that more than two-thirds of loan applicants did not indicate their gender when applying, and 17 loans don't even list the borrower's address!

Example 6-9. Recent data column summaries

```
LoanStatus
Exemption 4              549011
Paid in Full            110120
Active Un-Disbursed     107368
dtype: int64
766499

Gender
Unanswered       563074
Male Owned       168969
Female Owned      34456
dtype: int64
766499

17
```

So is this data "high volume"? Yes—while we're missing quite a lot of data overall, there seems to be useful information in a relatively high proportion of the rows and columns that we have. Keep in mind that in some cases, it's possible to generate useful insights about something with as little as a *few dozen* rows of data—as long as they contain truly meaningful information. That's why it's not sufficient to simply look at the size of a data file or even the number of rows it contains to confirm that it's truly

---

19 For more information on FOIA requests and exemptions, see "FOIA/L Requests" on page 377 and the full text of the exemption on the Department of Justice's website (*https://justice.gov/oip/exemption-4-after-supreme-courts-ruling-food-marketing-institute-v-argus-leader-media*).

"high volume"—we actually have to really examine the data in some detail in order to be sure.

Is It Consistent?

Another thing we know from our earlier completeness check is that the format of the PPP loan data absolutely was *not* consistent between August and later releases: the data published beginning in December 2020 was much more detailed than what had been released previously (*https://washingtonpost.com/business/2020/06/11/trump-administration-wont-say-who-got-511-billion-taxpayer-backed-coronavirus-loans*), and even most of the column names differed between the two files.

Since we're now relying only on the more recent data files, there is a different kind of consistency we need to think about: how consistent are the values within the dataset itself? We might hope, for example, that the same units will have been used in the dollar amount columns like `InitialApprovalAmount` and `CurrentApprovalAmount`. Still, it's better to check for errors just in case. In Example 6-10, we'll do another quick min/max confirmation to ensure that the figures for these fall within the range we expect.

Example 6-10. ppp_min_max_loan.py

```
# quick script for finding the minimum and maximum loans currently approved
# in our PPP loan dataset

# importing the `pandas` library
import pandas as pd

# read the recent data into a pandas DataFrame
ppp_data = pd.read_csv('public_150k_plus_recent.csv')

# use the pandas `min()` and `max()` methods to retrieve the
# largest and smallest values, respectively
print(ppp_data['CurrentApprovalAmount'].min())
print(ppp_data['CurrentApprovalAmount'].max())
```

Based on the title of our data file—*150k_plus*—we would expect that the *minimum* loan amount we'll find approved is $150,000. A quick web search for "maximum loan under ppp" leads to a document on the SBA website that indicates that for most types of businesses,[20] the maximum loan amount is $10 million. Indeed, running our script seems to confirm that this minimum and maximum are reflected in our data:

---

[20] Specifically, "Paycheck Protection Program: How to Calculate Maximum Loan Amounts for First Draw PPP Loans and What Documentation to Provide by Business Type," which can be found at *https://sba.gov/sites/default/files/2021-01/PPP%20--%20How%20to%20Calculate%20Maximum%20Loan%20Amounts%20for%20First%20Draw%20PPP%20Loans%20%281.17.2021%29-508.pdf*.

```
150000.0
10000000.0
```

At this point, we also want to check for one of the most common (and insidious) forms of inconsistency: spelling differences. *Anytime* you're dealing with data that has been entered by humans, there are going to be spelling issues: extra spaces, typos, and differences in punctuation, at minimum. This is a problem because if we want to be able to answer a seemingly simple question like "How many loans originated with lender X?" we need the spelling of that bank's name to be consistent throughout the data. And it's almost guaranteed that it won't be—at least at first.

Fortunately, because this is such a common data problem, there are a number of well-developed approaches for dealing with it. Here we're going to use an approach called *fingerprinting* to begin checking the consistency of bank name spellings in our dataset. While there are many ways that we could cluster these company names (phonetically, for example) when looking for differently spelled duplicates, we're choosing fingerprinting because it follows a simple, strict-but-effective *algorithm* (really, just a set of sets) that minimizes the risk that we'll end up matching up two names that really *shouldn't* be the same.

Specifically, the fingerprinting algorithm we'll be using does the following things:[21]

1. Removes leading and trailing whitespace
2. Changes all characters to their lowercase representation
3. Removes all punctuation and control characters
4. Normalizes extended Western characters to their ASCII representation (for example "gödel" → "godel")
5. Splits the string into whitespace-separated *tokens*
6. Sorts the tokens and removes duplicates
7. Joins the tokens back together

As usual, while we could write the code for this ourselves, we're lucky that someone in the Python community has already done this and has created the library *fingerprints*, which we can install using pip:

```
pip install fingerprints
```

For the moment, our main concern is confirming whether we have any spelling discrepancies to speak of; actually transforming our data to address these differences is something we'll look at in Chapter 7. So for now, we're just going to count all the unique bank names in our dataset and then see how many unique fingerprints

---

21 See *https://github.com/OpenRefine/OpenRefine/wiki/Clustering-In-Depth* for more information on clustering.

there are in that list. If all the bank names in the file are truly distinct, then in *theory* the two lists should be the same length. If, on the other hand, some of the bank names in our dataset are "unique" only because of minor punctuation and whitespace differences, for example, then our list of fingerprints will be *shorter* than our list of "unique" bank names. This would suggest that we'll need to do some data transformations in order to reconcile multiple spellings of the same bank name to ensure that, for example, we're really able to pull up *all* of the loans associated with a single bank if we want to (Example 6-11).

Example 6-11. ppp_lender_names.py

```
# quick script for determining whether there are typos &c. in any of the PPP
# loan data's bank names

# importing the `pandas` library
import pandas as pd

# importing the `fingerprints` library, which will help us generate normalized
# labels for each of the bank names in our dataset
import fingerprints

# read the recent data into a pandas DataFrame
ppp_data = pd.read_csv('public_150k_plus_recent.csv')

# use the pandas DataFrame `unique()` method to create a list of unique
# bank names in our data's `OriginatingLender` column
unique_names = ppp_data['OriginatingLender'].unique()

# confirm how many unique names there are
print(len(unique_names))

# create an empty list to hold the fingerprint of each of the unique names
fingerprint_list = []

# iterate through each name in the list of unique names
for name in unique_names:

    # for each name, generate its fingerprint
    # and append it to the end of the list
    fingerprint_list.append(fingerprints.generate(name))


# use the `set()` function to remove duplicates and sort `fingerprint_list`
fingerprint_set = set(fingerprint_list)

# check the length of `fingerprint_set`
print(len(fingerprint_set))
```

Running this script yields the output:[22]

```
4337
4242
```

The length difference between the two lists certainly suggests that there are some spelling discrepancies in our dataset: the number of "unique" names in the raw data is 4,337, but the number of distinct fingerprints for those names is only 4,242. While the difference here is "only" ~100 items, these discrepancies may well affect thousands of rows of data, since on average each bank has issued hundreds of loans (750,000/4337 = ~173). As a result, we cannot say how many rows of our original dataset contain a given "misspelled" name (nor can we be sure that this is exhaustive). In "Correcting for Spelling Inconsistencies" on page 244, we'll go through the process of transforming our data using these fingerprints to better identify specific lenders and borrowers.

Is It Multivariate?

In much the same way that a dataset is more likely to be high volume if it contains many rows, it is more likely to be multivariate if it has many columns. Just like our quality check for volume, however, determining whether the columns we have make our data truly multivariate means doing a quality check on the data they contain as well.

For example, while our PPP loan data contains 50 data columns, about a dozen of these are essentially expanded addresses, since the location of the borrower, originating lender, and servicing lender are each broken out into a separate column for street address, city, state, and zip code. While many of the remaining columns may contain unique data, we need to get a sense of what they contain to understand how many data characteristics or *features* we actually have to work with.

For example, how many of the loans in our dataset have reported requesting money for something other than payroll costs? While the data structure (and the loan program) allows borrowers to use the loans for other things (such as healthcare costs and rent (*https://sba.gov/funding-programs/loans/covid-19-relief-options/paycheck-protection-program/first-draw-ppp-loan*)), to what extent does that show up in the data?

Just as we did when assessing how high volume our data really was, we'll look at the contents of a few more columns to determine whether the detail that they appear to offer is really borne out in the amount of data they contain. In this instance

---

22 When you run this script, you may see a warning about installing pyICU. Installing this library is a little bit complicated, however, and won't change our results for this exercise. If you plan to use this fingerprinting process extensively, though, you may want to invest the additional time to setup pyICU. You can find more information about this process here: *https://pypi.org/project/PyICU*.

(Example 6-12), we'll look at how many rows for each of the PROCEED columns do *not* contain a value.

Example 6-12. ppp_loan_uses.py

```python
# quick script for determining what borrowers did (or really, did not) state
# they would use PPP loan funds for

# importing the `pandas` library
import pandas as pd

# read the recent data sample into a pandas DataFrame
ppp_data = pd.read_csv('public_150k_plus_recent.csv')

# print how many rows do not list a value for `UTILITIES_PROCEED`
print(ppp_data['UTILITIES_PROCEED'].isna().sum())

# print how many rows do not list a value for `PAYROLL_PROCEED`
print(ppp_data['PAYROLL_PROCEED'].isna().sum())

# print how many rows do not list a value for `MORTGAGE_INTEREST_PROCEED`
print(ppp_data['MORTGAGE_INTEREST_PROCEED'].isna().sum())

# print how many rows do not list a value for `RENT_PROCEED`
print(ppp_data['RENT_PROCEED'].isna().sum())

# print how many rows do not list a value for `REFINANCE_EIDL_PROCEED`
print(ppp_data['REFINANCE_EIDL_PROCEED'].isna().sum())

# print how many rows do not list a value for `HEALTH_CARE_PROCEED`
print(ppp_data['HEALTH_CARE_PROCEED'].isna().sum())

# print how many rows do not list a value for `DEBT_INTEREST_PROCEED`
print(ppp_data['DEBT_INTEREST_PROCEED'].isna().sum())

# create a new DataFrame that contains all rows reporting *only* payroll costs
# that is, where all _other_ costs are listed as "NA"
payroll_only = ppp_data[(ppp_data['UTILITIES_PROCEED'].isna()) & (ppp_data
    ['MORTGAGE_INTEREST_PROCEED'].isna()) & (ppp_data
    ['MORTGAGE_INTEREST_PROCEED'].isna()) & (ppp_data['RENT_PROCEED'].isna()) &
    (ppp_data['REFINANCE_EIDL_PROCEED'].isna()) & (ppp_data
    ['HEALTH_CARE_PROCEED'].isna()) & (ppp_data['DEBT_INTEREST_PROCEED'].isna())
    ]

# print the length of our "payroll costs only" DataFrame
print(len(payroll_only.index))
```

As we can see from the output shown in Example 6-13, the vast majority of businesses (all but 1,828) said that they intended to use money for payroll expenses when they applied, with less than one-third reporting that they would (probably also) use the money to pay utilities. Another portion provided information about using the money for rent. Our last test, meanwhile, shows that well over two-thirds of all businesses listed *only* payroll expenses as the intended use of their PPP funds.

Example 6-13. Reported uses of PPP loan funds

```
570995
1828
719946
666788
743125
708892
734456
538905
```

What does this mean about how "multivariate" our data is? Even if we decide to discount the additional columns dedicated to address details, or the seemingly underutilized PROCEED columns, there's still quite a lot of information in this dataset to explore. It seems likely that we'll be able to use it to at least begin to draw conclusions about who has received PPP loans and how they used the money. As always, however, we cannot take for granted that the columns or rows of our dataset have data content until we've checked and confirmed for ourselves.

Is It Atomic?

This is another instance where our previous work on the data lets us say "Yes!" fairly quickly on this measure of data integrity. While the August version of our data contained only loan amount ranges, we know that this dataset contains one loan per row, including their exact dollar amounts. Since we have specific numbers rather than summary or aggregate values, we can feel pretty confident that our data is sufficiently granular or "atomic" to support a wide range of possible data analyses later on.

Is It Clear?

Although this dataset did *not* turn out to be especially well annotated, we've been able to make our way through many of our data integrity checks nonetheless because, for the most part, its column labels and their meanings *are* fairly clear. For example, if we weren't sure what CD stood for, a peek at some of the values (such as SC-05) makes inferring that this stands for "congressional district" fairly straightforward. As we gain more experience working with public and government datasets (or working in a particular subject area), more of the codes and jargon will make sense more quickly.

For the columns whose labels weren't so clear, exchanging a few emails with Stephen Morris at the SBA was enlightening. For example, he confirmed that the appropriate units for the Term column was months (not weeks, as first seemed likely) and that the

PROCEED columns describe what the loan funds would be used for, according to "what the lender submitted to SBA (as stated by the borrower to them on the borrower application)."

My correspondence with Morris also illustrated why going to a primary source expert, if at all possible, is an essential step in conducting data integrity checks. If you recall, one of the column headers whose meaning was *not* clear at the start was `LMIIndicator`. Since my sample data rows did not contain values for this column, I started doing some web searches and ended up with results that included "lenders' mortgage insurance" (as shown in Figure 6-9); at the time, this *seemed* like a reasonable interpretation of the column heading.

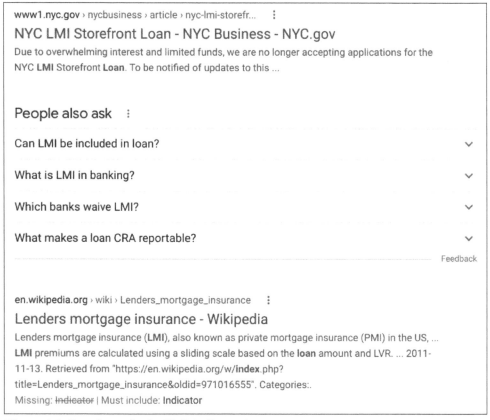

Figure 6-9. Search results for LMI indicator loans

The only problem? It's wrong. As Morris clarified via email, "The LMI Indicator tells whether a borrower is geographically located in a Low-Moderate Income zone."

The lesson here is that if you don't have an official data dictionary, you always want to be a bit cautious about how much you try to infer from column headers; even those that *seem* clear may not mean what you think. If there's any doubt, be sure to reach out to some experts (ideally the folks who compiled the data) to confirm your inferences.

Is It Dimensionally Structured?

If the idea of *dimensionally structured* data seemed a bit abstract when we discussed it in Chapter 3, hopefully it makes a bit more sense now that we have a real dataset in front of us. Dimensionally structured data includes information about useful categories or classes that we can use to group our data, alongside the more atomic features that help us conduct more granular analyses.

In the case of our PPP loan data, I would say that some of those usefully "dimensional" data columns include ones like `RuralUrbanIndicator`, `HubzoneIndicator`, the newly clarified `LMIIndicator`, `NAICSCode`, and to some extent even `SBAOffice Code`. Columns like `RaceEthnicity`, `Gender`, and `Veteran` could also be dimensionally useful, but as we know that many of them are "Unanswered," this limits what we can infer from them. The others, meanwhile, can help us answer useful questions about the location and types of businesses that have so far benefited from the PPP.

Even more than that, columns like `NAICSCode` offer the possibility of usefully *augmenting* our dataset by allowing us to understand what industries benefiting businesses belong to, which we can potentially compare to things like Bureau of Labor Statistics and other datasets about employment sectors in the United States. We'll dive into this process more deeply in "Augmenting Your Data" on page 253.

So far, we've been able to answer some of our data integrity questions with a resounding "Yes!", while others have been more qualified, suggesting the need for additional transformations and evaluations before we move on to the data analysis phase. Before we do that, however, we need to turn to the crucial question(s) of data *fit*: whether our data demonstrates the *validity*, *reliability*, and *representativeness* we need in order to draw meaningful conclusions about (in this case) how the PPP is affecting small businesses in the United States.

Assessing Data Fit

Now that we've evaluated our dataset's integrity with respect to nearly a dozen different measures, it's time to assess the extent to which it is *fit* for our purposes; that is, whether this data can really give us answers to the question(s) that we're asking. To do that, we'll turn to our three main criteria for data *fitness*: validity, reliability, and representativeness. Now is the time that we need to examine our dataset with our original question in mind: did the PPP help save American small businesses?

Validity

Remember that our working definition of validity is "the extent that something measures what it's supposed to." Even if our PPP loan data was perfect, we'd need to somehow determine whether it can answer that question in some way. At this point, we know that our dataset provides one essential piece of that answer, because we are pretty confident now that it accurately details which businesses currently have *approved* PPP loans. Through our investigations into its integrity (especially around completeness and in our search for annotating information, or *metadata*), we are also pretty confident that already *canceled* loans are not showing up in the dataset—we confirmed this both through the SBA's published information about the PPP program and by reaching out directly to businesses.

We can also use elements of the dataset (specifically `LoanStatus` and `LoanStatus Date`) to get a sense of which businesses—among the more than 750,000 that have been approved for a loan—have actually received the money. We can check this by first summarizing the `LoanStatus` column using the `value_counts()` method as we have before, as shown in Example 6-14.

Example 6-14. ppp_loan_status.py

```
# quick script for determining how many loans have been disbursed

# importing the `pandas` library
import pandas as pd

# read the recent data sample into a pandas DataFrame
ppp_data = pd.read_csv('public_150k_plus_recent.csv')

# print a summary of values in the `LoanStatus` column
print(ppp_data['LoanStatus'].value_counts())
print(sum(ppp_data['LoanStatus'].value_counts())) ❶
```

❶ Note that because the `value_counts()` method will *not* include NA values, I am also summing the entries to make sure every row has been accounted for.

The output from this script, shown in Example 6-15, confirms that of the 766,499 loans currently in our dataset, the funds for over 100,000 of them have not actually been sent to businesses yet, while more than another 100,000 businesses appear to have repaid their loans already.

Example 6-15. LoanStatus summary

```
Exemption 4           549011
Paid in Full          110120
Active Un-Disbursed   107368
Name: LoanStatus, dtype: int64
766499
```

If we're hoping to evaluate the fate of small businesses that received PPP loans, then, we need to start by making sure that we look only at those that have actually *received* the funds—meaning that we should restrict our inquiry to those whose LoanStatus value is either "Exemption 4" or "Paid in Full."

In theory, when businesses applied for PPP loans, they asked for enough money to keep their businesses afloat, so we might be tempted to assume that if a business has gotten the PPP money, it should be doing all right. But just as potentially too-loose criteria may have allowed many businesses to fraudulently get PPP loans (*https://papers.ssrn.com/sol3/papers.cfm?abstract_id=3906395*), the fact that a business *received* PPP money is no guarantee that it's still doing OK. This reality is exemplified by this *Wall Street Journal* article, which tells the story of one company that filed for bankruptcy despite receiving a PPP loan (*https://wsj.com/articles/hundreds-of-companies-that-got-stimulus-aid-have-failed-11605609180*). Since we already know that this business filed for bankruptcy, finding its record within our dataset can help give us a sense of what these records potentially look like, as shown in Example 6-16.

Example 6-16. ppp_find_waterford.py

```python
# quick script for finding a business within our dataset by (partial) name

# importing the `pandas` library
import pandas as pd

# read the recent data sample into a pandas DataFrame
ppp_data = pd.read_csv('public_150k_plus_recent.csv')

# create a DataFrame without any missing `BorrowerName` values
ppp_data_named_borrowers = ppp_data[ppp_data['BorrowerName'].notna()]  ❶

# because precise matching can be tricky,
# we'll use the pandas `str.contains()` method
bankruptcy_example = ppp_data_named_borrowers[ \
                        ppp_data_named_borrowers['BorrowerName']
                        .str.contains('WATERFORD RECEPTIONS')]  ❷

# transposing the result so it's easier to read
print(bankruptcy_example.transpose())
```

❶ Pandas cannot search for a string within any column that has NA values, so we need to create a DataFrame that doesn't have any of those in our target column, just for review purposes (obviously we might want to investigate loans with no named borrower).

❷ While str.contains() will match successfully on only part of a string, it *is* case-sensitive. This means that the fact that borrower names are in ALL CAPS matters!

The following output from this script is telling: the loan shows up with a status of "Exemption 4," and perhaps even more interestingly, with a LoanStatusDate of NA. But otherwise, there's no indicator that this business is, well, no longer in business.

```
LoanNumber                          7560217107
DateApproved                        04/14/2020
SBAOfficeCode                              353
ProcessingMethod                           PPP
BorrowerName             WATERFORD RECEPTIONS, LLC
BorrowerAddress              6715 COMMERCE STREET
BorrowerCity                       SPRINGFIELD
BorrowerState                               VA
BorrowerZip                              22150
LoanStatusDate                            NaN
LoanStatus                         Exemption 4
Term                                        24
SBAGuarantyPercentage                      100
InitialApprovalAmount                 413345.0
CurrentApprovalAmount                 413345.0
UndisbursedAmount                          0.0
FranchiseName                             NaN
ServicingLenderLocationID               122873
ServicingLenderName                   EagleBank
ServicingLenderAddress        7815 Woodmont Ave
ServicingLenderCity                    BETHESDA
ServicingLenderState                        MD
ServicingLenderZip                       20814
RuralUrbanIndicator                          U
HubzoneIndicator                             N
LMIIndicator                              NaN
BusinessAgeDescription   New Business or 2 years or less
ProjectCity                        SPRINGFIELD
ProjectCountyName                      FAIRFAX
ProjectState                                VA
ProjectZip                          22150-0001
CD                                       VA-08
JobsReported                              45.0
NAICSCode                             722320.0
RaceEthnicity                       Unanswered
UTILITIES_PROCEED                         NaN
PAYROLL_PROCEED                       413345.0
```

```
MORTGAGE_INTEREST_PROCEED                                         NaN
RENT_PROCEED                                                      NaN
REFINANCE_EIDL_PROCEED                                            NaN
HEALTH_CARE_PROCEED                                               NaN
DEBT_INTEREST_PROCEED                                             NaN
BusinessType                   Limited  Liability Company(LLC)
OriginatingLenderLocationID                                   122873
OriginatingLender                                          EagleBank
OriginatingLenderCity                                       BETHESDA
OriginatingLenderState                                            MD
Gender                                                    Male Owned
Veteran                                                  Non-Veteran
NonProfit                                                        NaN
```

In fact, if we quickly check how many loans appear with a `LoanStatusDate` of NA by adding the following line to the end of our script, we see that it is a perfect match for those with a `LoanStatus` of `Exemption 4`:

```
print(sum(ppp_data['LoanStatusDate'].isna()))
```

So does this PPP loan data *measure what it is supposed to measure*? I would say yes, but that's not the whole story. As we saw from our summary of the `LoanStatus` information, not all of the businesses that appear in this dataset *have actually gotten a loan*; they have been approved and still *could* receive the money (we know their loans have not been canceled)—but 107,368 of them have not yet taken the money, and we can't know for sure if they ever will.

We also can't say from this dataset alone what has happened to the businesses that have received the money. Some may still be in operation; others have gone bankrupt. Still others could have liquidated without filing for bankruptcy. In other words, while the PPP data has strong validity when it comes to answering certain parts of our question, answering the whole question will require much more than just this one dataset.

Reliability

When it comes to *reliability*, the primary criteria we are interested in are *accuracy* and *stability*. In other words, how well does the PPP data reflect who has gotten PPP loans, and how likely is it that the picture of who has gotten those loans will change over time?

Thanks to our previous investigations, we know by now that the *stability* of this dataset is far from perfect. Several thousand businesses that were approved for loans and appeared in the August dataset do *not* appear in the current one (we'll address the implications this has for *representativeness* in the next section), which comports with documentation from the SBA[23] that canceled loans are not included.[24] It's also not clear whether, as updates are made, previous versions of the data will still be available, making it difficult to determine what has changed unless we begin downloading and archiving each release ourselves.

Even the figures within the dataset itself may not be especially stable over time. For example, we know that 538,905 businesses reported that they would only be using their PPP loan for payroll costs. But as SBA representative Stephen Morris explained via email, "This data is speculative to some extent because it's not required that the borrower use the funds for the purpose they selected on their application." In other words, unless some part of the loan forgiveness or repayment process *requires* that PPP loan recipients detail how the money was spent (and that information is subsequently updated in this dataset), we can't know for sure whether the figures we see in the various PROCEED columns are either accurate or stable.

Representativeness

Is the PPP loan data representative of everyone who actually received a PPP loan? Most likely. After a public outcry led many large and/or publicly traded companies to return early PPP loans (*https://nbcnews.com/business/business-news/which-companies-are-returning-their-ppp-loan-here-s-list-n1194566*), the SBA indicated that they would be closely scrutinizing loans over $2 million, and almost $30 billion in loans had been returned or canceled by early July (*https://cnbc.com/2020/07/06/companies-returned-30-billion-in-small-business-loans-from-ppp.html*). After our relatively exhaustive comparisons between the August and February datasets, we can feel pretty confident that the dataset we have is at least representative of who has received PPP loans to date.

At the same time, this doesn't really tell us as much as we might think. We already know that the vast majority of PPP loan recipients that appear in this data did not disclose their gender, race, ethnicity, or veteran status, meaning that we have no real way of knowing how well (if at all) the demographics of PPP loan recipients reflect the population of small business owners in the United States. In fact, as we'll see in Chapter 9 it's very unlikely that we can draw conclusions about the demographics of PPP loan recipients at all, because the number of applicants who included this information is so small.

---

23 Which can be downloaded from *https://sba.gov/document/report-paycheck-protection-program-ppp-loan-data-key-aspects*.

24 Again, understanding why and how these loans were canceled might be instructive, but we won't find that information here—only some bread crumbs about where to start looking.

But the question of representativeness actually goes deeper than that, back to (and beyond) those 7,207 loans that disappeared between the August data release and the more recent one(s). Those missing loans reflect businesses that applied for loans and were approved, but in the words of one employee: "The money just never arrived." That means that while we know how many businesses *got* a PPP loan, we have no way of knowing *how many applied*. Because those canceled loans have been removed from the data, we are now left with an instance of what I like to call the "denominator" problem.

The denominator problem

The denominator problem is recognized—albeit under different names—across almost every field of data-driven inquiry. Sometimes called the *benchmarking* or *baseline* problem,[25] the denominator problem encapsulates the difficulty of trying to draw meaning from data when you lack sufficient comparative information to put it into context. In most cases, this is because the comparison data you really need was never collected.

In our exploration of the PPP data, we've already encountered one version of this problem: we know which businesses have received loans, but we don't know who applied and was rejected or why (in at least some cases, it seems, the recipients don't know, either). This is a problem for assessing the PPP loan process, because we don't know if legitimate applicants have been rejected even as some businesses are granted multiple rounds of loans. If we want to know whether the distribution of loans was fair—or even effective—knowing who *hasn't* been included is as important as finding out who *has*.

Some of the denominator problems we've encountered so far may be answerable using complementary data of some kind—that's what *The Wall Street Journal* did in comparing PPP loan data to bankruptcy filings. In others, the solution will be for us to build our own archive if—as seems to be the case here—the earlier datasets are not being offered by the data provider along with the updated versions.

---

25 The term *denominator problem* appears to have a very specific meaning when it comes to US property law, but needless to say, that is not precisely how I am using it here.

Conclusion

So, did the Paycheck Protection Program help save small businesses? *Maybe*. On the one hand, it's hard to imagine that so much money could be spent without *some* positive benefit. On the other hand, both the real world—and the data we have about it—is a complicated, interdependent mess. If a PPP loan recipient pivoted its business model and found new revenue streams, would we put it in the "saved by the PPP" category or not? Similarly, if a business that didn't receive a loan fails, is that *because* it didn't receive a loan, or would it have failed anyway? The more of these "what ifs" we propose, the more likely it is that a couple of things will happen:

1. We'll develop a violent headache, decide it isn't possible to *really* know anything, and look for a reassuring way to procrastinate.

2. After enough time playing games/reading the internet/complaining to confused friends and relations about how we spent all this time wrangling a dataset that we're not sure is worth anything and we can hardly remember why we started this whole thing in the first place, we'll come across something that gives us an idea for a *slightly* different, possibly *much* narrower question to explore, and excitedly return to our dataset, eager to see if we can somehow answer this new question any better than the last one.

Is this process arduous and circuitous? Yes. It is also reminiscent of our discussion about construct validity in "How? And for Whom?" on page 75. In the end, it is also *actually how new knowledge is formed*. The uncertain, frustrating, and slippery work of considering new options, thinking them through, testing them out, and then (potentially) starting the whole process over again with a bit more information and understanding the next time is how genuinely *original* insights are made. It's the thing that every algorithmic system in the world is desperately trying to approximate, or imitate. But if you're willing to put the effort in, *you can* actually succeed.

At this point, I feel like I've learned quite a bit about this dataset—enough that I know I probably *cannot* answer my original question with it but can still imagine some interesting insights it could yield. For example, I feel confident that the most recent data accurately reflects the state of currently approved loans, because I confirmed that loans missing from more recent files were (for some reason or other) probably never actually made. At the same time, while the SBA announced that as of early January 2021, over $100 billion in PPP loans had been forgiven (*https://sba.gov/article/2021/jan/12/11-million-paycheck-protection-program-loans-forgiven-so-far-totaling-over-100-billion*), there didn't seem to be a distinct value in the LoanStatus column to indicate forgiven loans, even more than six weeks later. While the SBA's Stephen Morris stopped responding to my emails in early

March, as of early May 2021, a data dictionary does seem to be available,[26] even if neither it—nor the updated data—contains this information, either.

Of course, there's still plenty more to learn here: about who has received loans and where they're located, how much they were approved for, and who is making those loans. And while the data is far from perfect, I can keep copies of past datasets on hand to reassure myself that if anything in the future changes significantly, I will at least have the resources on hand to spot it. Given that, it's time to move on from the assessment phase of our work and apply ourselves to the task of actually cleaning and transforming our data, which we'll tackle in Chapter 7.

---

26 And can be found at *https://data.sba.gov/dataset/ppp-foia/resource/aab8e9f9-36d1-42e1-b3ba-e59c79f1d7f0*.

# CHAPTER 7

Cleaning, Transforming, and Augmenting Data

Most of the time, the data that we initially find, collect, or acquire doesn't quite suit our needs in one way or another. The format is awkward, the data structure is wrong, or its units need to be adjusted. The data itself might contain errors, inconsistencies, or gaps. It may contain references we don't understand or hint at additional possibilities that aren't realized. Whatever the limitation may be, in our quest to use data as a source of insight, it is inevitable that we will have to clean, transform, and/or augment it in some way in order to get the most out of it.

Up until now, we have put off most of this work because we had more urgent problems to solve. In Chapter 4, our focus was on getting data out of a tricky file format and into something more accessible; in Chapter 6, our priority was thoroughly assessing the quality of our data, so we could make an informed decision about whether it was worth the investment of augmentation and analysis at all.

Now, however, it's time to roll up our sleeves and begin what to me is sort of the second phase of data wrangling and quality work: preparing the data we have for the analysis we want to perform. Our data is in the table-type format we need, and we've determined that it's of high enough quality to yield *some* useful insights—even if they are not precisely the ones we first imagined.

Since it's obviously impossible to identify and address every possible problem or technique related to cleaning, transforming, and/or augmenting data, my approach here will be to work through the actual examples we've already encountered where one or more of these tasks is required. For example, we'll look at different ways we might need to transform date-type information using datasets we encountered in Chapters 2 and 4. We'll also look at different ways we can clean up the "cruft" in data files that contain both structured data *and* metadata. We'll even explore *regular expressions*, which offer us a powerful way to select only certain parts of a data field or match particular terms and patterns irrespective of capitalization and/or punctuation. In the process, we'll manage to cover a decent range of the tools and strategies you're likely to need when cleaning and transforming most datasets. At the very least, the approaches outlined in this chapter will give you a useful starting place if you encounter a challenge that's truly gnarly or unique.

Selecting a Subset of Citi Bike Data

Way back in "Hitting the Road with Citi Bike Data" on page 62, we used Citi Bike system data to test out some of our freshly unboxed Python concepts, like `for...in` loops and `if/else` conditionals. For the sake of convenience, we started with a sample dataset that I had excerpted from the September 2020 system data file (*https://s3.amazonaws.com/tripdata/index.html*).

There are any number of situations where we'll want to segment large datasets for analysis—either because we don't have the time or computational resources to process everything at once or because we're only interested in a subset of the dataset to begin with. If all we wanted to do was select a specific number of rows, we could write a `for...in` loop using the `range()` function described in "Adding Iterators: The range Function" on page 101. But we might also want to excerpt the data based on its values as well. I did this in selecting all of the rides from September 1, 2020, but we might also want to do something a bit more nuanced, like evaluating weekday Citi Bike rides separately from those taken on weekends and holidays.

Let's start with the first task, of excerpting just the September 1, 2020, rides from the larger dataset.[1] Conceptually, this is simple enough: we just want to keep every row in our dataset containing a ride that started on the first day of September. If we briefly revisit the dataset, however, it becomes clear that even this task is not so simple.

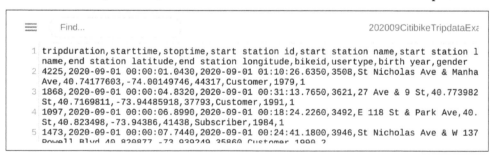

Figure 7-1. First few lines of Citi Bike trip data

---

[1] While the data format for Citi Bike data files changed in early 2021, files from before that date still follow the format in these examples.

As you can see in Figure 7-1, the `starttime` column is not simply a date but some kind of date/time format that includes not just the month, day, and year but also the hours, minutes, and seconds (to four decimal points!). The first entry in this data file, for example, the value of the `starttime`, looks like this:

```
2020-09-01 00:00:01.0430
```

Obviously, if we want to analyze just the first day of rides—or just rides during the morning "rush hour" commute or just weekday rides—we need a way to effectively filter our data based on just *part* of the information that's stored in this column. But what options do we have for accomplishing this? In the next few sections, we'll look at each of these tasks—finding just rides on a particular date, in a particular time frame, and on a particular "type" of day—in turn. In the process, we'll learn some of the tools Python offers for solving problems like these, as well as when and why we might choose one over another.

A Simple Split

Solving the first problem—excerpting just the rides that started on September 1, 2020—is actually relatively easy to do if we combine some of the tools that we've used already in some previous examples. It starts with recognizing that when we read in a basic CSV file with Python, most of our data will be treated as strings.[2] This means that, even though we humans clearly know that `2020-09-01 00:00:01.0430` is meant to be *interpreted* as a date and time, Python just sees it as a collection of numbers and characters.

Looking at the `starttime` field this way, the question of how to find all the rides that started on September 1, 2020, becomes a bit more straightforward, because the part of our data that contains the "date" information is *always* separated from the "time" information by a single space. This means that if we can find a way to look only at what comes *before* that space, we can easily set up an `if`/`else` conditional to compare that to our target date string—in this case, `2020-09-01`—and use that comparison to keep only the rows we want.

While it may not seem glamorous, the built-in string `split()` is going to be our hero here. It's already played a supporting role in previous exercises when we needed to break up filenames or URLs; we actually used it way back in "Verbs ≈ Functions" on page 42 to illustrate the difference between functions and methods! As a refresher, this method lets us specify a single character that should be used to split a string into parts. The output of this method is a list, which contains the "leftover" pieces of the string in the order in which they appeared, with the character you `split()` on

---

2 And even if they weren't, we could always convert them to strings.

removed. So splitting the string 2020-09-01 00:00:01.0430 on a space will yield the list ['2020-09-01', '00:00:01.0430'].

To see how simple and effective this is, let's modify our script from "Hitting the Road with Citi Bike Data" on page 62. In Example 7-1, I've edited down some of the comments because these tasks are much more familiar now, but it's still a good idea to outline your script's objective at the top.

Example 7-1. citibike_september1_rides.py

```
# objectives: filter all September 2020 Citi Bike rides, and output a new
#             file containing only the rides from 2020-09-01

# program outline:
# 1. read in the data file: 202009-citibike-tripdata.csv
# 2. create a new output file, and write the header row to it.
# 3. for each row in the file, split the `starttime` value on space:
#        a. if the first item in the resulting list is '2020-09-01', write
#             the row to our output file
# 4. close the output file

# import the "csv" library
import csv

# open our data file in "read" mode
source_file = open("202009-citibike-tripdata.csv","r")

# open our output file in "write" mode
output_file = open("2020-09-01-citibike-tripdata.csv","w")

# pass our source_file to the DictReader "recipe"
# and store the result in a variable called `citibike_reader`
citibike_reader = csv.DictReader(source_file)

# create a corresponding DictWriter and specify that the
# header should be the same as the `citibike_reader` fieldnames
output_writer = csv.DictWriter(output_file, fieldnames=citibike_reader.fieldnames)

# write the header row to the output file
output_writer.writeheader()

# use a `for...in` loop to go through our `citibike_reader` list of rows
for a_row in citibike_reader:

    # get the value in the 'starttime' column
    start_timestamp = a_row["starttime"]

    # split the value in 'starttime' on the space character
    timelist = start_timestamp.split(" ")

    # the "date" part of the string will be the first item, position 0
```

```
    the_date = timelist[0]

    # if `the_date` matches our desired date
    if the_date == "2020-09-01":

        # write that row of data to our output file
        output_writer.writerow(a_row)

# close the output file
output_file.close()
```

Pretty simple, right? Of course, you could easily modify this script to capture a different date, or even multiple dates if you wanted to. For example, you could modify the if statement to be something like:

```
    if the_date == "2020-09-01" or the_date == "2020-09-02":
```

Of course, while this or statement works perfectly well if you're looking for two or three specific dates, it starts to get *very* messy if you need to look for more than that (you may recall that we ended up with a similarly awkward conditional in Example 6-12). In order to filter our data with the precision we need without generating extraordinarily complex, awkward, and error-prone code, we'll be better served by a whole different toolkit: *regular expressions*.

Regular Expressions: Supercharged String Matching

A *regular expression* (often shortened to *regex*), allows you to quickly and efficiently search for string patterns within a larger string or piece of text. In most cases, if you're trying to solve a matching or filtering problem and find that the solution involves *lots* of and or or statements, it's an early sign that what you really need is a regular expression.

Regular expressions are found in most programming languages and are concise, powerful, and, at times, *extremely* tricky to work with. While a single regular expression can encapsulate even a very complex search pattern, designing regexes that work as expected can be extremely time-consuming, often requiring quite a bit of trial and error to get right. Since our goal is for our data wrangling work to be both efficient *and* comprehensible, we'll focus here on short regexes that offer unique functionality not easily achieved through other means. While there are certain tasks where regular expressions are indispensable, they are not the tool for solving every problem and usually work best when paired with other techniques.

To get started, let's use a regular expression to tackle the problem of filtering out rides that take place within the typical "morning commute" hours, which we'll estimate here as being from 7 a.m. to 9 a.m. Any regex process begins with distinguishing for ourselves what we *want* to match from what we *don't*. Here, we'll start with an example `starttime` entry that is *outside* of our identified time range (hence, something we *don't* want to match):

```
2020-09-01 00:00:01.0430
```

Now let's look at a `starttime` entry that falls *within* it:

```
2020-09-01 00:08:17.5150
```

Now, let's acknowledge first that we *could* address this problem with the string-splitting method we saw previously. We could start by splitting on the `:` character, which would, in the second instance, give us this:

```
['2020-09-01 00', '08', '17.5150']
```

Then we could take the middle item from the list and use a *compound conditional*— that is, an `if` statement that joins two or more tests—to see if it matches the strings `'07'`, `'08'`, or `'09'`.

This approach certainly *works*, but it feels a little awkward. It requires multiple steps and a three-part conditional that will quickly get difficult to read. A regular expression, meanwhile, will let us narrow in on those hour values in a single step while still being fairly readable. Before we dive into writing the regex itself, though, let's do a quick overview of the vocabulary of Python regular expressions.

Because a regular expression has to use characters and strings to describe *patterns* of characters and strings, the Python regular expression "language" uses a set of *metacharacters* and special sequences to make describing the pattern you're searching for simpler. In Table 7-1 I've included some of the most useful ones, drawn from a more complete list on W3Schools (*https://w3schools.com/python/python_regex.asp*).

Table 7-1. Common regular expression building blocks

Expression	Description
[]	A set of characters
"\"	Signals a special sequence (can also be used to escape special characters)
.	Any character (except newline character)
*	Zero or more occurrences
+	One or more occurrences
{}	Exactly the specified number of occurrences
|	Either or
()	Capture and group
\d	Returns a match where the string contains digits (numbers from 0–9)
\D	Returns a match where the string DOES NOT contain digits
\s	Returns a match where the string contains a whitespace character
\S	Returns a match where the string DOES NOT contain a whitespace character

Expression	Description
\w	Returns a match where the string contains any word characters (characters from a to Z, digits from 0–9, and the underscore _ character)
\W	Returns a match where the string DOES NOT contain any word characters

As always with writing, regular expressions give us more than one way to "capture" the pattern we're looking for. In most cases, our goal is to define a pattern that will match what we need to find while avoiding *accidentally* matching on anything else. For our "rush hour" problem, we can take advantage of the fact that the "hours" digits in the starttime column are surrounded by colons (:), *and nothing else is*. This means that we can use this "surrounded by colons" pattern as part of our regular expression and feel confident that we won't accidentally match some other part of the string. To see if this works as we hope, let's set up a few sample regular expressions to test against some (real and constructed) sample data to see how they do, as shown in Example 7-2.

Example 7-2. regex_tests.py

```
# the goal of this script is to try out how a couple of regular expressions
# fare with some sample test data. ❶

# import the regular expression library
import re

# using the `re.compile()` method is a helpful way of keeping a reference to
# our various regular expressions
bookend_regex = re.compile("\s0[7-9]:") ❷

# always try to be descriptive with the variable names
one_sided_regex = re.compile("0[7-9]:")

# this example should *fail*
sample1 = "2020-09-01 00:00:01.0430"

# this example should *match*
sample2 = "2020-09-01 09:04:23.7930"

# this example should *fail*
sample3 = "2020-09-01 10:07:02.0510"

# let's see what happens!
print("bookend_regex:")
print(bookend_regex.search(sample1))
print(bookend_regex.search(sample2))
print(bookend_regex.search(sample3))

print("one_sided_regex:")
print(one_sided_regex.search(sample1))
```

```
print(one_sided_regex.search(sample2))
print(one_sided_regex.search(sample3))
```

❶ In addition to sample files like this, you can also test out your Python regex online using the W3Schools regex demo (*https://w3schools.com/python/try python.asp?filename=demo_regex*).

❷ Even if you only use them once in a script, I *strongly* recommend defining your regex at the top of your file using an aptly named variable. It is the simplest, most efficient way to keep track of their functionality, especially if you're using more than one!

When you run the script in Example 7-2, your output should look something like this:

```
bookend_regex:
None
<re.Match object; span=(10, 14), match=' 09:'>
None
one_sided_regex:
None
<re.Match object; span=(11, 14), match='09:'>
<re.Match object; span=(14, 17), match='07:'>
```

As you can see, the "bookended" regex, where we specified both of the colons, correctly matches (*and* fails to match) in all three cases; the "one-sided" regex, on the other hand, erroneously finds a match on the *seconds* value of sample3. This is precisely why defining the string you're looking for as precisely as possible is important. If you look at the Match object printed out previously, you'll see that it contains information about what was matched (e.g., match='07:') and where (e.g., from index positions 14–17 in the string).

So far, this seems pretty straightforward. Things can still get a little tricky, however, when the *structure* of the thing we want to match changes. For example, what if we wanted to expand the hours we're interested in to range from 7 a.m. to 10 a.m.? Our bookend_regex won't work as written, because it specifies that the first character after the colon has to be a 0. We could try just adding the digits 1 and 0 as options to our digit ranges, like so:

```
plus_ten = re.compile("\s[01][0789]:")

print("plus_ten")
print(plus_ten.search("2020-09-01 18:09:11.0980"))
```

which produces the output:

```
plus_ten
<re.Match object; span=(10, 14), match=' 18:'>
```

The problem, as we can see from the output, is that our data uses a 24-hour clock and will end up matching on a whole range of times that we don't want. That's because regular expressions don't "see" numbers in the way we think of them—all they see are sequences of characters. That's why 18 comes back as a match—our regex allows any string that starts with a 0 or a 1 and is followed by a 0, 7, 8, or 9. While we obviously wrote it with the numbers 07, 08, 09, and 10 in mind, our code opens the door to many more.

The solution, in this case, is to use the "either/or" *pipe* character (|), which we can use to combine to (otherwise) completely distinct regular expressions. In this case, that will look something like what's shown in Example 7-3.

Example 7-3. Capturing 7 to 10

```
seven_to_ten = re.compile("\s0[7-9]:|\s10:")
```

Try it out yourself with a few sample data points, just to confirm that it captures what we're looking for (and nothing else).

I'm not going to go too much further with regular expressions than this; as with the web scraping we explored in "Web Scraping: The Data Source of Last Resort" on page 173, no two regular expression problems (or solutions) are alike. However, I hope you can see the potential these offer for doing pattern matching that would be very awkward with compound conditionals and basic string functions alone.

Making a Date

One of the reasons it's appealing to treat date-like data as strings is that, as we saw in our work with various source formats of unemployment data in Chapter 4, the way they are interpreted can vary dramatically across data sources and even Python libraries. Still, there are situations and tasks where converting date-like data to an actual `datetime` type is very useful. For example, if we want to isolate the weekday rides from our Citi Bike data, we *could* try to essentially "brute force" it by looking at a calendar, identifying the dates of all the weekdays, and then creating a giant string comparison list or writing a regular expression to match them. In the case of the September 2020 data, such a regular expression object might look something what's in Example 7-4.

Example 7-4. Weekday regex for September 2020

```
september2020_weekday = re.compile("-0[123489]-|-1[0145678]-|-2[1234589]-|-30-")
```

Ugh. This certainly *works*, but it's nearly impossible to read and is still basically one giant compound conditional—even if it's captured in fewer characters because it's a regular expression. Moreover, it's not a solution that scales very well. If we wanted to extend our analysis to any *other* month, it would mean getting out the calendar all over again.

Fortunately, a well-constructed Python `datetime` object has a number of built-in methods that can help with exactly this kind of task. In fact there is a simple `weekday()` method that returns a number from 0 to 6 (with 0 being Monday and 6 being Sunday (*https://docs.python.org/3/library/datetime.html#datetime.date.week day*)) based on the day of the week on which a certain date falls. This means that if we convert the contents of our `starttime` column to a date, as shown in Example 7-5, we can use this method to quickly identify the day of the week corresponding to *any* date. This will help us apply our code to additional data sources—say, a different month or year of ridership data—without having to do a thing!

Example 7-5. weekday_rides.py

```python
# objectives: filter all September 2020 Citi Bike rides, and output a new
#             file containing only weekday rides

# program outline:
# 1. read in the data file: 202009-citibike-tripdata.csv
# 2. create a new output file, and write the header row to it.
# 3. for each row in the file, make a date from the `starttime`:
#       a. if it's a weekday, write the row to our output file
# 4. close the output file

# import the "csv" library
import csv

# import the "datetime" library
from datetime import datetime

# open our data file in "read" mode
source_file = open("202009-citibike-tripdata.csv","r")

# open our output file in "write" mode
output_file = open("202009-citibike-weekday-tripdata.csv","w")

# convert source data to a DictReader; store the result in `citibike_reader`
citibike_reader = csv.DictReader(source_file)

# create a corresponding DictWriter and specify its fieldnames
output_writer = csv.DictWriter(output_file, fieldnames=citibike_reader.fieldnames)

# actually write the header row to the output file
output_writer.writeheader()
```

```
# use a `for...in` loop to go through our `citibike_reader` list of rows
for a_row in citibike_reader:

    # convert the value in the 'starttime' column to a date object
    the_date = datetime.strptime(a_row['starttime'], '%Y-%m-%d %H:%M:%S.%f') ❶

    # if `the_date` is a weekday
    if the_date.weekday() <= 4: ❷
        # write that row of data to our output file
        output_writer.writerow(a_row)

# close the output file
output_file.close()
```

❶ As mentioned in Example 6-1, providing the format of our source data (*https://docs.python.org/3/library/datetime.html#strftime-strptime-behavior*) will help our script run faster and more reliably.

❷ The `weekday()` method puts Monday at position 0 (*https://docs.python.org/3/library/datetime.html#datetime.date.weekday*), so looking for anything up to and including 4 will capture the values for Monday through Friday.

Depending on your device, you may notice that the script in Example 7-5 takes a while to run. For example, on my (not very powerful) device, it takes more than 85 seconds to complete. Accomplishing the same task using the regular expression in Example 7-4, meanwhile, takes only 45 seconds. I can also more easily tweak the regular expression to skip days that are officially weekdays but are also holidays (like Labor Day).

So which approach is better? As usual, *it depends*. What will actually work best for your particular data wrangling/cleaning/transformation process will be specific to your needs and your resources. If answering your question means looking for weekday commute patterns in a decade's worth of Citi Bike data, you're probably better off using the `weekday()` method, because you don't have to change your code to deal with different months or years. On the other hand, if you don't have very many months to work with and execution speed (and absolute precision) is your top concern, you might prefer to go the regular expression route. You may also just find that regexes make you want to tear your hair out or that using multiple steps to get perfect results drives you crazy. As we'll explore more in Chapter 8, all of these can be legitimate reasons for a particular design choice—just make sure the choice is *yours*.[3]

---

3 Unless, of course, you're working in a team—then you need to consider everyone's needs. You'll be glad when it's your turn to work with *their* code.

De-crufting Data Files

In Chapter 4, we encountered a number of instances where we needed to "clean up" a dataset that was otherwise awkward or unintelligible. When we went through the process of parsing an old-school-style *.xls* file in Example 4-6, for example, we encountered a couple of distinct issues. First, the spreadsheet contained both table-type data *and* descriptive header information that, despite being useful in principle, will inevitably need to be relocated in order for us to analyze the rest of it. Second, the *.xls* format's lack of support for "real" dates means that our initial transformation from *.xls* to *.csv* left us with a bunch of nonsense numbers where the dates should have been. While I chose to put off solving those problems at first, the time has come to confront them.

In thinking about the first problem, I want to stress that we *definitely* don't want to just "throw out" the information that's currently stored at the top of the *fredgraph.xls* file. As is hopefully clear from our work in Chapter 6, metadata is a precious resource, and we *never* want to discard metadata from a primary source (*https://loc.gov/programs/teachers/getting-started-with-primary-sources*). Rather, my preference in cases like this is to turn one file into two. We'll strip out the metadata and store it in a separate—but congruently named—text file while also parsing and saving the table-type data into an analysis-friendly *.csv* format.

Convention over Configuration

Even in this book's simplest examples, there are lots of decisions to be made—like naming variables, programming files, data output files, and more. While it may not be perfectly "Pythonic" (*https://en.wikipedia.org/wiki/Convention_over_configuration*), I find that the concept of "convention over configuration" has a lot to offer when it comes to collecting, generating, and reorganizing files in the data wrangling process. In particular, using a shared naming convention, our metadata file and our table-type data file can save us headaches both when it comes to creating our files now and finding them again later. While you don't have to follow the precise pattern I do here, choosing a consistent method for naming these files across your projects is something that will save you time, effort, and anxiety in the long run.

Looking at our source *.xls* file in a spreadsheet program, it's easy enough to see visually where the metadata ends and the table-type data begins. The real question is: how will we detect this transition in our script? As is so often the case with data cleaning, the most effective solution is not always an elegant one. The metadata ends where the table-type data begins, in the row containing its column headers. If we look at the first value in each row as we work our way through the file, we can *stop* writing to the metadata file and *start* writing to the *.csv* as soon as we encounter the first column header. Since the value `observation_date` is the first column header for this dataset, we'll make that transition as soon we find that at the beginning of our current row.

 Before you begin, check your source file carefully to see *where* the metadata appears within it. Especially in cases where the data contains estimates or other qualifiers, you're likely to find metadata both before and *after* the table-type data in your source file.

To see what's involved in creating these two purpose-built files from our single source file, take a look at the script in Example 7-6 (if you need a refresher on some of the code choices in this example, you may want to refer back to Example 4-6).

Example 7-6. xls_meta_parsing.py

```python
# converting data in an .xls file with Python to csv + metadata file
# using the "xrld" library. First, pip install the xlrd library:
# https://pypi.org/project/xlrd/2.0.1/

# import the "xlrd" library
import xlrd

# import the `csv` library, to create our output file
import csv

# pass our filename as an ingredient to the `xlrd` library's
# `open_workbook()` "recipe"
# store the result in a variable called `source_workbook`
source_workbook = xlrd.open_workbook("fredgraph.xls")

# open and name a simple metadata text file
source_workbook_metadata = open("fredgraph_metadata.txt","w") ❶

# an `.xls` workbook can have multiple sheets
for sheet_name in source_workbook.sheet_names():

    # create a variable that points to the current worksheet by
    # passing the current value of `sheet_name` to the `sheet_by_name` recipe
    current_sheet = source_workbook.sheet_by_name(sheet_name)

    # create "xls_"+sheet_name+".csv" as an output file for the current sheet
    output_file = open("xls_"+sheet_name+".csv","w")

    # use the `csv` library's "writer" recipe to easily write rows of data
    # to `output_file`, instead of reading data *from* it
    output_writer = csv.writer(output_file)

    # create a Boolean variable to detect if we've hit our table-type data yet
```

```
    is_table_data = False ❷

    # now, we need to loop through every row in our sheet
    for row_num, row in enumerate(current_sheet.get_rows()):

        # pulling out the value in the first column of the current row
        first_entry = current_sheet.row_values(row_num)[0]

        # if we've hit the header row of our data table
        if first_entry == 'observation_date':

            # it's time to switch our "flag" value to "True"
            is_table_data = True

        # if `is_table_data` is True
        if is_table_data:

            # write this row to the data output file
            output_writer.writerow(current_sheet.row_values(row_num))

        # otherwise, this row must be metadata
        else:

            # since we'd like our metadata file to be nicely formatted, we
            # need to loop through the individual cells of each metadata row
            for item in current_sheet.row(row_num):

                    # write the value of the cell
                    source_workbook_metadata.write(item.value)

                    # separate it from the next cell with a tab
                    source_workbook_metadata.write('\t')

            # at the end of each line of metadata, add a newline
            source_workbook_metadata.write('\n')

    # just for good measure, let's close our output files
    output_file.close()
    source_workbook_metadata.close()
```

❶ While we're only creating a single metadata file here, we could easily move this part of the process inside the for loop and create a unique metadata file for every worksheet, if necessary.

❷ This type of Boolean (True/False) variable is often described as a *flag* variable. The idea is that we set its value *outside* of a loop and then "flip" its value when some particular thing has happened—this saves us from having to loop through all our data twice. Here, we'll use it to check when we should start writing to our "data" file instead of our "metadata" file.

Before we move on to dealing with the (still inexplicable) dates in this file, I want to highlight a new technique introduced in Example 7-6: the use of a so-called *flag variable*. This term typically refers to any Boolean (True/False) variable that is used to keep track of whether a certain event has taken place or condition has been met, especially within a loop. In Example 7-6, for example, we are using the `is_table_data` variable as a way to keep track of whether we have yet encountered the row of data that marks the beginning of our table data. Since a given row of data in our `for...in` loop is essentially "forgotten" as soon as the next one is read, we need to create this variable *before* our loop. This keeps the `is_table_data` variable available beyond the *scope* of our loop—a concept we'll look at more closely in Chapter 8.

Decrypting Excel Dates

We can avoid the issue of those Excel dates no longer. While hopefully you will not encounter this situation often, I'm including it here for completeness and because it illustrates a few different ways that code tends to evolve—usually getting more complicated and less readable—as we add even seemingly small bits of functionality to it. For example, in Example 7-7, we'll need to check whether a variable contains a number or not, and believe it or not, we need a library for this—it is aptly called *numbers*. While that part is fundamentally straightforward, you'll quickly see in Example 7-7 how the need to transform these date values requires adapting our approach to writing the table-type data to our output file.

Example 7-7. xls_meta_and_date_parsing.py

```
# converting data in an .xls file with Python to csv + metadata file, with
# functional date values using the "xrld" library.
# first, pip install the xlrd library:
# https://pypi.org/project/xlrd/2.0.1/

# then, import the `xlrd` library
import xlrd

# import the csv library
import csv

# needed to test if a given value is *some* type of number
from numbers import Number

# for parsing/formatting our newly interpreted Excel dates
from datetime import datetime

# pass our filename as an ingredient to the `xlrd` library's
# `open_workbook()` "recipe"
# store the result in a variable called `source_workbook`
source_workbook = xlrd.open_workbook("fredgraph.xls")
```

```
# open and name a simple metadata text file
source_workbook_metadata = open("fredgraph_metadata.txt","w")

# an `.xls` workbook can have multiple sheets
for sheet_name in source_workbook.sheet_names():

    # create a variable that points to the current worksheet by
    # passing the current value of `sheet_name` to the `sheet_by_name` recipe
    current_sheet = source_workbook.sheet_by_name(sheet_name)

    # create "xls_"+sheet_name+".csv" as an output file for the current sheet
    output_file = open("xls_"+sheet_name+"_dates.csv","w")

    # use the `csv` library's "writer" recipe to easily write rows of data
    # to `output_file`, instead of reading data *from* it
    output_writer = csv.writer(output_file)

    # create a Boolean variable to detect if we've hit our table-type data yet
    is_table_data = False

    # now, we need to loop through every row in our sheet
    for row_num, row in enumerate(current_sheet.get_rows()):

        # pulling out the value in the first column of the current row
        first_entry = current_sheet.row_values(row_num)[0]

        # if we've hit the header row of our data table
        if first_entry == 'observation_date':

            # it's time to switch our "flag" value to "True"
            is_table_data = True

        # if `is_table_data` is True
        if is_table_data:

            # extract the table-type data values into separate variables
            the_date_num = current_sheet.row_values(row_num)[0]
            U6_value = current_sheet.row_values(row_num)[1]

            # create a new row object with each of the values
            new_row = [the_date_num, U6_value]

            # if the `the_date_num` is a number, then the current row is *not*
            # the header row. We need to transform the date.
            if isinstance(the_date_num, Number):

                # use the xlrd library's `xldate_as_datetime()` to generate
                # a Python datetime object
                the_date_num = xlrd.xldate.xldate_as_datetime(
                    the_date_num, source_workbook.datemode) ❶
```

```
            # overwrite the first value in the new row with
            # the reformatted date
            new_row[0] = the_date_num.strftime('%m/%d/%Y')  ❷


        # write this new row to the data output file
        output_writer.writerow(new_row)

    # otherwise, this row must be metadata
    else:

        # since we'd like our metadata file to be nicely formatted, we
        # need to loop through the individual cells of each metadata row
        for item in current_sheet.row(row_num):

                # write the value of the cell
                source_workbook_metadata.write(item.value)

                # separate it from the next cell with a tab
                source_workbook_metadata.write('\t')

        # at the end of each line of metadata, add a newline
        source_workbook_metadata.write('\n')

# just for good measure, let's close our output files
output_file.close()
source_workbook_metadata.close()
```

❶ Converting these *.xls* "dates" using the *xlrd* library's xldate_as_datetime() method requires both the number value *and* the workbook's datemode (*https:// xlrd.readthedocs.io/en/latest/api.html#xlrd.book.Book.datemode*) in order to generate the Python datetime object correctly.[4]

❷ Here, I've decided to write the date to my table-type data file as MM/DD/YYYY using the appropriate strftime() format, but you could use another format if you prefer.

While the *xlrd* library makes the process of converting our strange Excel dates to something understandable relatively straightforward, I think the code in Example 7-7 demonstrates how the idiosyncrasies of wrangling a particular dataset can quickly add complexity—especially in the form of additional, nested if statements—to what started as a very simple program. This is just one of the reasons why we'll spend Chapter 8 exploring strategies and techniques for effectively and efficiently streamlining our code: we want to make sure it does everything we need but *also* that it is sufficiently readable and reusable to stand the test of time.

---

4 Of course, Macs and PCs use a different "base" date because…*reasons*.

Generating True CSVs from Fixed-Width Data

Another instance where we also had only moderate success in transforming our data was in Example 4-7, where we converted our fixed-width source data into a *.csv*. While technically we succeeded in creating an output file that was comma separated, the result was honestly pretty unsatisfactory: it retained many of the formatting artifacts of the original file that could easily stymie our future efforts at data analysis.

Fortunately, the specific problem we encountered—that of "leading" and/or "trailing" whitespace—is very well-known, since the data technologies that typically generate it have been around for a long time. As a result, fixing this problem is pretty simple: the solution exists in the form of the built-in Python `strip()` function, as illustrated in Example 7-8.

Example 7-8. fixed_width_strip_parsing.py

```python
# an example of reading data from a fixed-width file with Python.
# the source file for this example comes from the NOAA and can be accessed here:
# https://www1.ncdc.noaa.gov/pub/data/ghcn/daily/ghcnd-stations.txt
# the metadata for the file can be found here:
# https://www1.ncdc.noaa.gov/pub/data/ghcn/daily/readme.txt

# import the `csv` library, to create our output file
import csv

filename = "ghcnd-stations"

# reading from a basic text file doesn't require any special libraries
# so we'll just open the file in read format ("r") as usual
source_file = open(filename+".txt", "r")

# the built-in "readlines()" method does just what you'd think:
# it reads in a text file and converts it to a list of lines
stations_list = source_file.readlines()

# create an output file for our transformed data
output_file = open(filename+".csv","w")

# use the `csv` library's "writer" recipe to easily write rows of data
# to `output_file`, instead of reading data *from* it
output_writer = csv.writer(output_file)

# create the header list
headers = ["ID","LATITUDE","LONGITUDE","ELEVATION","STATE","NAME","GSN_FLAG",
           "HCNCRN_FLAG","WMO_ID"]

# write our headers to the output file
output_writer.writerow(headers)
```

```
# loop through each line of our file (multiple "sheets" are not possible)
for line in stations_list:

    # create an empty list, to which we'll append each set of characters that
    # makes up a given "column" of data
    new_row = []

    # ID: positions 1-11
    new_row.append((line[0:11]).strip()) ❶

    # LATITUDE: positions 13-20
    new_row.append((line[12:20]).strip())

    # LONGITUDE: positions 22-30
    new_row.append((line[21:30]).strip())

    # ELEVATION: positions 32-37
    new_row.append((line[31:37]).strip())

    # STATE: positions 39-40
    new_row.append((line[38:40]).strip())

    # NAME: positions 42-71
    new_row.append((line[41:71]).strip())

    # GSN_FLAG: positions 73-75
    new_row.append((line[72:75]).strip())

    # HCNCRN_FLAG: positions 77-79
    new_row.append((line[76:79]).strip())

    # WMO_ID: positions 81-85
    new_row.append((line[80:85]).strip())

    # now all that's left is to use the
    # `writerow` function to write new_row to our output file
    output_writer.writerow(new_row)

# just for good measure, let's close the `.csv` file we just created
output_file.close()
```

❶ If you compare this code with the code in Example 4-7, you'll see that it's identical apart from our having applied the strip() method to each string before appending it to our data row.

Once again, we see that modifying our original code to solve a formatting or "cleaning" issue isn't necessarily that hard, but the resulting script isn't *exactly* elegant, either. Stripping the whitespace from our output with the strip() method is definitely straightforward, but we've had to add a whole lot of parentheses in the process—leaving us with code that is far less readable than we'd like.

This illustrates yet another way in which creating good, quality Python code mirrors more typical writing processes. If we view our first efforts in Chapter 4 as something like the "outline" of our final program—where we solve the high-level problem of getting the data format we have into at least the table-type *structure* that we're after—it gives us space to come back later and revise that work, filling in the details that allow it to be more nuanced in its handling of the specific dataset we're working with.

Similarly, in Chapter 8 we'll take that revision process one step further, refining these programs—which already do everything we need them to do—so that they are more concise and easier to understand, just as we might do with any piece of writing. This iterative approach to programming not only means that we eventually end up with better, more useful code; it also helps us break down big, complicated programming problems into a series of less intimidating ones that we can solve one step at a time. Equally important, no matter what stage of the process we're in, we have a functioning program we can fall back on if needed. This incremental approach is especially useful when we take on more complex data-cleaning tasks like the one we'll look at next: resolving the unintentional spelling differences.

Correcting for Spelling Inconsistencies

In Chapter 6, we used a "fingerprinting" process to help address the possibility that information about banks in our Paycheck Protection Program (PPP) data might have spelling inconsistencies—a common issue in *any* dataset that relies on human data entry. Of course, the code we wrote in Example 6-11 only estimated the number of genuinely unique entries in the OriginatingLender column by counting how many of them resulted in a distinct fingerprint. We found that our dataset contained 4,337 unique bank names but only 4,242 unique fingerprints—an indicator that as many as 95 bank names might actually *be* the same but contain typos because they generated the same fingerprint.

Because those 95 potential typos could affect thousands of rows of data, we need a way to transform our dataset so that we can confidently aggregate it by lender. At the same time, we also don't want to *overcorrect* by grouping together entries that don't actually belong together.

This is an instance where *transforming* our data is invaluable: we don't want to risk losing any of our original data (retaining it is essential for validation and spot-checking), but we *also* need to transform it in order to support our future analysis efforts. Because our dataset is large, grouping and filtering it to meet our needs is likely to be time-consuming, so we want to preserve the results of that work by actually *adding* new columns to the dataset. This lets us both preserve our original data *and* the benefits of our transformation work in a single file.

Fortunately, we've got some go-to libraries that will make this process pretty straight-forward. Since we already know how to aggregate names using the fingerprinting process from Example 6-11, the trickier piece may be determining when banks that share the same fingerprint should actually be treated as distinct organizations. Looking back at the output from Example 6-7 (reproduced in Example 7-9 for convenience), we see that there are not a lot of fields that contain "originating" lender information, so our most likely option for deciding if two originating banks whose names share all the same words (and will therefore have the same fingerprint, e.g., "First Bank Texas" and "Texas First Bank") will be to compare the value included in `OriginatingLenderLocationID`.

Example 7-9. Recent sample data transposed

```
LoanNumber                                      9547507704
DateApproved                                    05/01/2020
SBAOfficeCode                                          464
ProcessingMethod                                       PPP
BorrowerName                          SUMTER COATINGS, INC.
BorrowerAddress                      2410 Highway 15 South
BorrowerCity                                        Sumter
BorrowerState                                         <NA>
BorrowerZip                                    29150-9662
LoanStatusDate                                  12/18/2020
LoanStatus                                    Paid in Full
Term                                                    24
SBAGuarantyPercentage                                  100
InitialApprovalAmount                          769358.78
CurrentApprovalAmount                          769358.78
UndisbursedAmount                                        0
FranchiseName                                         <NA>
ServicingLenderLocationID                           19248
ServicingLenderName                         Synovus Bank
ServicingLenderAddress                      1148 Broadway
ServicingLenderCity                              COLUMBUS
ServicingLenderState                                   GA
ServicingLenderZip                             31901-2429
RuralUrbanIndicator                                     U
HubzoneIndicator                                       N
LMIIndicator                                         <NA>
BusinessAgeDescription        Existing or more than 2 years old
ProjectCity                                        Sumter
ProjectCountyName                                  SUMTER
ProjectState                                           SC
ProjectZip                                     29150-9662
CD                                                 SC-05
JobsReported                                           62
NAICSCode                                          325510
RaceEthnicity                                  Unanswered
UTILITIES_PROCEED                                    <NA>
```

```
PAYROLL_PROCEED                                          769358.78
MORTGAGE_INTEREST_PROCEED                                     <NA>
RENT_PROCEED                                                  <NA>
REFINANCE_EIDL_PROCEED                                        <NA>
HEALTH_CARE_PROCEED                                          <NA>
DEBT_INTEREST_PROCEED                                        <NA>
BusinessType                                          Corporation
OriginatingLenderLocationID                                 19248
OriginatingLender                                   Synovus Bank
OriginatingLenderCity                                   COLUMBUS
OriginatingLenderState                                        GA
Gender                                                Unanswered
Veteran                                               Unanswered
NonProfit                                                    <NA>
```

Before we proceed, of course, we want to make sure that we understand what the data in OriginatingLenderLocationID actually *means*. Lucky for us, a web search for the words "originating lender location id" brings up yet another document from the SBA website (*https://sba.gov/sites/default/files/articles/ETran_Origination_01_2014.pdf*) as the first result. Searching through this PDF for the term "location" brings us to the page shown in Figure 7-2, which reassures us that the "Location ID" value entered should not change from branch to branch of the same bank but indicates the *main* branch of a given bank.

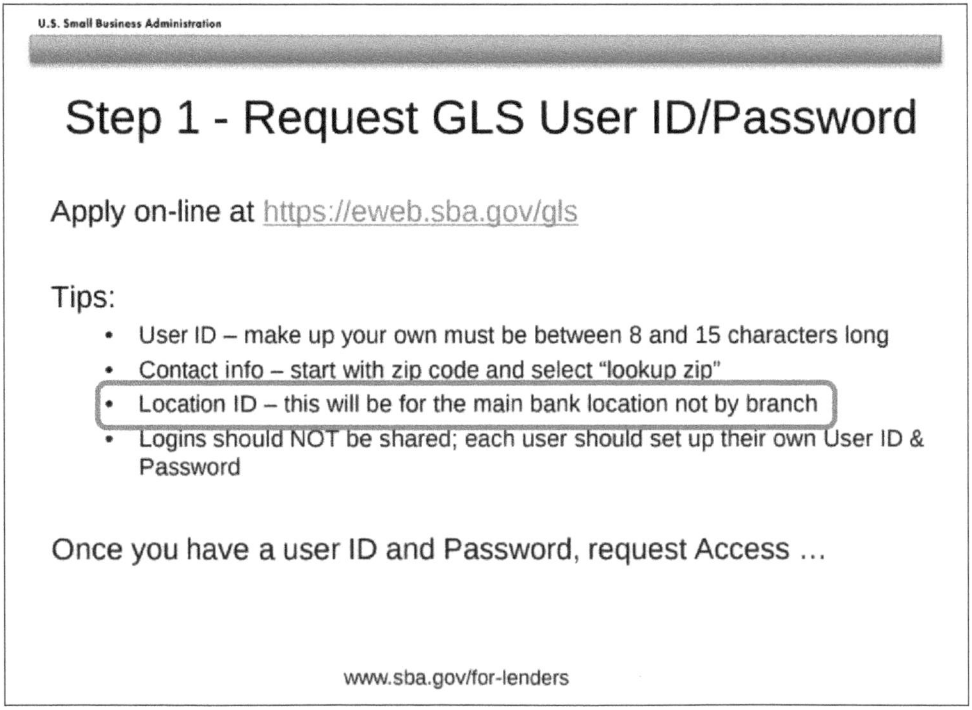

U.S. Small Business Administration

Step 1 - Request GLS User ID/Password

Apply on-line at https://eweb.sba.gov/gls

Tips:

- User ID – make up your own must be between 8 and 15 characters long
- Contact info – start with zip code and select "lookup zip"
- Location ID – this will be for the main bank location not by branch
- Logins should NOT be shared; each user should set up their own User ID & Password

Once you have a user ID and Password, request Access …

www.sba.gov/for-lenders

Figure 7-2. Information about lender location ID

With this additional information, we can go about creating a version of our PPP loan data that includes a new column, `OriginatingLenderFingerprint`, that contains a combination of the `OriginatingLender` fingerprint and the `OriginatingLenderLocationID`, as shown in Example 7-10. Later on, we can then use this value to quickly aggregate our data by originating lender while being (reasonably) confident that we are neither failing to match entries due to typos *nor* treating what should be two separate banks as one.

Example 7-10. ppp_add_fingerprints.py

```python
# quick script for adding a "fingerprint" column to our loan data, which will
# help us confirm/correct for any typos or inconsistencies in, e.g., bank names

# import the csv library
import csv

# importing the `fingerprints` library
import fingerprints

# read the recent data sample into a variable
ppp_data = open('public_150k_plus_recent.csv','r')

# the DictReader function makes our source data more usable
ppp_data_reader = csv.DictReader(ppp_data)

# create an output file to write our modified dataset to
augmented_ppp_data = open('public_150k_plus_fingerprints.csv','w')

# create a "writer" so that we can output whole rows at once
augmented_data_writer = csv.writer(augmented_ppp_data)

# because we're adding a column, we need to create a new header row as well
header_row = []

# for every column header
for item in ppp_data_reader.fieldnames:   ❶

    # append the existing column header
    header_row.append(item)

    # if we're at 'OriginatingLender'
    if item == 'OriginatingLender':

        # it's time to add a new column
        header_row.append('OriginatingLenderFingerprint')

# now we can write our expanded header row to the output file
augmented_data_writer.writerow(header_row)

# iterate through every row in our data
```

```
for row in ppp_data_reader:

    # create an empty list to hold our new data row
    new_row = []  ❷

    # for each column of data in the *original* dataset
    for column_name in ppp_data_reader.fieldnames:

        # first, append this row's value for that column
        new_row.append(row[column_name])

        # when we get to the 'OriginatingLender' column, it's time
        # to add our new "fingerprint" value
        if column_name == 'OriginatingLender':

            # our fingerprint will consist of the generated fingerprint PLUS
            # the OriginatingLenderLocationID
            the_fingerprint = fingerprints.generate(row[column_name]) + \
                              " " + row['OriginatingLenderLocationID']

            # append the compound fingerprint value to our row
            new_row.append(the_fingerprint)

    # once the whole row is complete, write it to our output file
    augmented_data_writer.writerow(new_row)

# close both files
augmented_ppp_data.close()
ppp_data.close()
```

❶ While it may seem excessive, this first loop actually exists *only* to create our new header row. As always, we want to avoid introducing typos whenever and wherever possible, so in this instance, the whole extra loop is worth it (*way* better than typing out this list by hand).

❷ Since we're adding a column of data, we need to build the new data row as a list, item by item—just as we did with the header row.

The structure of the resulting file is the same as the original, except that a new OriginatingLenderFingerprint column has now been added between OriginatingLender and OriginatingLenderCity, as you can see in Example 7-11.

Example 7-11. PPP data with fingerprints

```
LoanNumber                               9547507704
DateApproved                             05/01/2020
SBAOfficeCode                                   464
ProcessingMethod                                PPP
BorrowerName                   SUMTER COATINGS, INC.
```

```
BorrowerAddress                                2410 Highway 15 South
BorrowerCity                                                  Sumter
BorrowerState                                                   NaN
BorrowerZip                                              29150-9662
LoanStatusDate                                          12/18/2020
LoanStatus                                            Paid in Full
Term                                                            24
SBAGuarantyPercentage                                          100
InitialApprovalAmount                                   769358.78
CurrentApprovalAmount                                   769358.78
UndisbursedAmount                                             0.0
FranchiseName                                                  NaN
ServicingLenderLocationID                                   19248
ServicingLenderName                                  Synovus Bank
ServicingLenderAddress                               1148 Broadway
ServicingLenderCity                                      COLUMBUS
ServicingLenderState                                           GA
ServicingLenderZip                                      31901-2429
RuralUrbanIndicator                                             U
HubzoneIndicator                                                N
LMIIndicator                                                  NaN
BusinessAgeDescription         Existing or more than 2 years old
ProjectCity                                                 Sumter
ProjectCountyName                                          SUMTER
ProjectState                                                   SC
ProjectZip                                              29150-9662
CD                                                          SC-05
JobsReported                                                 62.0
NAICSCode                                                325510.0
RaceEthnicity                                           Unanswered
UTILITIES_PROCEED                                             NaN
PAYROLL_PROCEED                                         769358.78
MORTGAGE_INTEREST_PROCEED                                     NaN
RENT_PROCEED                                                  NaN
REFINANCE_EIDL_PROCEED                                        NaN
HEALTH_CARE_PROCEED                                           NaN
DEBT_INTEREST_PROCEED                                         NaN
BusinessType                                          Corporation
OriginatingLenderLocationID                                 19248
OriginatingLender                                    Synovus Bank
OriginatingLenderFingerprint                 bank synovus 19248
OriginatingLenderCity                                    COLUMBUS
OriginatingLenderState                                         GA
Gender                                                 Unanswered
Veteran                                                Unanswered
NonProfit                                                     NaN
```

While this transformation will help us easily aggregate our data by a particular "originating" lender, we could quickly duplicate it with the "servicing" lender as well. We could *even* write a script that compares the value of these two resulting fingerprints to create a "flag" column indicating whether the servicing and originating banks for a particular loan are the same.

The Circuitous Path to "Simple" Solutions

While I hope that you found the Example 7-10 exercise simple to follow, I want you know that the preceding script was *not* the first solution I tried—it wasn't even the second or third. In fact, I probably spent about a dozen hours, all told, thinking, hacking, wrangling, and failing before I *finally* realized that my eventual approach to the problem was the fastest, simplest, and most effective way to strike a balance between making sure that loans from the same bank were grouped together without accidentally conflating two different institutions.

I'm going to describe how I actually worked my way through this process because—as is hopefully *also* starting to become clear—data wrangling (and programming in general) is not so much about coding as it is about reasoning and problem-solving. This means that thinking through the problem in front of you, trying different solutions, and, perhaps most importantly, being willing to change course even if it feels like "throwing out" a bunch of work are *all* much more important to data wrangling than being able to write more than two lines of Python code from memory.[5] So in an effort to illustrate what just one of these problem-solving efforts entails, I'm going to (comparatively) briefly give you an overview here of the different approaches I tried before settling on the solution in "Correcting for Spelling Inconsistencies" on page 244.

At first, I started out by minimally adapting the script from Example 6-11, creating a new column that contained *just* those fingerprints and writing a new CSV that added this new column. But I realized that there was a strong likelihood that some banks with similar names would share the same "fingerprint," so I wrote a script that did the following:

1. Created a list of the unique fingerprints.

2. For every unique fingerprint, created a new list (actually a `pandas` DataFrame) of all the unique `OriginatingLenderLocationID` values.

3. If there was more than one distinct `OriginatingLenderLocationID` value, I then *updated* the "fingerprint" column to incorporate the `OriginatingLenderLocationID`, much as we ended up doing for *all* the entries in Example 7-10.

Even creating *that* script, however, was much more involved than this numbered synopsis would make it seem. The first step was easy, of course—we'd pretty much

---

5 Believe me, most professional programmers are looking things up online every five minutes.

done that already. But when it came time to working with the new file in `pandas`, my scrappy little Chromebook didn't have enough memory, so I moved my work to Google Colab. This gave me more memory to work with (sort of), but now every time I stepped away for more than a few minutes, I had to authenticate and reload the data from my Google Drive file all over again—that took an additional couple of minutes every time. Also, while I was *pretty* confident that I had figured out how to update the values in my DataFrame correctly, attempting to check my work by searching for a new fingerprint that I was sure should exist wasn't working reliably: sometimes I got matches, and sometimes I got an empty DataFrame! Add to this that it took about 3 or more minutes to run step 3 each time, and you can imagine how many hours (and how much frustration!) it took to be sure my code actually worked as intended.

Of course, once I had managed to code up (and check) that multistep solution, I realized that the result wasn't all that different from what I'd started with. In fact, it was a little *less* satisfying because now the format of my new `OriginatingLender Fingerprint` column was inconsistent: some had the `OriginatingLenderLocationID` appended, some didn't. But since the actual *value* of the fingerprint didn't matter—only that it could be used accurately to both aggregate and disambiguate banks—why was I going to all the trouble of only adding location IDs to the ones that had several entries? Couldn't they *all* just have the location IDs appended?

Well, of course it was only at *that* point that I bothered to look up the documentation shown in Figure 7-2, which confirmed that adding location IDs wouldn't break up fingerprints that should be the same.[6] And that's how I came full circle: rather than assigning potentially overlapping fingerprints and then trying to "weed out" the problems with an awkward and time-consuming search process, the best solution was just to make the `OriginatingLenderLocationID` part of the new "fingerprint" column right from the start.

Having spent hours working out how to "fix" the original fingerprints—and in the process, contending with the limits of my device, the vagaries of Google Colab, and the tedium of making a small change to a script and then having to wait several minutes for it to run—I won't pretend that it didn't feel like a bit of a letdown to realize that the best solution really just involved a small tweak on my original script (though not the one I had started with).

But if there's one thing that I've learned after years of data wrangling, it's that learning when to let go and start over (or go back to the beginning) is one of the most important skills you can develop. Sometimes you have to let go of a dataset, even if you've sunk hours into researching, evaluating, and cleaning it. Likewise, sometimes

---

6 At first I was concerned that the `OriginatingLenderLocationID` might refer to an individual bank branch, for example.

you have to let go of a programming approach, even if you've spent hours reading documentation and experimenting with new methods just to get the result you're after. Because in the end, the goal is *not* to use a particular dataset, or to use a particular library or coding method. *It's to use data to understand something about the world.* And if you can keep your focus on that, letting go when you need to will be much easier.

You will also probably find it easier to accept this process—whether it involves letting go of a dataset or a scripting solution you've already spent hours on—when you start to experience firsthand that you have learned something valuable even from something you eventually "abandon." Before my detour into "fixing" my original, text-only fingerprints, for example, I didn't really know how to update values within a `pandas` DataFrame; now I do (I *really* do). I also now know a bit more about Google Colab's strengths and inconsistencies and was reminded about some key "gotchas" to working with diverse datasets (more on that in the next section).

The same goes for datasets that might not turn out to be usable for answering a particular question: just because they aren't right for your current project doesn't mean they might not be for another one. But whether or not you ever look at them again, working with those datasets will teach you so many things: about the subject of the data, about the pitfalls and possibilities of certain data types, about experts on the topic, and more. In other words, letting go of a dataset or a coding approach is *never* a "waste": the experience you gain will only make your next effort better, if you let it.

Gotchas That Will Get Ya!

One of the reasons why it is so important to document your work is that very often the person you're writing that documentation for is really just "future you," who may be returning to a particular dataset or script—or even Python altogether—after days, weeks, or months away. In that time, things that were once obvious will seem confusing and obscure unless you document them thoroughly, and even common "lessons" can get overlooked when you're in a hurry or focused on something else. I had that experience myself as I worked through the exercises in the last few chapters, especially as I made an effort to check my own work. For me, that experience was just another reminder that when something's wrong with your script, it's usually something simple ;-)

Here are some common gotchas to keep in mind:

Confirm the case
> Anytime you are checking to see if two strings are the same, remember that capitalization matters! When I was working on Example 6-16, I at first overlooked that all of the business names (but not the bank names!) were in all caps. I had a frustrating few minutes thinking that my dataset did *not* contain the WATERFORD

`RECEPTIONS` example, until I finally looked at the data again and realized my error.

Insist on the data type

As I worked my way through the process described in "The Circuitous Path to "Simple" Solutions" on page 250, I once again had trouble finding matches for values that I felt certain should be in the dataset. I had forgotten, however, that the *pandas* library (unlike the *csv* library) actually tries to apply data types to the columns of data it reads into a DataFrame. In this case, that meant that `OriginatingLenderLocationID` became a number (instead of a string), so my efforts to find particular values for that column were failing because I was trying to match, for example, the number `71453` to the string `"71453"`—which definitely doesn't work!

In that instance, I found the simplest solution was simply to add a parameter to the `read_csv()` function call, specifying that all the data should be read as strings (e.g., `fingerprinted_data1 = pd.read_csv('public_150k_plus_fin gerprints.csv', dtype='string')`).[7] This also prevented some of the larger dollar amounts in the data from being converted to scientific notation (e.g., `1.21068e+06` rather than `1210681`).

After basic typos, the sort of data-type "gotchas" described here are probably the next most common data wrangling "errors" you're likely to encounter. So if you find you've made an oversight like these at some point, try not to be too frustrated. It's really just a sign that your programming logic is good and some of your formatting needs to be fixed.

Augmenting Your Data

Adding the `OriginatingLenderFingerprint` column in Example 7-10 was a valuable way to increase the utility and usability of the PPP loan data, but another good way to add value to a dataset is to look for *other* datasets that you can use to augment it. This is usually easiest when the dataset is *dimensionally structured*, in that it already references a widely used standard of some kind. In the case of our PPP loan data, we have an example of this in the column called `NAICSCode`, which a quick web search[8] confirms is the:

> …North American Industry Classification System. The NAICS System was developed for use by Federal Statistical Agencies for the collection, analysis and publication of statistical data related to the US Economy.

---

7 As a case in point, I didn't even end up using this approach in the final code for Example 7-10, but I *did* find a use for it in Example 7-12!

8 Which leads us to *https://naics.com/what-is-a-naics-code-why-do-i-need-one*.

Given this, we can probably find a way to augment our data by adding more information about the NAICS code for each entry, which might, for example, help us understand more about what industries and types of businesses are participating in the PPP loan program. While we could probably pull a comprehensive list of NAICS codes from the main website, a web search for `naics sba` brings up some interesting options. Specifically, the SBA offers a PDF that provides information about Small Business Administration size guidelines for businesses by NAICS code (*https://sba.gov/sites/default/files/2019-08/SBA%20Table%20of%20Size%20Standards_Effective%20Aug%2019%2C%202019.pdf*), in either millions of dollars or number of employees. In addition to providing us with more human-readable descriptions of the NAICS codes themselves, augmenting our PPP loan data with this additional information can help us answer more general questions about what actually qualifies as a "small business."

Our process for this won't be too much different from data merges we've done previously, both in the process we'll follow *and* the issues it introduces. To start off with, we'll look for a non-PDF version of the SBA size guidelines. Clicking on the "SBA's Size Standards Webpage" link on the first page of the PDF brings us to a more general page on the SBA website (*https://sba.gov/federal-contracting/contracting-guide/size-standards*), where in the "Numerical Requirements" section we find a link labeled "table of small business size standards" (*https://sba.gov/document/support-object-object-table-size-standards*). Scrolling down that page turns up a downloadable XLSX version (*https://sba.gov/sites/default/files/2019-08/SBA%20Table%20of%20Size%20Standards_Effective%20Aug%2019%2C%202019.xlsx*) of the earlier PDF document. From there, we can export the second sheet (which contains the actual codes and descriptions) as a CSV file. Now, we can import and match this with our PPP loan data.

As you'll see in Example 7-12, anytime we integrate a new data source, it means we have to evaluate, clean, and transform it just as we have our "primary" dataset. In this case, that means that we want to proactively update any <NA> values in the `NAICSCode` column of our PPP loan data to a flag value (I have chosen the string "None"), in order to prevent their being matched with essentially random <NA> values in our SBA NAICS code file. Similarly, once we've done our merge, we still want to see what codes from our PPP loan file *didn't* get matched successfully. For now, we'll leave open the decision about how to handle these until we've done a bit more digging around in our analysis phase to see whether we want to "fill them in" (e.g., with the regular NAICS values/interpretations), flag them as being atypical for the SBA, or some combination thereof.

Example 7-12. ppp_adding_naics.py

```python
# script to merge our PPP loan data with information from the SBA's NAICS
# size requirements, found here:
# https://www.sba.gov/document/support--table-size-standards

# import pandas to facilitate the merging and sorting
import pandas as pd

# read our PPP loan data into a new DataFrame
ppp_data = pd.read_csv('public_150k_plus_fingerprints.csv', dtype='string') ❶

# read the NAICS data into a separate DataFrame
sba_naics_data = pd.read_csv('SBA-NAICS-data.csv', dtype='string')

# if there's no value in the 'NAICSCode' column, replace it with "None"
ppp_data['NAICSCode'] = ppp_data['NAICSCode'].fillna("None") ❷

# merge the two datasets using a "left" merge
merged_data = pd.merge(ppp_data, sba_naics_data, how='left',
                       left_on=['NAICSCode'], right_on=['NAICS Codes'],
                       indicator=True)

# open a file to save our merged data to
merged_data_file = open('ppp-fingerprints-and-naics.csv', 'w')

# write the merged data to an output file as a CSV
merged_data_file.write(merged_data.to_csv())

# print out the values in the '_merge' column to see how many
# entries in our loan data don't get matched to an NAICS code
print(merged_data.value_counts('_merge'))

# create a new DataFrame that is *just* the unmatched rows
unmatched_values = merged_data[merged_data['_merge']=='left_only']

# open a file to write the unmatched values to
unmatched_values_file = open('ppp-unmatched-naics-codes.csv', 'w')

# write a new CSV file that contains all the unmatched NAICS codes in our
# PPP loan data, along with how many times it appears
unmatched_values_file.write(unmatched_values.value_counts('NAICSCode').to_csv())
```

❶ Use the dtype='string' parameter to force pandas to treat our entire dataset as strings; this will make later matching and comparison tasks more predictable.

❷ If we don't do this replacement, our data will match to unpredictable NA values from the *SBA-NAICS-data.csv* file.

Augmenting a dataset as we have in Example 7-12 can help us expand the types of questions we can use it to answer, as well as helping support faster, more comprehensive data analysis and interpretation. At the same time, anytime we introduce new data, we need to complete the same life cycle of evaluation, cleaning, transformation, and (maybe even) augmentation that we applied to our "primary" dataset. This means that we'll always need to strike a balance between making our primary data more elaborate (and possibly useful) with the time and effort involved in finding and wrangling the "secondary" data that we use to augment it.

Conclusion

While the variety of data cleaning, transformation, and augmentation possibilities is as varied as both datasets and analysis possibilities, the primary goal of this chapter was to illustrate common issues in data cleaning, transformation, and augmentation and introduce some key methods for resolving them.

Before we move on to actually trying to generate insights with our data, however, we're going to take a small "detour" in Chapter 8, which will focus on some programming best practices that can help us make sure our code is as clear, efficient, and effective as possible. Because while using Python to do data wrangling already lets us do things that would be impossible with other tools, optimizing our code for both use and reuse is another way to make sure we get the most out of each program and piece of code we write, too. In most cases, this means structuring our files so that they are more versatile, composable, and readable, as we'll see right now!

# CHAPTER 8

Structuring and Refactoring Your Code

Before we move on to the analyzing and visualizing aspects of data wrangling, we're going to take a brief "detour" to discuss some strategies for making the most of everything we've done so far. In the last few chapters, we've explored how to access and parse data from a variety of data formats and sources, how to evaluate its quality in practical terms, and how to clean and augment it for eventual analysis. In the process, our relatively simple programs have evolved and changed, becoming—inevitably—more convoluted and complex. Our `for` loops now have one or (more) nested `if` statements, and some of those now have apparently "magic" numbers embedded in them (like our `the_date.weekday() <= 4` in Example 7-5). Is this just the price of more functional code?

Remember that commenting our code can do a lot to help keep the logic of our scripts understandable, both to potential collaborators and our future selves. But it turns out that detailed documentation (much as I love it) isn't the only way that we improve the clarity of our Python code. Just like other types of written documents, Python supports a range of useful mechanisms for structuring and organizing our code. By making judicious use of these, we can make it simpler to both use and reuse our programming work down the line.

So in this chapter, we're going to go over the tools and concepts that will allow us to refine our code in such a way that it is both readable and reusable. This process, known as *refactoring*, exemplifies yet another way that using Python for our data wrangling work makes it possible to get more output for our effort: while we can rely on the functionality that *someone else*'s library offers when we need to, we can *also* create new coding "shortcuts" that are customized to exactly our own preferences and needs.

Revisiting Custom Functions

When we were covering the Python fundamentals way back in Chapter 2, one of the things we touched on was the concept of "custom" or *user-defined* functions.[1] In Example 2-7, we saw how a custom function could be used to encapsulate the simple task of printing out a greeting when a particular name was provided—but of course we can create custom functions that are as simple or as complex as we like. Before we dive into the mechanics of writing our own custom functions, however, let's take a step back and think about which design considerations can best help us decide *when* writing a custom function is likely to be most helpful. Of course, like all writing, there are few hard-and-fast rules, but what follows are a few heuristics that can help you decide when and how refactoring is likely to be worth it.

Will You Use It More Than Once?

Like variables, one way to identify parts of your code that could benefit from being repackaged into custom functions is to look for any particular task that gets done more than once. From validating input to formatting output (as we did, say, in Example 7-7) and everything in between, if your current script includes lots of fiddly conditionals or repetitive steps, that's an indicator that you may want to think about designing some custom functions. Keep in mind, too, that the repetition you're considering doesn't need to exist within a single script for refactoring to be worthwhile. If you find that there are particular tasks that you're doing frequently *across* the scripts that you're writing (for example, testing to see if a given day is a weekday, as we did in Example 7-5), you can always put the custom function into an external script and include it anywhere you might need it, just as we did with our credentials files in Chapter 5.

Is It Ugly and Confusing?

Documenting your work as you go is a gift to both current collaborators and your future self.[2] At the same time, thoroughly commenting your code—especially if you include not just the *how* but the *why* of your approach, which I still recommend—can eventually make it a bit unwieldy to read. Creating really comprehensible code, then, is a balancing act between providing enough detail to be comprehensive while *also* being sufficiently concise so your documentation actually gets read.

Packaging relevant bits of code into custom functions is actually a key way you can help thread this needle: like variables, custom functions can (and should!) have descriptive names. Just by *reading* the function name, whoever is looking at your code

---

1 In this case, the programmer is actually considered the "user."

2 Truly, good documentation will save your $h!t sometimes.

will get some essential information about what is happening, without your needing to add multiple lines of descriptive comments immediately around it. If the function name is descriptive enough and/or a particular reader doesn't need more detail right away, they can just move on. Meanwhile, they'll still be able to find your lovely, descriptive documentation for that function if they need it—neatly tucked away in another part of the program (or another file altogether). This means that the *inline* comments for your main script can stay relatively succinct without sacrificing the completeness of your documentation.

Do You Just Really Hate the Default Functionality?

OK, so this is maybe not the *best* reason to write a custom function, but it is a real one. Over time, you may find that there are tasks you need to complete over and over again as part of your data wrangling endeavors, and that there's something about the existing functions and libraries that just *bugs* you. Maybe it's a function name that you find confusing so you *always* have to remind yourself precisely what it's called. Or maybe there's a parameter you consistently forget to add that just makes everything more difficult (I'm looking at you, pd.read_csv(), with your dtype='string' parameter!). If you're working alone or in a small team, it's perfectly fine to write custom functions that help make your life easier just because they *do*. You don't need a grand rationale. If it will make your life easier, go ahead! That's the power of being the programmer.

Of course, there are some limits to this. Unless you want to take a much more formal and involved approach to writing Python code, you can't very effectively do things like define a new function that has the same name as an existing function or make operators like + or - behave differently.[3] However, if you just really wish that an existing function you have to use all the time worked a *little* bit differently, go with it—just make sure you document the heck out of your version!

Understanding Scope

Now that we've gone over some of the *reasons* you might refactor your code with custom functions, it's time to discuss the mechanics a little bit. Probably the most important concept to understand when you start writing custom functions is *scope*. Although we haven't used this term before, *scope* is something that we've actually been working with since we declared our first variables way back in "What's in a name?" on page 41. In that example, we saw that we could:

---

[3] Doing these things is definitely possible but is well beyond the scope of most data wrangling activities, and therefore this book.

1. Create and assign a value to a variable (`author = "Susan E. McGregor"`).

2. Use that variable to refer to its contents later and pass its value to a function (`print(author)`).

At the same time, we know that if we created a program that simply consisted of the line:

```
print(author)
```

we'd get an error, because in the universe of our one-line script, there is no memory-box labeled `author`. So Python chucks an error at us and declines to go any further.

When we talk about *scope* in programming, what we're actually talking about is the current "universe" from the perspective of a particular piece of code. An individual script has a scope that evolves as each line of code is read by the computer, from top to bottom, which is what leads to the (very much expected) behaviors of the scripts in Examples 8-1 and 8-2.

Example 8-1. No author variable in scope

```
# no variable called "author" exists in the same "universe"
# as this line of code; throw an error
print(author)
```

Example 8-2. An author variable in scope

```
# create variable "author"
author = "Susan E. McGregor"

# variable "author" exists in the "universe" of this line of code; carry on!
print(author)
```

Just as every time we create a new variable, a new "box" is created in the computer's memory, each time we define a new custom function, a new little universe, or *scope*, is created for it as well. This means that when we use custom functions, we are compartmentalizing our code not just *visually* but *logically* and *functionally*. This means that we can treat our *own* custom functions much the way we do the built-in Python methods and library functions that we've been using throughout this book: as "recipes" to which we provide "ingredients" and which return to us some value or freshly made Python object in return. The only difference is that with custom functions, we are the chefs!

To get a handle on what this all means in practice, let's revisit Example 2-7 from Chapter 2 but with a couple of tweaks, as shown in Example 8-3.

Example 8-3. greet_me_revisited.py

```python
# create a function that prints out a greeting
# to any name passed to the function
def greet_me(a_name):
    print("Variable `a_name` in `greet_me`: "+a_name)
    print("Hello "+a_name)


# create a variable named `author`
author = "Susan E. McGregor"

# create another variable named `editor`
editor  = "Jeff Bleiel"

a_name = "Python"
print("Variable `a_name` in main script: "+a_name)

# use my custom function, `greet_me` to output "Hello" messages to each person
greet_me(author)
greet_me(editor)

print("Variable `a_name` in main script again: "+a_name)
```

This yields the following output:

```
Variable `a_name` in main script: Python
Variable `a_name` in `greet_me`: Susan E. McGregor
Hello Susan E. McGregor
Variable `a_name` in `greet_me`: Jeff Bleiel
Hello Jeff Bleiel
Variable `a_name` in main script again: Python
```

Because any custom function automatically gets its own scope, that function can only "see" the variables and values that are explicitly passed into it. In turn, the values and variables inside that function are effectively "hidden" from the primary script. One consequence of this is that when we write custom functions, we don't need to worry about what variable names have already been used in the primary script, or vice versa. As a result, we need to define fewer unique variable names in general, which is helpful as we begin to write longer and more complex scripts. It *also* means that once we have a custom function working as we expect, we can use—and even modify—the details of how it functions *without* having to make adjustments to the variables and functions in the surrounding script.

Defining the Parameters for Function "Ingredients"

We already have a fair amount of experience with providing "ingredients" (officially known as *arguments*) to the methods and functions that come built into Python, or that we've had access to through the many libraries we've used so far. As we begin to write custom functions, however, we need to explore in more detail what the process is for defining the *parameters* that those functions will accept.[4]

First, know that—unlike some programming languages—Python doesn't require (or even really allow) you to *insist* that a function's parameters have specific data types.[5] If someone wants to pass entirely the wrong types of data into your function, they can absolutely do that. As the function author, then, it's up to you to decide whether and how you want to confirm (or *validate*) the appropriateness of the arguments or "ingredients" that have been passed into your custom functions. In principle, there are three ways to approach this:

- Check the data types of all the arguments that have been passed into your function and complain to the programmer if you find something you don't like.

- Wrap your code in Python's `try...except` blocks (*https://w3schools.com/python/python_try_except.asp*) so that you can capture certain types of errors without halting the entire program. You can also use this to customize the message to the programmer about what went wrong.

- Not worry about it and let the user of the function (in other words, the programmer) work through any problems using the default Python error messages.

While it may seem a bit laissez-faire, my primary recommendation at this point is actually to go with option three: don't worry about it. Not because errors won't happen (they will—you can revisit "Fast Forward" on page 46 if you need a refresher on what some of them look like) but because our primary interest here is wrangling data, not writing enterprise-level Python. As with the scripts we wrote in Chapter 4, we want to strike a balance between what we try to handle programmatically and what we rely on the programmer (whoever they may be) to investigate and handle for themselves. Since the programs we're writing won't bring down a website or corrupt the only copy of our data if they work incorrectly, not trying to anticipate and handle every possible error that might arise seems more than reasonable. Of course, if you document your functions clearly—a process we'll look at in more detail in

---

4 Technically, *parameters* describe the variable names assigned in the function definition, while *arguments* are the actual values that are passed to the function when it is called. In practice, though, these terms are often used interchangeably.

5 So-called "statically typed" programming languages will actually complain *before* your code runs if you've passed the wrong data type to a function or method.

"Documenting Your Custom Scripts and Functions with pydoc" on page 277—then other programmers will have everything they need to avoid errors in the first place.

What Are Your Options?

Even if we're not trying to write custom functions for use by thousands of people, we can still make them flexible and fully featured. One of the simplest ways to do this is to write our functions to solve the most common version of our problem but allow optional arguments—like those we've seen in *pandas*[6] and other libraries—that make them somewhat adaptable. For example, we could modify our greet_me() function to have a default greeting of "Hello" that can *also* be overridden by an optional value passed in by the programmer. This lets us craft functions that can be used effectively in multiple contexts. As an example, let's look at the modified version of greet_me shown in Example 8-4.

Example 8-4. greet_me_options.py

```
# create a function that prints out a greeting to any name
def greet_me(a_name, greeting="Hello"):
    print(greeting+" "+a_name)

# create a variable named author
author = "Susan E. McGregor"

# create another variable named editor
editor  = "Jeff Bleiel"

# use `greet_me()` to output greeting messages to each person

# say "Hello" by default
greet_me(author)
# let the programmer specify "Hi" as the greeting
greet_me(editor, greeting="Hi")
```

As you can see, adding optional arguments is really as simple as specifying a default value in the function definition; if the programmer passes a different value, it will simply overwrite that default when the function is called.

Getting Into Arguments?

Providing a default value in the function declaration is not the only way to add optional arguments to your custom functions. Python also supports two generic types of optional arguments, *args and **kwargs:

---

6 There's that dtype='string' again!

`*args`

The `*args` parameter is useful when you want to be able to pass a list of several values into a function and giving all of them names and/or default values would be tedious. Values passed in as `*args` are stored as a list, so they can be accessed within the function by writing a `for...in` loop to go through them one by one (e.g., `for arg in args`).

`**kwargs`

The `**kwargs` parameter is similar to `*args`, except that it allows an arbitrary number of keyword arguments to be passed to the function without assigning any of them a default value, as we did for `greeting` in Example 8-4. Values passed this way can be accessed via the `kwargs.get()` method (e.g., `my_var = kwargs.get("greeting")`).

If using `*args` and `**kwargs` seems like a handy way to (literally) leave your options open when writing custom functions, I'm here to tell you that it's *always* better to write custom functions (and scripts!) that solve the problems you *have*—not the ones you *think* you might have somewhere down the line. While the idea of extreme flexibility may seem attractive at first, it will usually lead to spending lots of time *thinking* about "someday" problems, rather than *actually* solving the ones right in front of us. And who has time for that? We've got data to wrangle!

Return Values

So far, our variations on the `greet_me()` function have been of pretty limited ambition; we've really just used them to print (slightly) customized messages to the console. By comparison, the functions we've used from external libraries have proven incredibly powerful; they can take a humble *.csv* and transform it into a *pandas* DataFrame or convert a whole *.xls* file into a collection of detailed lists and attributes that capture almost every aspect of this multitiered file type. While that level of Python programming is beyond the scope of this book, we can still create clean, super-useful custom functions harnessing the power of *return values*.

If parameters/arguments are the "ingredients" in our function "recipes," then *return values* are the final dish—the outputs that get consumed by the rest of our program. Really, return values are just pieces of data; they can be *literals* (like the string "Hello"), or they can be variables of any data type. They are useful because they let us hand off to a function whatever it needs and get back the thing that we need, without worrying (at least from the perspective—or *scope*—of the main program) how the proverbial sausage gets made. If we restructure the basic `greet_me()` function in Example 8-3 to use a return value, it might look something like Example 8-5.

Example 8-5. make_greeting.py

```python
# create a function that **returns** a greeting to any name passed in
def make_greeting(a_name):
    return("Hello "+a_name)


# create a variable named author
author = "Susan E. McGregor"

# create another variable named editor
editor  = "Jeff Bleiel"


# use my custom function, `greet_me()` to build and store
# the "Hello" messages to each person
author_greeting = make_greeting(author)
editor_greeting = make_greeting(editor)

# now `print()` the greetings built and returned by each function call
print(author_greeting)
print(editor_greeting)
```

At first you might be thinking, "How did that help?" While it's true that our main program actually got *longer*, it also arguably became a little bit more flexible and easier to understand. Because my `make_greeting()` function *returns* the greeting (rather than just printing it directly), I can do more things with it. Sure, I can just print it as we did in Example 8-5, but I can now also store its return value in a variable and do something else with it later. For example, I could add the line:

```python
    print(editor_greeting+", how are you?")
```

While that new message might not seem so exciting, it lets me both compartmentalize *some* work into the function (in this case, adding "Hello" to any name) while *also* giving me more flexibility about what to do with the output (for example, add more text to one but not the other).

Climbing the "Stack"

Of course, creating a whole new variable just to store a simple greeting, as we did in Example 8-5, does seem like a little bit more trouble than it's worth. And in fact, there's no rule that says we have to stash the output from a function in a variable before passing it to another function—we can actually "nest" our function calls so that the first function's *output* just becomes the next function's *input*. This is a strategy that we've actually used before, usually when we were manipulating strings and passing them to the `print()` function, as we did when we added the `strip()` function call to our *.csv* building process in Example 7-8. But we can do this with *any* set of functions, assuming the first one returns what the next one needs. To see how this works in practice, take a look at the rewrite of Example 8-5 shown in Example 8-6, where I've added a new function to append the ", how are you?" text to a greeting message.

Example 8-6. make_greeting_no_vars.py

```python
# function that returns a greeting to any name passed in
def make_greeting(a_name):
    return("Hello "+a_name)

# function that adds a question to any greeting
def add_question(a_greeting):
    return(a_greeting+", how are you?")

# create a variable named author
author = "Susan E. McGregor"

# create another variable named editor
editor  = "Jeff Bleiel"

# print the greeting message
print(make_greeting(author))

# pass the greeting message to the question function and print the result!
print(add_question(make_greeting(editor)))
```

While the code statement print(make_greeting(author)) is still fairly easy to interpret, things start to get more complicated with print(add_question(make_greeting(editor))), which I hope helps illustrate that there's a limit to the utility of function call nesting. The more function calls you nest, the more difficult it is to read the code, even though the "order of operations" logic stays the same: the "innermost" function is always executed first, and its return value "bubbles up" to become the input for the next function. *That* return value then bubbles up to the next function, and so on and so forth. In traditional programming terminology this, is known as the *function stack*, where the innermost function is the "bottom" of the stack and the outermost is the "top."[7] An illustration of the function stack for the last line of Example 8-6 is shown in Figure 8-1.

While this sort of function-call nesting is at the heart of an entire programming philosophy (*https://en.wikipedia.org/wiki/Functional_programming*), for the sake of readability it is best used sparingly in most instances.

---

7 This term is also why the forum is called *Stack* Exchange.

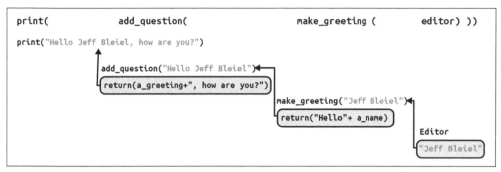

Figure 8-1. A nested function call stack

Refactoring for Fun and Profit

Now that we've explored some of the key principles and mechanisms for refactoring our code, let's see how it can be used to improve the clarity of some of our scripts from previous chapters. As we move through the follwoing examples, remember that choices about what to refactor and how (as with *any* kind of editing process) are partly a matter of preference and style. To that end, I'll describe the reasoning behind my choices below each example; you may find these to be useful models when it comes to developing your *own* refactoring practice.

A Function for Identifying Weekdays

In Example 7-5, we created a small script designed to read in our Citi Bike rides data (*https://s3.amazonaws.com/tripdata/index.html*) and output a new file containing only the rides that took place on a weekday. While there was nothing fundamentally wrong with the approach we used in that example, I think it is a good candidate for refactoring for a couple of reasons.

First, the existing script relies on a couple of ugly and not-very-descriptive function calls. The first one is required to convert the available date string into an actual `datetime` format that Python can evaluate meaningfully:

```
the_date = datetime.strptime(a_row['starttime'], '%Y-%m-%d %H:%M:%S.%f')
```

Similarly, though the built-in `weekday()` method is reasonably straightforward (although it might be better named `dayofweek()`), we have to compare it to the "magic number" 4 in order to determine if `the_date` is, in fact, a weekday:

```
if the_date.weekday() <= 4:
```

Overall, I think these parts of the code would be more readable without these relatively obscure formats and comparisons.

Second, checking whether a particular date-like string is a Monday-through-Friday weekday seems like the kind of thing that might come up reasonably frequently in data wrangling work. If I encapsulate this task into a custom function, I can easily reuse it in other scripts.

To see how I've gone about refactoring the Example 7-5 script, take a look at Example 8-7.

Example 8-7. weekday_rides_refactored.py

```
# objective: filter all September, 2020 Citi Bike rides, and output a new
#            file containing only weekday rides

# program outline:
# 1. read in the data file: 202009-citibike-tripdata.csv
# 2. create a new output file, and write the header row to it.
# 3. for each row in the file, make a date from the `starttime`:
#      a. if it's a weekday, write the row to our output file
# 4. close the output file

# import the "csv" library
import csv

# import the "datetime" library
from datetime import datetime

def main(): ❶
    # open our data file in "read" mode
    source_file = open("202009-citibike-tripdata.csv","r")

    # open our output file in "write" mode
    output_file = open("202009-citibike-weekday-tripdata.csv","w")

    # pass our source_file to the DictReader "recipe"
    # and store the result in a variable called `citibike_reader`
    citibike_reader = csv.DictReader(source_file)

    # create a corresponding DictWriter; specify its fieldnames should
    # be drawn from `citibike_reader`
    output_writer = csv.DictWriter(output_file,
                                   fieldnames=citibike_reader.fieldnames)

    # actually write the header row to the output file
    output_writer.writeheader()

    # loop through our `citibike_reader` rows
    for a_row in citibike_reader:

        # if the current 'starttime' value is a weekday
        if is_weekday(a_row['starttime']): ❷
            # write that row of data to our output file
```

```
            output_writer.writerow(a_row)

    # close the output file
    output_file.close()

def is_weekday(date_string, date_format='%Y-%m-%d %H:%M:%S.%f'): ❷

    # convert the value in the 'date_string' to datetime format
    the_date = datetime.strptime(date_string, date_format)

    # if `the_date` is a weekday (i.e., its integer value is 0-5)
    if the_date.weekday() <= 4:
        return(True)
    else:
        return(False)

if __name__ == "__main__": ❸
    main()
```

❶ Wrapping our top-level script into a function called `main()` is a Python convention that also serves an important functional purpose. Because the computer reads Python top to bottom, if we *don't* wrap this code in a function, then the computer won't have gotten to the definition of `is_weekday()` when it reaches `if is_weekday(a_row['starttime'])` and will throw an error.

❷ We can use the `is_weekday()` function to handle the finicky details of converting our date string to both a "real" date and its weekday value. The descriptive function name conveys what is happening at a high level without forcing the reader to wade through the particulars.

❸ The computer still reads from top to bottom as usual, but while it encounters both the `main()` and `is_weekday()` function definitions first, we aren't asking it to execute anything until the very bottom of the script.

As you can see, while the bulk of the code (and even many of the comments) in Example 8-7 are the same as those in Example 7-5, things have been reorganized in a way that makes the `main()` part of the program much more concise and readable. Sure, if the programmer *wants* to know the details of how weekdays are identified, the specifics are available right there in the `is_weekday()` function definition. Otherwise, though, they can just read through the primary part of the script and very easily confirm that it is doing what the outline alleges.

Metadata Without the Mess

In Example 7-7, we built on code from Examples 4-6 and 7-6 to create a single script that both effectively interpreted Microsoft Excel dates *and* split our source data file into a metadata text file and a structured *.csv*. While the resulting script did everything we needed, its code became leggy and hard to read, full of hard-to-interpret conditionals and obscure date-formatting function calls.

Here we can clean things up a little bit by handling the formatting of the different types of row content (for the *.csv* or the *.txt* file, respectively) in separate functions. This requires rearranging (and clarifying) our script's logic somewhat. It also illustrates some of the challenges that can arise when it comes to getting all the requisite information *into* our custom functions. The approach outlined in Example 8-8 illustrates my currently preferred way of handling these issues.

Example 8-8. xls_meta_and_date_parsing_refactored.py

```
# converting data in an .xls file with Python to csv + metadata file, with
# functional date values using the "xrld" library.
# first, pip install the xlrd library:
# https://pypi.org/project/xlrd/2.0.1/

# then, import the `xlrd` library
import xlrd

# import the csv library
```

---

8 You can find a helpful description/demonstration of the reasoning behind this convention at *https://freecode camp.org/news/if-name-main-python-example*.

```
import csv

# needed to test if a given value is *some* type of number
from numbers import Number

# for parsing/formatting our newly interpreted Excel dates
from datetime import datetime

def main():

    # use `open_workbook()` to load our data in the `source_workbook` variable
    source_workbook = xlrd.open_workbook("fredgraph.xls")

    global the_datemode ❶

    the_datemode = source_workbook.datemode ❶

    # open and name a simple metadata text file
    source_workbook_metadata = open("fredgraph_metadata.txt","w")

    # an `.xls` workbook can have multiple sheets
    for sheet_name in source_workbook.sheet_names():

        # create a variable that points to the current worksheet
        current_sheet = source_workbook.sheet_by_name(sheet_name)

        # create "xls_"+sheet_name+".csv" as current sheet's output file
        output_file = open("xls_"+sheet_name+"_dates.csv","w")

        # use the `writer()` recipe to write `.csv`-formatted rows
        output_writer = csv.writer(output_file)

        # Boolean variable to detect if we've hit our table-type data yet
        is_table_data = False

        # now, we need to loop through every row in our sheet
        for row_num, row in enumerate(current_sheet.get_rows()):

            # pulling out the value in the first column of the current row
            first_entry = current_sheet.row_values(row_num)[0]

            # if we've hit the header row of our data table
            if first_entry == 'observation_date':

                # it's time to switch our "flag" value to "True"
                is_table_data = True

            # if `is_table_data` is True
            if is_table_data:

                # pass the requisite data to out `create_table_row()` function
                new_row = create_table_row(current_sheet, row_num) ❷
```

```
                # write this new row to the data output file
                output_writer.writerow(new_row)

            # otherwise, this row must be metadata
            else:

                # pass the requisite data to our `create_meta_text()` function
                metadata_line = create_meta_text(current_sheet, row_num)

                # write this new row to the metadata output file
                source_workbook_metadata.write(metadata_line)

        # just for good measure, let's close our output files
        output_file.close()
        source_workbook_metadata.close()

def create_table_row(the_sheet, the_row_num):

    # extract the table-type data values into separate variables
    the_date_num = the_sheet.row_values(the_row_num)[0]
    U6_value = the_sheet.row_values(the_row_num)[1]

    # create a new row object with each of the values
    new_row = [the_date_num, U6_value]

    # if the `the_date_num` is a number, then the current row is *not*
    # the header row. We need to transform the date.
    if isinstance(the_date_num, Number):

        # use the xlrd library's `xldate_as_datetime()` to generate
        # a Python datetime object
        the_date_num = xlrd.xldate.xldate_as_datetime(the_date_num, the_datemode)

        # create a new list containing `the_date_num` (formatted to MM/DD/YYYY
        # using the `strftime()` recipe) and the value in the second column
        new_row = [the_date_num.strftime('%m/%d/%Y'),U6_value]

    # return the fully formatted row
    return(new_row)

def create_meta_text(the_sheet, the_row_num):

    meta_line = ""

    # since we'd like our metadata file to be nicely formatted, we
    # need to loop through the individual cells of each metadata row
    for item in the_sheet.row(the_row_num):

            # write the value of the cell, followed by a tab character
            meta_line = meta_line + item.value + '\t'
```

```
        # at the end of each line of metadata, add a newline
        meta_line = meta_line+'\n'

        # return the fully formatted line
        return(meta_line)

if __name__ == "__main__":
    main()
```

❶ Though they should be used sparingly, creating a *global* variable here called `the_datemode` means its value can be accessed by *any* function (the `global` here refers to its scope). Note that in Python, global variables cannot be assigned a value in the same line they are declared, which is why this has been done across two separate code statements.

❷ For example, if we *didn't* create a global variable, for the date mode, we would have to pass it as another argument to `create_table_row()`, which feels a bit incongruous.

If you compare Example 8-8 with Example 8-7, you'll see they have several key features in common: instead of code that executes automatically, everything in this script has been compartmentalized into functions, with the conventional `main()` function call protected by an `if __name__ == "__main__":` conditional. This example also overlaps with Example 7-7 almost perfectly: the includes are all the same, and while it has been rearranged into three functions instead of a single, linear script, most of the code is almost identical.

Part of what I want to illustrate here is that refactoring your code doesn't have to be an enormous undertaking, but the results are invaluable. As a program, the structure of Example 8-8 is now basically all logic and no particulars—fiddly details are handled by our new functions. If I suddenly needed to download and parse a new data series from the FRED database, I would feel comfortable just throwing it at this script to see what happens, because if there are problems, *I know exactly where to go to fix them.* Instead of having to wade through the entire program, any formatting issues that might arise with a new data source are almost certainly going to be the result of code in either `create_table_row()` or `create_meta_text()`—and even then, problems will probably only appear in one or the other. That means that in order to adapt this script to work with new (similar) data sources, I'll probably only have to look at (maybe) a dozen lines of code. That's certainly better than wading through close to 100!

In other words, while refactoring your data wrangling scripts usually doesn't mean *writing* too much more code, it can really save you from *reading* more than you need to when you want to use, reuse, or adapt it later—and that's yet another way that Python can help you scale your data wrangling work.

Going Global?

In Python, global variables like the one used in Example 8-8 differ from typical variables in two ways:

1. Using the *global* keyword indicates that this variable can be accessed—and modified—from inside *any* function in our program (that is, its *scope* is "global").

2. A global variable (like `the_datemode`) cannot be declared and assigned a value in the same code statement the way we do with most variables (e.g., `is_table_data = False`). Instead, we have to declare it with the *global* keyword on one line and assign a value to it on a subsequent line.

Right now you might be thinking, "Hey, this *global* keyword is handy. Why don't I just make *all* my variables global?" Even though global variables can be quite useful at times, they should always be used cautiously—even as a last resort.

True, adding global variables to our code may help minimize how much you have to re*write* your code in order to re*factor* it. At the same time, the drawbacks of using lots of global variables can quickly overtake the advantages of refactoring in the first place—most especially the ability to reuse variable names across functions and scripts. As you write code over time, you'll almost certainly start to develop your own conventions for naming variables, along with your collection of commonly used functions. But if one of your scripts contains a global variable that *shares* a name with a variable used by an included function, you'll start to get strange and inexplicable behavior from your code. This kind of overlap can lead to the bug hunt of your life, because you'll have to go through your code line by line in order to uncover the mix-up. In other words, use global variables *extremely* sparingly—and not at all if you can avoid it!

Given all the reasons *not* to use global variables, why did I ultimately decide to use one here? First, there is only *one* possible value for `source_workbook.datemode`, because there is only one `datemode` attribute per Excel spreadsheet. So even if a particular workbook had 20 different sheets each containing 100 columns of data, there would still only be one, single, unchanging value for `datemode` for all of them. So conceptually, the value of `datemode` is actually "global"; it's reasonable that the variable we use to store this value would be as well. And since the value of `datemode` will never need to be updated within the script, there is less risk of retrieving an unexpected value from it.

As with all writing, however, these choices are partly a matter of taste—and even our own taste can change over time. While at first I liked the symmetry of creating one function to "build" each row of table data and another function to "build" each line of metadata text, there's also something to be said for breaking that symmetry and avoiding the use of the global datemode variable altogether, as shown in Example 8-9.

Example 8-9. xls_meta_and_date_parsing_refactored_again.py

```python
# converting data in an .xls file with Python to csv + metadata file, with
# functional date values using the "xrld" library.
# first, pip install the xlrd library:
# https://pypi.org/project/xlrd/2.0.1/

# then, import the `xlrd` library
import xlrd

# import the csv library
import csv

# needed to test if a given value is *some* type of number
from numbers import Number

# for parsing/formatting our newly interpreted Excel dates
from datetime import datetime

def main():

    # use `open_workbook()` to load our data in the `source_workbook` variable
    source_workbook = xlrd.open_workbook("fredgraph.xls")

    # open and name a simple metadata text file
    source_workbook_metadata = open("fredgraph_metadata.txt","w")

    # an `.xls` workbook can have multiple sheets
    for sheet_name in source_workbook.sheet_names():

        # create a variable that points to the current worksheet
        current_sheet = source_workbook.sheet_by_name(sheet_name)

        # create "xls_"+sheet_name+".csv" as the current sheet's output file
        output_file = open("xls_"+sheet_name+"_dates.csv","w")

        # use the `writer()` recipe to write `.csv`-formatted rows
        output_writer = csv.writer(output_file)

        # Boolean variable to detect if we've hit our table-type data yet
        is_table_data = False

        # now, we need to loop through every row in our sheet
        for row_num, row in enumerate(current_sheet.get_rows()):

            # pulling out the value in the first column of the current row
            first_entry = current_sheet.row_values(row_num)[0]
```

```
            # if we've hit the header row of our data table
            if first_entry == 'observation_date':

                # it's time to switch our "flag" value to "True"
                is_table_data = True

            # if `is_table_data` is True
            if is_table_data:

                # extract the table-type data values into separate variables
                the_date_num = current_sheet.row_values(row_num)[0]
                U6_value = current_sheet.row_values(row_num)[1]

                # if the value is a number, then the current row is *not*
                # the header row, so transform the date
                if isinstance(the_date_num, Number):  ❶
                    the_date_num = format_excel_date(the_date_num,
                                                     source_workbook.datemode)

                # write this new row to the data output file
                output_writer.writerow([the_date_num, U6_value])

            # otherwise, this row must be metadata
            else:

                # pass the requisite data to our `create_meta_text()` function
                metadata_line = create_meta_text(current_sheet, row_num)

                # write this new row to the metadata output file
                source_workbook_metadata.write(metadata_line)

        # just for good measure, let's close our output files
        output_file.close()
        source_workbook_metadata.close()


def format_excel_date(a_date_num, the_datemode):

    # use the xlrd library's `xldate_as_datetime()` to generate
    # a Python datetime object
    a_date_num = xlrd.xldate.xldate_as_datetime(a_date_num, the_datemode)

    # create a new list containing the_date_num (formatted to MM/DD/YYYY
    # using the `strftime()` recipe) and the value in the second column
    formatted_date = a_date_num.strftime('%m/%d/%Y')

    return(formatted_date)

def create_meta_text(the_sheet, the_row_num):

    meta_line = ""
```

```
# since we'd like our metadata file to be nicely formatted, we
# need to loop through the individual cells of each metadata row
for item in the_sheet.row(the_row_num):

        # write the value of the cell, followed by a tab character
        meta_line = meta_line + item.value + '\t'

    # at the end of each line of metadata, add a newline
    meta_line = meta_line+'\n'

    return(meta_line)

if __name__ == "__main__":
    main()
```

❶ Although I no longer pass parallel information to a custom function in order to generate the table-type and metadata output files, abandoning that symmetry prevents my having to create a global variable.

Which of these is the better solution? As with all writing, it depends on your preferences, your use cases, and your *audience*. Some groups or institutions will be "opinionated" about the choice to use—or avoid—global variables; some will feel that shorter solutions are preferable, while others will prize structural symmetry, or reusability. While Example 8-9 sacrifices some structural symmetry, it *generates* a function that may be more broadly reusable. The choice of which is more important is, as always, up to you to determine.

Documenting Your Custom Scripts and Functions with pydoc

Up until now, we've taken a thorough but free-form approach to documenting our code. There's nothing wrong with this in principle, especially if it helps ensure you actually *do* the documentation in the first place. As your inventory of Python scripts (and their potential audience) expands, however, it is useful to be able to review your personal collection of custom functions without individually opening up and reading through each and every Python file. If nothing else, having lots of files open makes it that much more likely that a stray keystroke will introduce an error into a function you rely on in lots of other scripts—which is a really quick way to ruin your day.

Fortunately, with just a little bit of formatting we can adapt our existing program descriptions and comments to work with a command-line function called pydoc. This will let us print out our script and function descriptions to the command line just by providing the relevant filename.

To see this in action, let's start by refactoring one more script. In this case, we'll revise Example 7-8 to make it a little bit more concise. In the process, I'll also update the comments at the top of the script (and add some to our new function) to make them compatible with the pydoc command. You can see what this looks like in Example 8-10.

Example 8-10. fixed_width_strip_parsing_refactored.py

```
""" NOAA data formatter ❶
Reads data from an NOAA fixed-width data file with Python and outputs
a well-formatted CSV file.

The source file for this example comes from the NOAA and can be accessed here:
https://www1.ncdc.noaa.gov/pub/data/ghcn/daily/ghcnd-stations.txt

The metadata for the file can be found here:
https://www1.ncdc.noaa.gov/pub/data/ghcn/daily/readme.txt

Available functions
-------------------
* convert_to_columns: Converts a line of text to a list

Requirements
------------
* csv module

"""
# we'll start by importing the "csv" library
import csv

def main():
    # variable to match our output filename to the input filename
    filename = "ghcnd-stations"

    # we'll just open the file in read format ("r") as usual
    source_file = open(filename+".txt", "r")

    # the "readlines()" method converts a text file to a list of lines
    stations_list = source_file.readlines()

    # as usual, we'll create an output file to write to
    output_file = open(filename+".csv","w")

    # and we'll use the `csv` library to create a "writer" that gives us handy
    # "recipe" functions for creating our new file in csv format
    output_writer = csv.writer(output_file)

    # we have to "hard code" these headers using the contents of `readme.txt`
    headers = ["ID","LATITUDE","LONGITUDE","ELEVATION","STATE","NAME",
                "GSN_FLAG","HCNCRN_FLAG","WMO_ID"]

    # create a list of `tuple`s with each column's start and end index
    column_ranges = [(1,11),(13,20),(22,30),(32,37),(39,40),(42,71),(73,75),
```

```
                    (77,79),(81,85)]  ❷

    # write our headers to the output file
    output_writer.writerow(headers)

    # loop through each line of our file
    for line in stations_list:

        # send our data to be formatted
        new_row = convert_to_columns(line, column_ranges)

        # use the `writerow` function to write new_row to our output file
        output_writer.writerow(new_row)

    # for good measure, close our output file
    output_file.close()


def convert_to_columns(data_line, column_info, zero_index=False):  ❸
    """Converts a line of text to a list based on the index pairs provided

    Parameters
    ----------
    data_line : str
        The line of text to be parsed
    column_info : list of tuples
        Each tuple provides the start and end index of a data column
    zero_index: boolean, optional
        If False (default), reduces starting index position by one

    Returns
    -------
    list
        a list of data values, stripped of surrounding whitespace
    """

    new_row = []

    # function assumes that provided indices are *NOT* zero-indexed,
    # so reduce starting index values by 1
    index_offset = 1

    # if column_info IS zero-indexed, don't offset starting index values
    if zero_index:
        index_offset = 0

    # go through list of column indices
    for index_pair in column_info:

        # pull start value, modifying by `index_offset`
        start_index = index_pair[0]-index_offset
```

```
            # pull end value
            end_index = index_pair[1]

            # strip whitespace from around the data
            new_row.append((data_line[start_index:end_index]).strip())

    # return stripped data
    return new_row

if __name__ == "__main__":
    main()
```

❶ By starting and ending the file and the convert_to_columns() function descriptions with a set of three double quotation marks ("""), they visually stand from the rest of the comments in the file and will now be accessible to pydoc by running the following in a terminal:[9]

    `pydoc fixed_width_strip_parsing_refactored`

This will display all of the file and function descriptions within the command-line interface (use the arrow keys to scroll up and down, or the space bar to move an entire "page" down at once). To exit the documentation and return to the command line, just hit the q key.

❷ Instead of writing a unique line of code to pull each column of data out of a given line of text, I've put all the start/end values for each column into a list of Python tuples (*http://docs.python.org/3.3/library/stdtypes.html?high light=tuple#tuples*), which are essentially unchangeable lists.

❸ By passing the column start/end information to the convert_to_columns() function along with each line of data, we can use a for...in loop to convert the text to columns. This makes our main script easier to read *and* results in a function that could be reused with *any* line of text we need to split into columns, as long as we pass in the start/end index pairs in the correct format. I've even added a flag value called zero_index, which lets us use this function with start/end pairs that consider zero to be the first position (the default value assumes—as this dataset does—that the first position is "1").

Note that in addition to viewing the documentation for the whole file, it is possible to use pydoc to view the documentation for a single function (for example, the convert_to_columns() function) by running:

---

9 The actual structure/formatting I've used here a mashup of different styles derived from the guide at *https://realpython.com/documenting-python-code/#documenting-your-python-code-base-using-docstrings*. While using a standard approach may matter if you are working with a large team, if you are working alone or in a small group, find a style that works for you!

```
pydoc fixed_width_strip_parsing_refactored.convert_to_columns
```

and moving through/exiting its documentation in the same way as you did for the entire file.

Navigating Documentation in the Command Line

Generically, you can view the documentation of any Python script (if its description has been properly formatted) using the command:

```
pydoc __filename_without_.py_extension__
```

Likewise, you can access the documentation of any function in a script using:

```
pydoc __filename_without_.py_extension__.__function_name__
```

And since you can't use your mouse to get around these files, the following keyboard shortcuts will be especially helpful:

arrow up/arrow down
    Move one line up/down

spacebar
    Move one entire page down

q
    Quit/exit documentation

The Case for Command-Line Arguments

Refactoring one long script into a series of functions isn't the only way we can make our data wrangling code more reusable. For multistep data wrangling processes (such as those that involve downloading data, like Example 5-8, or converting PDF images to text, like Example 4-16), breaking up our *code* into multiple scripts is yet another way to save time and effort. For one thing, this approach lets us minimize how often we do resource-intensive tasks, like downloading data or actually converting PDF pages to images. Even more, these tasks tend to be pretty rote—it doesn't make much difference *what* data we're downloading or *which* PDF we're converting to images; our script will pretty much always be doing the same thing. As a result, all we need are a few additional tricks to transform our currently bespoke data wrangling scripts into standalone code that we can reuse as is—over and over again.

As an example, let's look back at Example 5-8. In this script, the main thing we're doing is downloading the contents of a web page; it's just that in this instance we've "hard-coded" the target file (*http://web.mta.info/developers/turnstile.html*) specifically. Likewise, the code that downloaded the XML and JSON files in Example 5-1 was almost identical—the only real difference was the source URLs and the filenames of the local copies. If there was a way that we could refactor these scripts so that the *whole thing* acted more like a function, that could potentially save us a lot of time and effort in the long run.

Fortunately, this is very achievable with standalone Python files, thanks to the built-in *argparse* Python library, which lets us write our scripts to both require—and use—arguments passed in from the command line. Thanks to *argparse*, we don't need to write a new script for every individual web page we want to download, because it lets us specify both the target URL *and* the name of our output file right from the command line, as shown in Example 8-11.

Example 8-11. webpage_saver.py

```
""" Web page Saver!

Downloads the contents of a web page and saves it locally

Usage
-----
python webpage_saver.py target_url filename


Parameters
----------
target_url : str
    The full URL of the web page to be downloaded
filename : str
    The desired filename of the local copy

Requirements
------------
* argparse module
* requests module


"""
# include the requests library in order to get data from the web
import requests

# include argparse library to pull arguments from the command line
import argparse

# create a new `ArgumentParser()`
parser = argparse.ArgumentParser()

# arguments will be assigned based on the order in which they were provided
parser.add_argument("target_url", help="Full URL of web page to be downloaded") ❶
parser.add_argument("filename", help="The desired filename of the local copy")
args = parser.parse_args()
```

```
# pull the url of the web page we're downloading from the provided arguments
target_url = args.target_url

# pull the intended output filename from the provided arguments
output_filename = args.filename

# create appropriate header information for our web page request
headers = {
    'User-Agent': 'Mozilla/5.0 (X11; CrOS x86_64 13597.66.0) ' + \
                  'AppleWebKit/537.36 (KHTML, like Gecko) ' + \
                  'Chrome/88.0.4324.109 Safari/537.36',
    'From': 'YOUR NAME HERE - youremailaddress@emailprovider.som'
}

# because we're just loading a regular web page, we send a `get` request to the
# URL, along with our informational headers
webpage = requests.get(target_url, headers=headers)

# opening up a local file to save the contents of the web page to
output_file = open(output_filename,"w")

# the web page's code is in the `text` property of the website's response
# so write that to our file
output_file.write(webpage.text)

# close our output file!
output_file.close()
```

❶ Here we're assigning the parameter name we can use to access the values passed via the command-line from within our script. The help text is important! Be descriptive but concise.

Help Me!

We've written this code to use *positional* arguments in the command line, rather than *optional* arguments, because our code can't do anything useful unless it has at least a target_url and a filename to save it to.

But how would someone new to our script know that? Well, we obviously have our pydoc-compatible documentation, but we *also* have the "help" text we added along with each argument. If someone encounters our script and only wants to know what the required arguments are, they can run:

```
python webpage_saver.py -h
```

which will print out a concise "how-to" guide for our script (with respect to required arguments, at least) to the command line.

Now we *should* have an easy way to download any web page to our device, without having to write a script for every unique URL. For example, if we run:

```
python webpage_saver.py "http://web.mta.info/developers/turnstile.html" \
"MTA_turnstiles_index.html"
```

we will get exactly the same result as in Example 5-8, but we can *also* run:

```
python webpage_saver.py \
"https://www.citibikenyc.com/system-data/operating-reports" \
"citibike_operating_reports.html"
```

to get the Citi Bike operating reports without having to even *open*, much less modify, our script. Handy, no?

 Using command-line arguments with your task-specific scripts can save you time, but not if you end up copying complex URLs into your command-line interface character by character. To make things simpler, here's a quick overview of how to copy/paste to the command line, depending on your operating system:

Linux (including Chromebook)
Highlight the URL/text you want to copy, then context-click and select Copy. In your command-line window, just click and it will automatically paste.

Windows/Macintosh
Highlight the URL/text you want to copy, then context-click and select Copy. In your command-line window, context-click again and select Paste.

Where Scripts and Notebooks Diverge

By now you may have noticed that in the preceding sections, I *didn't* describe a way to get arguments from the command line into a Jupyter notebook, nor have I talked much about generating and interacting with script and function documentation for Jupyter notebooks, either. This is not because these things are impossible but because Jupyter notebooks are designed to let you interact with Python differently than standalone scripts, and some of these concepts are less applicable to them. As someone who started working with Python before Jupyter (formerly IPython) notebooks existed, my bias is still toward standalone scripts for the majority of my rubber-to-the-road Python data wrangling. While notebooks are (generally) great for testing and tweaking chunks of code, I almost always end up migrating back to standalone scripts once I've identified the approach that works for a particular data wrangling task. This is mostly because as I move further along in a project, I often get impatient even with the process of opening and modifying a script unless I have to—much less launching a webserver or waiting for a web page to load (I might not even have an internet connection!). These are some of the reasons why I favor using command-line arguments and standalone scripts for common, straightforward tasks.

As we'll soon see, however, the interactivity of Jupyter notebooks makes them somewhat superior to standalone Python scripts when it comes to experimenting with —and especially sharing—the data analysis and visualization portion of our data wrangling work. As a result, you'll find more references to Jupyter notebooks in particular as we turn to those topics in Chapters 9 and 10.

Conclusion

In this chapter, we've taken a bit of a break from data wrangling per se to revisit some of our prior work where the code had gotten unwieldy. Through the process of refactoring, we explored how we can reorganize code that *works* into code that *works well*, because it is more readable and reusable. As our data wrangling projects evolve, this will help us build up and make use of our own collection of custom functions that meet our own particular data wrangling needs. Similarly, by applying a bit more structure to our documentation, we made it accessible—and useful—right from the command line so that we can find the script or function that we're looking for without opening a single script. And in a similar vein, we applied that refactoring logic to our scripts so that we can customize their functionality without having to open *them*, either!

In the next chapter, we'll return to our focus on data with an overview of some of essential data analysis techniques. After that, in Chapter 10 we'll (briefly) cover the core visualization approaches that will help you understand and present your data effectively so that you can better share your data wrangling insights with the world!

CHAPTER 9
Introduction to Data Analysis

So far, this book has focused mostly on the logistics of acquiring, assessing, transforming, and augmenting data. We've explored how to write code that can retrieve data from the internet, extract it from unfriendly formats, evaluate its completeness, and account for inconsistencies. We've even spent some time thinking about how to make sure that the tools we use to do all this—our Python scripts—are optimized to meet our needs, both now and in the future.

At this point, though, it's time to revisit the *why* of all this work. Back in "What Is "Data Wrangling"?" on page 2, I described the purpose of data wrangling as transforming "raw" data into something that can be used to generate insight and meaning. But unless we follow through with at least *some* degree of analysis, there's no way to know if our wrangling efforts were sufficient—or what insights they might produce. In that sense, stopping our data wrangling work at the augmentation/transformation phase would be like setting up your mise en place and then walking out of the kitchen. You don't spend hours carefully prepping vegetables and measuring ingredients unless you want to *cook*. And that's what data analysis is: taking all that beautifully cleaned and prepared data and turning it into new insight and knowledge.

If you fear we're slipping into abstractions again, don't worry—the fundamentals of data analysis are simple and concrete enough. Like our data quality assessments, however, they are about one part technical effort to four parts judgment. Yes, the basics of data analysis involve reassuring, 2 + 2 = 4–style math, but the insights depend on *interpreting* the outputs of those very straightforward formulas. And that's where you need logic and research—along with human judgment and expertise—to bridge the gap.

Over the course of this chapter, then, we'll be exploring the basics of data analysis—specifically, the simple measures of *central tendency* and *distribution* that help us give data meaningful context. We'll also go over the rules of thumb for making appropriate inferences about data based on these measures and the role that both numerical and *visual* analysis play in helping us understand the trends and anomalies within our dataset. Toward the end of the chapter, we'll address the limits of data analysis and why it *always* takes more than traditional "data" to get from the "what" to the *why*. Along the way, of course, we'll see how Python can help us in all these tasks and why it's the right tool for everything from quick calculations to essential visualizations.

Context Is Everything

If I offered to sell you an apple right now for $0.50, would you buy it? For the sake of this example, let's imagine that you like apples, and you're feeling like a snack. Also, this is a beautiful apple: shiny, fragrant, and heavy in the hand. Let's also suppose you're confident that I'm not trying to harm you with this apple. It's just a nice, fresh, apple, for $0.50. Would you buy it?

For most people, the answer is: *it depends*. Depends on what? Lots of things. No matter how much you trust me (and my almost-too-perfect apple), if someone standing next to me was selling also-very-good-looking apples for $0.25 each, you might buy one of those. Why? Well, obviously they're cheaper, and even my *incredibly* awesome apple probably isn't *twice* as awesome as the next one. At the same time, if your cousin was standing on the other side of me selling tasty apples for $0.60 each, you might well buy one of those instead, just to show support for your cousin's new apple-selling start-up.

This might seem like a pretty complicated decision-making process for choosing a piece of fruit, but in reality we make these kinds of choices all the time, and the results are sometimes surprising. Economists like Dan Ariely (*https://danar iely.com/all-about-dan*) and Tim Harford (*https://timharford.com/articles/undercovere conomist*) have conducted research illustrating things like how influential a "free" gift is, even if it creates an added cost, or how our satisfaction with our own pay can go down when we learn what people around us are earning.[1] Most of our priorities and decisions depend on value judgment, and in order to make those effectively we need to know what our options are. Would I buy a fairy-tale-perfect apple for $0.50? Maybe. Probably not if I could get a really similar one at the next corner for half the price. But I probably would if I was in a hurry and had to walk a mile to get one otherwise. Though we all understand what we mean by it, a more precise way of saying "It depends" would be to say, "It depends on the *context*."

The importance of context is why a data point in isolation is meaningless; even if it is factually "true," a single data point can't help us make decisions. Generating

---

1 See *Predictably Irrational* by Dan Ariely (Harper) for more information.

and acquiring new knowledge, in general, is about connecting new information to information we already know. In other words, the knowledge isn't "in the data" itself but in its *relationship* to other things. Since we can't exhaustively explore the context of every situation where decisions are required (including your concerns about your cousin's new apple startup and the importance of supporting family efforts), we often have to restrict ourselves to examining those parts of the context that we can (or have chosen to) consistently measure and quantify. In other words, we turn to data.

How do we derive context from data? We do things like investigate its provenance, asking questions about who collected it and when and why—these answers help illuminate both what the data includes and what might be missing. And we look for ways to systematically compare each data point to the rest, to help understand how it conforms to—or breaks—any patterns that might exist across the dataset as a whole. Of course, none of this is likely to offer us definitive "answers," but it will provide us with insights and ideas that we can share with others and use to inspire our *next* question about what's happening in the world around us.

Same but Different

While building context is essential for generating insight from data, how do we know *which* contexts matter? Given that there are infinite relationship *types* we could identify, even among the data points in a pretty small dataset, how do we decide which ones to pay attention to? Take, for example, the data in Example 2-9, which was just a simple (fictional) list of page counts:

```
page_counts = [28, 32, 44, 23, 56, 32, 12, 34, 30]
```

Even with just this handful of numbers, there are lots of types of "context" we can imagine: we could describe it in terms of even versus odd values, for example, or which ones can be evenly divided by 8. The problem is, most of these relationships are not all that interesting. How can we tell which ones will be?

It turns out, the human brain is pretty well wired to notice—and care about—two types of relationships in particular: sameness and differentness. Trends and anomalies in almost any type of stimulus—from seeing patterns in clouds or lottery results (*https://archive.is/20130121151738/http://dbskeptic.com/2007/11/04/apophenia-definition-and-analysis*) to quickly identifying a difference in orientation among similar objects (*https://csc2.ncsu.edu/faculty/healey/PP*)—tend to catch our attention. This means *trends* and *anomalies* are interesting, almost by definition. So a pretty good place to start when we want to build meaningful context for our data is with the ways that individual records in a given dataset are similar to—or different from—each other.

What's Typical? Evaluating Central Tendency

What does it mean for something to be "average"? When we use that term in day-to-day life, it's often a stand-in for "unremarkable," "expected," or "typical." Given its specifically *un*extraordinary associations, then, in many cases "average" can also be a synonym for "boring."

When it comes to analyzing data, however, it turns out that what's "average" is actually what interests us, because it's a basis for comparison—and comparisons are one thing humans care about a lot. Remember the research on wages? As humans, we want to know how things that affect us compare to what is "typical" for other people. So even if we never hope to *be* "average," in general we still want to know both what it is and how our own experience compares.

What's That Mean?

You may already be familiar with the process for calculating the "average" of a set of numbers: add them all up and divide by how many you have. That particular measure of *central tendency* is more precisely known as the *arithmetic mean*, and it's calculated just the way you remember. So for our page_counts variable, the math would be:

    mean_pgs = (28+32+44+23+56+32+12+34+30)/9

And this would give us (roughly) a mean value of:

    32.333333333333336

As a representation of the "typical" chapter length, this seems pretty reasonable: many of our chapters have page counts that are pretty close to 30, and there are even two chapters that have *precisely* 32 pages. So a mean per-chapter page count of just over 32 seems about right.

While the mean may have served us well in this instance, however, there are many situations where using it as a measure of "typicality" can be deeply misleading. For example, let's imagine one more, *really* long chapter (like, 100 pages long) got added to our book. Our method of calculating the mean would be the same:

    mean_pgs = (28+32+44+23+56+32+12+34+30+100)/10

But now the mean value would be:

    39.1

All of a sudden, our "average" chapter length has increased by almost 6 pages, even though we only added a single new chapter, and fully *half* of our chapters are 28–34 pages long. Is a chapter that's roughly 39 pages truly "typical" in this case? Not really.

What we're seeing even in this small example is that while in *some* cases the mean is a reasonable measure of "typicality," it's also heavily influenced by extreme values—and just one of these is enough to make it useless as a shorthand for what is "typical" of a dataset. But what are our alternatives?

Embrace the Median

Another way to think about "typical" values in a dataset is to figure out what is—quite literally—in the "middle." In data analysis, the "middle" value in a series of records is known as the *median*, and we can find it with even *less* math than we used when calculating the mean: all you need to do is sort and count. For example, in our original set of chapter lengths, we would first sort the values from lowest to highest:[2]

```
page_counts = [28, 32, 44, 23, 56, 32, 12, 34, 30]
page_counts.sort()
print(page_counts)
```

Which gives us:

```
[12, 23, 28, 30, 32, 32, 34, 44, 56]
```

Now, all we have to do is choose the "middle" value—that is the one that is positioned halfway between the beginning and end of the list. Since this is a nine-item list, that will be the value in the fifth position (leaving four items on either side). Thus, the *median* value of our page_count dataset is 32.

Now, let's see what happens to the median when we add that extra-long chapter. Our sorted data will look like this:

```
[12, 23, 28, 30, 32, 32, 34, 44, 56, 100]
```

And what about the median? Since the list now has an *even* number of items, we can just take the *two* "middle" values, add them together, and divide by two.[3] In this case, that will be the values in positions 5 and 6, which are both 32. So our median value is (32 + 32) / 2 = 32. Even when we add our extra-long chapter, the median value is still the same!

Now at first you might be thinking, "Hold on, this feels wrong. A whole new chapter was added—a really *long* chapter, but the median value didn't change *at all*. Shouldn't it move, at least a little bit?"

The real difference between the mean and the median is that the mean is powerfully affected by the specific *values* in dataset—as in how high or low they are—while the median is influenced mostly by the *frequency* with which certain values appear. In a

---

2 You can technically also sort from highest to lowest, but starting with lower values is conventional and will make things easier in the long run.

3 There are actually multiple methods of choosing the median value for an even number of data points, but as long as you're consistent, any of them is fine. Anecdotally, this is the approach that feels most intuitive and that I've seen used most often.

sense, the median is much closer to a "one value, one vote" sort of approach, whereas the mean lets the most extreme values speak "loudest." Since our current goal is to understand what values are "typical" in our dataset, the median will usually be the most representative choice.

Think Different: Identifying Outliers

In "Same but Different" on page 289, I noted that human beings, in general, are interested in "sameness" and "differentness." In looking at our two possible measures of central tendency, we were exploring ways in which values in a dataset are similar. But what about the ways in which they are different? If we look again at our original `page_count` list, we'd probably feel confident that a 32-page chapter is reasonably "typical," and maybe even a 30-, 28-, or 34-page chapter, too. But what about a 12-page chapter? Or a 56-page chapter? They certainly don't seem typical, but how do we know which values are different *enough* to be truly "unusual?"

This is where we have to start mixing math with human judgment. Measures of central tendency can be pretty unequivocally calculated, but determining which values in a dataset are truly unusual—that is, which are *anomalies* or *outliers*—cannot be definitively assessed with arithmetic alone. As datasets get larger and more complex, however, it gets harder for humans to interpret them effectively as sets of data points.[4] So how can we possibly apply human judgment to large datasets? We need to engage our largest and most comprehensive data-processing resource: the human visual system.[5]

Visualization for Data Analysis

The role of visualization in data work is twofold. On the one hand, visualization can be used to help us *analyze* and make sense of data; on the other, it can be used to *convey* the insights that we've generated from that analysis. Using data for the latter purpose—as a communication tool to share insights about our data with a broader audience—is something that we'll explore in-depth in Chapter 10. Here, we're going to focus on the ways in which visualization can offer us insight into the data we have.

In order to understand how visualization can help us identify extreme values in our data, we first need to look—quite literally—at the data itself. In this case, I don't mean

---

4 While the precise estimates for the number of items that humans can hold in *working memory* differ, researchers *do* agree that this capacity has limits. See *https://ncbi.nlm.nih.gov/pmc/articles/PMC2864034* and *https://pnas.org/content/113/27/7459*.

5 Although there is a long way to go, there is some exciting research being done on tactile graphics (*https://dl.acm.org/doi/abs/10.1145/3373625.3418027*) to reduce the vision dependency of these approaches, especially for folks who are blind or visually impaired. See *http://shape.stanford.edu/research/constructiveVizAccess/assets20-88.pdf*.

that we're going to open up our CSV file and start reading through data records. Rather, we're going to create a special kind of bar chart known as a *histogram*, in which each bar represents the number of times a particular value appears in our dataset. For example, we can see a very simple histogram of our (expanded) `page_count` data in Figure 9-1.

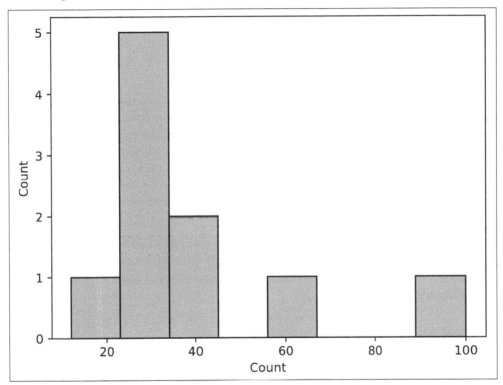

Figure 9-1. A basic histogram

For a dataset as small as our `page_counts` example, a histogram can't tell us much; in fact, a dataset with only 10 values arguably has too few data points for either the concepts of *central tendency* (like the *mean* and the *median*) or outliers to have much meaning. Even so, in Figure 9-1 you can see the *beginnings* of what looks like a pattern: the two chapters of equal length form a double-height spike, with the unique page-lengths of most of the remaining chapters becoming single-height bars clustered reasonably close it. *Way* out on the right end, meanwhile, is our 100-page chapter, with no other values anywhere near it. While we might have already been tempted to conclude that the 100-page chapter was an anomaly—or *outlier*—based on the math, this histogram certainly reinforces that interpretation.

Of course, in order to really appreciate the power of visualization for data analysis, we'll want to look at a dataset with values we couldn't even hope to "eyeball" the way that we did with our list of page counts. Fortunately, the Paycheck Protection Program (PPP) data that we worked through in Chapter 6 is *definitely* not lacking in this regard, since it contains hundreds of *thousands* of loan records. To see what we can learn about what is and isn't "typical" in the loan amounts approved through the PPP, we'll write a quick script to generate a histogram of the currently approved loan values in the PPP. Then, we'll label that histogram with both the mean and median values in order to see how well each might serve as a potential measure of central tendency. After that, we'll return to the question of identifying possible outliers in the approved loan amounts, using both our visualization of the data and some math to back it up.

For this to work, we'll once again be leveraging some powerful Python libraries—specifically, *matplotlib* and *seaborn*—both of which have functions for calculating and visualizing data. While *matplotlib* remains the foundational library for creating charts and graphs in Python, we're also using *seaborn* for its helpful support of more advanced calculations and formats. Because the two are highly compatible (*seaborn* is actually built on *top* of *matplotlib*), this combination will offer us the flexibility we need both to quickly create the basic visualizations we need here and also customize them for presenting data effectively in Chapter 10.

For now, though, let's focus on the analytical size of our visualization process. We'll start this by creating a basic histogram of our PPP loan data using the `CurrentApprovalAmount` values. We'll also add mean and median lines for more context, as shown in Example 9-1.

Example 9-1. ppp_loan_central_measures.py

```
# `pandas` for reading and assessing our data
import pandas as pd

# `seaborn` for its built-in themes and chart types
import seaborn as sns

# `matplotlib` for customizing visual details
import matplotlib.pyplot as plt

# read in our data
ppp_data = pd.read_csv('public_150k_plus_221.csv')

# set a basic color theme for our visualization
sns.set_theme(style="whitegrid")

# use the built-in `mean()` and `median()` methods in `pandas
mean = ppp_data['CurrentApprovalAmount'].mean()  ❶
median = ppp_data['CurrentApprovalAmount'].median()

# create a histogram of the values in the `CurrentApprovalAmount` column
```

```
approved_loan_plot = sns.histplot(data=ppp_data, x="CurrentApprovalAmount")
```

```
# get the min and max y-values on our histogram
y_axis_range = approved_loan_plot.get_ylim() ❷
```

```
# add the vertical lines at the correct locations
approved_loan_plot.vlines(mean, 0, y_axis_range[1], color='crimson', ls=':') ❸
approved_loan_plot.vlines(median, 0, y_axis_range[1], color='green', ls='-')
```

```
# the matplotlib `show()` method actually renders the visualization
plt.show() ❹
```

❶ The `CurrentApprovalAmount` column in our PPP data tells us the dollar amount of each loan that is currently approved (whether or not it has been disbursed).

❷ The `get_ylim()` method returns the lowest and highest y-axis value as a list. We'll mostly be using this to set a legible length for our mean and median lines.

❸ We can add vertical lines anywhere on our histogram (or other visualization) by specifying the "x" position, "y" starting point, "y" ending point, color, and line style. Note that the units for "x" and "y" values are relative to the dataset, *not* the visual size of the chart.

❹ While calling the *matplotlib* `show()` method is not explicitly required in Jupyter notebooks, like `print()` statements, I prefer to include them for clarity and consistency. By default, the chart will render in "interactive" mode (in Jupyter, you'll need to include the `%matplotlib notebook` "magic" command, as I have in the provided files), which allows us to zoom, pan, and otherwise explore our histogram in detail without writing more code.

Most likely, you're looking at the chart that displayed as a result of running this script (which hopefully looks something like Figure 9-2) and thinking, "Now what?" Admittedly, this initial visualization seems a bit lackluster—if not downright confusing. Fear not! If anything, take this as your first case study in why visualization for analysis and visualization for communication are *not* one and the same. Analytical visualizations like this one, for example, require far more effort to read, understand, and refine than *any* visualization we would want to use for general communications. For generating insight about our data, however, this is actually just the right place to start.

Before we forge ahead with our data analysis, though, let's take a moment to appreciate the distinctly old-school—but incredibly useful—interface that Python has given us for this chart. Rather than just a static image, our Python script has *also* given us an entire toolbar (shown in Figure 9-2) that we can use to interact with it: to zoom, pan, modify, and even save the output. While of course we can (and eventually will) customize the contents and aesthetics of this chart using code, the fact that we can effectively explore our data without having to constantly modify and rerun our code is a huge time-saver. To get a feel for what's possible, take a few minutes to play with the controls yourself. When you're ready to move on with our data analysis, just click the "home" icon to return the chart to its initial view and follow along in the sections that follow.

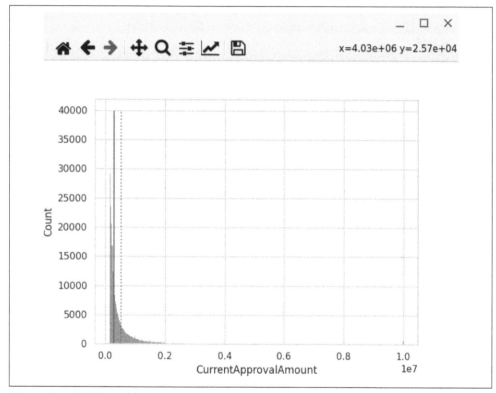

Figure 9-2. PPP loan histogram

What's Our Data's Shape? Understanding Histograms

When we were working with our data in a table-type format, we tended to think of its "shape" in terms of the number of rows and columns it had (this is actually *exactly* what the pandas.shape property of a DataFrame returns). In this context, the "shape" we're interested in is the literal shape of the histogram, which will help us identify potentially interesting or important patterns or anomalies. Some of the first things we'll look for in these instances are:

Symmetry

Is our data vertically symmetrical? That is, could we draw a vertical line somewhere over our visualized data such that the pattern of bars on one side looks (roughly) like a reflection of those on the other?

Density

Where are most of our data values clustered (if anywhere)? Are there multiple clusters or just one?

Unsurprisingly, these questions are about more than aesthetics. The shape of a dataset's histogram illustrates what is typically described as its *distribution*. Because certain distributions have specific properties, we can use our data's *distribution* to help us identify what is typical, what is unusual, and what deserves further scrutiny.

The Significance of Symmetry

In the natural world, symmetry is a common occurrence. Plants and animals tend to be symmetrical in many ways; for example, a dog's face and an oak leaf both exhibit what's known as *bilateral symmetry*—what we might describe as one side being a "mirror image" of the other. Across populations of living things, however, there is also often symmetry in the distribution of certain physical characteristics, like height or wing length. Our histogram lets us observe this symmetry firsthand, by illustrating the *frequency* of specific heights or wing lengths within a population. A classic example of this is shown in Figure 9-3, which shows the length of housefly wings as measured by a team of biologists in the mid-20th century.[6]

The symmetrical bell curve shown in Figure 9-3 is also sometimes described as the "normal," "standard," or "Gaussian" distribution. If you've ever had an academic grade "curved," this was the distribution that the grades in your cohort were being transformed to fit: one with very few scores at the top or bottom and most of them lumped in the middle.

The power of the Gaussian distribution is not just in its pretty shape, however; it's in what that shape means we can *do*. Datasets that demonstrate Gaussian distributions can be both described and compared to one another in ways that nonsymmetrical distributions cannot, because we can meaningfully calculate two measures in particular: the *standard deviation*, which quantifies the numerical range of data values within which most of them can be found, and each value's *z-score*, which describes its distance from the mean in terms of standard deviations. Because of the fundamental symmetry of Gaussian distributions, we can use the *standard deviation* and the *z-score* to compare two sets of functionally similar data *even if they use different scales*. For

---

6 See "A Morphometric Analysis of Ddt-Resistant and Non-Resistant House Fly Strains" by Robert R. Sokal and Preston E. Hunter, *https://doi.org/10.1093/aesa/48.6.499*; the relevant data is provided there.

example, if student grades demonstrate a Gaussian distribution, we can calculate and compare individual students' z-scores (that is, their performance relative to their cohort) even across different classes and instructors who may use different grading rubrics. In other words, even if the mean of student grades for one instructor is in the 90s and for another instructor in the 70s, if both sets of students' grades are truly Gaussian in their distribution, we can still determine which students are doing the best or need the most help across cohorts—something the *nominal* grades (e.g., 74 or 92) could never tell us.

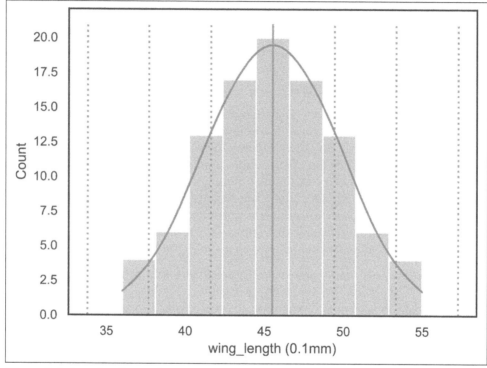

Figure 9-3. Length of housefly wings

These characteristics also inform how we can think about measuring central tendency and outliers. For example, in a "perfect" Gaussian distribution, the mean and the median will have the same value. What's more, a value's z-score gives us a quick way of identifying how typical or unusual that particular value is, because the percentage of data values that we expect to have a given z-score is well-defined. Confused yet? Don't worry. Just like any other complex data relationship, this all makes much more sense if we visualize it.

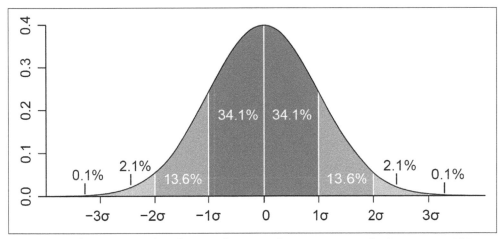

Figure 9-4. The Gaussian distribution, showing what percentage of values exist within 1, 2, and 3 standard deviations (σ) from the mean

As you can see in Figure 9-4,[7] if our data's distribution is Gaussian, more than two-thirds of the data values (34.1% + 34.1% = 68.2%) can be found within one standard deviation (often designated as it is here, by the Greek letter σ) of the mean. Another 27.2% can be found between one and two standard deviations from the mean, and a final 4.2% can be found between two and three standard deviations from the mean. This means that for a Gaussian distribution, *99.7% of all values can be found within 3 standard deviations of the mean.*

So what? Well, remember that one of our fundamental objectives in data analysis is to understand what values are typical for our dataset and which ones are truly extreme. While the mean and the median offer a quick shorthand for a dataset's "typical" value, measures like the standard deviation—and the z-scores we can calculate from it—help us systematically evaluate which values might or might not be truly unusual.

Unsurprisingly, calculating these values using Python is quite straightforward. Using either *pandas* or the *statistics* library, we can quickly find the value of the standard deviation for our dataset (σ) and then use it to place lines over our histogram where the relevant z-score values are. For this example, we'll build on the data used to generate Figure 9-3, as shown in Example 9-2.

---

7 M. W. Toews, "CC BY 2.5," *https://creativecommons.org/licenses/by/2.5*, via Wikimedia Commons (*https://en.wikipedia.org/wiki/Normal_distribution#/media/File:Standard_deviation_diagram.svg*).

Example 9-2. wing_length_with_sd.py

```python
# `pandas` to read in our data
import pandas as pd

# `seaborn` for built-in themes and chart types
import seaborn as sns

# `matplotlib` for customizing visual details
import matplotlib.pyplot as plt

# `statistics` easily calculating statistical measures
import statistics

# read in our data
wing_data = pd.read_csv('wing_length - s057.csv')

# set a basic color theme for our visualization
sns.set_theme(style="white")

# create the histogram, allowing `seaborn` to choose default "bin" values
wing_plot = sns.histplot(data=wing_data, x="wing_length (0.1mm)", kde="True") ❶

# calculate the standard deviation via the `statistics` `stdev()` method
sd = statistics.stdev(wing_data['wing_length (0.1mm)']) ❷

# get the min and max y-values on our histogram
y_axis_range = wing_plot.get_ylim()

# plot the mean as a solid line
mean = wing_data['wing_length (0.1mm)'].mean()
wing_plot.vlines(mean, 0, y_axis_range[1], color='gray', ls='-')

# plot the three standard deviation boundary lines on either side of the mean
for i in range(-3,4): ❸

    # find the current boundary value
    z_value = mean + (i*sd)

    # don't draw a second line over the mean line
    if z_value != mean:

        # plot a dotted gray line at each boundary value
        wing_plot.vlines(z_value, 0, y_axis_range[1], color='gray', ls=':')

# show the plot!
plt.show()
```

❶ Each "bin" is a range of *actual* data values that will be lumped together into a single histogram bar; the `kde` parameter is what adds a smoothed line to our visualization. This line approximates the pattern we would expect if our dataset had infinite data points.

❷ We could also have used the *pandas* `std()` method: `wing_data['wing_length (0.1mm)'].std()`.

❸ Recall that our loop will stop *before* the second value provided to `range()`, so to get three positive lines, we set the second value to 4. By starting with a negative number, we actually *subtract* from the mean at first—which we want to do because we want to capture values both above *and* below the mean.

As you review the output of Example 9-2 you might be thinking, "Great, we've drawn some lines on data about bugs. How will this help me interpret *real* data?" After all, the prototypically Gaussian distribution of this housefly wing-length data doesn't look much like the output we got when we charted our PPP loan data, which was distinctly asymmetrical, as most of your data is likely to be.

So what do we do when our data distribution lacks symmetry? We already know how to find the "middle" of an asymmetric distribution like the one in Example 9-1: by calculating the median, rather than the mean. But what about identifying extreme values? Since asymmetric or *skewed* distributions aren't, well, symmetric, there is no single "standard" deviation, nor can we use it to calculate z-scores. We can, however, still usefully subdivide an asymmetric dataset in a way that will let us generate insight about possibly unusual or extreme values.

Like finding the median, this subdivision process is really quite simple. First, we find the middle value of our sorted dataset—in other words, the median. Now we look at each half of the data records as if it were a standalone dataset and find *their* median values. The median of the lower half is traditionally labeled Q1, while the median of the upper half is traditionally labeled Q3. At this point, we've split our dataset into four parts, or *quartiles*, each of which contains an equal number of data values.

What does this do for us? Well, remember that a big part of what z-scores tell us is the *percentage of data points that have similar values*. Looking at Figure 9-4, for example, we can see that a data point with a z-score of 0.75 is (as we would expect) less than one standard deviation from the mean—something we know will be true for roughly 68.2% of all the data values in the set as a whole. By dividing our data into quartiles, we have started along a similar path. For example, any value in our dataset that is *numerically* less than the value of Q1 is, by definition, smaller than at least 75% of all the data values we have.

Still, what we're *really* looking for are ways to identify potentially unusual values. Being smaller—or larger—than 75% of all data values is something, but it's hardly *extreme*. Identifying our quartile boundaries alone won't quite be enough.

Fortunately, we can use our Q1 and Q3 values to calculate what's known as the *lower bound* and *upper bound* of our dataset. If our data's distribution was secretly Gaussian, these boundaries would line up almost perfectly with the values found at three standard deviations below and above the mean. While of course we're using them precisely because our data *isn't* Gaussian, I make the comparison to illustrate that we can use them to help identify extreme values in an asymmetrically distributed dataset.

Like finding the median, calculating the upper and lower bounds is actually quite straightforward. We start by finding a value called the *interquartile range* (IQR)—a fancy-sounding name for the numerical difference between the values of Q3 and Q1. We then multiply that value by 1.5 and subtract it from Q1 to get the lower bound, and add it to Q3 to get the upper bound. That's it!

IQR (interquartile range) = Q3 – Q1

Lower bound = Q1 – (1.5 × IQR)

Upper bound = Q3 + (1.5 × IQR)

On a Gaussian distribution, our upper and lower bound values will be about three standard deviations above or below the mean—but does this mean that every value beyond our upper and lower bounds is automatically an *outlier*? No. But finding these boundaries does let us narrow down where we might start *looking* for outliers. And just as importantly, these measures help us understand what values are *not* outliers, even if they might seem, numerically, to be pretty different from the "typical" or "expected" value provided by the median or mean.

As an example, let's return to our PPP loan data. A $1 million loan seems like a lot, even if—as we are—you're only looking at loans that were over $150,000 to begin with. But is a $1 million loan truly *unusual*? This is where our measures of central tendency and spread—in this case, the median, quartiles, and lower and upper bound values—can really help us out. Let's take a look at what our histogram looks like with these values added, as shown in Example 9-3, and see what we think.

Example 9-3. ppp_loan_central_and_dist.py

```
# `pandas` for reading and assessing our data
import pandas as pd

# `seaborn` for its built-in themes and chart types
```

```
import seaborn as sns

# `matplotlib` for customizing visual details
import matplotlib.pyplot as plt

# read in our data
ppp_data = pd.read_csv('public_150k_plus_221.csv')

# set a basic color theme for our visualization
sns.set_theme(style="whitegrid")

# use the built-in `mean()` and `median()` methods in `pandas
mean = ppp_data['CurrentApprovalAmount'].mean()
median = ppp_data['CurrentApprovalAmount'].median()

# Q1 is the value at the position in our dataset
# that has 25% of data readings to its left
Q1 = ppp_data['CurrentApprovalAmount'].quantile(0.25)

# Q3 is the value at the position in our dataset
# that has 75% of data readings to its left
Q3 = ppp_data['CurrentApprovalAmount'].quantile(0.75)

# IQR is the difference between the Q3 and Q1 values
IQR = Q3-Q1

# and now we calculate our lower and upper bounds
lower_bound = Q1 - (1.5*IQR)
upper_bound = Q3 + (1.5*IQR)

# use `seaborn` to plot the histogram
approved_loan_plot = sns.histplot(data=ppp_data, x="CurrentApprovalAmount")

# get the min and max y-values on our histogram
y_axis_range = approved_loan_plot.get_ylim()

# add mean line in gray
approved_loan_plot.vlines(mean, 0, y_axis_range[1], color='gray', ls='-')

# other lines in black (median solid, others dotted)
approved_loan_plot.vlines(median, 0, y_axis_range[1], color='black', ls='-')
approved_loan_plot.vlines(lower_bound, 0, y_axis_range[1], color='black', ls=':')
approved_loan_plot.vlines(Q1, 0, y_axis_range[1], color='black', ls=':')
approved_loan_plot.vlines(Q3, 0, y_axis_range[1], color='black', ls=':')
approved_loan_plot.vlines(upper_bound, 0, y_axis_range[1], color='black', ls=':')

# show the plot!
plt.show()
```

As you can see from the zoom-in view of the resulting graph (shown in Figure 9-5), there's really no support for the claim that a loan of \$1 million is out of the ordinary; that amount falls well below the upper bound we've calculated for this dataset. So even though a loan of that amount is larger than three-quarters of all loans approved so far (because the $1 million mark, currently labeled as 1.0 1e6 on the graph's x-axis, is to the *right* of our Q3 line), it's still not *so* much that any loan of $1 million is likely to be worth investigating further. At least, that's probably not where we'd want to start.

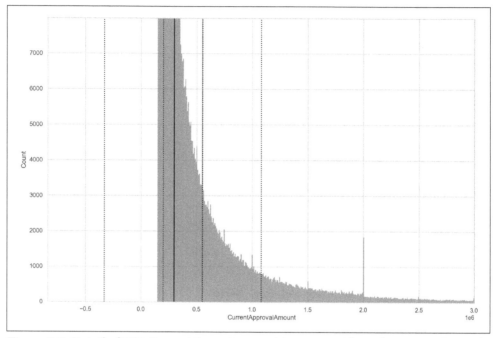

Figure 9-5. Detail of PPP Current Loan Amount histogram with median, quartiles, and bounds in black and mean plotted in gray

So where should we look next for potentially interesting patterns in the data? *Right in front of us*, at the graph we already have. Because while we *could* start looking for more complex statistical measures to calculate and evaluate, even this basic visualization is showing some intriguing patterns in the data. The first one worth noting—if only to reassure ourselves about our choice of statistical measures—is that the mean of this dataset is at nearly the same position in the distribution as our Q3 value. If we had any concern about selecting the median over the mean as a measure of central tendency for this dataset, that fact should set it to rest. The other thing that we can see—in the data view shown in Figure 9-5 and if we were to scroll farther to the right—is that there are curious little spikes in our data, indicating that a particular loan amount was approved with relatively high frequency.[8] Given how clearly these stand out from the data patterns immediately around them, we should probably look at those values next.

---

8 Specifically relative to the loan amounts just above or below these values.

Counting "Clusters"

Imagine you're walking down a crowded street and you notice a group of people gathered on the corner across from you. What do you do? On a busy avenue where most pedestrians are concerned with getting from one place to another, more than one or two people stopped in the same place at the same time is enough to signal that *something* is going on. Whether "something" turns out to be a busker playing music, a vendor of especially popular snacks, or a box full of kittens,[9] the fact remains that our visual system is drawn to anomalies, and that's precisely because deviating from a trend indicates that something at least a little bit out of the ordinary is going on.

This is also why visualizing data is such a valuable tool for analyzing it—our eyes and brain are wired to both quickly perceive patterns and to just as quickly notice deviations from them. Sometimes the reason for a pattern is easy to guess, sometimes less so. But in any predictable pattern—whether it's the flow of people on a street, a bell-shaped data distribution, or one that forms a smoothly sloping curve—something that breaks that pattern is worth investigating.

In the case of Figure 9-5, we can see a range of such pattern violations. The first is the sharp line at the lefthand side of the graph, which serves as a good reminder that our dataset contains *only* approved loan amounts of $150,000 or more, rather than all of the loans that have been approved within the program. In case we had lost sight of that, the obvious and hard cutoff our data shows at the lefthand edge is a good reminder.

Bu there is also another set of pattern violations: little spikes in our histogram around particular points along the x-axis, at data values like $2 million. Where are these coming from? While we can't say for sure, scanning our histogram reveals that similar spikes appear at roughly $500,000 intervals, especially as the loan amounts increase. To some degree, these are probably the result of a tendency toward "round" numbers: if you're going to ask for $1,978,562.34, why not just "round it up" to $2 million? Of course, that would still be $21,437.66 more than maybe you need—and to most of us it is a *lot* of money. Given that PPP loans are intended to support specific costs, it does seem a little strange that *so* many loans—nearly 2,000 of them, based on our graph—would happen to work out to precisely $2 million.

So what's going on? This is where we need to do some additional research to effectively interpret what we're seeing in the data. Based on my experience, my first step would be to look through the rules for PPP loans to see if I can work out why $2 million might be such a popular amount to request. For example, is $2 million a minimum or maximum allowed amount based on specific attributes of the business or what it's requesting support for?

---

9 It happens.

A little bit of searching around the Small Business Administration's (SBA) website (*https://sba.gov/funding-programs/loans/covid-19-relief-options/ paycheck-protection-program/second-draw-ppp-loan*) seems to offer at least part of the answer:

> For most borrowers, the maximum loan amount of a Second Draw PPP loan is 2.5x the average monthly 2019 or 2020 payroll costs up to $2 million. For borrowers in the Accommodation and Food Services sector (use NAICS 72 to confirm), the maximum loan amount for a Second Draw PPP loan is 3.5x the average monthly 2019 or 2020 payroll costs up to $2 million.

Since $2 million is a ceiling for essentially *all* types of businesses applying for so-called second-draw (or second-round) PPP loans—including those that might have initially qualified for *more* money—it makes sense that the cluster of loans approved for *precisely* $2 million is so large.

This "answer," of course, just leads to more questions. According to the documentation, $2 million was the upper limit for second-round PPP loans; first-round loans could be up to $10 million. If so many businesses were requesting the upper limit for *second*-round loans, it indicates that many businesses 1) have already received a first-round loan, and 2) their first-round loan may have been even *larger* than $2 million, since they would have had to round *down* to $2 million if they qualified for more than that in the first round. In other words, we might expect those businesses that requested *precisely* $2 million in second-round loans are among those that were approved for the largest total amounts of PPP loan relief. And of course, if they *did* get some of the largest pots of money, we (and probably a lot of other people!) certainly want to know about it.

The $2 Million Question

In order to understand what (if any) shared characteristics there may be among companies that requested $2 million for their second-round PPP loans, we first have to effectively isolate their records within our dataset. How might we do this? Well, we know that we're interested in companies approved for more than one loan, which means that their `BorrowerName` *should* appear more than once in our data. We *also* know that no second-round loans were issued before January 13, 2021. By combining these two insights, we can probably use our data wrangling skills to do a decent job of identifying the companies that requested precisely $2 million for their second-round loan.

In order to accomplish this, we'll do a couple of key transformations on our dataset:

1. We'll create a new column for each loan, containing the label `first_round`, or `maybe_second`, based on whether it was issued before January 13, 2021. While we can't be sure that all loans after that date were "second round," we *can* be sure that all loans *before* that date were "first round."

2. Look for duplicate entries in our dataset. Each approved loan creates a separate record, so if the same business was approved for two loans, that means its information would appear twice in the records.

The logic here is that if we find a given business name twice in our data *and* those records have different "round" labels, it probably indicates a business that has, in fact, been approved for two separate loans.

As usual, we're going to call in the help of some Python libraries to get this work done. We'll need to use *pandas*, as usual, but we're also going to use another library called *numpy* that has lots of useful array/list functions (*pandas* actually relies heavily on *numpy* under the hood). I'm also going to pull in *seaborn* and *matplotlib* again so that we have the option of generating visualizations to help us evaluate our evolving dataset as we go along.

Although what we're trying to do with this data is conceptually pretty straightforward, the wrangling involved in performing this analysis takes a fair number of steps, as you can see in Example 9-4.

Example 9-4. who_got_2_loans_by_date.py

```python
# `pandas` for data loading/transformations
import pandas as pd

# `seaborn` for visualization
import seaborn as sns

# `matplotlib` for detailed visualization support
import matplotlib.pyplot as plt

# `numpy` for manipulating arrays/lists
import numpy as np

# load our data
ppp_data = pd.read_csv('public_150k_plus_borrower_fingerprint_a.csv')  ❶

# convert the `DateApproved` column to an actual datetime data type
ppp_data['DateApproved'] = pd.to_datetime(ppp_data['DateApproved'])  ❷

# create a variable to hold the second-round start date
second_round_start =  pd.to_datetime('2021-01-13')

# treat today's date to use as the "upper" limit on possible second-round loans
```

```
todays_date = pd.to_datetime('today')

# use 1/1/2020 as a "lower" limit, since it's before the PPP launched
program_start = pd.to_datetime('2020-01-01')

# pass our boundaries and category labels to the pandas `cut()` function
loan_round = pd.cut(ppp_data.DateApproved,
                    bins=[program_start,second_round_start, todays_date],
                    labels=['first_round', 'maybe_second']) ❸

# insert the new column at the position we specify
ppp_data.insert(2,'Loan Round',loan_round)

# this "pivot table" will return a Series showing the number
# of times a particular 'BorrowerNameFingerprint' appears in the dataset
loan_count = ppp_data.pivot_table(index=['BorrowerNameFingerprint'], aggfunc='size')

# convert our Series to a DataFrame and give it a name
loan_count_df = loan_count.to_frame('Loan Count') ❹

# use the `describe()` method to print out summary statistics
print("Description of duplicate borrower table:")
print(loan_count_df.describe()) ❺
```

❶ This file was generated by running our fingerprinting process on BorrowerName, as described in "Finding a Fingerprint" on page 311.

❷ We want to know which loans were approved *before* January 13, 2021. The fastest way to do this will be to convert our DateApproved strings to "real" dates and compare them to that.

❸ The pandas cut() function lets us create a new column by applying boundaries and labels to an existing one. In this case, we label each record according to whether it was approved before or after January 13, 2021.

❹ We do this for convenience so we can use the describe() method.

❺ We expect the maximum value in this table to be 2, since no business is allowed to get more than two loans under the PPP.

If you run the code from Example 9-4 and nothing happens for a minute, don't despair. On my Chromebook, this script takes about 40 to 90 seconds to execute (depending on how many other Linux apps I'm running alongside).[10] When it's finished, however, your output will look something like this:

---

10 If it's *too* many, the output will say Killed. This is a sign you either need to close some apps or maybe move into the cloud.

```
Description of duplicate borrower table:
          Loan Count
count  694279.000000
mean        1.104022
std         0.306489
min         1.000000
25%         1.000000
50%         1.000000
75%         1.000000
max        12.000000
```

From this first effort something seems…off. The output from our `.describe()` command gives us a quick way of getting almost all the summary statistics we're interested in (the Q1, median, and Q3 are labeled here according to the percentage of values that would appear to their left on a histogram—so 25%, 50%, and 75%, respectively). These values suggest that fewer than 25% of all businesses have received more than one loan (otherwise the 75% value would be greater than 1), which makes sense. But the max value is troubling, since the PPP rules don't appear to allow a single business to receive more than two loans, much less 12! Let's take a closer look by adding the code shown in Example 9-5 to what we wrote in Example 9-4 and see what we find.

Example 9-5. who_got_2_loans_by_date.py (continued)

```
# start by sorting our DataFrame of loan counts from greatest to least
sorted_loan_counts = loan_count_df.sort_values(by=['Loan Count'], ascending=False)

# create a new DataFrame with *only* those that have more than two loans
more_than_two = sorted_loan_counts[sorted_loan_counts['Loan Count'] > 2]

# print one instance of each business name that appears in `more_than_two`
print("Businesses that seem to have gotten more than 2 loans:")
print(more_than_two.shape)

print("Number of businesses that appear to have gotten precisely 2 loans:")
precisely_two = sorted_loan_counts[sorted_loan_counts['Loan Count'] == 2]
print(precisely_two.shape)
```

Now we get the additional output shown here:

```
Businesses that seem to have gotten more than 2 loans:
(58, 1)
Number of businesses that appear to have gotten precisely 2 loans:
(72060, 1)
```

This suggests that there are only a (relative) handful of businesses that may have been approved for more than two loans, and we can probably attribute those cases to a combination of our chosen fingerprinting approach (a combination of BorrowerName, BorrowerCity, and BorrowerState) along with the possibility that there are multiple instances of a single franchise in the same city that applied for PPP funds.[11] In any case, there are few enough of them that they are unlikely to change the outcome of our analysis considerably, so we won't focus on tracking down their details right now. At least the second piece of output showing that 72,060 individual businesses got *exactly* two loans seems reasonable so far, since this is definitely less than 25% of our total dataset, and therefore aligns with the summary statistics we got from our Loan Count DataFrame (because the value of Q3 was still 1, meaning that fewer than 25% of all business names appeared in our dataset more than once).

Of course, this is still just an estimate; it would be much better if we had a more official count of second-round loans to work with. As noted at the end of Chapter 6, the Small Business Administration *did* actually release an official data dictionary (*https://data.sba.gov/dataset/ppp-foia/resource/aab8e9f9-36d1-42e1-b3ba-e59c79f1d7f0*) for the PPP loan data, and while it doesn't contain all of the information we might hope, it *does* indicate that the ProcessingMethod field distinguishes between first-round (PPP) and second-round (PPS) loans. Let's look at our data this way and compare it to our name-matching-based estimate by adding the code in Example 9-6 further down in our file.

Example 9-6. who_got_2_loans_by_date.py (continued again)

```
# use `ProcessingMethod` value to identify second-round loans
pps_loans = ppp_data[ppp_data['ProcessingMethod'] == 'PPS']

# print out the `shape` of this DataFrame to see how many businesses we have
print("Number of loans labeled as second round:")
print(pps_loans.shape)
```

Rerunning our script yields the additional output:

```
Number of loans labeled as second round:
(103949, 52)
```

Wow! Even with our possibly too-lax fingerprinting method, we still failed to find more than 300,000 businesses with both of their loans. What do we do?

First of all, recognize that this isn't even an unusual situation. We're dealing with around 750,000 data records, each one of which is a combination of data entry done by multiple individuals, including the borrower, the lender, and possibly the SBA. The fact that there are still so many discrepancies is not really surprising (I illustrate some of them in the following sidebar), but all is not lost. Remember that our original interest was in those businesses that got precisely $2 million for their second-round

---

11 See *https://sba.gov/document/support-faq-ppp-borrowers-lenders* and *https://sba.gov/document/support-sba-franchise-directory* for more information.

loan, which is likely to be just a fraction of all the businesses that got two loans. We can still move ahead with that part of the analysis in order to (1) test how effective our date-based estimate of second-round loans was, and (2) see what we can learn about that specific subset of businesses that got exactly $2 million in the second round.

Finding a Fingerprint

Since we have already covered how to use the *fingerprints* library in previous chapters, I skipped over the exact process used to prepare the data we're looking at here.[12] As always, however, the effectiveness of the matching process depends not just on the fingerprinting algorithm itself but also the data it's applied to. While the combination of `BorrowerName`, `BorrowerCity`, and `BorrowerState` is clearly far from perfect, I settled on it only after having first tried to match up loans based on `BorrowerName` directly, and then on a combination of the fingerprinted `BorrowerName` and `Borower Zip`. In both instances, I could find matches for less than half of the second-round loans.

Wondering what the data discrepancies look like? Here's one example:

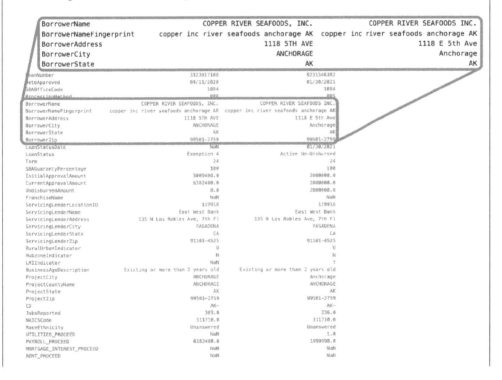

---

12 Though you can find it in the file *ppp_fingerprint_borrowers.py*.

As you can see, while the `BorrowerName` field is *similar*, it's not the same, nor is the value in `BorrowerAddress` or the capitalization of `BorrowerCity`. The zip codes *are* the same, but many other columns—such as `Gender`, `Veteran`, and even `LMIIndica` `tor`—don't match up, either. That's real-world data for you!

At this point, we're going to use the information from the `PaymentProcessingMethod` column to *validate* our earlier work using name-matching and date-based loan round estimates. To do this, we're going to merge our `Loan Count` DataFrame back onto our original dataset. Then we'll select only the $2M loans that we *estimate*, based on their date, were second-round loans. Finally, we'll compare that number of loans with the number of $2M loans we *know* were second draw, based on their `ProcessingMethod` value of PPS. Obviously, this will mean adding yet more code to our file, as shown in Example 9-7.

Example 9-7. who_got_2_loans_by_date.py (continued more)

```
# how many loans in our derived data frame were approved for precisely $2M
# during the (possibly) second-round timeframe?

# merge our `loan_count_df` back to keep track of businesses
# we labeled as having precisely two loans
ppp_data_w_lc = pd.merge(ppp_data, loan_count_df,
                         on=['BorrowerNameFingerprint'], how='left')

# now get *all* the records of business names we associated with two loans
matched_two_loans = ppp_data_w_lc[(ppp_data_w_lc['Loan Count'] == 2)]

# select those loans our `maybe_second` loans that have a value of $2M
maybe_round2_2M = matched_two_loans[(matched_two_loans[
                                    'CurrentApprovalAmount'] == 2000000.00) &
                                    (matched_two_loans[
                                    'Loan Round'] == 'maybe_second')]
print("Derived $2M second-round loans:")
print(maybe_round2_2M.shape)

# select those loans that we *know* are second round and have a value of $2M
pps_got_2M = pps_loans[pps_loans['CurrentApprovalAmount'] == 2000000.00]
print("Actual $2M second-round loans:")
print(pps_got_2M.shape)
```

Adding this code to our main files give us another few lines of output:

```
Derived $2M second-round loans:
(1175, 53)
Actual $2M second-round loans:
(1459, 52)
```

If we compare these results to previous ones, it looks like we're doing a bit better. Across *all* loans, we appear to have matched up 72,060 out of 103,949 actual second-round loans, or about 70%. For those organizations approved for $2M in second-round loans, we've found 1,115 out of 1,459, or about 80%.

So what can we say about businesses that got $2M in the second round? We can't say anything with 100% confidence unless and until we find matches for those 284 companies whose `BorrowerNameFingerprint` isn't the same between their first- and second-round loans. But we can still look at our 80% sample and see what we discover. To do this, I'm going to take the following steps:[13]

1. Find all the unique `BorrowerNameFingerprint` values for businesses that definitely got $2M second-round loans.

2. Create a DataFrame (`biz_names_df`) based on this list and fill it out with the flag value `2Mil2ndRnd`.

3. Merge that DataFrame back onto my dataset and use the flag value to pull *all* loan records for those businesses (both first and second round).

4. Do some basic analyses of how much money those businesses were approved for across both rounds, and visualize those amounts, comparing the official second-round designation (that is, `ProcessingMethod == 'PPS'`) with our derived, date-based category.

And of course, now that I've written out in a list the steps my script should take (this is exactly the kind of thing that you'd want to put in your data diary and/or program outline), it's just a matter of coding it up below our existing work; for clarity I've put it into a second script file, the complete code of which is shown in Example 9-8.

Example 9-8. who_got_2M_with_viz.py

```
# `pandas` for data loading/transformations
import pandas as pd

# `seaborn` for visualization
import seaborn as sns

# `matplotlib` for detailed visualization support
import matplotlib.pyplot as plt

# `numpy` for manipulating arrays/lists
import numpy as np
```

---

13 Note that I'm intentionally doing this in a *slightly* roundabout way in order to demonstrate a few more data-wrangling and visualization strategies, but feel free to rework this code to be more efficient as an exercise!

```
# load our data
ppp_data = pd.read_csv('public_150k_plus_borrower_fingerprint_a.csv')

# convert the `DateApproved` column to an actual datetime data type
ppp_data['DateApproved'] = pd.to_datetime(ppp_data['DateApproved'])

# create a variable to hold the second-round start date
second_round_start =  pd.to_datetime('2021-01-13')

# treat today's date to use as the "upper" limit on possible second-round loans
todays_date = pd.to_datetime('today')

# use 1/1/2020 as a "lower" limit, since it's before the PPP launched
program_start = pd.to_datetime('2020-01-01')

# pass our boundaries and category labels to the pandas `cut()` function
loan_round = pd.cut(ppp_data.DateApproved,
                    bins=[program_start,second_round_start, todays_date],
                    labels=['first_round', 'maybe_second'])

# insert the new column at the position we specify
ppp_data.insert(2,'Loan Round',loan_round)

# this "pivot table" will return a Series showing the number
# of times a particular 'BorrowerNameFingerprint' appears in the dataset
loan_count = ppp_data.pivot_table(index=['BorrowerNameFingerprint'],
                                  aggfunc='size')

# convert our Series to a DataFrame and give it a name
loan_count_df = loan_count.to_frame('Loan Count')

# use the `describe()` method to print out summary statistics
print("Description of duplicate borrower table:")
print(loan_count_df.describe())

# start by sorting our DataFrame of loan counts from greatest to least
sorted_loan_counts = loan_count_df.sort_values(by=['Loan Count'],
                                               ascending=False)

# create a new DataFrame with *only* those that have more than two loans
more_than_two = sorted_loan_counts[sorted_loan_counts['Loan Count'] > 2]

# print one instance of each business name that appears in `more_than_two`
print("Businesses that seem to have gotten more than 2 loans:")
print(more_than_two.shape)

print("Number of businesses that appear to have gotten precisely 2 loans:")
precisely_two = sorted_loan_counts[sorted_loan_counts['Loan Count'] == 2]
print(precisely_two.shape)

# use `ProcessingMethod` value to identify second-round loans
```

```python
pps_loans = ppp_data[ppp_data['ProcessingMethod'] == 'PPS']

# print out the `shape` of this DataFrame to see how many businesses we have
print("Number of loans labeled as second round:")
print(pps_loans.shape)

# how many loans in our derived data frame were approved for precisely $2M
# during the (possibly) second-round timeframe?

# merge our `loan_count_df` back to keep track of businesses
# we labeled as having precisely two loans
ppp_data_w_lc = pd.merge(ppp_data, loan_count_df,
                          on=['BorrowerNameFingerprint'], how='left')

# now get *all* the records of business names we associated with two loans
matched_two_loans = ppp_data_w_lc[(ppp_data_w_lc['Loan Count'] == 2)]

# select those loans our `maybe_second` loans that have a value of $2M
maybe_round2_2M = matched_two_loans[
                    (matched_two_loans['CurrentApprovalAmount'] == 2000000.00) &
                    (matched_two_loans['Loan Round'] == 'maybe_second')]
print("Derived $2M second-round loans:")
print(maybe_round2_2M.shape)

# select those loans that we *know* are second round and have a value of $2M
pps_got_2M = pps_loans[pps_loans['CurrentApprovalAmount'] == 2000000.00]
print("Actual $2M second-round loans:")
print(pps_got_2M.shape)

# isolate the fingerprints of businesses that got $2M second-round loans approved
biz_names = pd.unique(pps_got_2M['BorrowerNameFingerprint'])

# convert that list to a DataFrame
biz_names_df = pd.DataFrame(biz_names, columns=['BorrowerNameFingerprint'])

# create a new array of the same length as our biz_names_df and fill with
# a flag value
fill_column = np.full((len(biz_names),1), '2Mil2ndRnd')
biz_names_df['GotSecond'] = fill_column

# now merge this new, two-column DataFrame back onto our full_data list,
# so that we (hopefully) find their first-round loans as well
second_round_max = pd.merge(ppp_data_w_lc, biz_names_df,
                            on='BorrowerNameFingerprint')

# now all the loans that share fingerprints with the ones that got the max
# amount in the second round should have the flag value '2Mil2ndRnd' in the
# 'GotSecond' column
second_max_all_loans = second_round_max[
                            second_round_max['GotSecond'] == '2Mil2ndRnd']

# we expect this to be twice the number of businesses that received $2M
```

```
# second-round loans
print('Total # of loans approved for most orgs that got $2M for second round:')
print(second_max_all_loans.shape)

# how much money were these businesses approved to get from the PPP, total?
total_funds = second_max_all_loans['CurrentApprovalAmount'].sum()
print("Total funds approved for identified orgs that could have " + \
      "second-round max:")
print(total_funds)

# plot our date-based `Loan Round`-labeled data next to records
# separated by `ProcessingMethod`. Do we get the same results?

# set the seaborn theme
sns.set_theme(style="whitegrid")

# use `matplotlib` `subplots()` to plot charts next to each other
# use `tuples` to access the different subplots later
fig, ((row1col1, row1col2)) = plt.subplots(nrows=1, ncols=2)

# plot the histogram of our date-based analysis
date_based = sns.histplot(data=second_max_all_loans, x='CurrentApprovalAmount',
                          hue='Loan Round', ax=row1col1)

# plot the histogram of our data-based analysis
data_based = sns.histplot(data=second_max_all_loans, x='CurrentApprovalAmount',
                          hue='ProcessingMethod', ax=row1col2)

# show the plot!
plt.show()
```

Running this script will give us all the output from previous examples, along with yet a few more lines of additional output:

```
Total # of loans approved for most orgs that got $2M for second round:
(2634, 54)
Total funds approved for identified orgs that could have second-round max:
6250357574.44
```

At first, it looks like something's off, because we might have expected our total number of loans to be 2 × 1,175 = 2,350. But remember that we matched up loans based on whether they got approved for *exactly* $2M in round two, *and* we failed to match 284 loans on BorrowerNameFingerprint. This means we have *all* second-round loans but are missing 284 first-round loans in these numbers. In other words, we'd *expect* to have (2 × 1,175) + 284 = 2,634—and we do! Good! It's always nice when *something* matches up. This means that our "total" figure, while still not 100% accurate, is a somewhat reasonable estimate of the *minimum* total loan amount this group of businesses were approved for in PPP funds: around $6 billion dollars.

Finally, let's take a look at the visualization shown in Figure 9-6, which is a view of the graphic generated by the script in which we can compare how our Loan Round classification matches up against the designated PPS loans. This is a rough (but still useful) way to validate our work—and the results look pretty good![14]

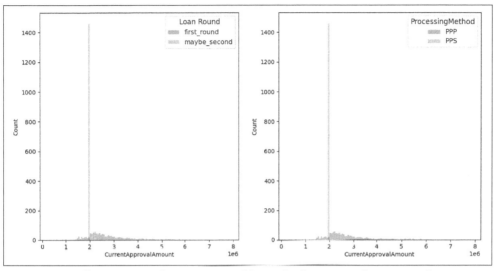

Figure 9-6. Dollar amount of most approved loans for businesses that received two PPP loans, by loan round

Interestingly, though, Figure 9-6 also illustrates something else: it seems that a fair number of the businesses approved for $2M in second-round loans violate our earlier hypothesis that companies approved for $2M in second-round loans were approved for *more* than that amount in their first-round loans, when the limits were higher. As usual, in answering one question, we've generated another! And of course the work we've already done would give us a head start down the road to answering it. Before we let loose on our next round of question-and-answer, though, we need to talk about one more essential component of data analysis and interpretation: *proportionality*.

Proportional Response

Imagine you go out to eat with some friends. You've eaten recently, so you just order a drink, but your three friends are ravenous and each order a full meal. How do you decide who owes what when the check arrives? Most of us would agree that the most sensible thing to do would be to calculate—or at least estimate—what *proportion* of

---

14 If we compare the results numerically, we'll find they're identical, at least for our subset of companies approved for $2M in the second round.

the total bill each person's order accounted for, and then have each person pay that, along with that same proportion of, say, the tax and tip.

The same sort of logic applies when we're analyzing data. In "The $2 Million Question" on page 306, we looked at the *total* funds that had been approved for a certain subset of businesses through the PPP, and while $6B sounds like a lot, we should arguably be more interested in how those businesses *used* that money, rather than the absolute number of dollars they got. Since the PPP was designed to keep people on the payroll, one thing we might want to know is how much money those businesses received *in relation to how many jobs they preserved*, a process I think of as *rationalizing* the data.[15]

Fortunately, the process of rationalizing our data is extremely simple: we calculate the *ratio* between two data values by dividing one number by the other. For example, if we want to know how many dollars per job the companies identified in "The $2 Million Question" on page 306 spent, we can (after some sanity checking) divide the value in PAYROLL_PROCEED by the value in JobsReported for each record, as shown in Example 9-9.

Example 9-9. dollars_per_job_2M_rnd2.py

```
# `pandas` for data loading/transformations
import pandas as pd

# `seaborn` for visualization
import seaborn as sns

# `matplotlib` for customizing visuals
import matplotlib.pyplot as plt

# `numpy` for manipulating arrays/lists
import numpy as np

# load our data
ppp_data = pd.read_csv('public_150k_plus_borrower_fingerprint_a.csv')

# first, sanity check our data
print(ppp_data[ppp_data['JobsReported'] <= 0]) ❶

# drop the records with no value in `JobsReported`
ppp_data.drop(labels=[437083,765398], axis=0) ❶

# calculate the dollars per job
dollars_per_job = ppp_data['CurrentApprovalAmount']/ppp_data['JobsReported']
```

---

15 This term has more specific meanings in the business and statistics/data-science worlds, but *proportionalizing* just sounds kind of awkward. Plus, it better matches the actual calculation process!

```
# insert the new column into our original dataset
ppp_data.insert(3, 'Dollars per Job', dollars_per_job)

# use `ProcessingMethod` value to identify second-round loans
pps_loans = ppp_data[ppp_data['ProcessingMethod'] == 'PPS']

# select all second-round loans that have a value of $2M
pps_got_2M = pps_loans[pps_loans['CurrentApprovalAmount'] == 2000000.00]
print("Actual $2M second-round loans:")
print(pps_got_2M.shape)

# pull fingerprints of businesses approved for $2M second-round loans
biz_names = pd.unique(pps_got_2M['BorrowerNameFingerprint'])

# convert that list to a DataFrame
biz_names_df = pd.DataFrame(biz_names, columns=['BorrowerNameFingerprint'])

# create an array of the same length as `biz_names_df`; fill with flag value
fill_column = np.full((len(biz_names),1), '2Mil2ndRnd')
biz_names_df['GotSecond'] = fill_column

# now merge this new, two-column DataFrame back onto our full_data list
second_round_max = pd.merge(ppp_data, biz_names_df, on='BorrowerNameFingerprint')

# all loans whose fingerprints match those of businesses that got $2M
# in the second round should have `2Mil2ndRnd` in the `GotSecond` column
second_max_all_loans = second_round_max[
                            second_round_max['GotSecond'] == '2Mil2ndRnd']

# sbould be 2x the number of businesses approved for $2M second-round
print('Total # of loans approved for most orgs that got $2M for second round:')
print(second_max_all_loans.shape)

# how much money were these businesses approved to get from the PPP, total?
total_funds = second_max_all_loans['CurrentApprovalAmount'].sum()
print("Total funds approved for identified orgs that could have " + \
      "second-round max:")
print(total_funds)

# now, let's plot that new column on our selected dataset

# set the seaborn theme
sns.set_theme(style="whitegrid")

# the `matplotlib` `subplots()` to plot charts side by side
fig, ((row1col1)) = plt.subplots(nrows=1, ncols=1)

# plot the histogram of our date-based analysis
date_based = sns.histplot(data=second_max_all_loans, x='Dollars per Job',
                          hue='ProcessingMethod', ax=row1col1)
```

```
# show the plots!
plt.show()
```

❶ It turns out that a couple of businesses didn't report *any* jobs, which will break our calculation. Since there are only two records guilty of this, we'll just drop them, using their *pandas*-assigned row labels.

While the text output here confirms that we're looking at the same set of loans that we examined in "The $2 Million Question" on page 306, our rationalized data highlights some noteworthy anomalies in some of the first-round loans, where a handful of companies appear to have had loans approved that allocated more for payroll than the $100,000-per-job limit allowed, as shown in Figure 9-7.

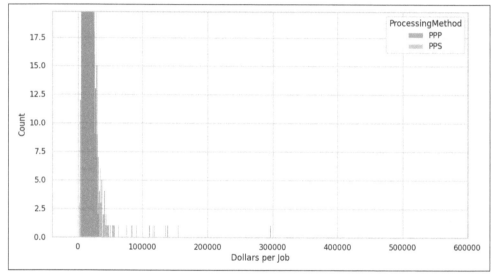

Figure 9-7. Detail of dollars per job of companies approved for $2M in second-round loans

What do we make of this? You may notice that by now we've veered a rather long way from the question we posed back in "The Pandemic and the PPP" on page 187, where we started out trying to assess whether the PPP had helped "save" American businesses. While that focus helped us work our way through our data quality evaluations, doing some contextual analysis has opened up a number of new questions and directions—which I think you'll find is a pretty common occurrence when it comes to data wrangling. Hopefully, though, this will just encourage you to keep working with new datasets to see what else you can find!

Conclusion

After all these analyses, we've learned a few new things—some of which are specific to this dataset but many of which are far more generally applicable:

- A relatively small number of companies were approved for the maximum allowable second-round amount in the PPP loan program. While many of them had filed for much more than that for their first-round loan, some did not.

- A handful of companies that were approved for a $2M second-round loan claimed more than $100,000 per reported job in their first-round loan.

- Human-entered data is always a mess. That's why data cleaning is an ongoing, iterative process. Documenting your work is essential to being able to defend your results.

So, our introductory data analysis left us with far more questions than answers. At this point, there's only one way we're going to find out more: talking to people. Sure, some of the patterns we uncovered look questionable (*https://papers.ssrn.com/ sol3/papers.cfm?abstract_id=3906395*), but we have far too many unknowns to make any well-supported claims at this point. For example, many of the $2M second-round loans had yet to be disbursed when this data was released, so some companies might have actually gotten or used far less than that. Since the PPP rules only require that a minimum percentage of a loan is spent on payroll in order to be forgivable, companies that appear to have been approved for too much may have simply used the difference on other allowable expenses, like mortgage interest or health care costs. In other words, while we can learn a little bit from this type of numerical data analysis, it will never be enough to tell us the whole story—either the how or the why. That is something for which we need direct human input.

Once we've done that work, and are clear about what insights we want to share, we are ready to begin thinking about the most effective way to convey what we've learned to others. Just as our data analysis relies on both data *and* human judgment and input, the most effective data communications almost always involve a balance between words and visualizations. As we'll see in the next chapter, by crafting both our words *and* our visualizations with care, we can better ensure that our intended message truly gets heard.

# CHAPTER 10

Presenting Your Data

After all the effort we've put into accessing, assessing, cleaning, transforming, augmenting, and analyzing our data, we've finally reached the point where we're ready to start thinking about communicating what we've learned to others. Whether it's for a formal presentation to colleagues or a social media post for friends and followers, sharing the insights we've generated through our data wrangling work is an opportunity for our work to have impact beyond ourselves.

Like every other part of our data wrangling process, effectively and accurately conveying our insights involves applying only a few hard-and-fast rules but a whole lot of judgment. This is certainly true of written communications, but perhaps even more so when it comes to the aspect of data communication that often gets the most attention: *visualization*.

As we touched on in "Visualization for Data Analysis" on page 292, creating visualizations to effectively share our data insights with others requires a different focus and approach than we had when building the visualizations for generating those insights in the first place. For example, unless you're trying to reach a *pretty* specialized audience (say, through an academic publication), it's deeply unlikely that a histogram will find its way into your visualization vocabulary when it's time to share your findings with the world. At the same time, it is *extremely* likely that you will end up using some form of bar or column chart[1] to share your insights with a nonspecialist audience, since these widely used and highly legible graphic forms are relatively easy for most audiences to interpret accurately.

In other words, the way we choose to visually represent our data findings should be informed by not just the *data* we have (or used to reach our conclusions) but also

---

1 Of which a histogram is a special type.

the *audience* we are trying to reach. Many software packages (including some of the ones we have already used) will happily generate charts and graphs if you simply point them to a structured dataset and pass in a few optional parameters. While this will work in the bare-minimum sense of producing a visualization, the output will be much more like a machine translation than a poem. Yes, at a high level it may conform to the "rules" of the language, but the clarity of its meaning (to say nothing of its effectiveness or *eloquence*) is questionable. As such, using visualization to make our data insights truly accessible to others requires thinking carefully about *what* you want to convey, *which* visual form suits it best, and *how* you can tailor it to your specific needs.

Over the course of this chapter, we'll cover each of these tasks in turn, starting with some strategies designed to help you identify the key points in your data findings. After that, we'll do a review of the most common (and useful!) visual forms for data. In each instance, we'll cover the rules and best practices for using each of them, in addition to presenting some basic code for rendering them in Python using a combination of the *seaborn* and *matplotlib* libraries. Finally, we'll take a basic visualization of real-world data and work through how to customize and refine its various elements in order to turn the (usually) serviceable default presentation into something that is both accurate *and* appealing. Along the way, I hope you'll encounter at least a few new tools and approaches that will help you think more critically about data visualization in general—whether it's the result of your own data wrangling efforts or not.

Foundations for Visual Eloquence

As I've mentioned a few times, the process of writing good code mirrors that of writing well in most other circumstances. For example, in Chapter 8 we spent time revising and restructuring code that—while it already *worked*—evolved into scripts and functions that were ultimately clearer, cleaner, and more reusable. At a high level, this process was not dissimilar to how you might revise an essay or an article: once you have all your key ideas collected in one place, you can come back to the piece later and see how it might be reworded and reorganized so that the writing is more concise and the concepts flow more logically.

Though this same write-edit-polish cycle applies to data visualizations, however, the unit we are working with is much less like an essay and much more like a single *paragraph*—because in general, a single visualization should be used to convey just *one single* idea. This is true whether your visualization is printed or digital, static or interactive, whether it is part of a longer talk or will be a standalone social media post. One visualization = one key idea.

I'm emphasizing this now because if you came to this chapter hoping for examples of how to build Gapminder-style (*https://www.google.com/publicdata/directory*) interactives or elaborate stream graphs (*https://flowingdata.com/2008/02/25/ebb-and-flow-of-box-office-receipts-over-past-20-years*), I want to disappoint you promptly: in this chapter, my focus will be on the most commonly used visualization types, such as bar, column, and line charts. The reason is partly because they remain the simplest and most interpretable way to represent data that has only one independent variable—and that's all you should be trying to present most of the time, anyway. Yes, more complex visualizations *can* be used to plot multiple independent variables—the original Gapminder visualization is a rare good example of this—but without an endearing Swedish man to guide viewers through them in real time (*https://youtube.com/watch?v=jbkSRLYSojo*), they are more like pretty toys than informative tools. That's why our focus here will be on refining accessible visual forms into what I like to call *eloquent* graphics—visualizations that, like the best text, convey information clearly, simply, and accessibly. While making eloquent graphics doesn't preclude visual complexity or even interactivity, it *does* require that every aspect of the visualization contributes to the clarity and meaning of the graphic.

Achieving this kind of visual eloquence means thinking about data visualization in three main phases:

1. *Refining your focus*

   What *precisely* are you trying to communicate? In some ways, this parallels the process of choosing your original data wrangling question: no matter what your wrangling and analysis have revealed, you need to communicate *one* idea per visualization. How do you know if you've done this effectively? Most of the time, this means you will able to express it *in a single sentence*. As with your earlier data wrangling question, the data statement you craft will act as a kind of "ground truth" for making choices about your visualization. Anything that helps you convey your idea more clearly gets kept; *everything else* gets cut.

2. *Finding your visual form*

   Is your data best displayed as a column or line chart? Is it a map? A pie chart? A scatter plot or bubble chart? Identifying the best visual form for your data will always involve some experimentation. At the same time, choosing a visual form to express your data statement is not solely a matter of preference, or taste; there are a handful of incontrovertible rules about how certain types of data and data relationships must be visually encoded. Yes, aesthetics *do* play a role in the effectiveness of a visualization—but they cannot override the need for accuracy.

3. *Enhancing clarity and meaning*

   Even with the major visual form identified, there are a plethora of ways in which the details of your visualization can improve or degrade its clarity, accessibility, visual appeal, and eloquence. At minimum, you will need to make decisions about color, pattern, scales, and legends, as well as labels, titles, and annotations. If your data statement is especially complex, you will need to carefully layer on even more visual structure to capture these nuances, such as error bars or uncertainty ranges, or perhaps projected and/or missing data.

In the following sections, we'll not only discuss each of these phases conceptually, but we'll use real-world data to see how they are applied in practice using Python.

Making Your Data Statement

Many years ago, I was fortunate to have *The New York Times*' Amanda Cox (*https://en.wikipedia.org/wiki/Amanda_Cox*) as a guest speaker in one of my data visualization courses, where she shared an excellent tip for assessing whether a given data statement was truly appropriate for visualization: "If you don't have a verb in your headline, you have a problem."

Treated superficially, of course, this requirement is easy to meet.[2] The spirit of her statement, however, implies something much more rigorous: that your graphic's headline should clearly articulate some significant relationship or claim, and the supporting evidence should be visible in the graphic itself. Why is this so important? For one thing, putting your claims right in the headline will encourage readers to actually *look* at your graphic in the first place; naming them clearly helps ensure that viewers will—quite literally—know *where* to look for supporting evidence for those claims. Of course, it's our job as information designers to make sure that all of our graphic's visual cues do this too, but often it's the headline that draws people in (*https://psychologicalscience.org/news/how-headlines-change-the-way-we-think.html*).

If you simply can't manage to get an action verb in your graphic's headline, it's a clue that a visualization is probably *not* the best way to convey your insights. True, in the right circumstances humans can process visualizations incredibly quickly (*https://news.mit.edu/2014/in-the-blink-of-an-eye-0116*), but that advantage is only realized if the visualization has something to "say." In other words, while you may be able to generate a visually accurate chart titled "One Year of Daily Treasury Long-Term Rates," the reality is that even the biggest policy wonk will wonder why they should bother looking at it. Don't insist on visualization if it's not the right tool! Remember that our goal is to convey our data wrangling insights as effectively as possible—not to express them visually at all costs. By focusing first on refining your data statement—and confirming it has the power you need—you will avoid spending lots of time designing and building a visualization that doesn't really do what you want or what your audience needs. Sure, basic data visualizations can be quickly generated

---

2 Particularly if you give yourself credit for *linking verbs* (*https://merriam-webster.com/dictionary/link ing%20verb*).

with a dataset and a solid visualization library (like *seaborn*). But making really *eloquent* visualizations requires careful thought as well as detailed customization of even the best library's default charts. Before you commit all that time and energy, then, it's worth making sure that your complex visualization wouldn't have been better off as a single, highlighted statistic from your analysis.

Once you've got a powerful data statement "headline" in place, however, it's time to identify the graphic form that will help you most effectively present the data evidence for your claim.

Charts, Graphs, and Maps: Oh My!

Even if we limit ourselves to the more straightforward graphic forms, there are still enough options to make the process of finding the best one for our data a little bit overwhelming. Should you choose a line chart or a bar graph? If a bar graph is best, should it be horizontal or vertical? Are pie charts *ever* OK? Unfortunately, this is one situation where our Python libraries largely *cannot* help us, since in general they will just valiantly attempt to produce whatever type of chart you ask for with the data you give them. We need a better way.

This is where having a well-focused data statement comes in. Does your statement reference *absolute* values—like the CurrentApprovalAmount in our PPP loan data —or does it focus on the *relationship* between values, as in "The pandemic cut annual FDI flows by one-third" (*https://economist.com/graphic-detail/2021/06/21/the-pandemic-cut-annual-fdi-flows-by-one-third*)? While claims about *absolute* values are often best expressed through bar charts, data statements about relationships can be well supported through a wider range of visual forms. If your data statement includes a claim about change over time, for example, a line graph or scatter plot is a good place to start. Meanwhile some visual forms, like pie charts and maps, are difficult to adapt to anything except data from a single point in time.

In truth, there are few hard-and-fast rules for visualizing data,[3] but I have outlined those that exist in the sections that follow—along with some general tips for designing your graphics. While these guidelines will help you choose a form for your visualization that doesn't work *against* your data, that's only the next step. The choices that can really elevate your graphics are the ones that we'll cover in "Elements of Eloquent Visuals" on page 345. That section is where we'll move beyond the (still quite excellent) defaults of *seaborn* and begin digging more into *matplotlib* in order

---

3 Though even those few are often are violated publicly and frequently, e.g., Junk Chart's "Start at Zero Improves This Chart but Only Slightly" (*https://junkcharts.typepad.com/junk_charts/2021/06/start-at-zero-improves-this-chart-but-only-slightly.html*).

to control things like the labels, colors, and annotations that can really set your visualization apart.

Pie Charts

Pie charts are a surprisingly polarizing topic in visualization. Though pie charts are helpful for teaching children about fractions (*https://pbs.org/parents/recipes/pegs-pizza-fractions*), there are plenty of folks who feel they have little to no place in an effective visualization lexicon (*https://storytellingwithdata.com/blog/2011/07/death-to-pie-charts*).

Personally, I think there are specific—if limited—situations in which a pie chart is the best visualization for supporting your data statement. For example, if you are trying to make a point about what *proportion* or *share* of your data has a particular value and the remaining values can be sensibly grouped into four or fewer categories, then a pie chart may well be what you want. This is especially true if the resulting chart highlights values that correspond to some "recognizable" (*https://store.moma.org/for-the-home/kitchen-dining/cookware-kitchen-tools/visual-measuring-cups/8711-802262.html*) fraction of the whole (e.g., 1/4, 1/3, 1/2, 2/3, or 3/4), since the human eye is able to detect such differences in line orientation without much effort (*https://csc2.ncsu.edu/faculty/healey/PP*).

For example, looking at the results of the New York City Democratic primary for mayor in June 2021 (*https://washingtonpost.com/elections/election-results/new-york/nyc-primary*), we can imagine writing a data statement along the lines of "Despite Wide Field, Top 3 Candidates Capture Nearly 3/4 of First-Choice Votes." Because only four candidates received more than 10% of the first-choice votes, it is also reasonable to lump all the remaining candidates into a single "Other" category. In this instance, then, a pie chart is a perfectly reasonable way to both accurately present the results and support our claim—in part because it makes it easy to see how significantly the front-runners outpaced the other candidates.

Given the contentious nature of pie charts, it's not totally surprising that there is no pie chart option provided in the generally quite versatile *seaborn* library. We can, however, use *matplotlib* directly to get a very serviceable pie chart.[4] Still, there are a few idiosyncrasies in the *matplotlib* pie charting function that we have to overcome. For example, best practice dictates that pie charts are laid out with the largest section starting at "12 o'clock," with the rest added in descending size order clockwise from there. In *matplotlib*, however, the first section starts at "3 o'clock," and additional sections are added *counter*clockwise from there. As a result, we need to specify

---

4 Since both the *pandas* and *seaborn* libraries rely heavily on *matplotlib*, there are many instances where significant customization requires using *matplotlib* features directly, as we'll see in more detail in "Elements of Eloquent Visuals" on page 345.

startangle=90 and reverse the largest-to-smallest order of our segments.[5] Likewise, *matplotlib* also assigns each "slice" of the pie a different color hue (e.g., purple, red, green, orange, and blue) by default, in a particular range of colors that may be inaccessible to folks with certain kinds of colorblindness. Since our data statement is conceptually grouping the top three candidates, I've made all of these the same shade of green; and since *all* the candidates are from the same political party, I've kept all the slices in the green family. To see how this type of chart is coded (including these small customizations), take a look at Example 10-1 and the resulting visualization in Figure 10-1.

Example 10-1. a_humble_pie.py

```python
import matplotlib.pyplot as plt

# matplotlib works counterclockwise, so we need to essentially reverse
# the order of our pie-value "slices"
candidate_names = ['Adams', 'Wiley', 'Garcia', 'Yang', 'Others']
candidate_names.reverse()
vote_pct = [30.8, 21.3, 19.6, 12.2, 16.1]
vote_pct.reverse()

colors = ['#006d2c','#006d2c', '#006d2c', '#31a354','#74c476']
colors.reverse()

fig1, ax1 = plt.subplots()
# by default, the starting axis is the x-axis; making this value 90 ensures
# that it is a vertical line instead
ax1.pie(vote_pct, labels=candidate_names, autopct='%.1f%%', startangle=90,
        colors=colors) ❶
ax1.axis('equal')  # equal aspect ratio ensures that pie is drawn as a circle.

# show the plot!
plt.show()
```

❶ The argument that we pass to `autopct` should be a "formatted string literal," also known as an *f-string* (*https://docs.python.org/3/tutorial/inputoutput.html#formatted-string-literals*). This example specifies that the fraction be expressed as a *floating point* (decimal) number to one-point of precision. The double percent sign (`%%`) is used here to print a single one in the output (by escaping the reserved percent sign symbol with another one).

---

5 Obviously, we could simply reverse the order in which we originally specified the data, but I prefer to have the data order and the eventual visual order match up.

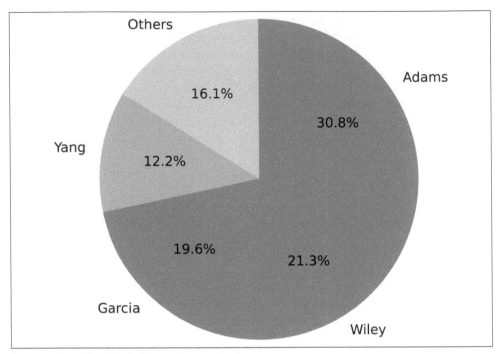

Figure 10-1. New York City primary pie chart

To recap, if you're considering a pie chart:

Rule
Your data categories must conceptually (and literally) sum to a single "whole."

Guideline
The number of categories should be condensed to five or fewer.

Guideline
The proportion of data you want to highlight should be 1/4, 1/3, 1/2, 2/3, or 3/4 of the total.

If your data doesn't fit one or more of those requirements, however, a bar chart may be the next graphic form to explore.

Bar and Column Charts

Bar charts are often the most effective way to highlight the relationships (including differences) among discrete, nominal (as opposed to proportional) data values. Unlike pie charts, bar charts can accurately represent datasets where the values do not sum to a single "whole." They can also effectively represent both positive and negative values (simultaneously, if needed) and can display both point-in-time comparisons of different categories of data and data values over time. The bars can also be oriented vertically (sometimes these graphics are described as *column* charts) or horizontally to make labels and data relationships more legible.

In other words, bar charts are *incredibly* flexible and offer many options for presenting the evidence for data claims effectively. There is, however, *one hard-and-fast rule* for working with bar charts: *data values MUST start at zero!* There are really no exceptions to this rule, though that doesn't stop some people from trying (*https:// datajournalism.com/read/longreads/the-unspoken-rules-of-visualisation*). Why is this rule so important? Because starting bars of a chart at a number *other* than zero means that their visual difference in length will no longer be proportional to their *actual* difference in value.

For example, imagine you were arguing for a raise at work, where you currently earn the US federal minimum wage of $7.25 per hour. You ask your boss to raise your hourly rate to $9.19 per hour (*https://data.bls.gov/cgi-bin/cpicalc.pl? cost1=7.25&year1=200907&year2=202107*), to account for the effect of inflation since the minimum wage was last raised in 2009.

"Well," says your boss, "let's see what that kind of raise would look like," and then shows you a chart like the one shown in Figure 10-2.

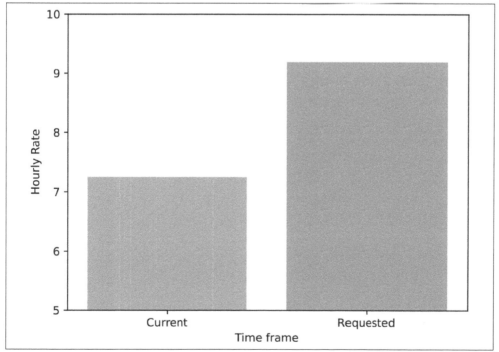

Figure 10-2. An inaccurate wage comparison

See the problem? By starting the bars at 5 rather than zero, the chart in Figure 10-2 makes it *look* like $9.19 per hour would be almost *double* your current wage. But of course some simple math (9.19 – 7.25 / 7.25 = ~.27) illustrates that it's just over 25% more than you're currently making. As you can see, starting bar charts at zero isn't a matter of taste, aesthetics or semantics—it's a visual lie (*https://flowing data.com/2017/02/09/how-to-spot-visualization-lies*).

Still, even professional graphics teams sometimes get this wrong. Take this example, highlighted on Kaiser Fung's excellent blog, *Junk Charts*, titled "Working Culture" (*https://junkcharts.typepad.com/junk_charts/2005/11/finally_a_tange.html*) and reproduced in Figure 10-3.

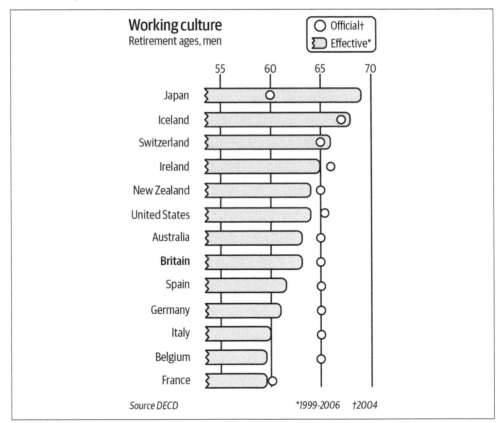

Figure 10-3. An inaccurate retirement age comparison

In Figure 10-3, a "broken" bar chart claims to display when men in different countries stop working, as compared to the official retirement age. As in Figure 10-2, failing to start the bars at zero grossly misrepresents their real value difference: according to the data labels, men in France retired roughly 10 years before men in Japan—a 15% difference in working years. But the actual bar for Japan is *more than twice as long* as the one for France. Of course, if the bars all started at zero, the difference in their values would not seem so dramatic.

What gives? Are the designers of this visualization really trying to trick us into thinking that men in Japan work twice as long as men in France? Almost certainly not. Graphics like the one in Figure 10-3 are the reason why expressing *one* idea per visualization is so important: trying to layer in more than that is where you're most likely to run into trouble and end up with an inaccurate and misleading visualization. In Figure 10-3, the designers are trying to show two different measures (difference between the official retirement age and the age men stop working *and* what that age is) whose scales are incompatible. Start the bars at zero, and readers won't be able to distinguish the ages where the dots are placed; change the scale so the dot placement is legible, and the bars become inaccurate. Either way, you're forcing the reader to do a lot of work—especially since the graphic's heading hasn't told them what they should be looking for ;-)

Let's see what happens when we start with a clear, action-verb headline and use that to redesign this graphic: "Men in Japan work years past retirement age, while others stop well before." Here, our headline/data statement is about highlighting the *difference* between official retirement and actual retirement. Now we can design a horizontal bar chart that both supports this claim *and* accurately represents the underlying data, as shown in Example 10-2 and the resulting Figure 10-4.

Example 10-2. retirement_age.py

```python
import matplotlib.pyplot as plt
import pandas as pd
import seaborn as sns
import numpy as np


# (abbreviated) list of countries
countries = ['Japan', 'Iceland', 'Switzerland', 'France', 'Ireland', 'Germany',
            'Italy', 'Belgium']

# difference in years between official and actual retirement age
retirement_gap = [9, 2, 2, -1, -2, -2, -7, -8]

# zip the two lists together, and specify the column names as we make the DataFrame
retirement_data = pd.DataFrame(list(zip(countries, retirement_gap)),
            columns =['country', 'retirement_gap'])

# in practice, we might prefer to write a function that generates this list,
# based on our data values
bar_colors = ['#d01c8b', '#d01c8b', '#d01c8b', '#4dac26','#4dac26','#4dac26',
            '#4dac26','#4dac26']

# pass our data and palette to the `seaborn` `barplot()` function
```

```
ax = sns.barplot(x="retirement_gap", y="country",
                 data=retirement_data, palette=bar_colors) ❶

# show the plot!
plt.show()
```

❶ By assigning our numerical values to the x-axis, and categorical values to the
   y-axis, *seaborn* will render this as a horizontal, rather than vertical, bar chart.

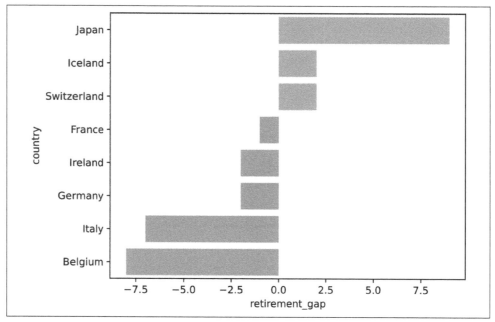

Figure 10-4. Retirement gap horizontal bar chart

Because my data statement/headline is now clearly about the *difference* in years
between official and actual retirement age, I've chosen to chart this difference
directly and also reorder the data: men in France only retire one year early, while
men in Belgium retire about eight years early. To further highlight the before/after
official retirement age distinction, I've also color-coded the bars according to their
positive/negative value.

The mix of positive and negative values in this dataset—along with the longer country name labels—makes this graphic much more readable as a horizontal bar chart
rather than a vertical one. If we want to test it out as a vertical chart for the sake of
comparison, however, we need to swap which data columns we pass as the x and y
arguments to the barplot() function. For example, by changing this:

```
ax = sns.barplot(x="retirement_gap", y="country", data=retirement_data,
                 palette=bar_colors)
```

to this:

```
ax = sns.barplot(x="country", y="retirement_gap", data=retirement_data,
                 palette=bar_colors)
```

While this change is easy enough to make, there can be real differences in the readability of a given dataset when it's rendered vertically or horizontally. Specifically, vertical bars tend to be better for data with shorter labels, less variation, and/or few to no negative values, while horizontal bars are usually better for divergent data (especially if there is a high proportion of negative values) and/or data that has longer labels.

While the visualization shown in Figure 10-4 is still quite simple, if you run the code you'll see for yourself the difference in quality that, for example, taking care with your color palette brings to a visualization. While I have chosen a binary magenta/green color encoding here, I could also have specified one of seaborn's 170 color palettes (*https://medium.com/@morganjonesartist/color-guide-to-seaborn-palettes-da849406d44f*) (e.g., `palette='BuGn'`), which would (mostly) align the color intensity with the value of each bar.

To recap, when working with bar charts:

Rule
    Bars must begin at zero!

Guideline
    Vertical bars are good for denser data with less variation.

Guideline
    Horizontal bars are better for more variation and/or longer labels.

Line Charts

When your data statement is about *rates of change* rather than *value differences*, it's time to explore line charts. Like bar charts, line charts can effectively display multiple categories of numerical data, but only as it *changes over time*. Because they don't visually encode the absolute data values, however, line chart scales do *not* need to start at zero.

At first, this might seem like an invitation for manipulation—and indeed, line charts have been at the center of some major political controversies.[6] For both bar charts and

---

6 "The Hockey Stick: The Most Controversial Chart in Science, Explained" by Chris Mooney, *https://theatlantic.com/technology/archive/2013/05/the-hockey-stick-the-most-controversial-chart-in-science-explained/275753*; that said, organizational charts (*http://voices.washingtonpost.com/ezra-klein/2009/07/when_health-care_reform_stops.html*) have also (expletive warning) had their day (*https://flickr.com/photos/robertpalmer/3743826461*).

line charts, however, what's actually driving the scale of the y-axis is the *data*: just as we cannot decide to start bar charts at a value other than zero, it would be absurd to scale the y-axis to many times the value of our largest data measure, as shown in Figure 10-5.

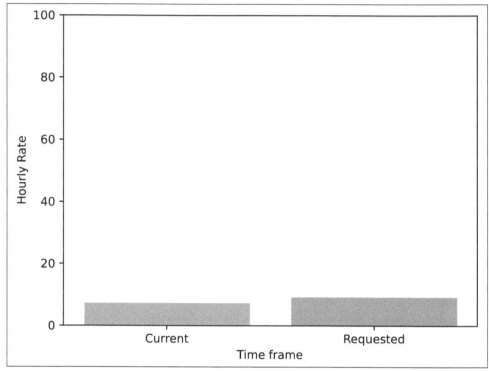

Figure 10-5. Another bad wage comparison graphic

While technically accurate, the hyperextended y-scale in Figure 10-5 has so compressed the data values that our eyes can no longer accurately or effectively distinguish the difference between them. For bar charts, then, the highest y-axis value should usually be at the next "whole" labeled increment (more about this in "Selecting Scales" on page 347). For line charts, visualization experts like Dona Wong recommend that the value range of the data occupy about two-thirds of the y-axis space.[7]

Of course, this approach highlights the influence that the *selection* of data points in a line chart has on the overall message. For example, consider this graphic from *The Economist* (*https://economist.com/graphic-detail/2021/06/21/the-pandemic-cut-annual-fdi-flows-by-one-third*), reproduced in Figure 10-6.

---

7 For more, see Wong's *The Wall Street Journal Guide to Information Graphics* (Norton).

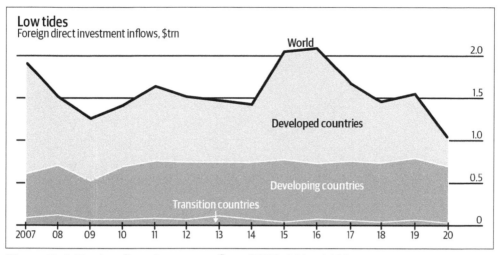

Figure 10-6. Foreign direct investment flows (FDI), 2007–2020

In this case, the original headline, "The pandemic cut annual FDI flows by one-third," is actually pretty effective; it's both active and specific. But while the data this headline describes is *included* in the accompanying chart, it's far from emphasized—the visualization includes more than a decade's worth of data even though the change described took place between 2019 and 2020. If we revise the graphic to focus *only* on what happened between those two years, as shown in Figure 10-7, we can both support the data statement more clearly *and* reveal an additional dimension of the data: though foreign direct investment dropped substantially in "developed" countries, it largely held steady in "developing" regions. As the article itself states, "Inflows to rich countries fell faster than those to developing ones—by 58% against just 8%."

This two-point line graph—also known as a *slope graph*—not only makes it easy for readers to see the evidence behind the headline claim, it also allows them to infer the disparate impact of the pandemic on FDI with respect to "developed" versus "developing" countries—thereby providing evidence for the article's later claim as well. As you can see in Example 10-3, generating this type of basic line chart takes just a few lines of code.

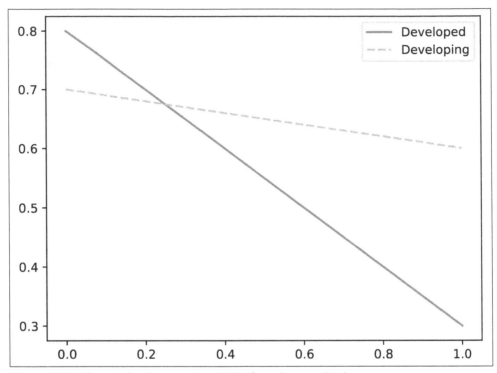

Figure 10-7. The pandemic cut annual FDI flows by one-third

Example 10-3. covid_FDI_impact.py

```
import matplotlib.pyplot as plt
import pandas as pd
import seaborn as sns
import numpy as np


# each individual array is a row of data
FDI = np.array([[0.8, 0.7], [0.3, 0.6]])

fdi_data = pd.DataFrame(data=FDI,
            columns=['Developed', 'Developing'])

ax = sns.lineplot(data=fdi_data)

# show the plot!
plt.show()
```

At this point, you may be wondering, though, whether it's somehow *wrong* to include only two years of data. After all, we have (at least) a decade's worth on hand.

The real question, of course, is not whether we *have* more data but whether the data claim we're making somehow misrepresents a broader trend. Looking at the original plot in Figure 10-6, it's clear that the FDI has only dropped this *quickly* twice in the past 15 years or so: from 2007 to 2008 and again between 2016 and 2017. Why? We don't know for sure—neither the original chart nor the full article text (I checked!) make it clear. What we *do* know is the absolute change in value (around $500B) and the proportional change in value are both large enough *and* unique enough that focusing just on the one-year change is not misleading. If we want to reassure our readers of this, we'd be better off providing the additional detail in a table, where they can review the precise numbers in detail without being distracted from the main point.

Line charts are essential visual forms when the *rate of change* (captured in the slope of each line) is central to the data statement's message. While this type of chart does not need to start at zero, it can *only* be used to represent data over time. To review, when working with line charts, the following apply:

Rule
    Data points must represent values *over time*.

Guideline
    Data lines should occupy roughly 2/3 of the vertical chart area.

Guideline
    Four or fewer lines should be distinctly colored/labeled.

While it may seem counterintuitive at first, it's actually OK to have a large number of lines on a line chart—as long as they are styled so that they don't compete with the evidence for our data statement. As we'll see in the next section, this kind of "background" data can actually be a useful way to provide additional context for readers, thereby supporting your headline claims even more effectively.

Scatter Charts

Although scatter plots are not frequently used in general data communications, they can be irreplaceable as a point-in-time counterpart to line charts, especially when you have a large number of data points that illustrate a clear trend—or deviation from that trend.

Consider, for example, the graphic in Figure 10-8, which reproduces one from this *New York Times* story (*https://nytimes.com/interactive/2021/06/29/upshot/portland-seattle-vancouver-weather.html*), and illustrates how, even among thousands of temperature readings taken over the course of more than four decades, three consecutive days in June 2021 were well outside the expected range in cities from Portland, Oregon, to Vancouver, Canada. While the headline could certainly be punchier, the visualization itself has a clear message: the maximum temperatures reached in

Portland, OR, on three days in late June were higher *than every other day* of the last 40 years.

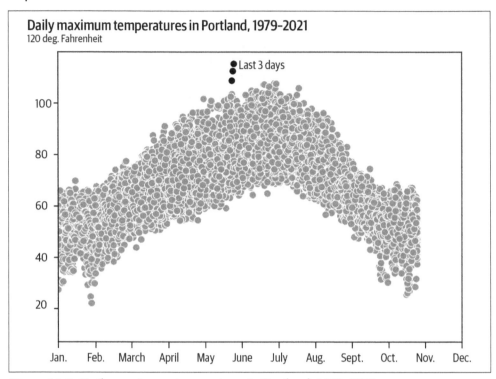

Figure 10-8. Daily maximum temperatures in Portland, 1979–2021

Most of the time, scatter plots are used to display data values captured either over the course of time (as in Figure 10-8) or across many individual members of some "group" (e.g., "schools," "large cities," "river-fed lakes," or "Marvel movies"). At times, scatter plots may include calculated trend lines that serve as a benchmark for comparing individual data points with "expected" average values; at other times, the benchmark might be a value determined by professional, legal, or social norms.

For example, drawing inspiration from a *Pioneer Press* story about schools where students perform better than the typical indicators would suggest,[8] we can use *seaborn* to plot historical data from the California school system to generate a scatter plot and highlight an unusual data point. The code for this example can be found in Example 10-4.

---

8 Megan Boldt et al., "Schools That Work: Despite Appearances, Schools Doing Better than Expected Have Traits in Common," July 9, 2010, *https://twincities.com/2010/07/09/schools-that-work-despite-appearances-schools-doing-better-than-expected-have-traits-in-common*.

Example 10-4. schools_that_work.py

```python
import matplotlib.pyplot as plt
import seaborn as sns
import pandas as pd

# import the school test data
school_data = pd.read_csv("apib12tx.csv")

# plot test scores against the percentage of students receiving meal support
sns.scatterplot(data=school_data, x="MEALS", y="API12B", alpha=0.6, linewidth=0) ❶

# highlight a high-performing school
highlight_school = school_data[school_data['SNAME'] == \
                                "Chin (John Yehall) Elementary"]
plt.scatter(highlight_school['MEALS'], highlight_school['API12B'],
            color='orange', alpha=1.0) ❷

# show the plot!
plt.show()
```

❶ The `alpha` argument governs the opacity of the dots; 60% opacity (0.6 as a decimal) proved the right balance here for legibility of individual as well as overlapping dots. The argument `linewidth=0` eliminates the outlines around each dot, which interferes with the heatmap effect of adjusting the opacity.

❷ To "highlight" a school, we are essentially just creating a one-dot scatter plot at the x and y coordinates of our selected data point.

One of the key challenges when using scatter plots is the problem of *occlusion*, in which data points may end up superimposed on one another, thus obscuring the true density of the data. One approach to this is to add *jitter*—a small amount of randomness to the placement of individual dots designed to minimize this visual overlap. As of *seaborn* 0.11.2, however, jitter is listed as an optional argument (*https://seaborn.pydata.org/generated/seaborn.scatterplot.html*) but is listed as "not supported." Fortunately, we can preserve the precision of our data without losing its interpretability by adjusting the opacity or *alpha* of the data points. By making all the dots in our visualization somewhat transparent, overlapping data points translate to a kind of opacity-driven *heatmap* that clarifies trends without losing specificity, as shown in Figure 10-9.

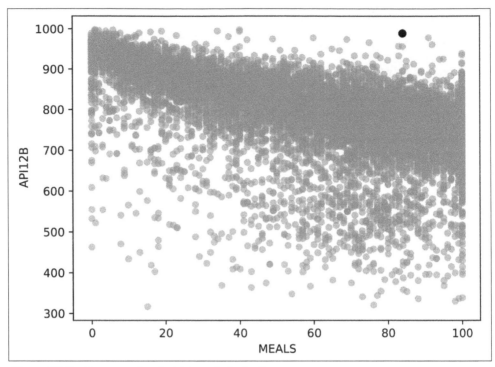

Figure 10-9. At some schools, history isn't destiny

So when do scatter plots make sense?

Guideline

Data must be high-volume enough for trends and outliers to be visible.

Guideline

Relevant benchmarks, whether arising from the data or outside rules, should be visualized.

Guideline

Most of the data should be a "background" color, with no more than a handful of points highlighted.

Guideline

Adjust opacity or apply jitter to minimize data occlusion.

Maps

For many of us, maps are one of the most familiar visualization types available; depending on your circumstances, you may use maps to plan your route to work or school, find a new shop or restaurant, or locate a new park or bike path. Maps are also a common visual form in mass communications, where they appear as weather maps, election maps, or even "locator" maps that provide a frame of reference for unfamiliar locations. If our data has a geographic component, then, it's natural to consider mapping it.

In reality, however, *unless your data is* about *geography, you really shouldn't be mapping it*. Why? Because maps represent *land area*. Not prevalence, or even population—which is usually what our data is about. For example, let's think back to our PPP loan data from Chapter 6. If you were to cluster the number of approved loans by state using `value_counts('ProjectState')`, you would end up with the following output (reformatted into columns to save space):

CA	99478	VA	18682	CT	10197	NH	4197	AK	2076
TX	60245	NC	18022	AL	9025	ID	3697	PR	2032
NY	54199	MN	16473	OK	8598	NM	3524	VT	1918
FL	46787	CO	15662	SC	8522	ME	3490	WY	1791
IL	33614	MD	15170	UT	7729	HI	3414	GU	305
PA	30768	WI	14729	KY	7623	DC	3175	VI	184
OH	26379	IN	13820	IA	7003	RI	3012	MP	55
NJ	24907	MO	13511	KS	6869	WV	2669	AS	18
MI	24208	TN	12994	NV	6466	MT	2648		
MA	21734	AZ	12602	NE	4965	ND	2625		
GA	20069	OR	10899	AR	4841	DE	2384		
WA	18869	LA	10828	MS	4540	SD	2247		

Without too much effort, you can probably guess that the order in which states appear in this table is similar to their order in this one (*https://en.wikipedia.org/wiki/ List_of_U.S._states_and_territories_by_population*), which ranks the states by population. In other words, if we were to "map" the data about PPP loan approvals, it would basically end up being a population map. But let's say we fixed this, and we normalized the number of loans by population, and so generated a new column called "Approved Loans Per Person" or something similar. Even now that we've converted our data from population to prevalence, we've really just given ourselves the bar chart problem in geographic form: the actual *visual area* occupied by a particular state is just *not* proportional to the data we're displaying. No matter how we choose our color palette or data ranges, Delaware will occupy 1/50 the visual space of Wyoming, even though it has 25% more approved loans. By mapping this, we're just guaranteeing that our visual representation is working against the actual data.

Obviously, there are a *lot* of map visualizations out there, and a fair number of them probably make one or both of the mistakes I've highlighted thus far. Mapping offers such a *seemingly* straightforward visual organizing principle that many people can't resist it, but using it for nongeographic data is really a disservice to both the data and your readers.

There are, of course, excellent maps of genuinely geographic phenomena out there: these *New York Times* census maps, for example, offer a thoughtful approach to presenting census data (*https://nytimes.com/interactive/2015/07/08/us/census-race-map.html*), while *ProPublicas*'s work on Houston's flood zones (*https://projects.propubl ica.org/graphics/harvey-maps*) illustrates how important geography (both natural and human-made) is during extreme weather events. And for a beautiful and original presentation of wind data, check out this wind map on hint.fm (*http://hint.fm/wind*).

Given how rarely maps will be the *right* visualization for supporting your data claims (as well as how complex building them can be in Python), we're not going to go through a code example for mapping here. If you're working with data that you feel you truly *must* map, I recommend looking at the *geopandas* library (*https://geo pandas.org/index.html*), which is designed to combine mapping-related shape information easily with *pandas* DataFrames to produce visualizations.

Pull Out the Paper

Though your visualizations are probably destined to live digitally, I strongly recommend that when it's time to begin your design process, you step away from your keyboard and pick up a pen (or pencil, or crayon) instead. Don't worry if you "can't draw"—your goal here is to identify (and possibly solve) visual challenges without being prejudiced by what your digital tools can and can't easily do. If this means that your visualization "paper prototypes" (*https://en.wikipedia.org/wiki/Paper_proto typing*) end up looking more like scratch paper than an illustration, that's actually all the better: user-experience research shows that if a sample design is too detailed or precise, viewers are more likely to fixate on details like the specific font size or colors used, rather than on "bigger picture" questions about layout and meaning. Sketching your visualization ideas out on paper (or a whiteboard) as a first step also offers an effective way to try out a variety of visual forms for your data while also being fast, cheap, and easy.

Personally, I find that making a sketch helps me see more quickly whether a given visual form (say, a bar chart) really illustrates the relationship among data elements that I need it to. It also makes it easy to consider—and change—things like the data highlights, annotations, scales, and axis labels that often constitute the difference between a serviceable graphic and an excellent one. I also find that starting with a pen or pencil makes generating the final (digital) visualization two to three times faster when it eventually is time to start coding.

One tip about this process: don't worry about painstakingly accounting for every single data point when you make these sketches. What you want is to get a general feel for what type of visualization will work best for your data, and to make key decisions about what will be highlighted and what will be left off. Even without precise data values at hand, sketching out your ideas will allow you to review, share, and get input on them in ways that you won't be able to once you've committed your ideas to code.

Elements of Eloquent Visuals

Although I have been an information designer for most of my career, I do not consider myself a true graphic designer. I cannot make you a good logo for your business, any more than you—having now learned a decent amount about Python programming—can troubleshoot a printer problem. Fortunately, through study, lots of reading, a few courses, and the generosity of the many talented designers with whom I've worked, I've learned a fair bit about effective visual design in general, and information design in particular. My takeaways from a couple of decades in the work are outlined here.

The "Finicky" Details Really Do Make a Difference

A million years ago, when I first started working as a frontend programmer for a web startup, my number-one priority was to make things that *worked*—and let me tell you, I was *really* glad when they did. Over time, I even refined and refactored my code in some of the same ways we did in Chapter 8, and I was pretty happy with those programming artifacts. From the perspective of a programmer, my work was pretty clean.

But I worked on a *design* team, and the designers I worked with were always pushing me to tweak little details that seemed to me more on the side of "nice to have," rather than essential. Did it *really* matter if the photos in a slideshow slowed down or rebounded just a bit as they slid into place? At the time, coding up effects like that meant writing and tweaking (very approximate) physics equations, which I did not love. Plus, all those customizations were cluttering up my code.

But one of the things I like most about programming is problem-solving, so eventually I hunkered down and made the changes they asked for. And once I saw it in action, I realized how much more polished and satisfying the end result really was. I began to appreciate that the *quality* of the design was in those "little" details and that "finicky" things—like a color change on tap or click—actually made my interfaces and graphics both clearer and more usable. In other words, don't dismiss the design "details"—they're not just about making things "look pretty." *Design is how it works.*

Trust Your Eyes (and the Experts)

Visual elements rendered digitally are necessarily expressed in quantitative terms: the mathematical origins of hexadecimal color codes (*https://computer hope.com/htmcolor.htm*) and x/y coordinate positioning might make it seem like finding the "correct" colors for a chart or the right positioning for an annotation label is a matter of doing the right math. It isn't. Color perception, for example, is both complex and highly individual—we can't really be sure that other people are seeing "the same" color that we are—and, of course, there are many types of color "blindness" that may prevent some people from perceiving the difference between certain pairs of complementary colors (e.g., red/green, blue/orange, yellow/purple) at all. There is no equation that can account for that.

In fact, every "color" that we might work with is, in fact, characterized by three different properties: hue (for example red versus blue), brightness (or luminosity), and saturation. Colors that "go" together align or contrast across these features in very particular ways. When it comes to visualizations, of course, we need colors to do much more than just look good together; they have to *meaningfully encode* information. But what does it mean for a color to be "20% more blue" than another? Whatever it is, it's not just a matter of flipping some numbers in your hexadecimal color value.[9]

Luckily, we have the help of experts. For more than two decades, anyone looking for color advice (mostly for maps, though it is also a great place to start for other types of charts) has been able to turn to the work of Cynthia Brewer (*http://personal.psu.edu/cab38*), a cartographer and professor of geography at Penn State, whose ColorBrewer (*https://colorbrewer2.org*) tool provides excellent, free color distributions for visual design. Likewise, Dona Wong's excellent book *The Wall Street Journal Guide to Information Graphics* (Norton) includes some of my personal favorites when it comes to color combinations for graphics.

If you feel really strongly about choosing your own color palette, then the next best approach is to turn to the greatest color authority we've got: nature. Find a photograph of the natural world (photos of flowers often work particularly well), and use a color capture tool to select contrasting colors, if you need them, or several shades of a single color. Use these to update the defaults on almost any visualization package, and you'll appreciate how much more appealing and professional-looking your graphic has become.

When it comes to things like font size and label placement, there are also no equations to follow—you mostly just have to *look* at your graphic and then nudge things around if they don't seem quite right. For example, I clearly remember coding up one of my colleague's designs at *The Wall Street Journal*, which contained a list of items in the layout, and naturally I had written a `for` loop to place them precisely. The problem was, something looked off when I ran the code and rendered it. Convinced that I just had estimated the spacing poorly, I asked him how many pixels of white space there should be between each element. "I don't know," he said, "I just looked at it."

---

9 Believe me, I've tried.

While I recognize that this kind of advice can be frustrating when you're just starting out with visual design, I can also promise that if you give yourself some time to experiment, you'll eventually learn to trust your *own* eyes. With that, some practice, and attention to the (well-defined) details laid out in the following sections, you'll soon be producing visualizations that are both accurate *and* eloquent.

Selecting Scales

Throughout "Charts, Graphs, and Maps: Oh My!" on page 327, we addressed the issue of scale with respect to the *accuracy* of our visualizations; here our focus is on clarity and readability. Packages like *seaborn* and *matplotlib* will automatically choose scales and axis limits based on your data, but these defaults may need tweaking for a variety of reasons. Once you've confirmed the appropriate *numerical* range for your data, you'll want to review how your graphic is actually rendering and make sure that it is also following these general rules:

- Axis limits and marked values should be whole numbers and/or multiples of 5 or 10.
- Value labels should *not* be in scientific notation.
- Units should only appear on the last element of each axis.
- Though not ideal, labels may need to be edited or (less preferably) angled in order to remain readable.

Choosing Colors

In addition to seeking expert advice on specific color selection, consider how many colors your data elements should have. Color can be an invaluable way to highlight a specific data point or distinguish between measured and projected values. When selecting colors for your chart or graph, remember:

One color per data category
If you are displaying several months of data about the PPP loan program, for example, all of the bars should be the *same* color. Likewise, different values of the same variable should be shades of a single color.

Avoid continuous color distributions
While adjusting the color of each visual element according to its value may *seem* more precise, like the visual compression of data we saw in Figure 10-5, continuous color palettes (or *ramps*) generate color differences so small that the human eye cannot really perceive them. This is where your distribution calculations (you

did do those, right?) will come in handy: create a color scale (or *ramp*) of up to five colors and then assign each one to a single *quintile* of your data.[10]

Use diverging color scales with care
Diverging color scales are really only suitable when there is a true "neutral" value that the data varies around. In some cases, this may be zero. In others, it may be an agreed-upon value in the field (for example, the US Federal Reserve views an inflation rate of about 2% (*https://federalreserve.gov/faqs/5D58E72F066A4DBDA80BBA659C55F774.htm*) to be ideal).

Never color-code more than four distinct categories of data
But, including contextual data in a background gray is fine.

Test for color accessibility
Tools like ColorBrewer include an option to produce only colorblind-safe combinations. If you are using your own colors, test your selections by converting your graphic to grayscale. If you can still distinguish all the colors in your visualization, your readers should be able to also.

Above All, Annotate!

The goal of our visualization process is to share our data insights and support our claims. While our action-verb headline should encapsulate the main idea of our graphic, it is often valuable to highlight or add context to specific data points within the visualization itself. This is *not* the place for asterisks and footnotes. Information needed to accurately or effectively understand the graphic needs to be part of the graphic's main visual field. Some of the key ways you can make the data within your visualization easier to understand include the following:

Label categorical differences directly
Rather than creating a separate legend, place data labels directly on the visualization. This saves readers from having to look back and forth between your graphic and a separate key to make sense of the information being presented.

Highlight relevant data points with color
If one key data point is central to your overall claim, highlight it in a contrasting color.

Add contextual annotations
These small amounts of text (connected to the relevant data element using a thin *leader* line, if necessary) could be a label, an explanation, or important contextual

---

10 You can accomplish this quickly in *pandas* by using the `quantile()` function and passing in the values `0.2`, `0.4`, `0.6`, and so on. For a more general refresher on how to calculate these values and what they represent, see Example 9-3 in Chapter 9

information. Whatever it is, make sure it appears as close to the data as possible and always within the visual bounds of the graphic itself.

From Basic to Beautiful: Customizing a Visualization with seaborn and matplotlib

One final word about design—visual or otherwise. While I made an effort in "Elements of Eloquent Visuals" on page 345 to break down the elements of effective visualization into component parts, a truly eloquent graphic is not a collection of swappable parts. Shifting one part of it—moving a label, changing a color—means that many, if not all, of its remaining elements will need to be adjusted to bring the whole back into balance. This is precisely why I haven't provided code examples for each individual design aspect outlined previously: seen in isolation, it can be hard to understand why any given element is so important. But viewed as part of a cohesive whole, it will (hopefully) become clear how each contributes to the impact of the graphic.

To actually realize these customized visuals in Python, we are still going to be relying on the *seaborn* and *matplotlib* libraries. But while we let *seaborn* do most of the heavy lifting in previous instances, in this example, it's the fine-grained control offered by *matplotlib* that will really shine. Yes, we'll still let *seaborn* handle the high-level tasks, like actually plotting the data values to scale. But *matplotlib* will give us the leverage we need to specify everything from label placement and orientation to units, labeling, annotation, and highlighting values—everything we need to truly tailor our visualization to our claims.

For this example, we're going to take a break from the PPP data and instead work with some COVID-19 data collated by a team of researchers based on data from Johns Hopkins University and made available at Our World in Data (*https://ourworl dindata.org/coronavirus-source-data*). Our goal with this visualization will be to highlight the spike in confirmed COVID-19 cases in the United States during July 2020, which at the time was attributed to the accelerated reopening[11] in many states earlier that spring[12] as well as gatherings over the July 4th holiday.[13] To understand the

---

11 Lazaro Gamio, "How Coronavirus Cases Have Risen Since States Reopened," *The New York Times*, July 9, 2020, *https://nytimes.com/interactive/2020/07/09/us/coronavirus-cases-reopening-trends.html*.

12 Anne Gearan, Derek Hawkins, and Siobhán O'Grady, "Coronavirus Cases Rose by Nearly 50 Percent Last Month, Led by States That Reopened First," *The Washington Post*, July 1, 2020, *https://washingtonpost.com/politics/coronavirus-cases-rose-by-nearly-50-percent-last-month-led-by-states-that-reopened-first/2020/07/01/3337f1ec-bb96-11ea-80b9-40ece9a701dc_story.html*.

13 Mark Olalde and Nicole Hayden, "California COVID-19 Cases Spiked after July 4th. Family Gatherings Helped the Spread, Experts Say." *USA Today*, August 2, 2020, *https://usatoday.com/story/news/nation/2020/08/02/covid-19-spike-california-after-july-4-linked-family-gatherings/5569158002*.

---

difference between relying on the defaults and customizing the axis ranges, labels, and colors, compare Figure 10-10 to Figure 10-11. The code to produce Figure 10-11 is shown in Example 10-5.

Example 10-5. refined_covid_barchart.py

```python
# `pandas` for data loading; `seaborn` and `matplotlib` for visuals
import pandas as pd
import seaborn as sns
import matplotlib.pyplot as plt

# `FuncFormatter` to format axis labels
from matplotlib.ticker import FuncFormatter

# `datetime` to interpret and customize dates
from datetime import datetime

# load the data
vaccine_data = pd.read_csv('owid-covid-data.csv')

# convert the `date` column to a "real" date
vaccine_data['date']= pd.to_datetime(vaccine_data['date'])

# group the data by country and month
country_and_month = vaccine_data.groupby('iso_code').resample('M',
                                                 on='date').sum()

# use `reset_index()` to "flatten" the DataFrame headers
country_and_month_update = country_and_month.reset_index()

# select just the United States' data
just_USA = country_and_month_update[country_and_month_update['iso_code']=='USA']

# make the foundational barplot with `seaborn`
ax = sns.barplot(x="date", y="new_cases", palette=['#bababa'], data=just_USA)


# loop through the bars rectangles and set the color for the July 2020
# bar to red
for i, bar in enumerate(ax.patches):
    if i == 6:
        bar.set_color('#ca0020')

# set the maximum y-axis value to 7M
ax.set_ylim(0,7000000)

# setting the axis labels
plt.xlabel('Month')
plt.ylabel('New cases (M)')

# modify the color, placement and orientation of the "tick labels"
```

```
ax.tick_params(direction='out', length=5, width=1, color='#404040',
               colors='#404040',pad=4, grid_color='#404040', grid_alpha=1,
               rotation=45) ❶


# functions for formatting the axis "tick labels"
# `millions()` will convert the scientific notation to millions of cases
def millions(val, pos): ❷
    modified_val = val*1e-6
    formatted_val = str(modified_val)
    if val == ax.get_ylim()[1]:
        formatted_val = formatted_val+'M'
    if val == 0:
        formatted_val = "0"
    return formatted_val

# `custom_dates()` will abbreviate the dates to be more readable
def custom_dates(val, pos): ❷
    dates_list = just_USA.date.tolist()
    date_label = ""
    if pos is not None: ❸
        current_value = dates_list[pos]
        current_month = datetime.strftime(current_value, '%b')
        date_label = current_month
        if date_label == 'Jan':
            date_label = date_label + " '"+ datetime.strftime(current_value,
                                                              '%y')
    return date_label

# assign formatter functions
y_formatter = FuncFormatter(millions)
x_formatter = FuncFormatter(custom_dates)

# apply the formatter functions to the appropriate axis
ax.yaxis.set_major_formatter(y_formatter)
ax.xaxis.set_major_formatter(x_formatter)

# create and position the annotation text
ax.text(4, 3000000, "Confirmed cases\noften lag infection\nby several weeks.") ❹

# get the value of all bars as a list
bar_value = just_USA.new_cases.tolist()

# create the leader line
ax.vlines( x = 6, color='#404040', linewidth=1, alpha=.7,
                       ymin = bar_value[6]+100000, ymax = 3000000-100000)

# set the title of the chart
plt.title("COVID-19 cases spike following relaxed restrictions\n" + \
          "in the spring of 2020", fontweight="bold")
```

```
# show the chart!
plt.show()
```

❶ Customizing the orientation, color, and other attributes of the "tick labels" that indicate the values on each axis of the chart can be done via the *matplotlib* `tick_params()` method (*https://matplotlib.org/stable/api/_as_gen/matplotlib.axes.Axes.tick_params.html*).

❷ The arguments that are supplied to any custom function assigned to any `FuncFor` `matter` function will be "value" and "tick" position.

❸ In "interactive mode," this function will throw errors if `pos` is `None`.

❹ By default, the positioning of text elements layered on top of the chart (*https://matplotlib.org/stable/api/_as_gen/matplotlib.pyplot.text.html*) is "data coordinates," e.g., a value of 1 will left-align the start of the text with the center point of the first column. The provided "y" value anchors the *bottom* of the text box.

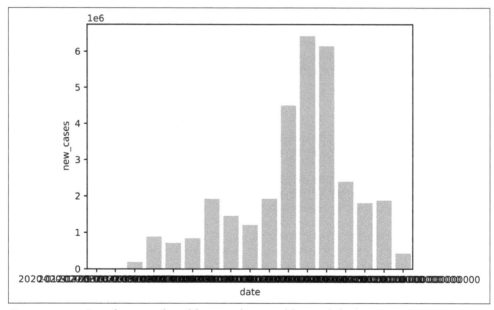

Figure 10-10. Bar chart produced by visualization library defaults

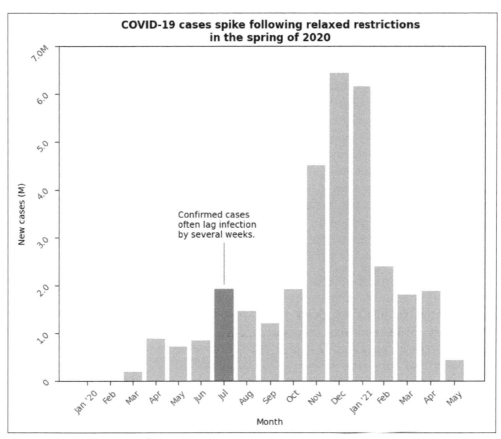

Figure 10-11. Customized visualization

As you can see from Example 10-5, the process of customizing our visualization in Python is somewhat involved; tailoring the look and feel of the default output has nearly tripled the lines of code required.

At the same time, the default output in this instance was basically illegible. By softening the colors, highlighting salient data points, and (perhaps most importantly) refining our data labels, we've managed to create a chart that could hold its own in most publication contexts. And obviously a good chunk of the code we have in here could be refined and repurposed to make this degree of customization a much less bespoke effort for future graphics.

Beyond the Basics

While I've aimed to cover the essentials of effective and accurate data visualization in this chapter, the truth is that valuable visualization ideas can come from anywhere—not just books or blogs that are dedicated to the topic. One of my favorite graphics from my time at *The Wall Street Journal* is the unemployment visualization (*https://jennifervalentinodevries.com/2009/09/16/grid-graphic-u-s-unemployment-rate*) shown in Figure 10-12, which was inspired by a similar form I encountered at a museum exhibit about climate change; the geometric heatmap format allows readers to visually compare decades of monthly unemployment rates at a glance. If you're interested in design, you can learn a lot about what does (and doesn't) work by simply looking critically at the media you see around you every day—whether it's an online advertisement or a restaurant menu. If something doesn't feel polished or appealing, look carefully at its components. Are the colors incongruous? Is the typeface hard to read? Or are there just too many things crowded together into too small a space?

Critiquing the work of others is easy, of course. If you really want to improve your own visualizations, challenge yourself to try to build better solutions, and you'll learn an enormous amount along the way. And if you find yourself searching for the right vocabulary to describe what isn't working, you may want to look through some of the resources in Appendix D, where you'll find some of my favorite resources for expanding and improving my own visualization work.

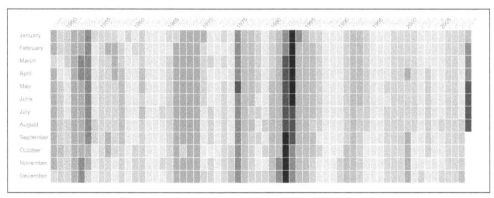

Figure 10-12. US unemployment over time (originally designed for The Wall Street Journal)

Conclusion

Like programming, visualization is an applied art: the only way to get better at it is to *do* it. If you don't have a project at hand to work on, start with a "found" visualization that you think is somehow subpar and redesign it yourself. You can use Python or other computational tools or just a pencil and paper—the point is to try to solve the problems you see in the original. Along the way, you'll experience firsthand the trade-offs inherent in every design decision, and you'll start building the skills needed to minimize those trade-offs in service of your visualization goals. Then when you're faced with your own data visualization challenges, you'll have a portfolio of prior work you can refer to when thinking about how best to present the data you have and make the point that you need to.

At this point, we've done just about all the data wrangling with Python that we set out to do—but there is a world of data and visualization tools *beyond* Python that can be amazingly useful in supporting your data wrangling and data quality work right alongside it. We'll turn to those in Chapter 11.

Beyond Python

Python is an exceptionally powerful and versatile tool for working with data, and if you've followed along with the exercises in this book, you are hopefully starting to feel confident about using it to move your own data wrangling projects forward. Thanks to the vibrant Python community and the constantly evolving suite of helpful libraries that its members create and maintain, the work you've put into learning the fundamentals in this book will still be valuable whether your next data wrangling project comes along tomorrow or next year. Also, while Python as a programming language is unique in many ways, the programming skills and vocabulary that you've acquired here will give you a head start with other programming languages, especially ones relatively object-oriented ones like JavaScript.

Still, one thing I've tried to clarify throughout this book is that there are times when the "programmatic" solution to a problem is not *really* the most efficient one. Our work with Excel and XML files in Chapter 4, for example, highlighted that sometimes trying to do things programmatically just doesn't make sense. For example, while in Example 4-12 we *could* have written a Python script to traverse our entire XML document in order to discover its structure, it was undoubtedly faster and easier to simply *look* at our data, identify the elements that interested us, and write our Python program to target them directly. Likewise, there are times when writing a Python program *at all* can be more effort than a particular data wrangling project really requires, especially if it is smaller or more exploratory. Though *pandas* is an incredibly useful library, you can still end up writing a fair amount of code just to get a basic sense of what a new dataset contains. In other words, while I fully believe that the power and versatility of Python makes it an indispensable data wrangling tool, I also want to highlight a few other free and/or open source tools that I think you'll find useful[1] as a complement to Python in your data wrangling projects.

Additional Tools for Data Review

Python offers great speed and flexibility when it comes to actually accessing and wrangling data, but it's not particularly well suited to letting you actually *look* at your data. So throughout this book we've relied on basic text editors (and occasionally web browsers) when we want to browse our dataset visually. While text editors are a great first step for this, you'll also want to get comfortable with at least one of each of the following program types to help you get a quick initial overview of your data—especially if the files you're working with are not too large.

Spreadsheet Programs

It's possible that before you began reading this book you were already familiar with spreadsheet programs—whether online versions like Google Sheets, paid local software options like Microsoft Excel, or contribution-supported, open source alternatives like Libre Office Calc. Spreadsheet programs typically come bundled with "office"-style software suites and offer basic calculation, analysis, and charting functionality. In general, there is not a huge variation in what these programs can do, though some are more flexible than others. I prefer LibreOffice (*https://libreoffice.org*), for example, because it is free, open source, and works across platforms (including less common ones, like Linux). It even has a certified app for Chromebooks and Android devices called Collabora (*https://collaboraoffice.com/press-releases/collabora-office-ships-for-chromebooks*). That said, if you already have or are familiar with a particular spreadsheet program, there is no important reason to switch to any other, as long as you are not going broke paying for it. Whatever you do, do *not* use pirated software; in a world where ransomware is running rampant—i.e., this one—it's simply not worth the risk to your devices and data!

While many spreadsheet programs have advanced functions that approximate what Python does (on a much smaller scale), I usually find myself turning to them for very specific data wrangling and assessment tasks. In particular, I will often use a spreadsheet program to quickly do the following:

Change file formats
    For example, if my data is provided as an multisheet XLSX file, I might open it in a spreadsheet program and save only the sheet I am interested in as a *.csv*.

---

1 I certainly do!

Rename columns

> If there are not many columns, I may change those with awkward or nondescript headers to be something more readable and/or intuitive for my purposes.

Get a "feel" for data values

> Are the values provided in a "date" column actually dates? Or are they simply years? Are there a lot of obviously missing data values? If my dataset is relatively small, just visually scanning through the data in a spreadsheet program can sometimes be enough to determine whether I have the data I need—or if I need to move on.

Generate basic summary statistics

> Of course I can do this in Python, and most of the time I do. But if I have only a few hundred rows of data, typing =MEDIAN() and then selecting the cells of interest is sometimes faster, especially if my original data file has metadata in it that would otherwise need to be stripped out (as we saw in Chapter 4 and again in Chapters 7 and 8).

Of course, every tool comes with its trade-offs, and previewing data in a spreadsheet program can create some unexpected results. As you might guess from our extended adventures in dealing with XLS-style "dates," previewing a file that contains date-like values can cause them to display very differently according to particular spreadsheet program and its default handling and rendering of dates. As a result, you should *always* inspect date-like values using a text editor if the original data format is text based (e.g., *.csv*, *.tsv*, or *.txt*). Likewise, be sure to confirm the formatting (whether default or applied) on any number-containing cells, as truncating or rounding of values can obscure important variations in your data.

OpenRefine

One of the tools I turn to most for my initial exploration of larger, structured datasets is OpenRefine (*https://openrefine.org*). In my experience, OpenRefine has proved to be a unique software tool that helps bridge the gap between traditional spreadsheet programs and full-on programming languages like Python. Like spreadsheet programs, OpenRefine operates through a graphical user interface (GUI), so most of your work with it will involve pointing and clicking with a mouse. *Unlike* spreadsheet programs, however, you don't scroll through rows of data to get a sense of what they contain; instead, you can use menu options to create *facets* that provide summary information similar to that provided by the pandas value_counts() method (*https:// pandas.pydata.org/docs/reference/api/pandas.Series.value_counts.html*)—but without needing to write any code. OpenRefine also supports batch editing, implements several algorithms for string matching (including the fingerprinting method we used in Example 6-11), and can import large files in segments (e.g., 100,000 rows at a time). In truth, OpenRefine is often my first stop when wrangling a new dataset, because it easily opens a variety of data formats and even offers a handy live preview of how the data will be parsed based on your selection of delimiters, for example. Once your dataset is loaded, OpenRefine can also provide almost one-click answers to questions like "What is the most common value in column *x*?" Finally, any time you make an actual change to a data file in OpenRefine (as opposed to just clustering or faceting it), it automatically records your actions in an exportable *.json* file that you can then apply to a *different* OpenRefine file in order to have those actions automatically repeated (usually in seconds). This is incredibly useful if you need to rename or rearrange data columns for a dataset that is regularly updated by the data provider. It's even *more* useful, however, if you need *someone else* to be able to do it and they don't have or cannot use Python.

For the most part, I use OpenRefine to easily do the following:

Preview small pieces of large datasets
OpenRefine allows you to load (and skip) as many rows in your dataset as you like. This is especially handy for large datasets when I want to get a reasonable sense of what they contain, but I know truly nothing about them. I can start by loading 50,000 or 100,000 rows and use facets and other functions to get an overview of, say, what the data types are and how the overall dataset is organized.

Get quick top-line information about a dataset
What's the most common type of film permit requested in New York City? And what is the most popular borough? As shown in Figure 11-1, OpenRefine can give you these counts in one or two clicks and allows you to create cross-tabulations just as quickly.

Do basic transformations that spreadsheet programs don't support
Some spreadsheet programs lack functionality, like the ability to split a string on a particular character, or may have limited regular expression support. One of my favorite features of OpenRefine is batch editing, which you can do quickly and easily through the lefthand facet window.

Autogenerate macros
Many spreadsheet programs will let you record *macros* that automate certain actions, but OpenRefine records these for you by default—making it a more powerful tool with a lower learning curve for this type of task.

Of course, there are some aspects of working with OpenRefine that can take some getting used to. First, while installation is getting more user friendly, it relies on having another programming language, called Java, installed on your computer, so getting it up and running can be a multistep process. Launching the program once it's installed is also a little unusual: You need to both click (or double-click) on the program icon to launch and, in some cases, open a browser window pointed to your "localhost" address (typically `http://127.0.0.1:3333/` or `http://localhost:3333`).

Like Jupyter Notebook, OpenRefine actually runs through a tiny web server on your computer, and the interface is just a web page that behaves sort of like a supercharged spreadsheet program. Despite these quirks, OpenRefine is *incredibly* useful and often a great place to start when you want to do some initial exploration of a (potentially messy) dataset.

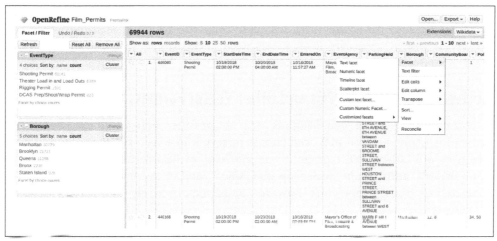

Figure 11-1. OpenRefine NYC film permit facets

Additional Tools for Sharing and Presenting Data

In Chapter 10, we focused on how to select and refine visualizations using Python and key libraries like `seaborn` and `matplotlib`. While the degree of customization that you can achieve using these tools is impressive, there are times when you may need to make a small tweak to a visualization and you may not want—or be able—to regenerate it from the original data source with Python.

If you need to quickly add or change something minor on a visualization, having access to image editing software is valuable. And while you're probably familiar with the very powerful—and very expensive—commercial software applications for editing images, you may not realize that there are similarly powerful tools that are free and open source.

Image Editing for JPGs, PNGs, and GIFs

For editing pixel-based images, the GNU Image Manipulation Program (GIMP) is an especially good option if you're looking for something powerful but you can't (or don't want to) pay a lot for it. GIMP (*https://gimp.org*) is free and open source, and it works across platforms. While the style of its user interface is decidedly outdated (the interface is being overhauled at the time of this writing), the reality is that the program itself can probably do whatever basic (and not-so-basic) high-quality image editing you may need, especially if you're just looking to add (or remove) some text or annotations from an image, update the axis labels, etc.

It's true that GIMP can have a somewhat steep learning curve. The keyboard shortcuts may not be what you expect, and the placement of some menus and the look of their icons do not match what you'll see in commercial software. That said, unless you are an expert in another image editing program and you are willing to pay (and continue to pay) for access to it, whatever time you invest in learning GIMP will be well worth it. Especially if what you need is occasional access to image editing software, GIMP is a powerful and flexible choice.

Software for Editing SVGs and Other Vector Formats

If you plan to use your visualizations for print or other high-resolution (or flexible-resolution) contexts, you may well choose to save it in a vector format. Although the file sizes are larger, vector graphics are much more flexible than their pixel-driven counterparts; they can be scaled up and down without losing quality by becoming pixelated or blurry. They can't, however, be edited effectively with bitmap software like GIMP.

Once again, if you have the budget for commercial software, you should go ahead and use it—but here, too, you have a free and open source option. Like GIMP, Inkscape (*https://inkscape.org*) is free, open source, and cross platform. And, like GIMP, it has almost all the same features as expensive commercial vector editing software. Even better, if you take the time to get comfortable with vector editing software, it won't just let you tweak your digital-to-print data graphics—vector editing software is also essential to T-shirt printing, laser cutting, and lots of other digital-to-physical work. If you're just starting out, Inkscape is also definitely the right price: free!

About FOSS

FOSS is an acronym for Free and Open Source Software, and many FOSS programs—like GIMP and Inkscape—have been around for decades. Despite the fact that most of us are much more familiar with brand-name software made by companies like Apple, Microsoft, Google, and others, the fact is that a large portion of the software that runs both computers and the internet today is based on programs, packages, and libraries that—like the Python packages and libraries we've used throughout this book—are free for anyone to access and use. In many cases, it's even legal to create and sell products that have FOSS software at their core—and this is something that lots of companies do.

While free and open source software helps ensure that the tools for innovation aren't locked away as the intellectual property of big companies, the reality is that building, maintaining, and enhancing these tools isn't *actually* free. It's made possible by the

---

work of volunteers—some of whom are allowed to use work hours paid for by their company to do it—but many of whom do it unpaid.

The fact that FOSS tools are free for everyone helps keep data wrangling work accessible, and I (obviously) recommend working with them if you can. At the same time, if you find yourself using them regularly and are able, I also recommend a small donation to the projects you use in order to help keep them going.

Reflecting on Ethics

The main focus of this book has been on building data wrangling skills—in large part to support our interest in assessing and improving data quality. Along the way, we've touched on the broader implications of data quality, both abstractly and concretely. Poor data quality can lead to analyses that produce a misleading, distorted, or discriminatory view of the world; couple this with the scale and ubiquity of data-driven systems today, and the resulting harms can be substantial and far-reaching. While you can use the methods in this book to test and improve the quality of your data, there is unfortunately still plenty of room for "good-quality" data to be obtained unethically. And just as with every other part of the data wrangling process, it's up to you to decide what kind of data you're comfortable working with and for what purposes.

One strategy for ensuring that your data wrangling work doesn't unintentionally violate your own ethical standards is to develop a checklist. By developing a list of questions you ask yourself about your data sources and how the output of your analysis will be used, you can determine early on if a given data wrangling project is one you're willing to pursue. The following checklist is adapted from one shared by data experts DJ Patil, Hilary Mason, and Mike Loukides (*https://oreilly.com/radar/of-oaths-and-checklists*). Like the list of data characteristics in Chapter 3, the purpose here is not to reject a data project unless the answer to every question is "yes"; the goal is to think critically about *all* aspects of data quality—including those that may be outside our control. True, we may only be able to decline (rather than change) a project that doesn't meet our ethical standards, but if you voice your concerns, you may help make room for others to do the same. At worse, the project is taken on by someone else and your conscience is (somewhat) clear. At best, you may inspire others to consider the ethical implications of their work before they take on their next project as well. Here are some questions that you might want to include:

1. Does the design of the data collection reflect the values of the community it is about?

2. Do the members of that community know that it was collected, and did they have a meaningful way to decline?

3. Has the data been evaluated for representativeness?

4. Is there a way to test the data for bias?

5. Are our data features accurate proxies for the phenomena we want to describe?

6. Will our analysis be replaced if and when the data becomes out of date?

Ultimately, you may decide that your own concerns about data have a different focus. Whatever you choose to include in your own checklist, however, you'll find your data principles much easier to stick to if you lay them out in advance.

Conclusion

Over the course of this book, we have covered everything from the basics of Python programming and data quality assessment to wrangling data from half-a-dozen file formats and APIs. We've applied our skills to some typically messy and problematic real-world data and refined our code to make future projects easier. We've even explored how to do basic data analysis and visually present our data in support of our insights.

If you've made it this far, then I imagine by this point you've caught some sort of "bug": for programming, for data, for analysis and visualization—or maybe all of the above. Whatever brought you to this book, I hope you've found at least some of what you were looking for, including, perhaps, the confidence to take the next step. Because whatever else may change about the world of data wrangling in the coming years, one thing is sure to be true: we need as many people as possible doing this work critically and thoughtfully. Why shouldn't one of them be you?

More Python Programming Resources

As this book has hopefully illustrated, Python is a robust and flexible programming language, with a wide range of applications. While I've introduced many key concepts and popular libraries in the preceding chapters, I've created this appendix to provide you with some helpful resources and references for taking your Python work to the next level.

Official Python Documentation

Yes, there are always search engines and StackOverflow (*https://stackover flow.com/questions/tagged/python*), but there's value in getting comfortable reading official documentation—whether it's for the Python language or for popular libraries like pandas, matplotlib, or seaborn. Though I wouldn't suggest you sit down and read *any* programming documentation end to end, looking through the parameters and options of a data type or function you want to use can give you a better sense of what (in general) can be done with it, as well as an idea of how its mechanisms are organized. This can be especially helpful when you want to do something completely new, because it will give you an idea of where to look for paths forward.

For example, I knew when I started writing this book that seaborn and pandas were both built on top of matplotlib, and I had done some hacking around with making and customizing graphics with both of them. It wasn't until I was looking through the latter's documentation, however, that I came to understand the difference between the figure and axes objects that I so often saw referenced in example code, and that understanding helped me find solutions more quickly as I experimented with ways to more fully customize my visualizations. Almost as important, official documentation is generally kept up to date, while it's not uncommon for the most popular forum posts about a topic to be months or even years old—meaning that the advice they include can sometimes be woefully out of date.

I also recommend regularly turning to the Python Standard Library (*https://docs.python.org/3/library/index.html*) because you might be surprised by how much built-in functionality it offers. Many of the methods you may recognize from working with libraries are built on top of (or to mimic) functions that exist in "vanilla" Python. And while libraries are often unique and useful, there are no guarantees that they will continue to be developed or maintained. If you can get the functionality you need by working with "plain" Python, the less likely it is that you'll find your code going out of date because it relies on a library that is no longer being updated.

Installing Python Resources

There are a lot of ways to install Python packages, depending on your programming environment. Whether you're using Homebrew on macOS, working on a Windows machine, or using Colab, the most reliable way to install Python packages will pretty much always be to use some version of `pip` (*https://packaging.python.org/tutorials/installing-packages*). In fact, you can even use `pip` to install a package on a Google Colab notebook (if you manage to find one that isn't already installed) using the following syntax (*https://colab.research.google.com/notebooks/snippets/importing_libraries.ipynb*):

```
!pip install librarynamehere
```

Whatever you choose, however, I suggest you make your choice and stick to it—things can get pretty unpredictable if you start using multiple tools to install and update your Python environment.

Where to Look for Libraries

For the most part, I recommend that you install Python packages that are available on the Python Package Index (*https://pypi.org*), also known as PyPI. PyPI has a clean structure and a robust tagging and search interface that make it easy to locate useful Python packages, and the fact that PyPI package documentation (usually) has a standard layout (as shown in Figure A-1) will really start to save you time if you're looking through lots of options.

Some projects (like Beautiful Soup `lxml`) may still keep much of their documentation in a standalone location, but their PyPI page will typically still contain a helpful summary of what the project does and even some getting-started tips. One of the things I personally like to look at is the "Release History" section, which shows when the project was first created, as well as how often and how recently the package was updated. Longevity is, of course, not a perfect metric for evaluating how reliable a given package is likely to be—since anyone can publish Python packages (and add them to PyPI)—but the ones that have been around longer and/or are updated more frequently (and recently) are usually a good place to start.

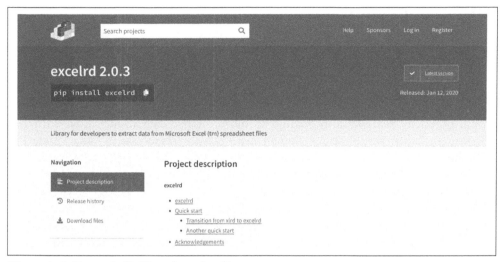

Figure A-1. Example PyPI package landing page

Keeping Your Tools Sharp

Programming tools are being updated all the time as the community identifies (and mostly fixes) new problems or comes to agree that some aspect of a software tool (or even Python itself!) ought to work differently. If you followed the instructions for installing Python and Jupyter Notebook provided in Chapter 1, then you can use the `conda` command to update both of these. You'll just need to run `conda update python` and `conda update jupyter` every once in a while. At the same time, because this book is intended for beginners, one thing I didn't address in Chapter 1 was the question of Python *environments*. In this context, a given *environment* is defined mostly by the major version of Python that will be used by default (for example, 3.9 versus 3.8) when you use the `python` command. While running `conda update python` will update, say, version 3.8.6 to 3.8.11, it *won't* ever automatically update your version to a different major release (e.g., 3.9). Often, this won't cause problems for you unless your Python installation is several years (and therefore major versions) out of date. If and when that happens, you'll want to create a new environment for the new version of Python, mostly because it can be hard for your computer to keep things straight otherwise. Fortunately, when the time comes for you to upgrade Python to the next major version, you can learn what you need to know about how to do this from the `conda` documentation page (*https://docs.conda.io/projects/conda/en/latest/user-guide/tasks/manage-environments.html*).

Where to Learn More

Because Python is such a popular programming language, there are thousands of resources online and in libraries for moving to the next level, whether you have a specific project to complete or just want to learn more about advanced topics like machine learning and natural languages processing.

For a practical, succinct introduction to more intense data science topics, my first recommendation would be the *Python Data Science Handbook* by Jake VanderPlas (O'Reilly)—it's a resource I've used myself when trying to get my head around some of the more advanced machine-learning work that Python can do, and Jake's clear writing style and concise examples offer an accessible way to both get an overview of machine learning with Python and learn about specific methods (like k-means clustering). Even better, you can access the entire book for free online (*https://jakevdp.github.io/PythonDataScienceHandbook*)—though if you're able to, I highly recommend buying a copy of the book.

Perhaps even more valuable than finding the right books, tutorials, or classes, however, is finding a community of people whom you can work and learn alongside as you continue your data wrangling journey. Whether through a school, community organization, or meetup, finding a small group of people that you can talk about your projects with or turn to for advice (and, sometimes, commiseration!) is probably the most invaluable resource for expanding your skills in both Python and data wrangling. There are also many cost-free programs that can help support and advance your work, especially for folks from communities that are underrepresented in technical fields. Check out groups like the Ada Developers Academy (*https://adadevelopersacademy.org*) or Free Code Camp (*https://freecodecamp.org*).

A Bit More About Git

For the most part, working with Git as the only programmer on a project is fairly straightforward: you make changes to your code, commit them, push them to GitHub (or another remote repository), and that's that.

Until..,it isn't. Maybe you updated your *README.md* file on GitHub and forgot to `git pull` before making changes to the same file on your device. Maybe you forgot to add a message when you ran `git commit`. While dealing with these kinds of hiccups is not really all that complicated, some of the error messages and default behaviors of Git in the terminal can be tricky to deal with if you've never encountered them before. While the guidance in this appendix is *far* from comprehensive, in my experience a basic working knowledge of Git is more than enough, unless and until you're working with a relatively large team in a large organization. So while you should definitely move beyond these simple fixes if you're planning to use Git with multiple collaborators on complex projects, for most of us, these examples cover the situations you'll find yourself in—and need help getting out of—most often.

You Run git push/pull and End Up in a Weird Text Editor

Like me, Git is relentless when it comes to documenting your work, to the point that *it will not let you commit changes without a commit message*. That means that if you run a `commit` command without including the `-m "Commit message here"`, for example:

```
git commit filename
```

you will most likely find your terminal window taken over, showing text similar to what's shown in Figure B-1.

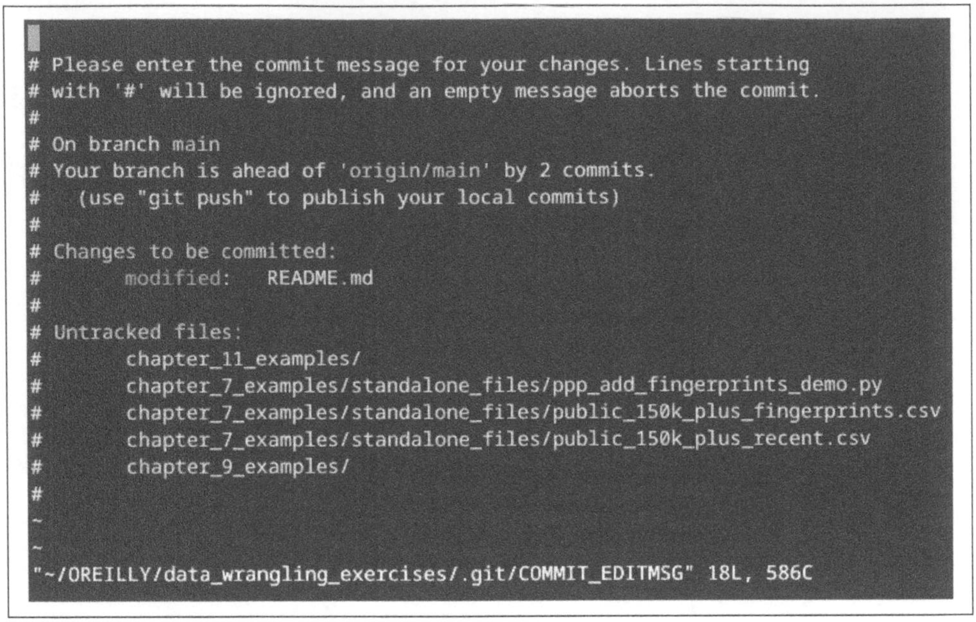

```
# Please enter the commit message for your changes. Lines starting
# with '#' will be ignored, and an empty message aborts the commit.
#
# On branch main
# Your branch is ahead of 'origin/main' by 2 commits.
#   (use "git push" to publish your local commits)
#
# Changes to be committed:
#       modified:   README.md
#
# Untracked files:
#       chapter_11_examples/
#       chapter_7_examples/standalone_files/ppp_add_fingerprints_demo.py
#       chapter_7_examples/standalone_files/public_150k_plus_fingerprints.csv
#       chapter_7_examples/standalone_files/public_150k_plus_recent.csv
#       chapter_9_examples/
#
~
~
~
"~/OREILLY/data_wrangling_exercises/.git/COMMIT_EDITMSG" 18L, 586C
```

Figure B-1. Terminal-based commit message editing

This can be pretty unsettling, especially the first time it happens. But since it *will* happen, here's how to get it sorted out quickly:

1. Start by typing the letter **i**. While not all editors actually require you to type i to enter INSERT mode, most of them will swallow the first character you type, so you may as well start with that one. You can see what this view looks like in Figure B-2.

2. To get *out* of INSERT mode, hit the Esc or Escape key. Then type **:x** as shown in Figure B-3, followed by Enter or Return. This will save your commit message as required and *also* get you out of that text editor and back into the terminal window you know and love.

Note that the editor you find yourself in may not look like what's shown in Figures B-2 and B-3; if not, don't panic. Now's the time to search online for how to edit, save, and exit in whatever program you have been bounced into. Whatever the specifics, the objective is the same.

Figure B-2. Terminal editor in INSERT mode

Figure B-3. Terminal editor with "save and exit" command

Your git push/pull Command Gets Rejected

It happens to all of us. You think you've been diligent about committing your code at the end of each work session—even writing individual commit messages to keep track of the changes you've made in individual files instead of just running `git com mit -a`. Even so, sometimes you run your `git push` command and it gets rejected. What do you do then?

If your `git push` command fails, you'll probably see an error like this:

```
 ! [rejected]        main -> main (non-fast-forward)
error: failed to push some refs to 'https://github.com/your_user_name/your_r
epo_name.git'
hint: Updates were rejected because the tip of your current branch is behind
hint: its remote counterpart. Integrate the remote changes (e.g.
hint: 'git pull ...') before pushing again.
hint: See the 'Note about fast-forwards' in 'git push --help' for details.
```

In general, this happens when (at least) one of the files in your local repository has been changed since the last commit, but *so has the version in your remote repository*, so Git doesn't know which one should take precedence. Not to worry!

Run git pull

If the changes in the file(s) can be merged automatically, Git will do that. This will resolve your file conflicts, but it can result in your being popped into the command line's built-in text editor, which can be pretty confusing to deal with in its own right. If you run `git pull` and suddenly you're looking at something like the text shown in Figure B-1, see "You Run git push/pull and End Up in a Weird Text Editor" on page 369.

If the changes in the file(s) *can't* be merged automatically, you'll get a message that looks something like this (you'll also see this message if you just run `git pull` without running `git push` first):

```
Auto-merging filename
CONFLICT (content): Merge conflict in filename
Automatic merge failed; fix conflicts and then commit the result.
```

This basically means that it's up to you, the human, to determine which file should take precedence and either manually bring them back into line (by directly editing one or both files) or by simply forcing one to overwrite the other.

Fixing conflicts manually

Imagine you have a repo with a *README.md* file, to which you have committed changes both on GitHub.com and on your device. You tried to `git push` and got an error, so you tried to `git pull`, but the automatic merge failed. To fix the conflicts

---

manually, start by opening the *local* copy of the file in your preferred text editor. What you might see for a markdown file is shown in Example B-1.

Example B-1. An example conflict in a markdown file

```
# This header is the same in both files

This content is also the same.

<<<<<<< HEAD


This content is what's currently in the local file.
=======
This content is what's currently in the remote file.
>>>>>>> 1baa345a02d7cbf8a2fcde164e3b5ee1bce84b1b
```

To resolve the conflict, simply edit the content of the file as you prefer, being sure to delete the lines that start with <<<<<<< and >>>>>>>, as well as the =======; if you leave those lines, they will appear in your final file. Now save the file as usual.

Next, run:

```
git add filename
```

Then run:

```
git commit -m "How I fixed the conflict."
```

Note that you *cannot* specify the filename in the `git commit` command, or Git will complain that you've asked it to do a partial commit during a merge.

Finally, run:

```
git push
```

And you should be all set!

"Fixing" conflicts by forcing an overwrite

While it's always a good idea to actually look at any files where conflicts have popped up, sometimes you're pushing to a repo that you know is way out of date, and you just want to overwrite what's on your remote repository. In that case, you *can* push the changes without manually reconciling the files by running:

```
git push --force
```

This will simply overwrite the remote file with your local version, but keep in mind that *all record of the overwritten version will be lost, including the commit history.* That means once you use `--force`, there's no going back—the remote content is gone. Obviously, this means that you should *never* use this option if other people are contributing to the same repository—use it only if you're the only one working on it and you're (very) confident that the material in the remote repo can be overwritten safely.

Git Quick Reference

Table B-1 is a very brief overview of the most useful/common `git` commands. A more comprehensive list can be found on the GitHub website (*https://training.git hub.com/downloads/github-git-cheat-sheet*).

Table B-1. Most-used `git` terminal commands

Command text	Command result
`git status`	Prints out the current state of the repo; doesn't modify anything. Lists all files[a] in the repo, grouped by whether they are *new*, *untracked*, or *modified*.
`git add filename`	*Stage* a specific file that is currently *untracked*. A file must be staged by a `git add` command before it can be committed to the repository. After this, `git status` will label staged files as *new*.
`git add -A`	Stage *all* currently untracked files at once. After this, `git status` will label staged files as *new*.
`git commit -m "Commit message here."` filename`	Commit a specific, already-staged file, attaching the message that appears between double quotation marks.
`git commit -a -m "Commit message here."`	Commit *all* currently staged files, attaching the same commit message to all of them.
`git push`	Push all local commits to the remote repo. Adding the `--force` command will overwrite any conflicting commits in the remote repo with the locally committed files.
`git pull`	Pull all remote files to the local repo. Adding the `--force` command will overwrite any conflicting commits in the local repo with the remote committed files.

[a] If you have an active *.gitignore* file for the repo, any ignored files will *not* be listed by `git status`.

Finding Data

In general, there are four main "sources" of data that you can turn to when you are trying to answer a question about the world. I put "sources" in quotes because these are really *types* of sources, not specific websites, databases, or even organizations. Instead, these represent the mechanisms that journalists, researchers, and other professionals use to collect data about the world in order to answer their questions.

Data Repositories and APIs

"Open data" access has increasingly become a feature of many governmental and scientific organizations, in an effort to improve transparency, accountability, and —especially in the scientific community—*reproducibility*. This means that many government agencies, nonprofit organizations, and scientific journals, for example, maintain websites where you can access structured data relevant to their work. For example, a simple web search for "nyc open data" or "baltimore open data" will bring you to those cities' "open data" portals; a similar search for "johannesburg open data" will bring you first to the South African Cities Open Data Almanac (SCODA) website, but a few links down you'll find more datasets from an organization called "DataFirst" as well as the South African Data Portal hosted at *http://opendataforafr ica.org*. All of these sites will have some data—though as we discussed in Chapter 3, the *quality* of that data—including its appropriateness for answering your particular question—can vary widely.

APIs are another valuable source of data, as they can provide access to highly detailed and customized datasets that won't show up in search engine results. This is because API data is part of what's sometimes referred to as the "deep web": data that is accessible *via* the web but only through specially constructed searches sent to particular URLs. For example, while a web search for "currently available citibikes, nyc" will eventually bring you to an interactive map where you can click on a Citi Bike station to see how many bikes are available, a query to Citi Bike API allows you to access information about the available bikes at *all* Citi Bike stations in New York City. Moreover, the API will return that data in a file reasonably well structured for analysis, unlike the interactive map or, for that matter, most web pages.

Data repositories and APIs are often a great way to access large quantities of structured data that is relatively clean and easy to use for data analysis. At the same time, however, these data sources come with a significant limitation: the company or agency that runs the portal or API has complete control over what data it contains. This mean that the data may be out of date, incomplete, or insufficiently contextualized—or it may simply omit information that the data owner doesn't want others to know. In other words, just because the data may be clean and "ready to use" does *not* mean that it is necessarily good-quality data. A critical evaluation of its quality is still essential.

More often than not, however, *all* of the information you need to answer your chosen question won't be accessible through one of the preceding types of interfaces, so you'll need to look toward other sources.

Subject Matter Experts

As discussed in Chapter 3, *all* data originates with humans in one way or another. Yet it can often seem easier, at the outset, to rely on automated interfaces like the web portals and APIs discussed previously. True, those resources are almost constantly available; there's no need to worry about telephone wait times, business hours, or vacation schedules when structuring an API call. At the same time, talking with human subject matter experts is often the fastest way to identify, if not obtain, the richest and most relevant data for answering your question. That's because many publicly available data sources, even if they are web accessible, are niche enough so that while you may not yet know the best search terms to find them, specialists will use them on a regular basis. As such, they'll not only be able to point you to portals and APIs that you would almost never be able to turn up in a web search, but they can also help you distinguish among seemingly similar data sources and provide important contextual information about their contents. Moreover, they may be able to voluntarily provide you with datasets that you might otherwise wait weeks or months for in response to a FOIA/L request.

In general, there are three places you'll find subject matter experts who may be able to help you locate or understand data. Colleges and universities are home to a dizzying array of experts on a seemingly infinite range of subjects. Start with a call or email to the public relations department, or just start reading the online profiles of faculty and researchers. Similarly, nongovernmental organizations (NGOs), such as nonprofits and think tanks, employ experts according to their focus who may similarly be familiar with specialized datasets that would otherwise be difficult to discover; they may also have data to share that they have personally collected and/or analyzed. Finally, government employees can be an extraordinary source of data and insight, since they are often the very individuals required to collect and process it on behalf of the government in the first place. And while negative stereotypes abound, in my experience, government workers are among the most kindest and most generous data "helpers" you'll find.

FOIA/L Requests

Freedom of Information Act (FOIA) and Freedom of Information Law (FOIL) requests are a mechanism by which any individual can request records about government activities at the federal, state, or local level, respectively,[1] which can be a source for data that is not already available through existing portals or publications. These requests are essentially a specialized letter that you can send to a designated office or individual within an agency, specifying your request for information.

A key requirement for using FOIA/L requests effectively is to be as specific and narrow as possible: while FOIA/L laws guarantee your right to *request* data, most only mandate that you receive *a* response within a specified time frame (often between 5 and 20 business days); they do *not* require that the response include the data you requested. In most cases, an initial response will (1) deny your request based on allowable exemptions and exclusions (*https://dhs.gov/foia-exemptions*); (2) acknowledge your request but classify it as "complex," thereby warranting an extended timeline for delivery; or (3) respond that a search request was performed but yielded no results. Successfully obtaining the data you seek will likely require at least one "appeal"—and lots and lots of patience.

A comprehensive introduction to FOIA/L requests is beyond the scope of this book, but there are a number of guides available online that provide templates and tips on how to construct your FOIA/L request, and even websites like MuckRock that provide tools to help you write, submit, and keep track of requests that you have submitted. In thinking about what to ask for, keep in mind the following:

FOIA/L requests only apply to government records
>   You'll need to think creatively about how the phenomenon you're interested in might generate such records. Think about any activities related to your question that may require permits, licensing, or taxation—all of these will generate government records. Also keep in mind that the activities of government employees—including their emails, calendars, and other records—are subject to FOIA/L laws as well.

---

1 Some states require that the requester be a resident of that state.

Don't "bundle" requests

If you are looking for records containing multiple terms, send a separate FOIA/L request for each term and file type (e.g., email, calendar etc.). This increases the number of FOIA/L requests you have to track but also reduces the chances that your request will be delayed because it has been classified as "complex."

Use publicly accessible forms

If you don't know what information an agency collects, use publicly accessible forms—such as those required for tax, licensing, and permitting purposes—to get an idea. You can then refer to those specific form numbers and fields in your request.

Look at past requests

FOIA/L requests are themselves subject to these laws. If you are looking for information that was part of a previously filled request, referring to it might expedite your own.

Politely reach out to the relevant personnel

FOIA/L officers can help you on your way—or make things difficult. Try to develop a cordial, if not friendly, relationship with them—either via email or telephone. They can offer you crucial tips on how to refine your request for greater success.

Custom Data Collection

Sometimes, your question just cannot be answered with any combination of existing datasets, no matter how many experts or APIs you use. This circumstance highlights the very human-constructed nature of data: it only exists because someone somewhere has decided to collect it, clean it, and make it available. If your question is especially timely or unique, it may turn out that that person is you.

At universities, you can find multiple courses dedicated entirely to various methods of data collection, from surveys to sensors. The method(s) you choose when collecting data will depend on both the nature of your question and the resources (including time) that you have to devote to the data-gathering process. If you are seeking exploratory or anecdotal data, then your data collection process might be as simple as posting a question or "poll" on social media and analyzing the responses you receive. If, on the other hand, you want to be able to make claims that *generalize*—that is, claims about a larger phenomenon than precisely the ones you have data for—then your data must be *representative*, as we discussed in Chapter 3.

Whichever type of data you're collecting—anecdotal or representative—there are two main methods for doing so: interviews and instrumentation. Interview techniques involve asking humans to provide a response, whether those responses are open-ended, multiple choice, or some other format. Instrumentation techniques involve some degree of automated data collection, whether of web-browsing habits or carbon monoxide levels. In either case, you'll need to read up on best practices or consult with experts in order to understand both the limitations of your measurement techniques and the appropriate methods for analyzing and interpreting your data. While collecting your own data can be a challenge, it can also be incredibly rewarding.

Resources for Visualization and Information Design

The evolution of visualization tools in the past decade has transformed the process of creating beautiful, informative graphics from something that required expensive specialty software and specialized training to something that almost anyone can do. As discussed in Chapter 10, however, making eloquent visualizations is about more than the tools you have at your disposal; it's about finding the design choices that best enhance and clarify your message. While there are many books and courses out there that focus on visualization for particular purposes (business or science communication, for example), the following list is more of an all-purpose reader—these are great books and resources for developing and understanding the history, purpose, and potential of visualization and information design if you want to understand this space more broadly.

Foundational Books on Information Visualization

Probably the most name-checked person in the world of information visualization is Edward Tufte, who wrote many of the earliest and more influential books on the subject. While all of them are beautiful objects, probably the most instructive will be the first three: *The Visual Display of Quantitative Information*, *Envisioning Information*, and *Visual Explanations* (all from Graphics Press). If you find yourself wanting to read his entire opus, he has also published a few shorter reports and pamphlets that excerpt his books and offer pointed critiques of, well, PowerPoint. All of his publications can purchased on his personal website, *https://edwardtufte.com*, but many are also available in public libraries.

Although technically books about typography, *Thinking with Type* by Ellen Lupton (*http://elupton.com*) (Princeton Architectural Press) is an excellent introduction to general graphic design principles that apply anywhere text is involved—which is most places, including data-driven visualizations. Lupton's book introduces readers to all the essential aspects of designing with text, providing the vocabulary needed to reason about everything from font choice and weight to size, color, and spacing. The book is both a great primer and reference, wonderful to have on hand if you can buy a copy. If you can't, a lot of the book's essentials are available for free on the corresponding website, *http://thinkingwithtype.com*.

The Quick Reference You'll Reach For

My number-one ready reference for information visualization remains *The Wall Street Journal Guide to Information Graphics* (Norton), written by my former colleague, Dona Wong. This book has all the tips and tricks you'll need to accurately and beautifully visualize data in one place. Need a pleasing color palette? Check. A reminder on how to calculate percent change? Check. Ideas on how to handle negative or missing values? Check. A quick read and an invaluable go-to resource; if there's only one book on information visualization that you actually purchase, this should be it.

Sources of Inspiration

There are hundreds of books and blogs about information visualization, and not all of them are created equal—because not all designers are focused on the accurate presentation of data. While many folks offer paid workshops in visualization (some of which may be quite good), there are also many talented practitioners sharing their work and ideas for free.

Kaiser Fung's blog *Junk Charts* (*https://junkcharts.typepad.com*) is a long-standing resource of visualization critique and redesign. Here you can find more than 15 years' worth of Fung's well-informed perspectives on information design, which includes highlighting the data fallacies that sometimes crop up in the visualizations of even major news organizations and businesses. A great resource for anyone looking to learn about the ways that even well-meaning visualizations can go wrong.

Mona Chalabi's work for *The Guardian* (*https://theguardian.com/profile/mona-chalabi*) and elsewhere demonstrates how great data visualizations can also be made by hand and reflect the individuality and the humanity of the people that data is about.

Stefanie Posavec (*http://stefanieposavec.com*) is an artist and designer who creates data-driven objects and visualizations across a range of media.

Index

Symbols
= (equal sign), as assignment operator, 42
| (pipe) either/or character, 233

A
access tokens (APIs), 160, 168-172
accessibility
  of colors, 346, 348
  of Python, 7
accounts
  FRED, creating, 149
  Twitter development, applying for, 160-162
Ada Developers Academy, 368
adding code to files, 23
Agricultural Marketing Service (USDA), 82
alpha (transparency) in visualizations, 341
annotations in visualizations, 348
anomalies, 292
  as meaningful, 289
  in Gaussian distribution, 299
API (application programming interface),
  145-146
  authentication, 148
    API key protection, 153-159
    API key requests, 149
    creating account, 149
    data requests with API key, 150
    OAuth, 159-172
  benefits of, 143
  as data sources, 375-376
  documentation, reading, 151-152
  endpoints, 119, 152
  ethical usage, 172-173
  risks of, 141

  search engines as, 146-148
API keys
  data requests with, 150
  in OAuth
    creating, 164-167
    encoding, 167-168
  protection in Python, 153-159
    creating credentials file, 155
    .gitignore file, 157-159
    importance of, 154
    importing credentials file, 155-157
  requesting, 149
apps (Twitter), creating, 162-164
argparse library, 282
*args parameter, 264
arguments, 55
  command-line, 281-284
  documentation of, 283
  positional, 283
arguments (for functions), 262-264
arithmetic mean, 290
assessing
  data fit, 73-79, 215-221
    reliability, 76, 219
    representativeness, 77-79, 220-221
    validity, 74-76, 216-219
  data integrity, 79-88, 187-215
    atomic, 85, 213
    clear, 87, 213-215
    complete, 83, 189-200
    consistent, 86-87, 208-211
    dimensionally structured, 87, 215
    high volume, 84, 206-208
    of known provenance, 81, 188-189

structured data
    feed-based (see feed-based data sources)
    file-based (see file-based data sources)
    unstructured versus, 93-97
subject matter experts, as data source, 376-377
subsets of data, 226-235
    matching with regular expressions, 229-233
    splitting strings, 227-229
sum() function, 51
SVG (Scalable Vector Graphics), 124
symmetry, 297-304
syntax errors, 56-58
syntax highlighting, 14, 39

T
tab-separated value (.tsv) files, 97
    fixed-width files versus, 115
    reading data from, 101-104
table-type data
    accessing in PDFs, 139
    feed-based (see feed-based data sources)
    file-based (see file-based data sources)
Tabula, 139
tags (XML), 121
terminal (see command line)
tesseract-ocr library, 136
testing Python/Jupyter installation, 19
text (.txt) files, 97
    reading data from, 101-104
    tab-separated versus fixed-width, 115
text editors, opening delimited files in, 104
text, image-based (see PDFs)
Thinking With Type (Lupton), 381
timely, in data integrity, 83, 189
timestamps
    datetime object, 233-235
    separating from dates, 227-229
to_datetime() function, 192
transforming data, 244-250
transposing data, 201-202
trends
    as meaningful, 289
    types of, 290-292
troubleshooting Git
    file conflicts, resolving, 372-374
    git commit, 369-370
.tsv files (tab-separated values), 97
    fixed-width files versus, 115
    reading data from, 101-104

Tufte, Edward, 381
Twitter
    access tokens, requesting, 168-172
    API keys
        creating, 164-167
        encoding, 167-168
    apps, creating, 162-164
    development account, applying for, 160-162
    ethical usage, 172-173
.txt files (text), 97
    reading data from, 101-104
    tab-separated versus fixed-width, 115

U
unemployment example, 105-107, 354-355
unstructured data sources, 134
    PDFs, 134-139
    structured versus, 93-97
updating software tools, 367
upper bound of dataset, 302
URLs, query strings in, 146-148
USDA Agricultural Marketing Service, 82
user-defined functions, 43-47
    arguments, 262-264
    command-line arguments, 281-284
    components of, 45
    documentation, 277-281
    errors in, 46
    libraries, 47
    nesting, 265-266
    return values, 264-265
    scope, 259-261
    when to use, 258-259

V
validating data, 312-317
validity, in data fit, 74-76, 216-219
variables, 39-42
    data types, 39-40
    errors, 59
    global, 274
    incrementing, 68
    naming, 40-42
vector-based images, editing software for, 362
versatility of Python, 6
version numbers
    for Chromebooks, 14-15
    in Python, 11
    in Windows 10+, 17

About the Author

Susan E. McGregor is a researcher at Columbia University's Data Science Institute, where she also cochairs its Center for Data, Media and Society. For over a decade, she has been refining her approach to teaching programming and data analysis to non-STEM learners at the professional, graduate, and undergraduate levels.

McGregor has been a full-time faculty member and researcher at Columbia University since 2011, when she joined Columbia Journalism School and the Tow Center for Digital Journalism. While there, she developed the school's first data journalism curriculum and served as a primary academic advisor for its dual-degree program in Journalism and Computer Science. Her academic research centers on security and privacy issues affecting journalists and media organizations, and is the subject of her first book, *Information Security Essentials: A Guide for Reporters, Editors, and Newsroom Leaders* (CUP).

Prior to her work at Columbia, McGregor spent several years as the Senior Programmer on the News Graphics team at the *Wall Street Journal*. She was named a 2010 Gerald Loeb Award winner for her work on WSJ's original "What They Know" series, and has spoken and published at a range of leading academic security and privacy conferences. Her work has received support from the National Science Foundation, the Knight Foundation, Google, and multiple schools and offices of Columbia University. McGregor is also interested in how the arts can help stimulate critical thinking and introduce new perspectives around technology issues. She holds a master's degree in Educational Communication and Technology from NYU and a bachelor's degree in Interactive Information Design from Harvard University.

Colophon

The animal on the cover of *Practical Python Data Wrangling and Data Quality* is a horseshoe whip snake (*Hemorrhois hippocrepis*).

Native to southwestern Europe and northern Africa, this snake can be found living in a variety of habitats including shrubby vegetation, rocky and sandy shores, pastureland, plantations, rural gardens, and some urban areas. Adults can grow to a total length of 5 feet (or 1.5 meters). The horseshoe whip snake has smooth scales and a yellowish/red body with a series of large black or dark brown spots edged with black running down its back. It gets its name from the light horseshoe-shaped mark on the neck and back of head.

The horseshoe whip snake climbs well and hunts birds, small reptiles, and small mammals from the tops of trees, roofs, or rocky cliffs. While it can be aggressive when handled and has a strong bite, this snake is not venomous or particularly dangerous to humans.

Thought to be highly adaptable, the current conversation status of the horseshoe whip snake is "Least Concern." Many of the animals on O'Reilly covers are endangered; all of them are important to the world.

The cover illustration is by Jose Marzan Jr., based on an antique line engraving from Lydekker's *Royal Natural History*. The cover fonts are Gilroy Semibold and Guardian Sans. The text font is Adobe Minion Pro; the heading font is Adobe Myriad Condensed; and the code font is Dalton Maag's Ubuntu Mono.

Milton Keynes UK
Ingram Content Group UK Ltd.
UKHW050619050424
440536UK00002B/7

9 781492 091509